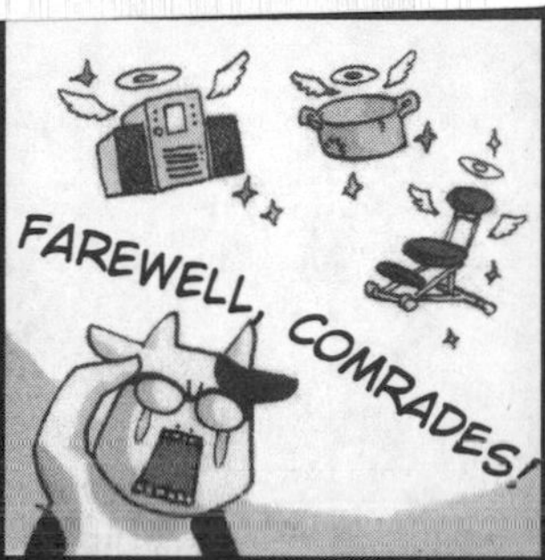
FAREWELL, COMRADES!

Recently, many of the items in my work space that have gone through good and bad times with me are breaking down, one after another. The pot that my assistants and I use to cook our lunch, the stereo, the ergonomic chair, etc.... You fools!! How dare you give up before the journey is done?! (sob)

—Hiromu Arakawa, 2008

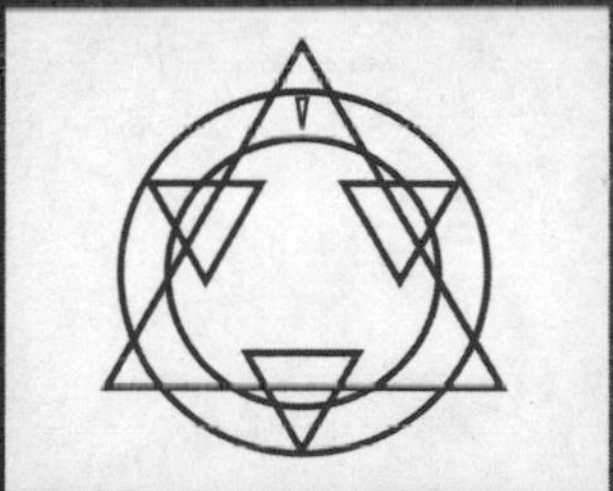

Born in Hokkaido (northern Japan), Hiromu Arakawa first attracted national attention in 1999 with her award-winning manga *Stray Dog*. Her series *Fullmetal Alchemist* debuted in 2001 in Square Enix's monthly manga anthology *Shonen Gangan*.

FULLMETAL ALCHEMIST
VOL. 20

VIZ Media Edition

Story and Art by Hiromu Arakawa

Translation/Akira Watanabe
English Adaptation/Jake Forbes
Touch-up Art & Lettering/Susan Daigle-Leach
Design/Julie Behn
Editor/Alexis Kirsch

Hagane no RenkinJutsushi vol. 20 © 2008 Hiromu Arakawa/SQUARE ENIX.
First published in Japan in 2008 by SQUARE ENIX CO., LTD. English translation
rights arranged with SQUARE ENIX CO., LTD. and VIZ Media, LLC.

Printed in the U.S.A.

Published by VIZ Media, LLC
P.O. Box 77010
San Francisco, CA 94107

11
First printing, September 2009
Eleventh printing, December 2021

www.viz.com

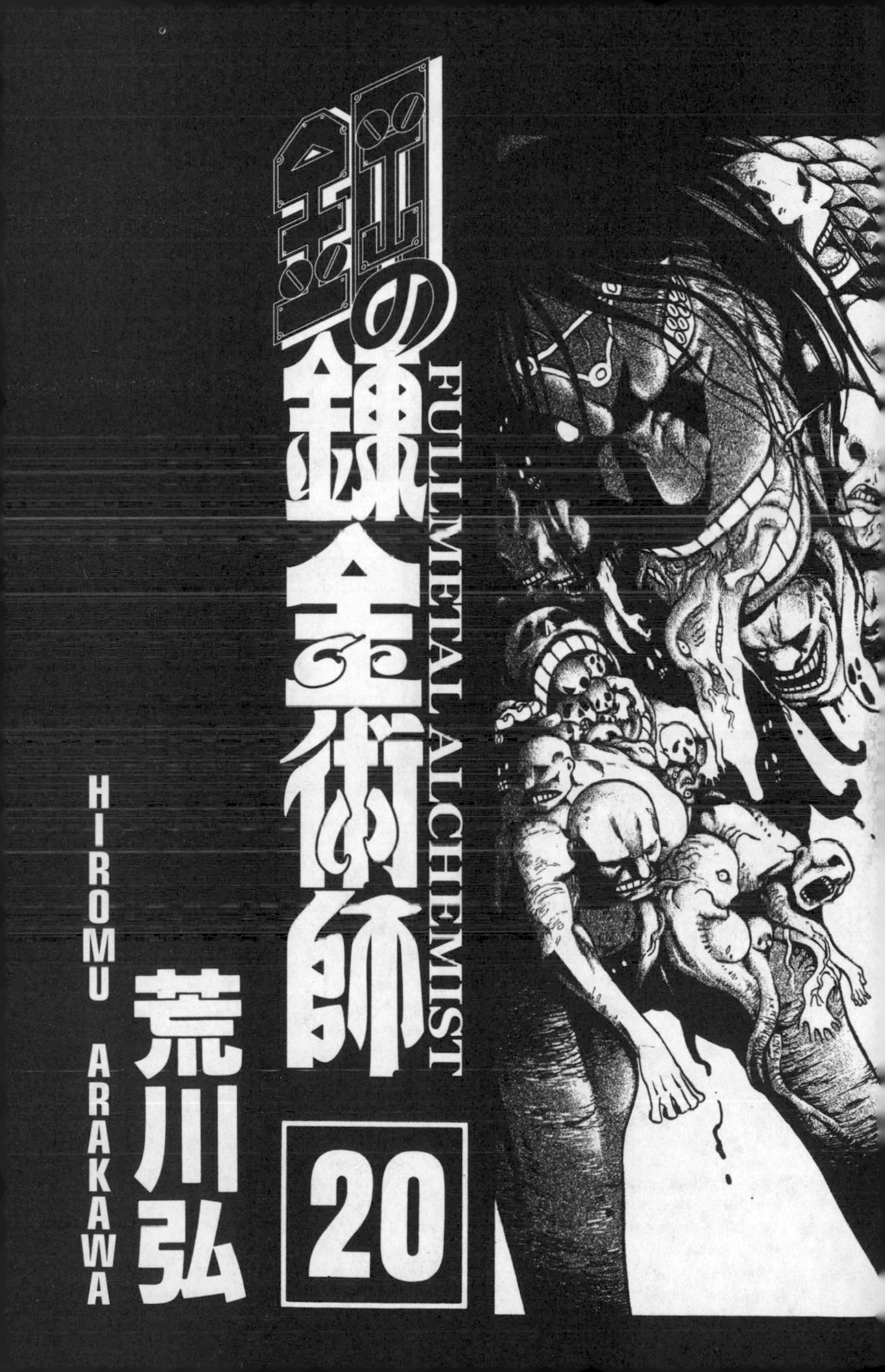

鋼の錬金術師

FULLMETAL ALCHEMIST

20

荒川弘

HIROMU ARAKAWA

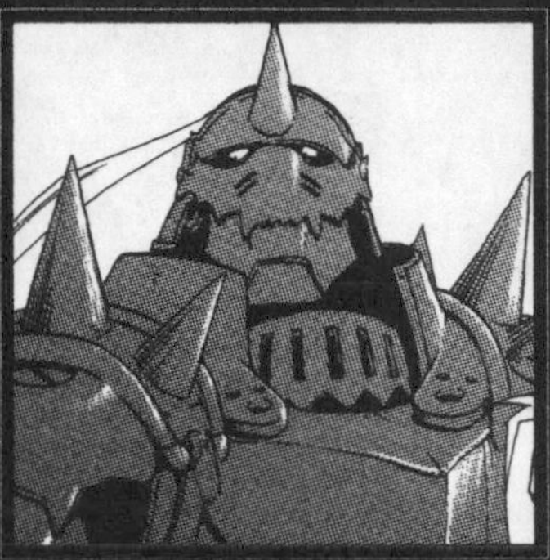

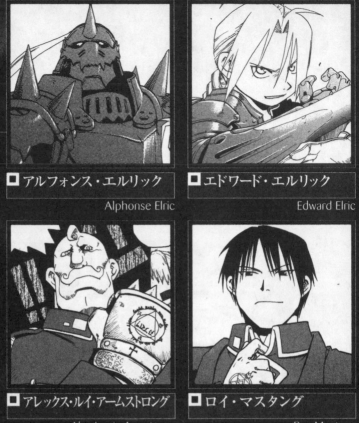

アルフォンス・エルリック

Alphonse Elric

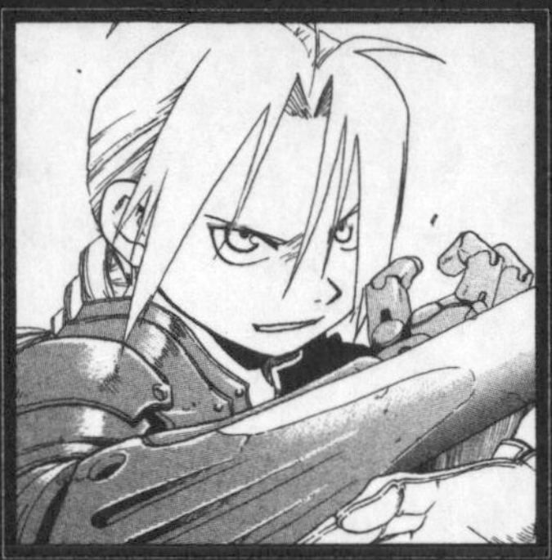

エドワード・エルリック

Edward Elric

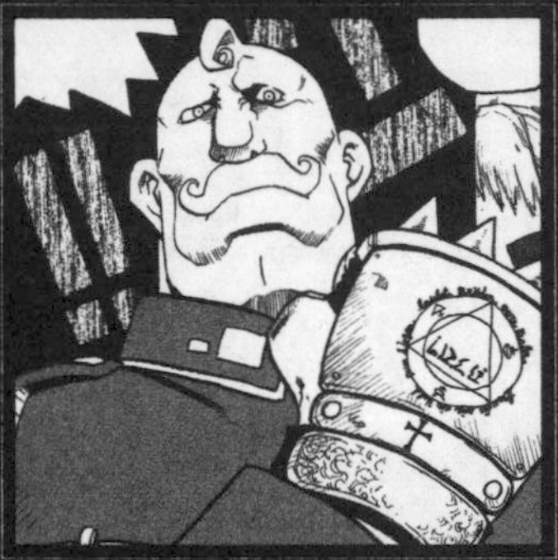

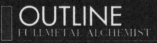

アレックス・ルイ・アームストロング

Alex Louis Armstrong

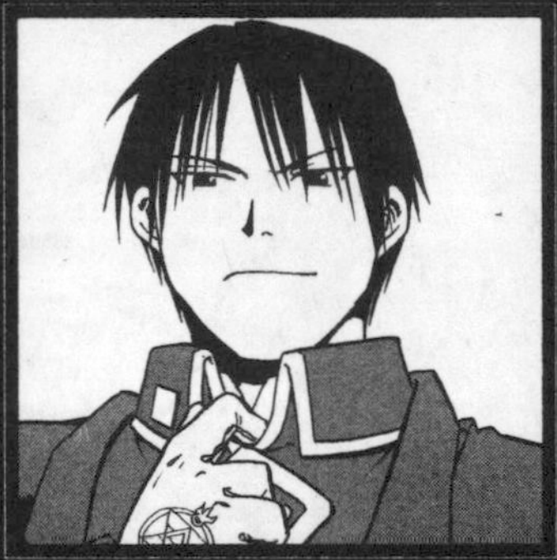

ロイ・マスタング

Roy Mustang

OUTLINE

FULLMETAL ALCHEMIST

Using a forbidden alchemical ritual, the Elric brothers attempted to bring their dead mother back to life. But the ritual went wrong, consuming Edward Elric's leg and Alphonse Elric's entire body. At the cost of his arm, Edward was able to graft his brother's soul into a suit of armor. Equipped with mechanical "auto-mail" to replace his missing limbs, Edward becomes a state alchemist in the hopes of finding a way to restore their bodies. Their search embroils them in a deadly conspiracy that threatens to take the innocence, if not the lives, of everyone involved.

For decades, the nation of Amestris has slowly expanded its borders into the shape of an enormous transmutation circle with the Homunculi's "Father" at its center. Now the circle is complete and calculated bloody wars at key points sanctify the circle for a final transmutation. Long ago, when a similar ceremony was performed in the city of Cselkcess, thousands of souls were lost so that the original Homunculus could be free. Only one person survived the massacre—Van Hohenheim, Ed and Al's father. Now this Philosopher's Stone in the shape of a man might hold the key to stopping the Homunculi before an even greater massacre consumes the world...

鋼の錬金術師
FULLMETAL ALCHEMIST

CHARACTERS
FULLMETAL ALCHEMIST

□ ウィンリィ・ロックベル

Winry Rockbell

□ スカー

Scar

□ オリヴィエ・ミラ・アームストロング

Olivier Mira Armstrong

□ キング・ブラッドレイ

King Bradley

□ ヴァン・ホーエンハイム

Van Hohenheim

□ メイ・チャン

May Chang

CONTENTS

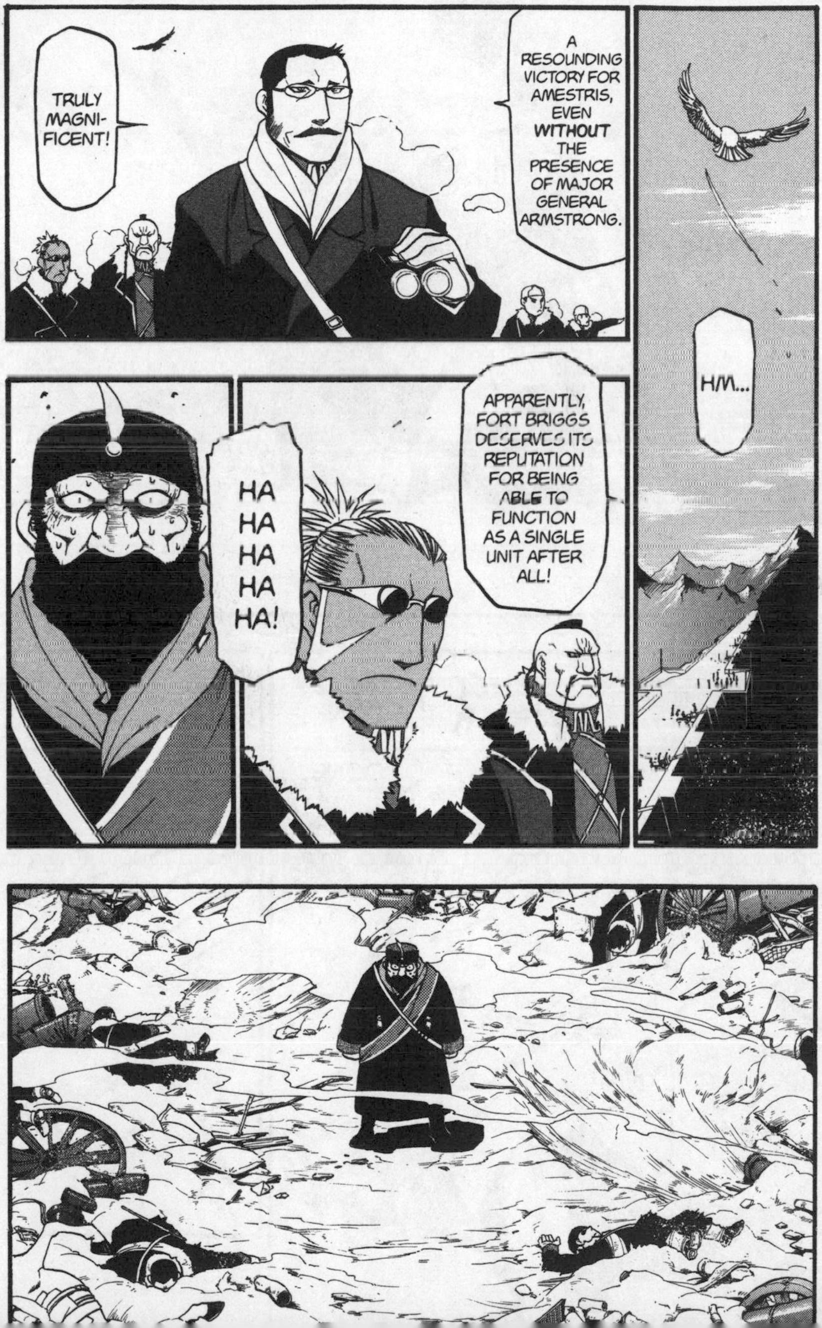
HM...
A RESOUNDING VICTORY FOR AMESTRIS, EVEN WITHOUT THE PRESENCE OF MAJOR GENERAL ARMSTRONG.
TRULY MAGNI-FICENT!
APPARENTLY, FORT BRIGGS DESERVES ITS REPUTATION FOR BEING ABLE TO FUNCTION AS A SINGLE UNIT AFTER ALL!
HA HA HA HA HA!

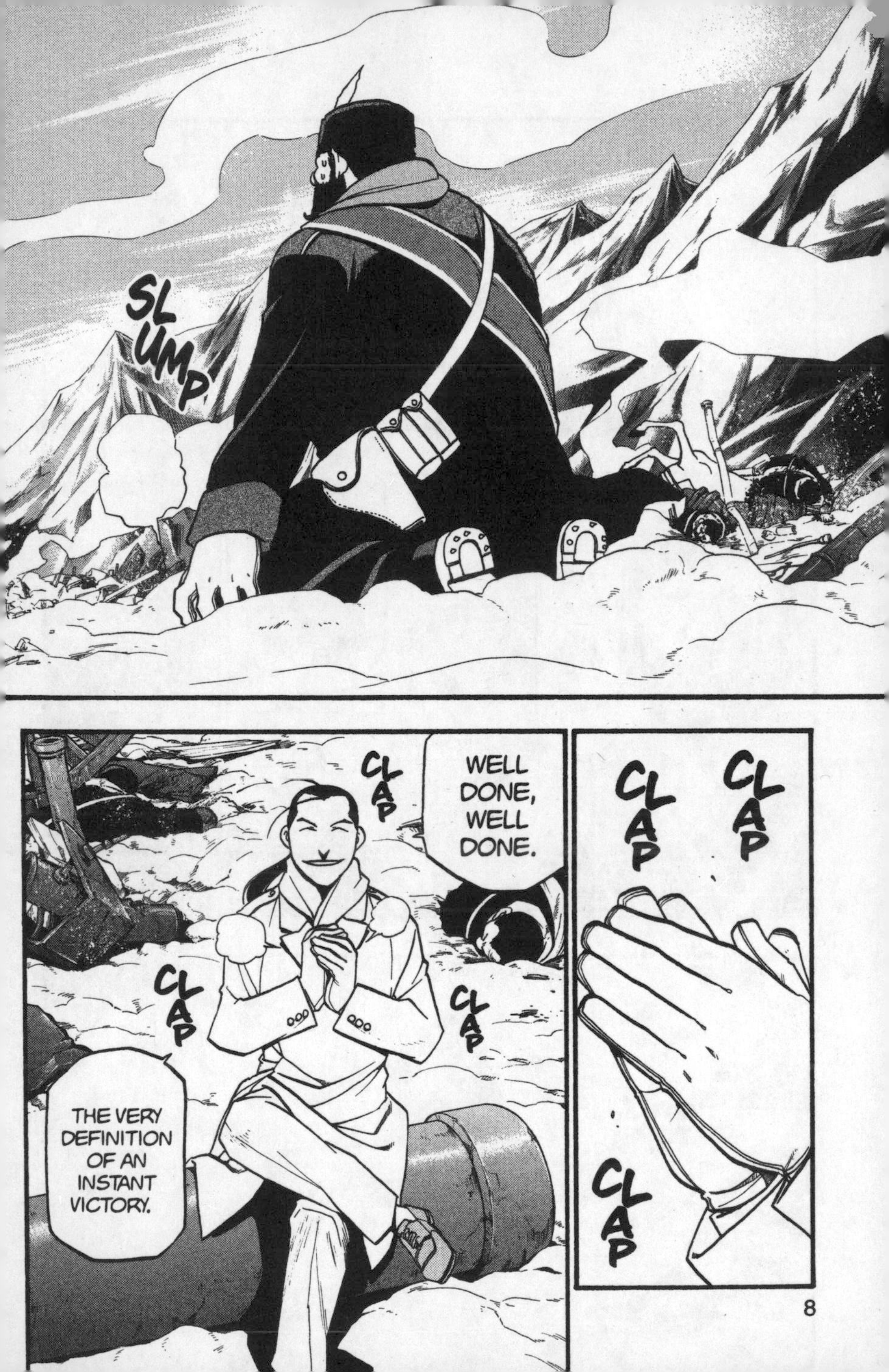
SLUMP
CLAP
CLAP
CLAP
CLAP
WELL DONE, WELL DONE.
CLAP
CLAP
CLAP
THE VERY DEFINITION OF AN INSTANT VICTORY.

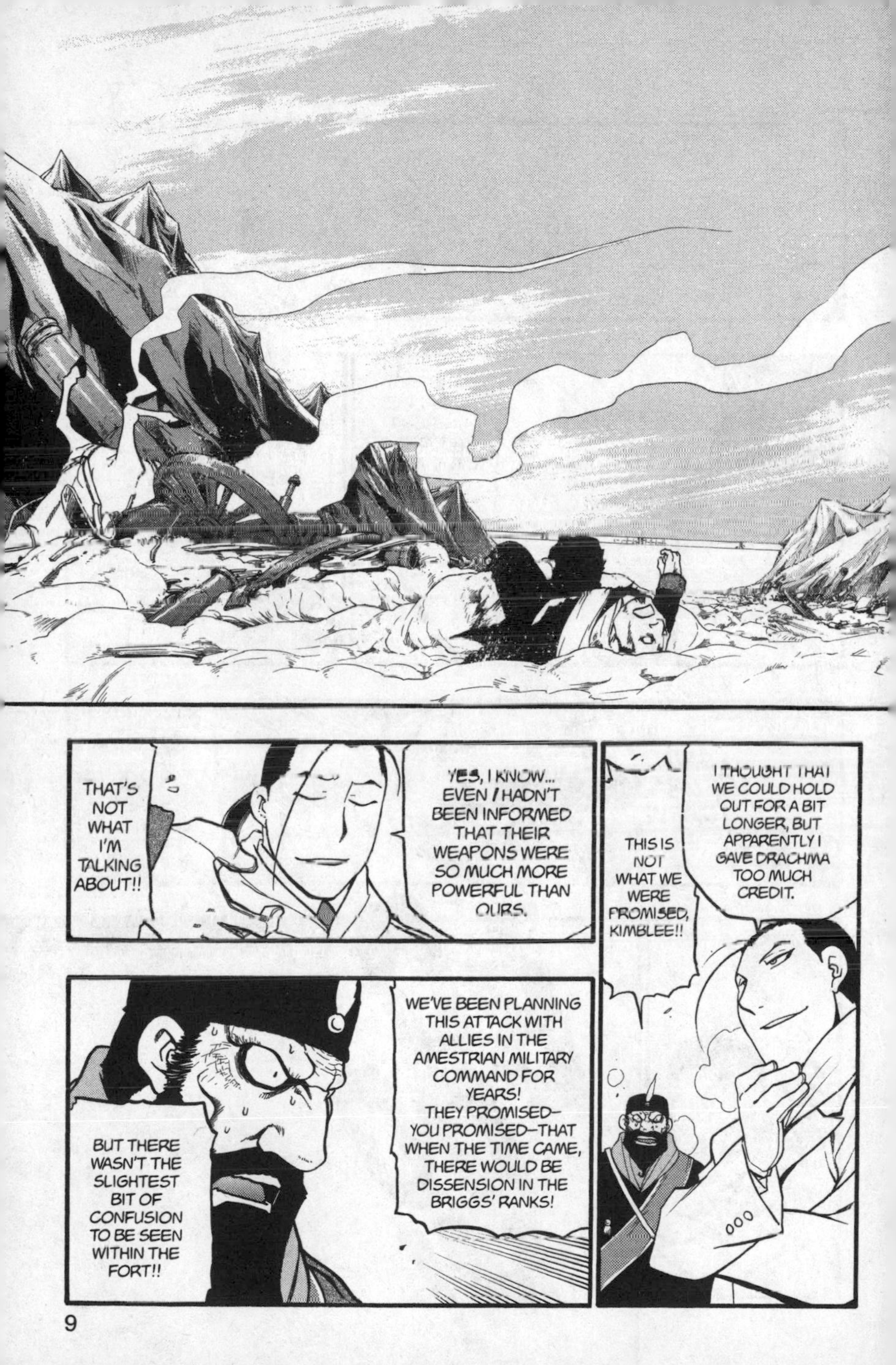
I THOUGHT THAT WE COULD HOLD OUT FOR A BIT LONGER, BUT APPARENTLY I GAVE DRACHMA TOO MUCH CREDIT.
THIS IS NOT WHAT WE WERE PROMISED, KIMBLEE!!
YES, I KNOW... EVEN I HADN'T BEEN INFORMED THAT THEIR WEAPONS WERE SO MUCH MORE POWERFUL THAN OURS.
THAT'S NOT WHAT I'M TALKING ABOUT!!
WE'VE BEEN PLANNING THIS ATTACK WITH ALLIES IN THE AMESTRIAN MILITARY COMMAND FOR YEARS!
THEY PROMISED— YOU PROMISED—THAT WHEN THE TIME CAME, THERE WOULD BE DISSENSION IN THE BRIGGS' RANKS!
BUT THERE WASN'T THE SLIGHTEST BIT OF CONFUSION TO BE SEEN WITHIN THE FORT!!

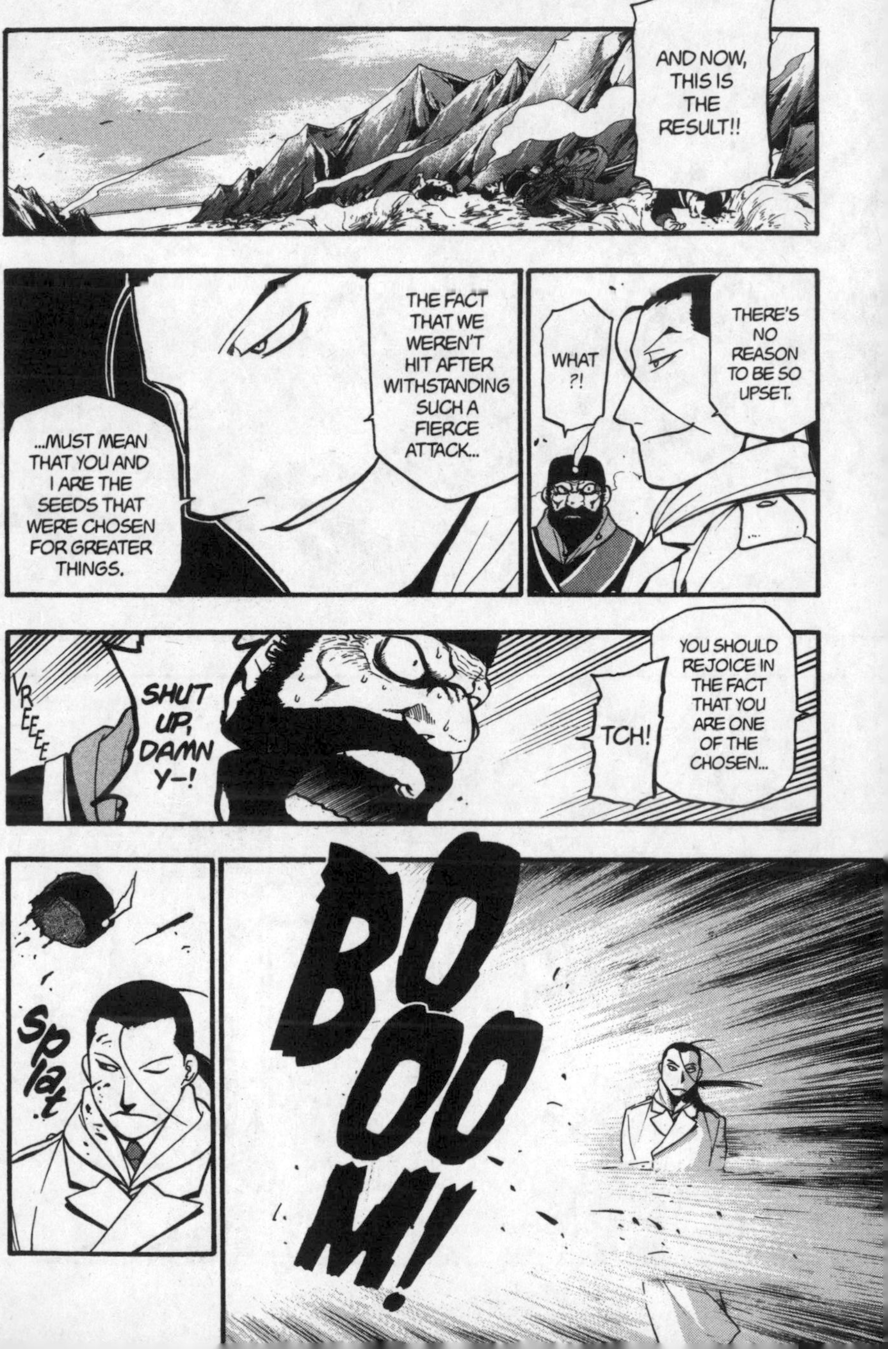
AND NOW, THIS IS THE RESULT!!
THERE'S NO REASON TO BE SO UPSET.
WHAT ?!
THE FACT THAT WE WEREN'T HIT AFTER WITHSTANDING SUCH A FIERCE ATTACK...
...MUST MEAN THAT YOU AND I ARE THE SEEDS THAT WERE CHOSEN FOR GREATER THINGS.
YOU SHOULD REJOICE IN THE FACT THAT YOU ARE ONE OF THE CHOSEN...
TCH!
SHUT UP, DAMN Y-!
VREEEEE
BOOOOM!
Splat

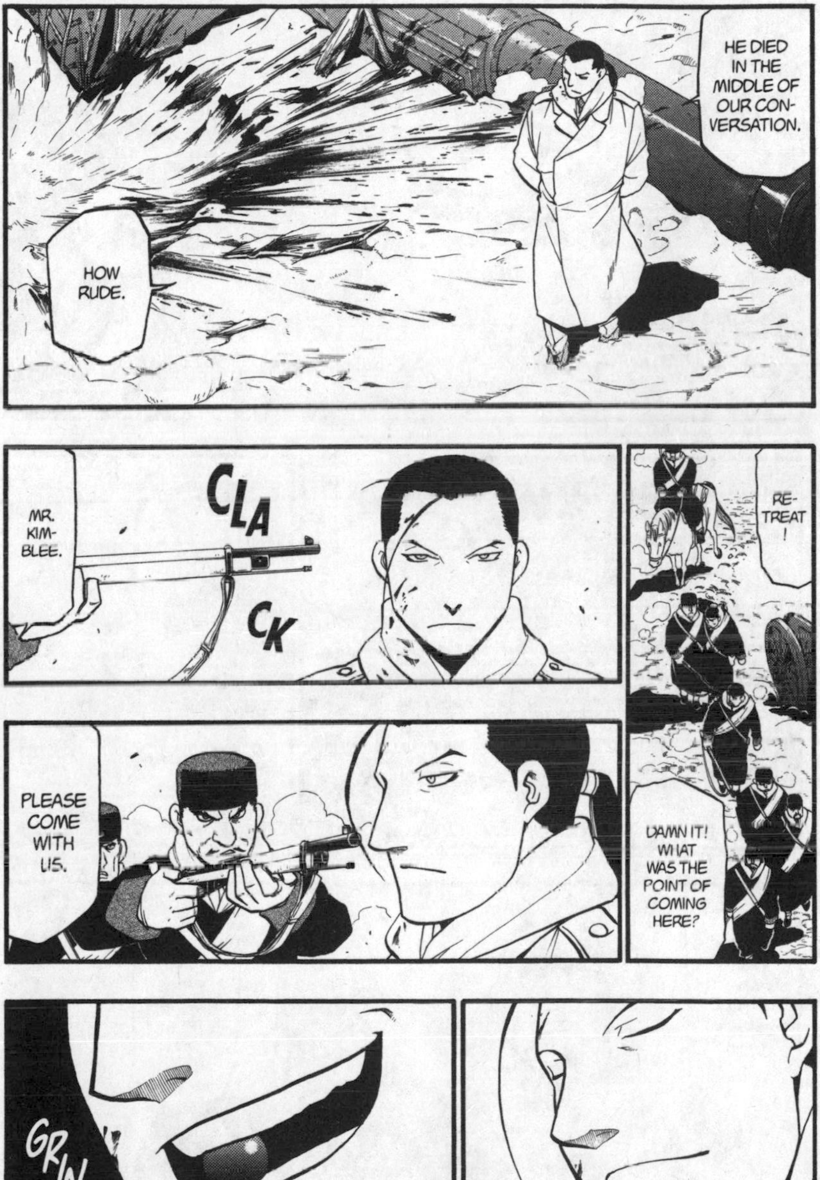
HE DIED IN THE MIDDLE OF OUR CON-VERSATION.
HOW RUDE.
RE-TREAT!
DAMN IT! WHAT WAS THE POINT OF COMING HERE?
CLACK
MR. KIM-BLEE.
PLEASE COME WITH US.
GRIN

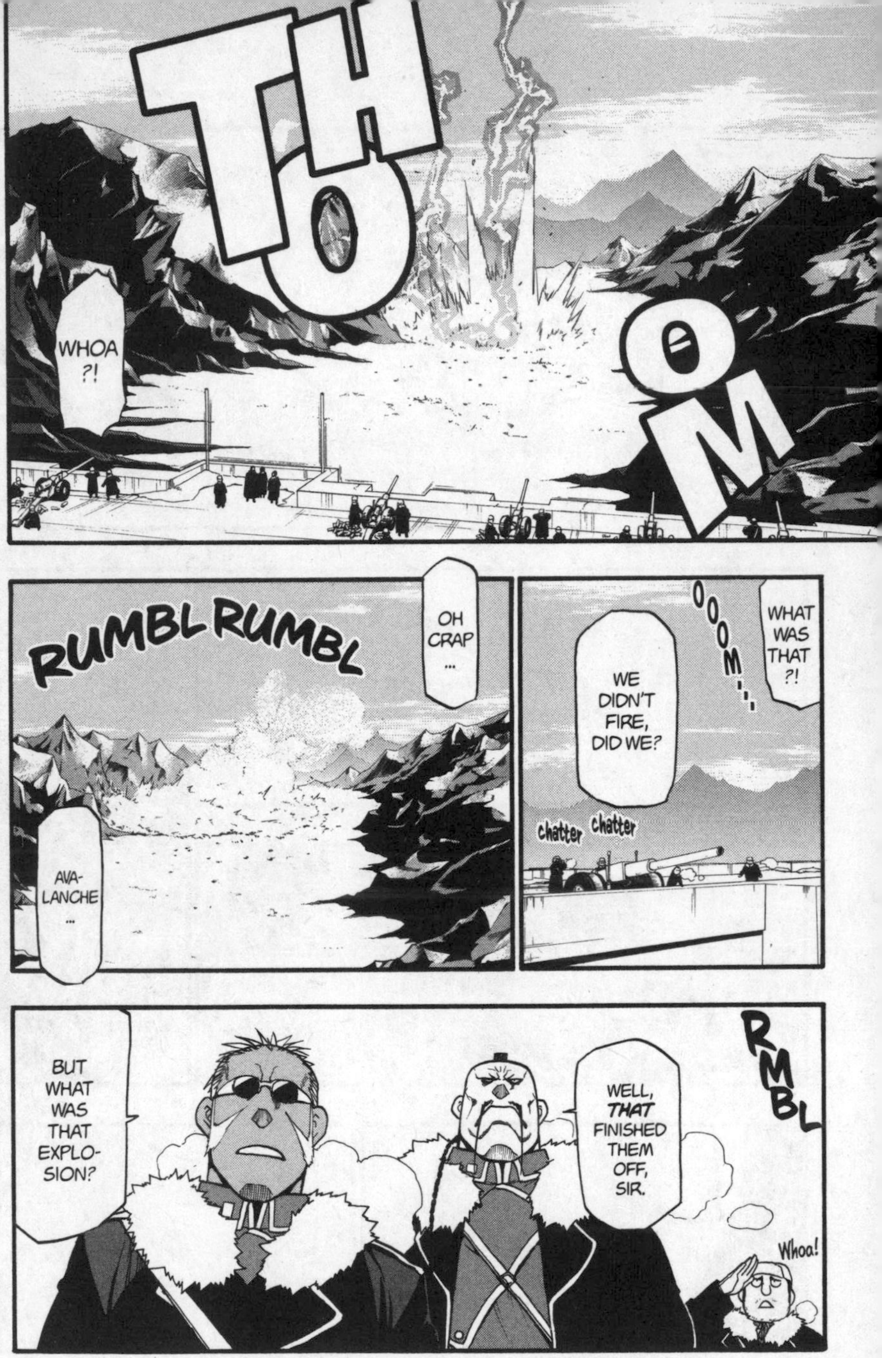
THOOM
WHOA?!
WHAT WAS THAT?!
OOOM...
WE DIDN'T FIRE, DID WE?
chatter chatter
OH CRAP...
RUMBL RUMBL
AVA-LANCHE...
RMBL
WELL, *THAT* FINISHED THEM OFF, SIR.
Whoa!
BUT WHAT WAS THAT EXPLOSION?

Chapter 79

Bug Bite

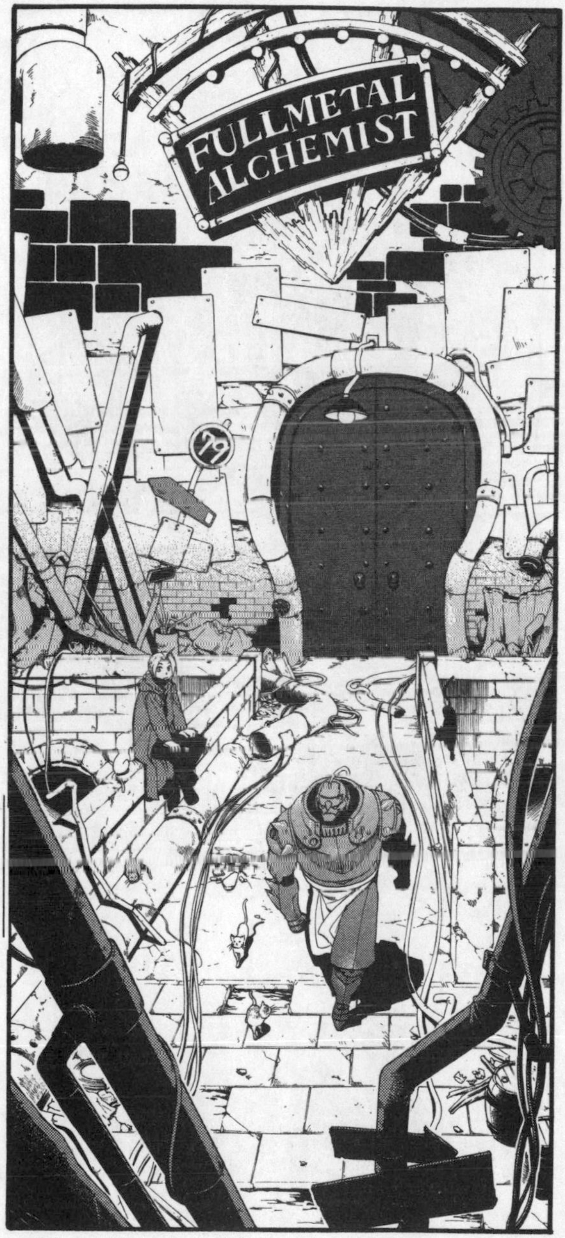
FULLMETAL ALCHEMIST
79

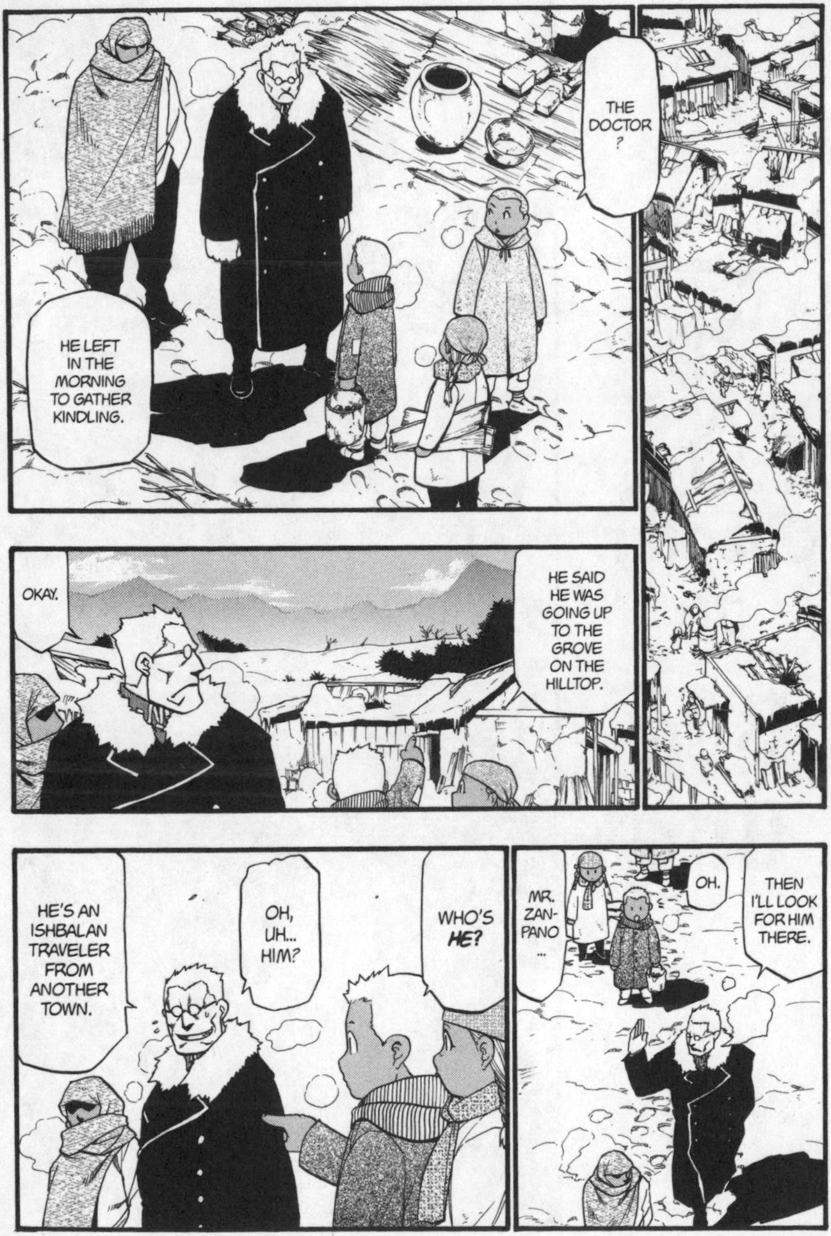
THE DOCTOR?
HE LEFT IN THE MORNING TO GATHER KINDLING.
HE SAID HE WAS GOING UP TO THE GROVE ON THE HILLTOP.
OKAY.
THEN I'LL LOOK FOR HIM THERE.
OH.
MR. ZAN-PANO...
WHO'S HE?
OH, UH... HIM?
HE'S AN ISHBALAN TRAVELER FROM ANOTHER TOWN.

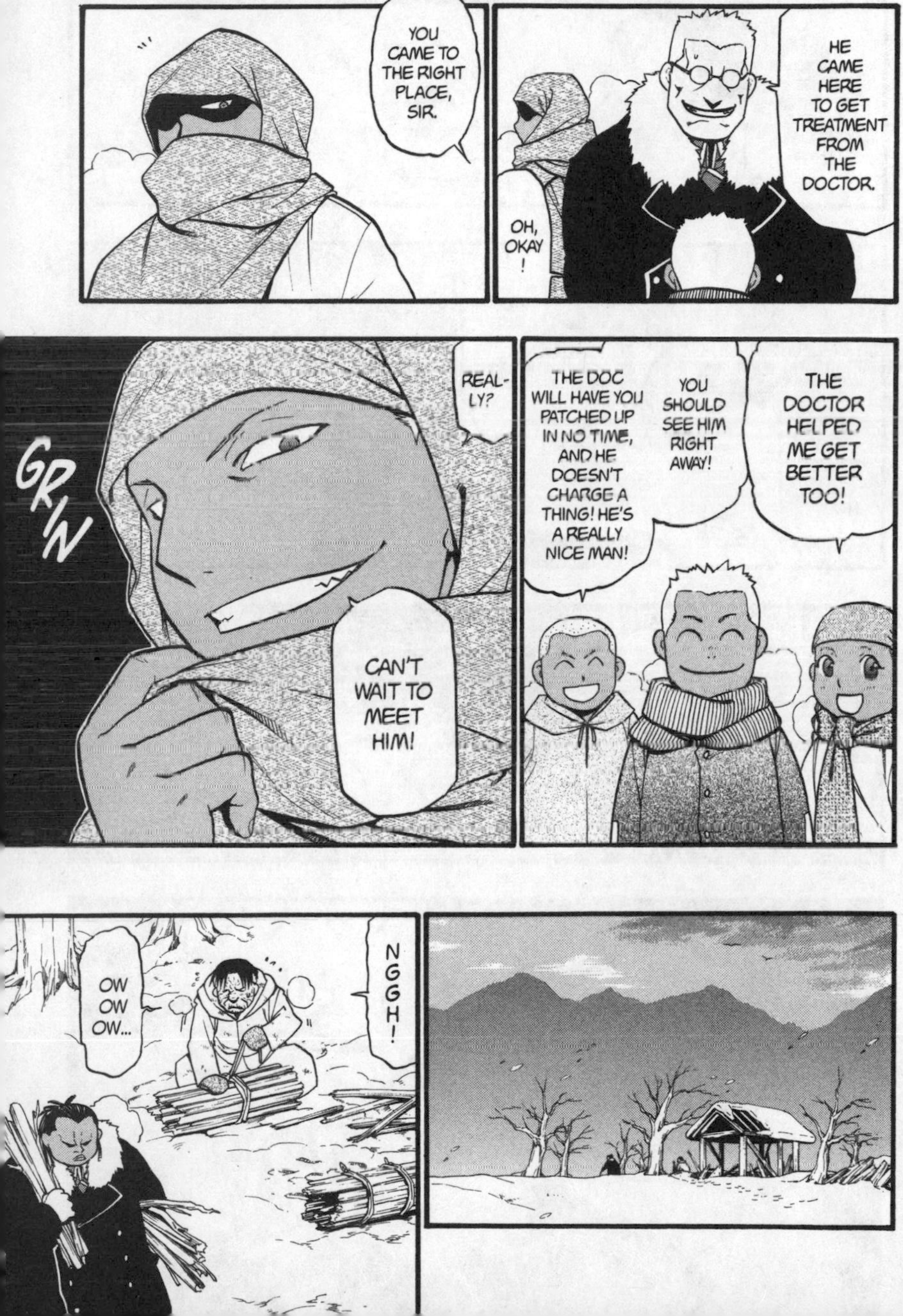
HE CAME HERE TO GET TREATMENT FROM THE DOCTOR.
OH, OKAY!
YOU CAME TO THE RIGHT PLACE, SIR.
THE DOCTOR HELPED ME GET BETTER TOO!
YOU SHOULD SEE HIM RIGHT AWAY!
THE DOC WILL HAVE YOU PATCHED UP IN NO TIME, AND HE DOESN'T CHARGE A THING! HE'S A REALLY NICE MAN!
REAL-LY?
GRIN
CAN'T WAIT TO MEET HIM!
NGGH!
OW OW OW...

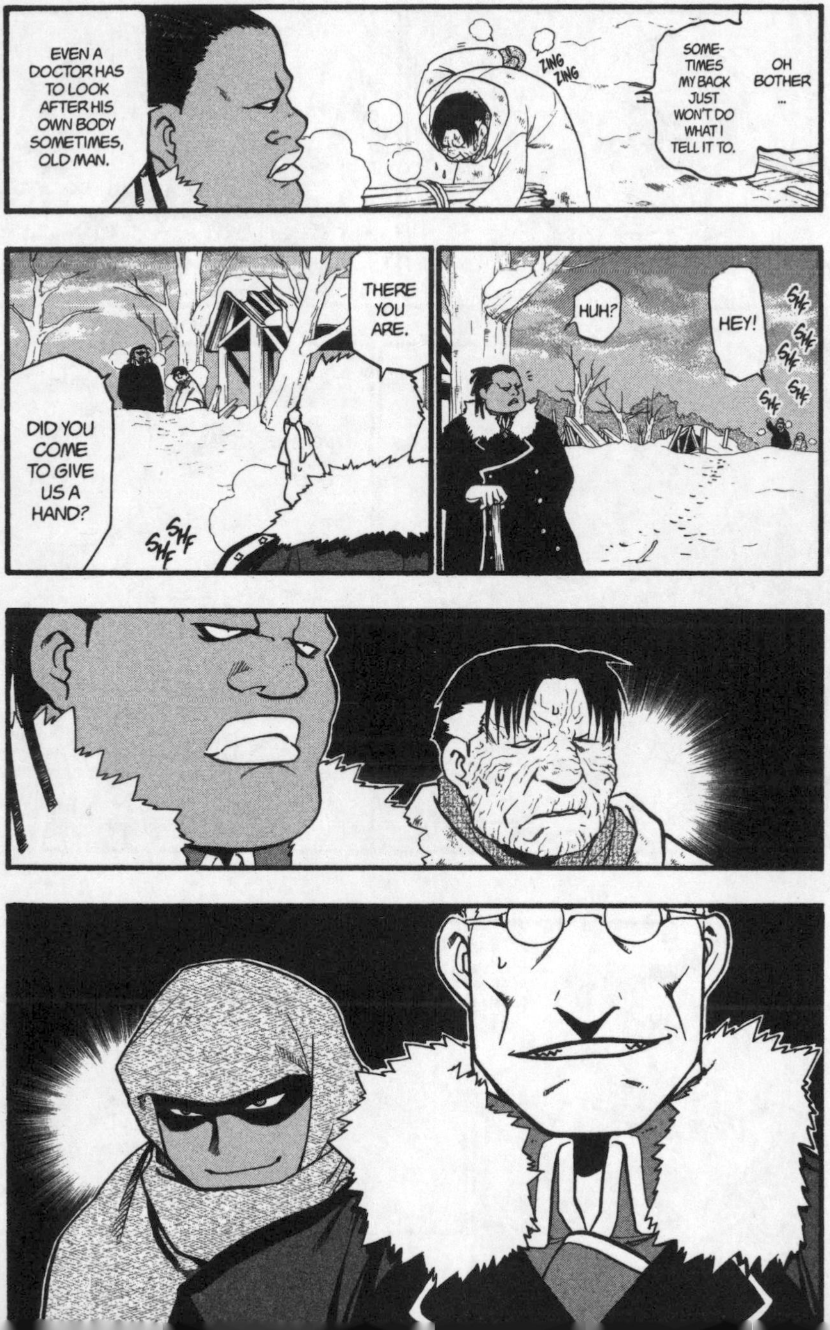
OH BOTHER ...
SOME-TIMES MY BACK JUST WON'T DO WHAT I TELL IT TO.
ZING ZING
EVEN A DOCTOR HAS TO LOOK AFTER HIS OWN BODY SOMETIMES, OLD MAN.
SHF SHF SHF SHF SHF
HEY!
HUH?
THERE YOU ARE.
DID YOU COME TO GIVE US A HAND?
SHF SHF

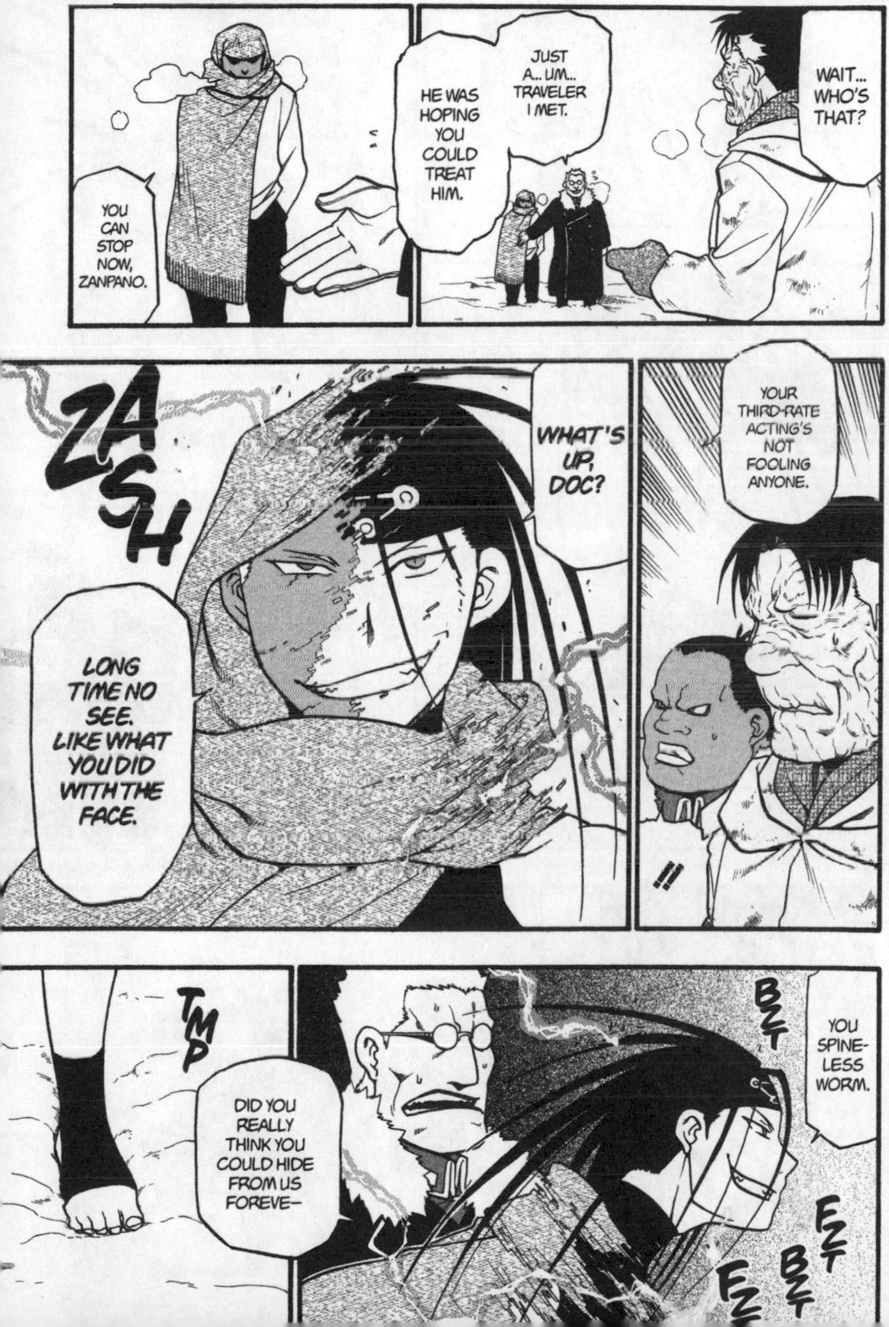
WAIT... WHO'S THAT?
JUST A... UM... TRAVELER I MET.
HE WAS HOPING YOU COULD TREAT HIM.
YOU CAN STOP NOW, ZANPANO.
YOUR THIRD-RATE ACTING'S NOT FOOLING ANYONE.
!!
WHAT'S UP, DOC?
ZASH
LONG TIME NO SEE. LIKE WHAT YOU DID WITH THE FACE.
BZZT
YOU SPINE-LESS WORM.
DID YOU REALLY THINK YOU COULD HIDE FROM US FOREVE–
FZZT
BZZT
TMP

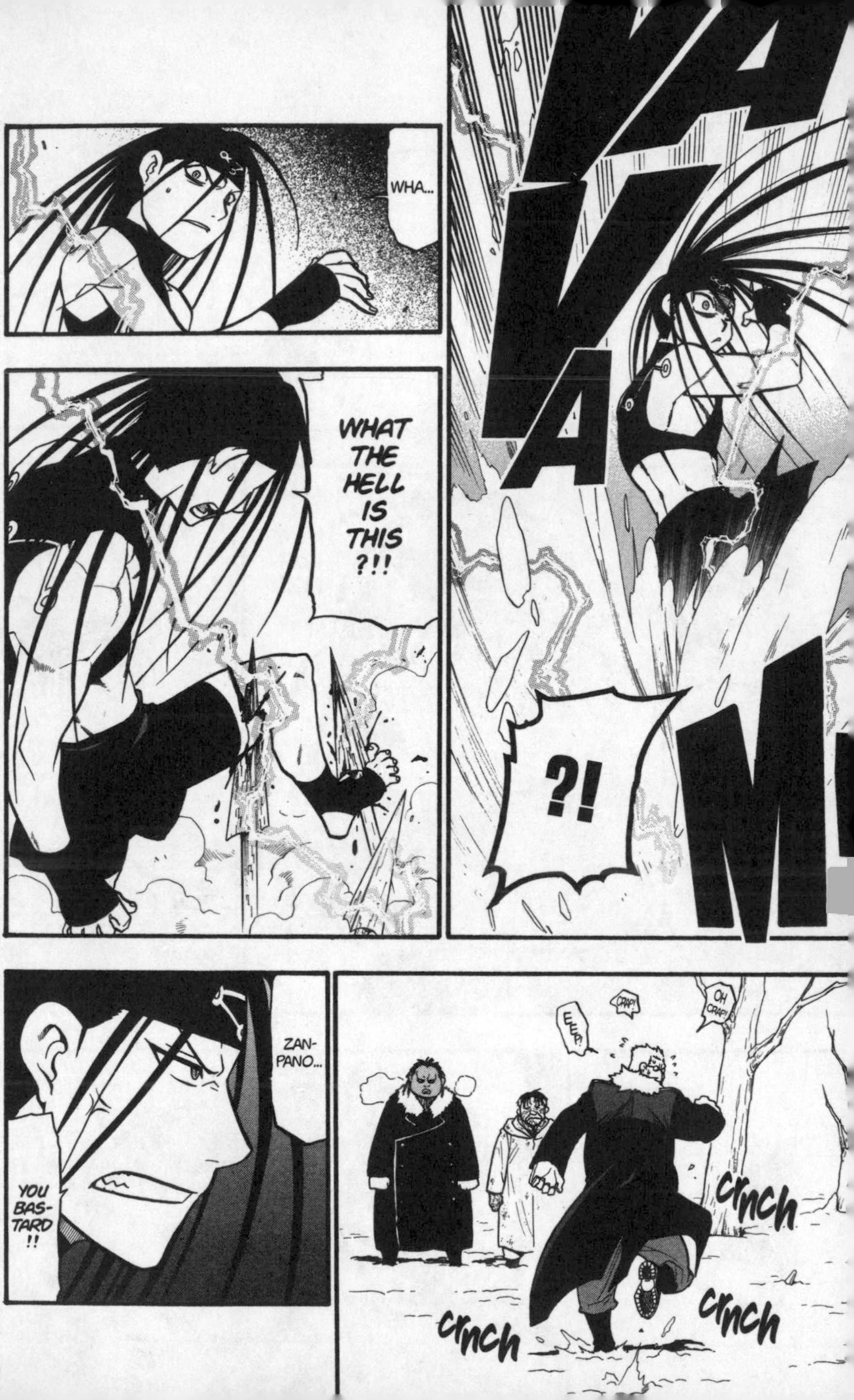
?!
WHA...
WHAT THE HELL IS THIS ?!!
OH CRAP!
CRAP!
EEEP!
crnch
crnch
crnch
ZAN-PANO...
YOU BAS-TARD !!

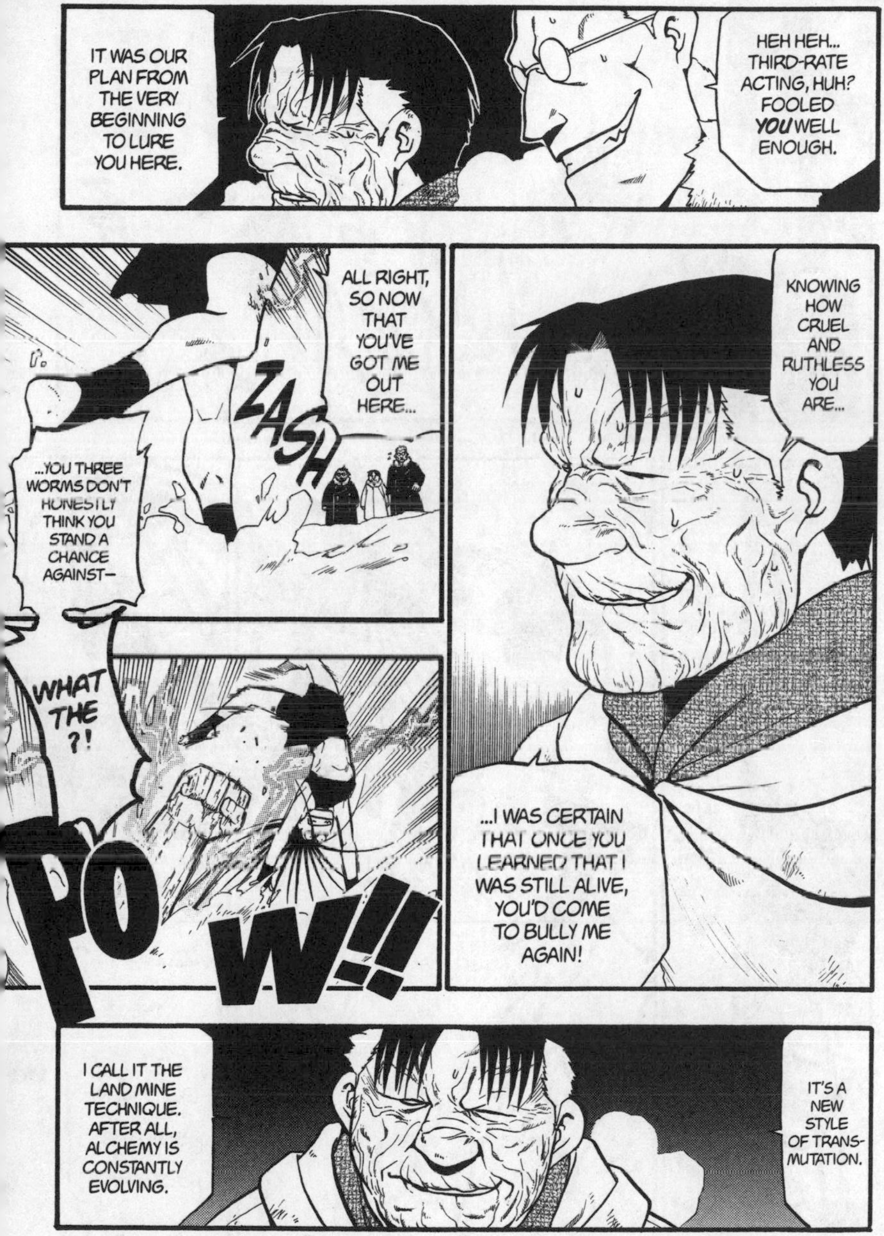
HEH HEH... THIRD-RATE ACTING, HUH? FOOLED YOU WELL ENOUGH.
IT WAS OUR PLAN FROM THE VERY BEGINNING TO LURE YOU HERE.
KNOWING HOW CRUEL AND RUTHLESS YOU ARE...
...I WAS CERTAIN THAT ONCE YOU LEARNED THAT I WAS STILL ALIVE, YOU'D COME TO BULLY ME AGAIN!
ALL RIGHT, SO NOW THAT YOU'VE GOT ME OUT HERE...
ZASH
...YOU THREE WORMS DON'T HONESTLY THINK YOU STAND A CHANCE AGAINST—
WHAT THE ?!
POW!!
IT'S A NEW STYLE OF TRANS-MUTATION.
I CALL IT THE LAND MINE TECHNIQUE. AFTER ALL, ALCHEMY IS CONSTANTLY EVOLVING.

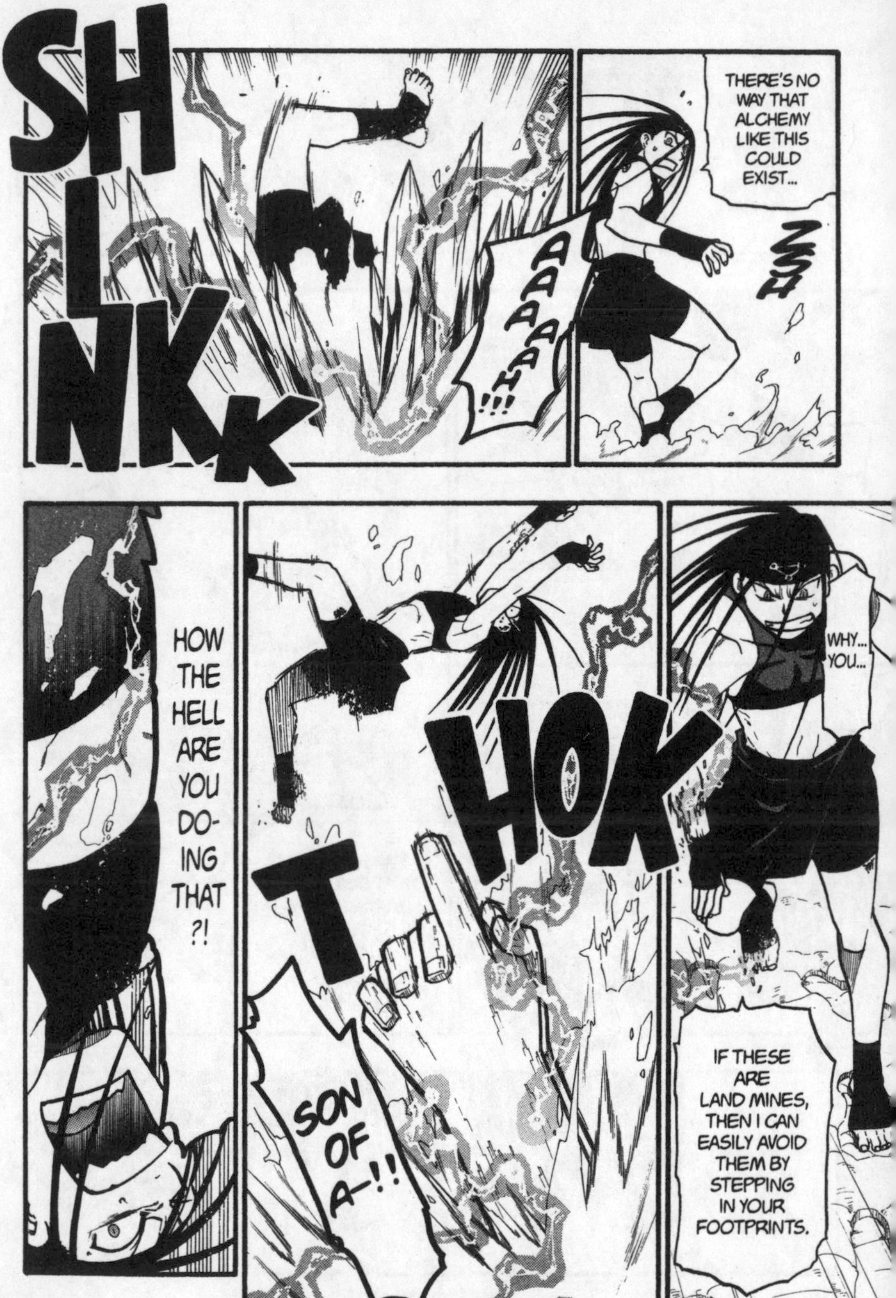
THERE'S NO WAY THAT ALCHEMY LIKE THIS COULD EXIST...
ZSH
AAAAAH!!!
SHLINKK
WHY... YOU...
IF THESE ARE LAND MINES, THEN I CAN EASILY AVOID THEM BY STEPPING IN YOUR FOOTPRINTS.
THOK
SON OF A—!!
HOW THE HELL ARE YOU DO-ING THAT?!

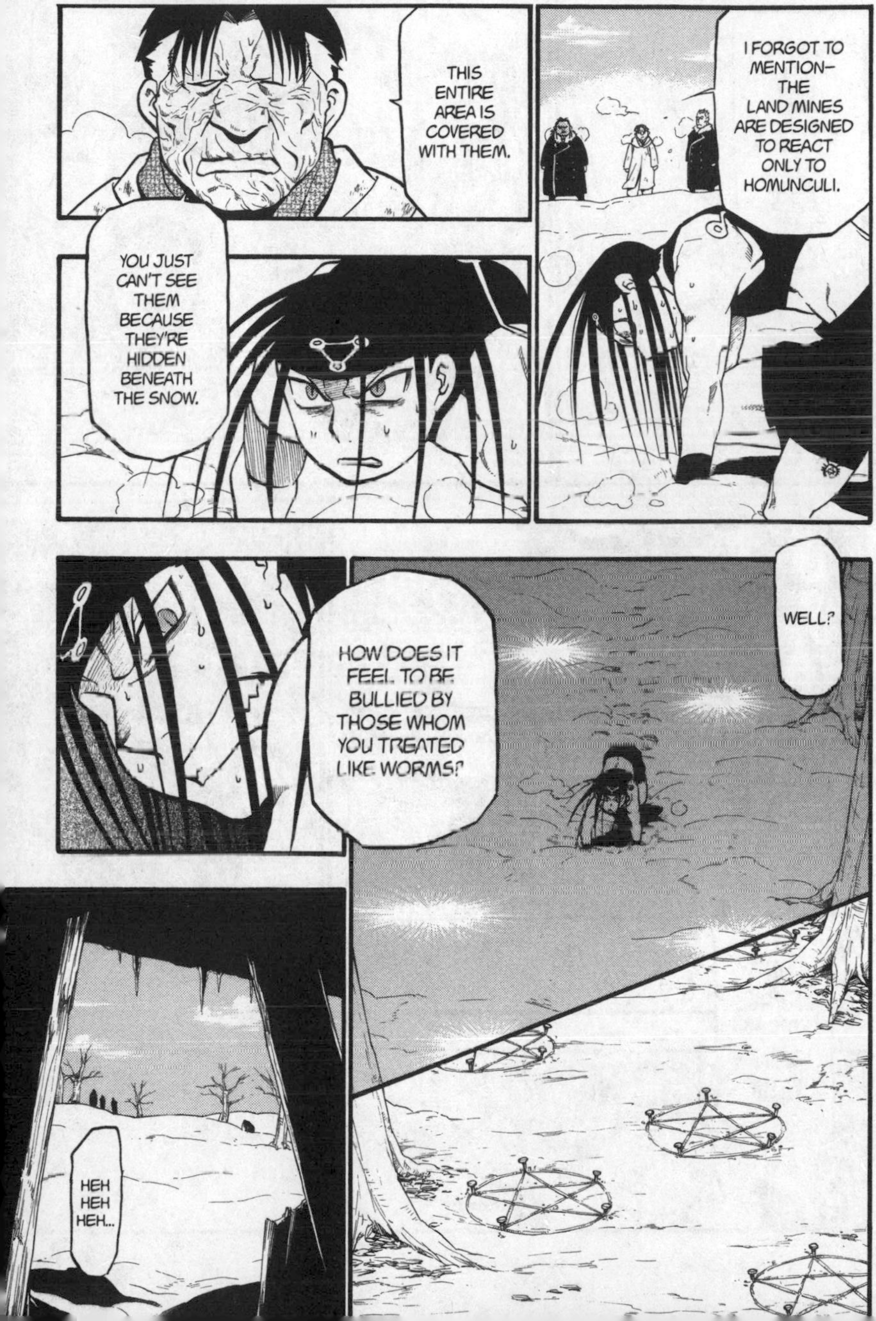
I FORGOT TO MENTION— THE LAND MINES ARE DESIGNED TO REACT ONLY TO HOMUNCULI.
THIS ENTIRE AREA IS COVERED WITH THEM.
YOU JUST CAN'T SEE THEM BECAUSE THEY'RE HIDDEN BENEATH THE SNOW.
WELL?
HOW DOES IT FEEL TO BE BULLIED BY THOSE WHOM YOU TREATED LIKE WORMS?
HEH HEH HEH...

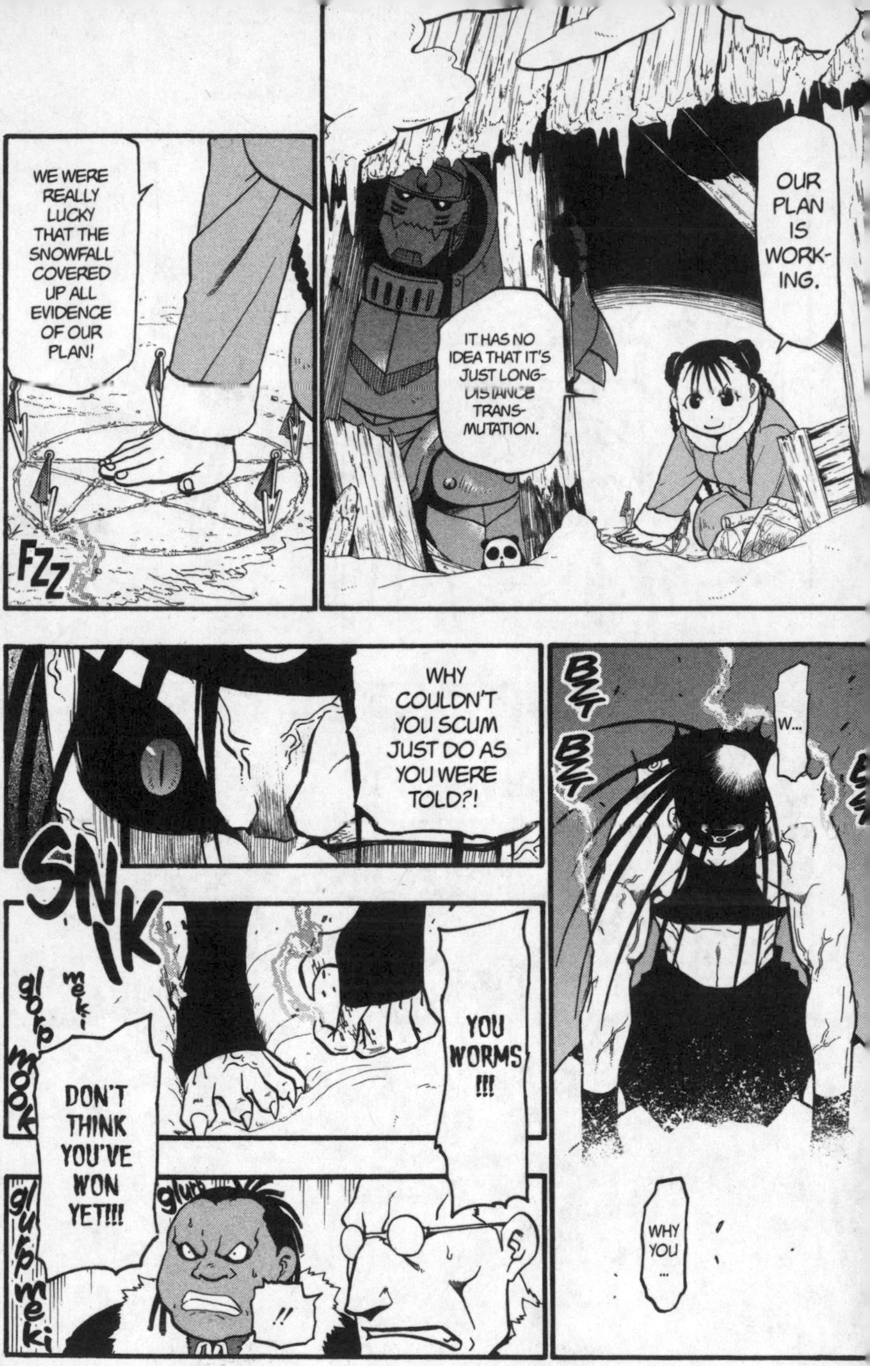
OUR PLAN IS WORKING.
IT HAS NO IDEA THAT IT'S JUST LONG-DISTANCE TRANSMUTATION.
WE WERE REALLY LUCKY THAT THE SNOWFALL COVERED UP ALL EVIDENCE OF OUR PLAN!
FZZ
BZZT
BZZT
W...
WHY YOU ...
WHY COULDN'T YOU SCUM JUST DO AS YOU WERE TOLD?!
SNIK
meki
glorp
mook
YOU WORMS!!!
DON'T THINK YOU'VE WON YET!!!
glurp
meki
glub
!!

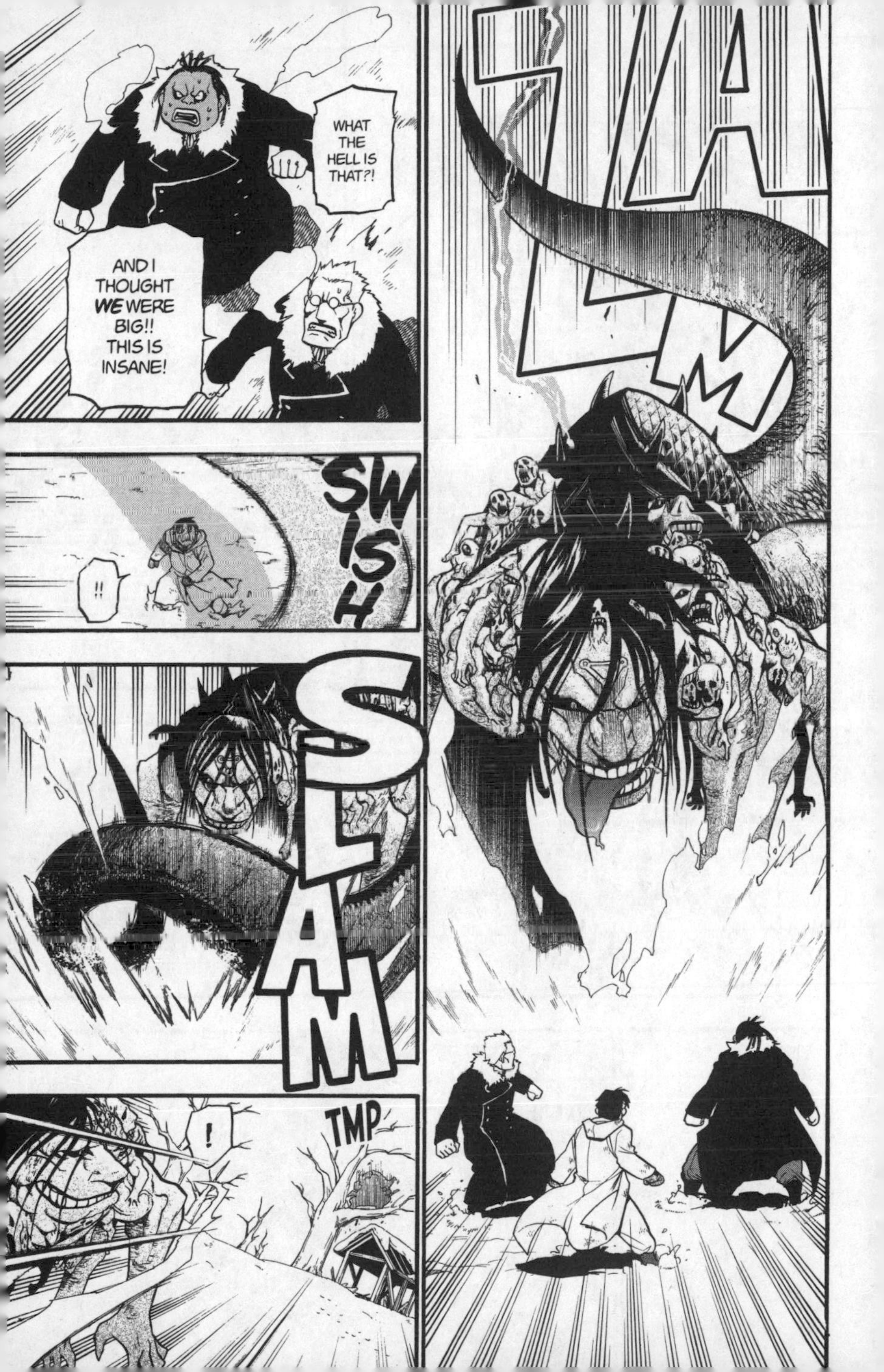
SLAM
WHAT THE HELL IS THAT?!
AND I THOUGHT WE WERE BIG!! THIS IS INSANE!
SWISH
!!
SLAM
TMP
!

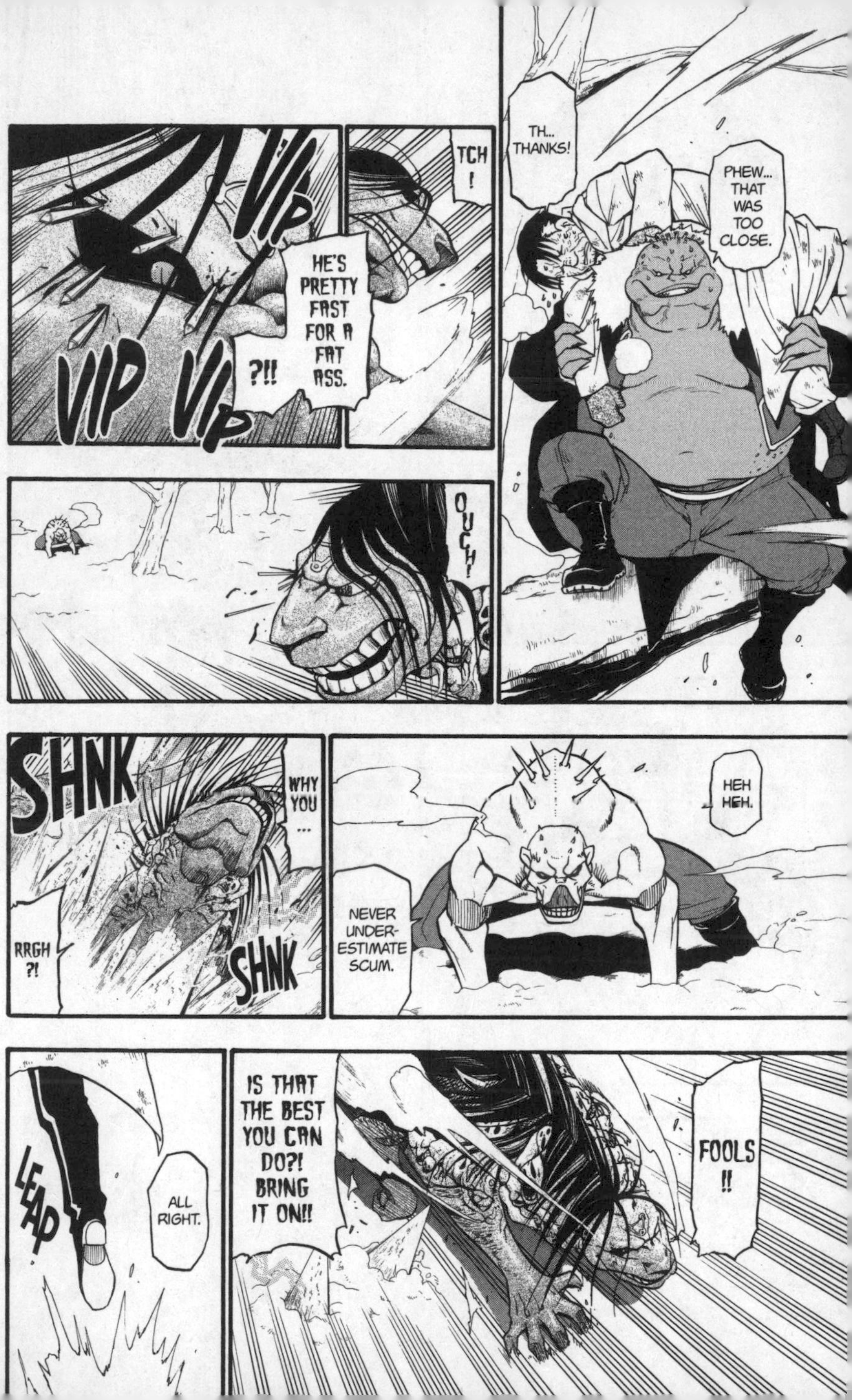
PHEW... THAT WAS TOO CLOSE.
TH... THANKS!
TCH!
HE'S PRETTY FAST FOR A FAT ASS.
?!!
VIP
VIP
VIP
OUCH!
HEH HEH.
NEVER UNDER-ESTIMATE SCUM.
SHNK
WHY YOU...
RRGH ?!
SHNK
FOOLS!!
IS THAT THE BEST YOU CAN DO?! BRING IT ON!!
ALL RIGHT.
LEAP

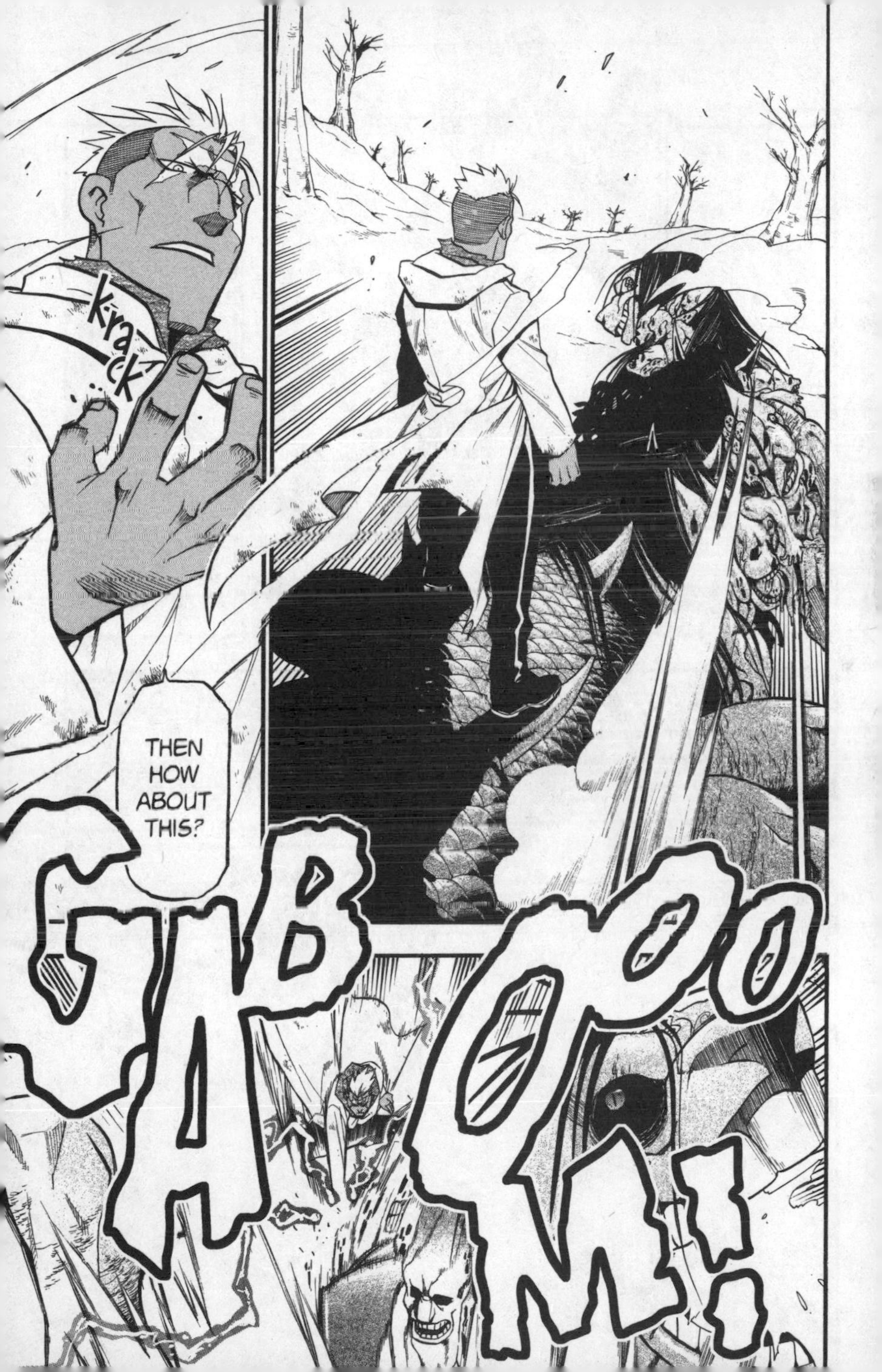

KRACK
THEN HOW ABOUT THIS?
KABOOM!

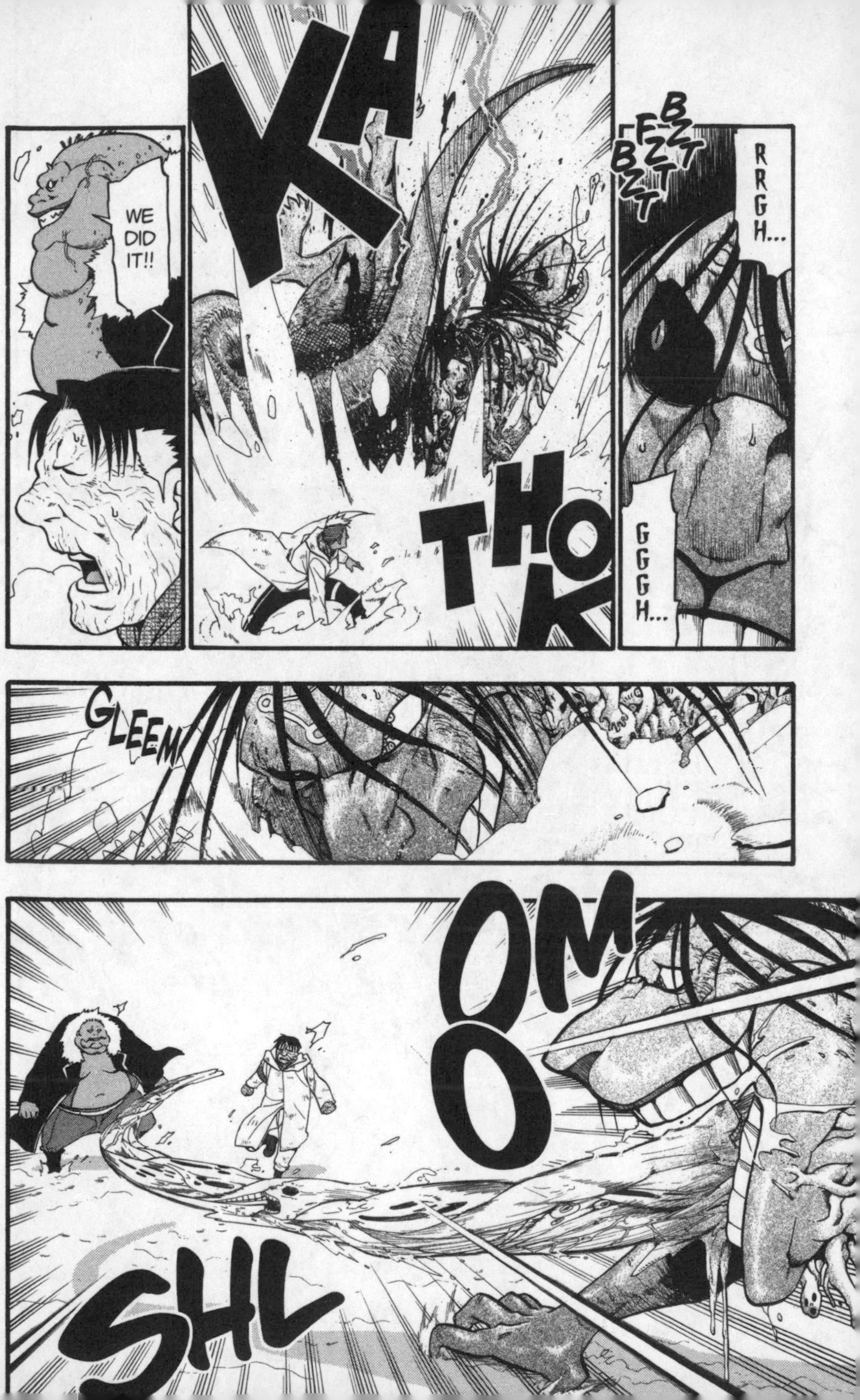
BZT
FZT
BZT
RRGH...
GGGH...
KA
THOK
WE DID IT!!
GLEEM
OMO
SHL

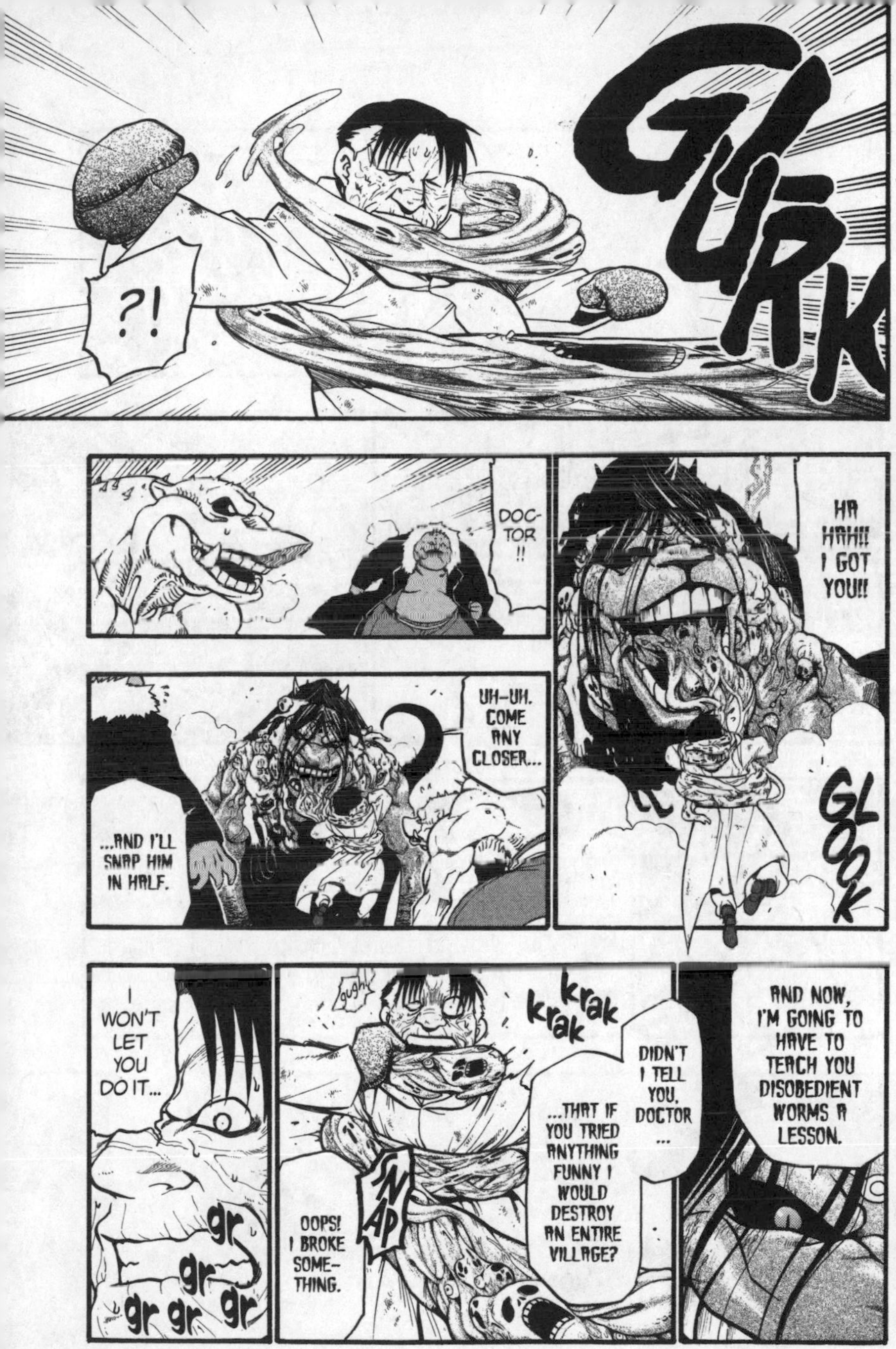
GURK
?!
HA HAH!! I GOT YOU!!
GLOOOK
DOCTOR!!
UH-UH. COME ANY CLOSER...
...AND I'LL SNAP HIM IN HALF.
AND NOW, I'M GOING TO HAVE TO TEACH YOU DISOBEDIENT WORMS A LESSON.
gugh
krak krak
DIDN'T I TELL YOU, DOCTOR...
...THAT IF YOU TRIED ANYTHING FUNNY I WOULD DESTROY AN ENTIRE VILLAGE?
SNAP
OOPS! I BROKE SOMETHING.
I WON'T LET YOU DO IT...
gr gr gr gr gr

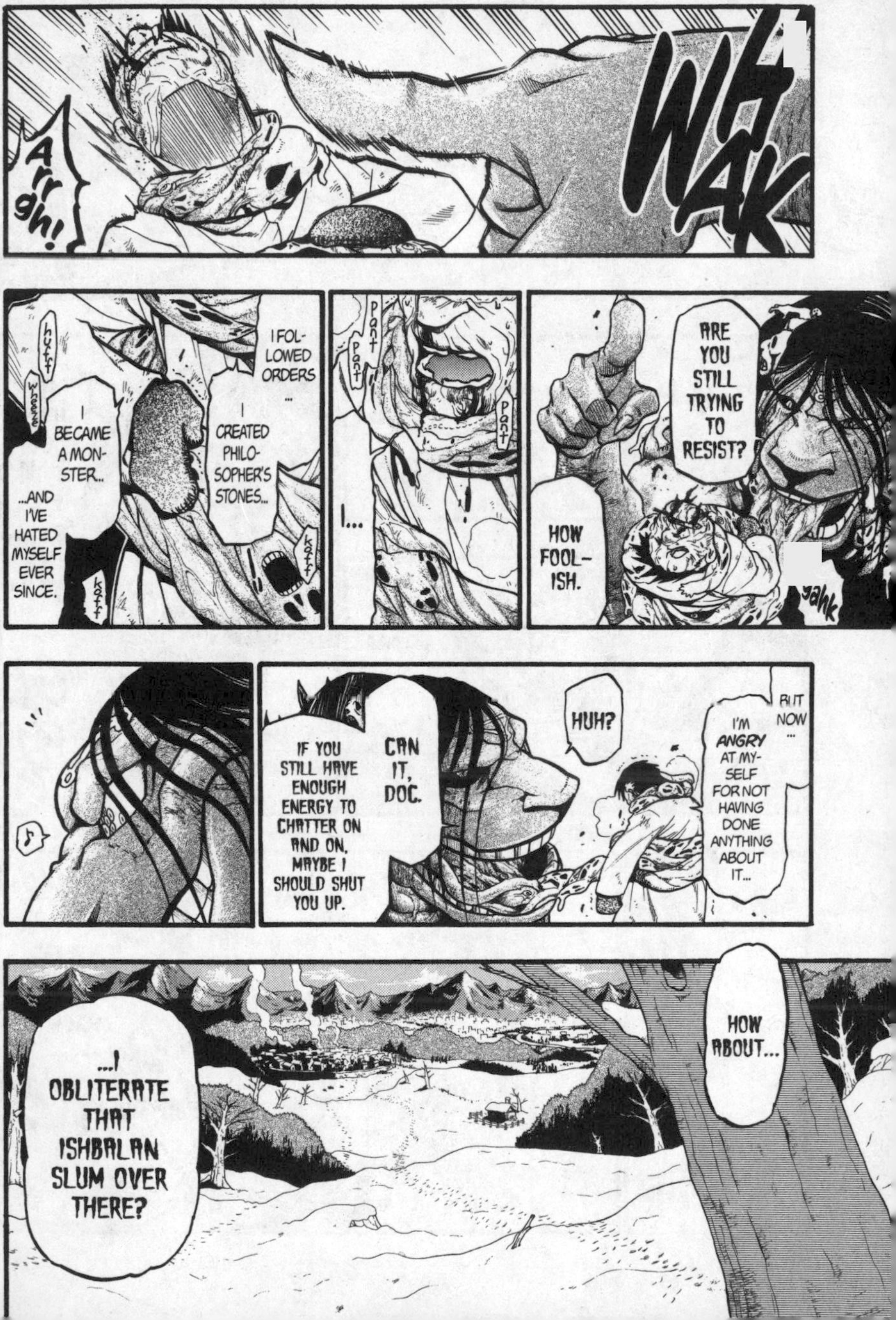
WHAK
Arrrgh!
ARE YOU STILL TRYING TO RESIST?
HOW FOOLISH.
gahk
pant
pant
pant
I...
I FOLLOWED ORDERS...
I CREATED PHILOSOPHER'S STONES...
I BECAME A MONSTER...
...AND I'VE HATED MYSELF EVER SINCE.
huff
wheeze
koff
koff
BUT NOW...
I'M ANGRY AT MYSELF FOR NOT HAVING DONE ANYTHING ABOUT IT...
HUH?
CAN IT, DOC.
IF YOU STILL HAVE ENOUGH ENERGY TO CHATTER ON AND ON, MAYBE I SHOULD SHUT YOU UP.
♪
HOW ABOUT...
...I OBLITERATE THAT ISHBALAN SLUM OVER THERE?

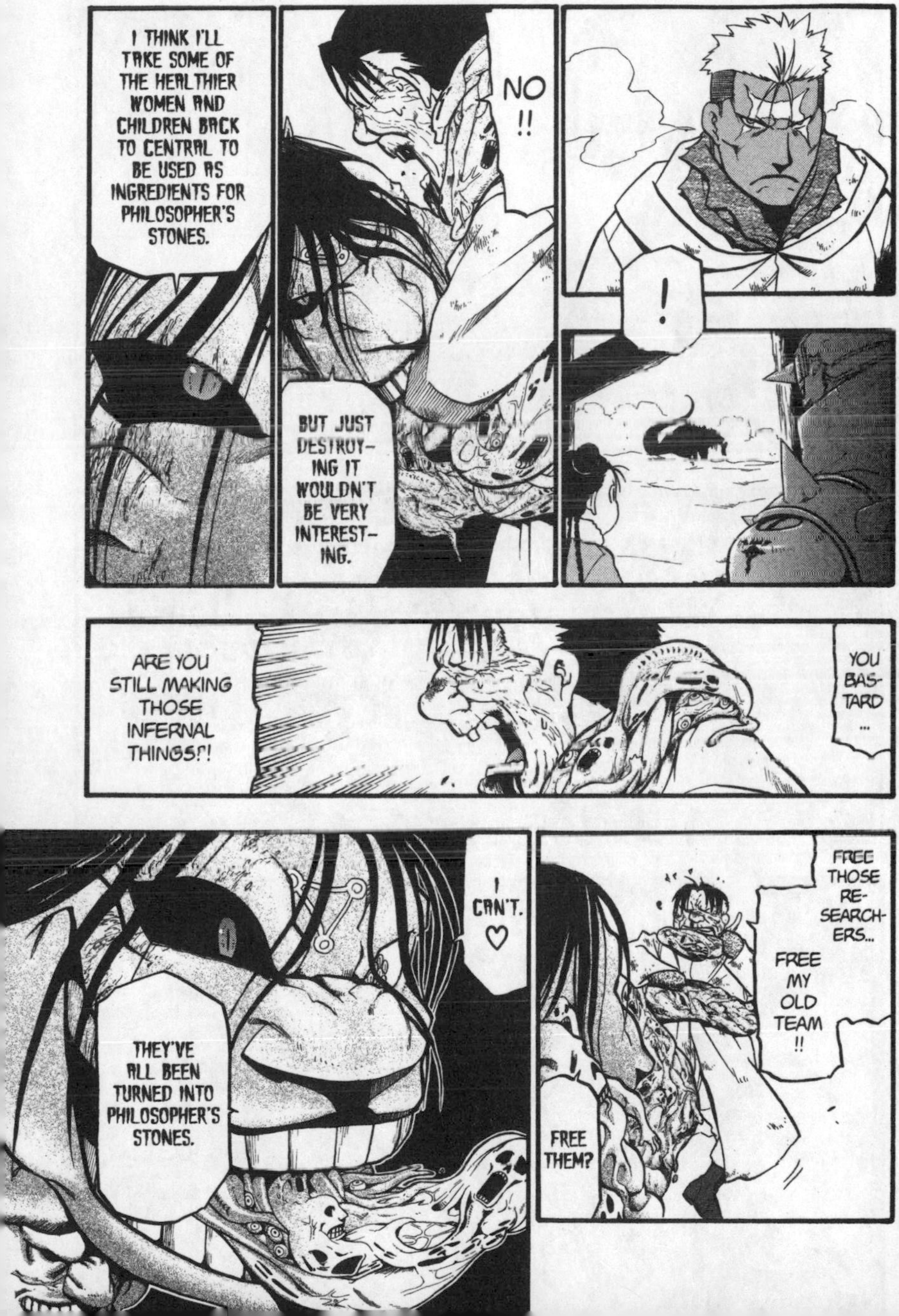
!
NO !!
BUT JUST DESTROYING IT WOULDN'T BE VERY INTERESTING.
I THINK I'LL TAKE SOME OF THE HEALTHIER WOMEN AND CHILDREN BACK TO CENTRAL TO BE USED AS INGREDIENTS FOR PHILOSOPHER'S STONES.
YOU BASTARD...
ARE YOU STILL MAKING THOSE INFERNAL THINGS?!
FREE THOSE RESEARCHERS...
FREE MY OLD TEAM !!
FREE THEM?
I CAN'T. ♡
THEY'VE ALL BEEN TURNED INTO PHILOSOPHER'S STONES.

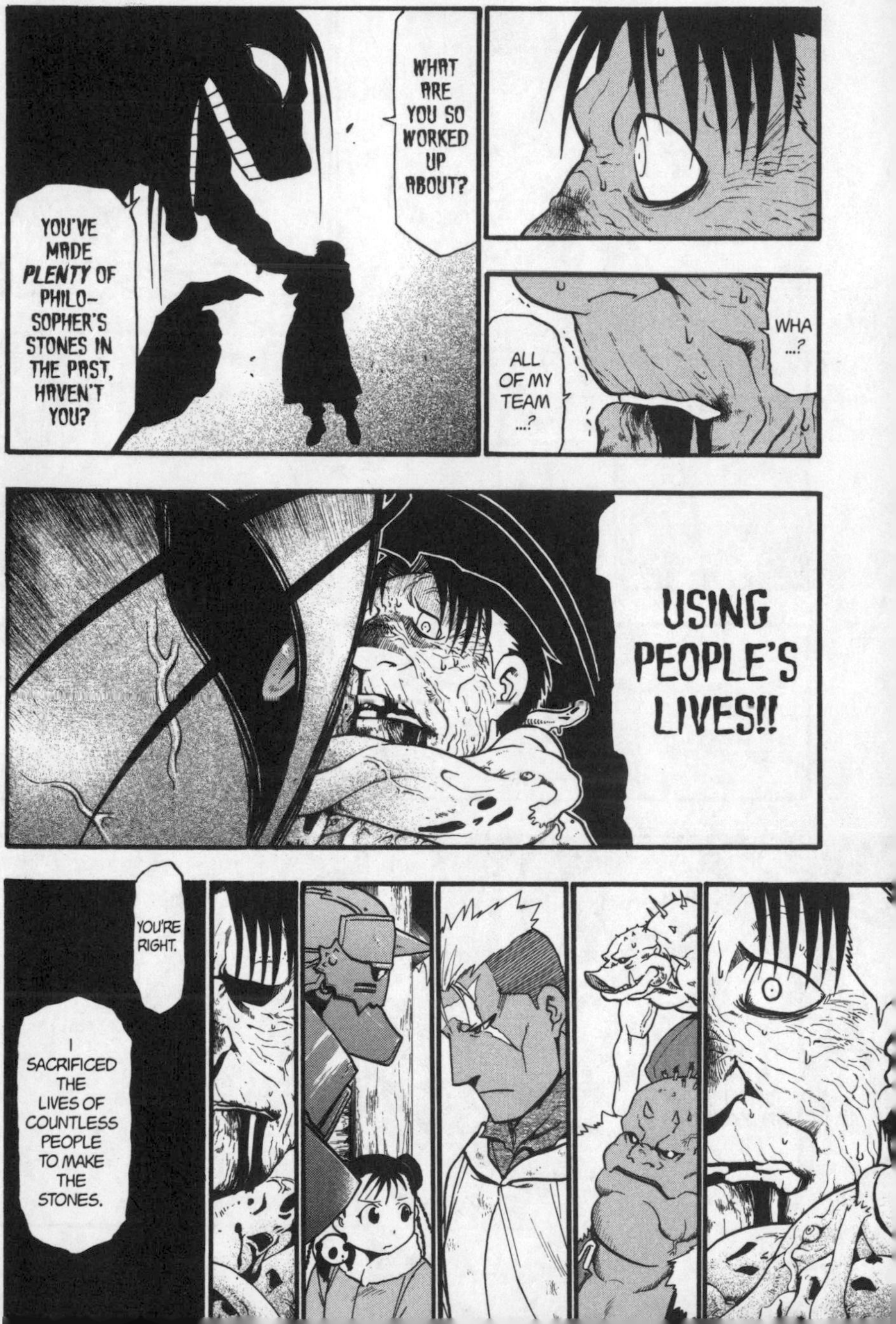
WHA ...?
ALL OF MY TEAM ...?
WHAT ARE YOU SO WORKED UP ABOUT?
YOU'VE MADE ***PLENTY*** OF PHILO-SOPHER'S STONES IN THE PAST, HAVEN'T YOU?
USING PEOPLE'S LIVES!!
YOU'RE RIGHT.
I SACRIFICED THE LIVES OF COUNTLESS PEOPLE TO MAKE THE STONES.

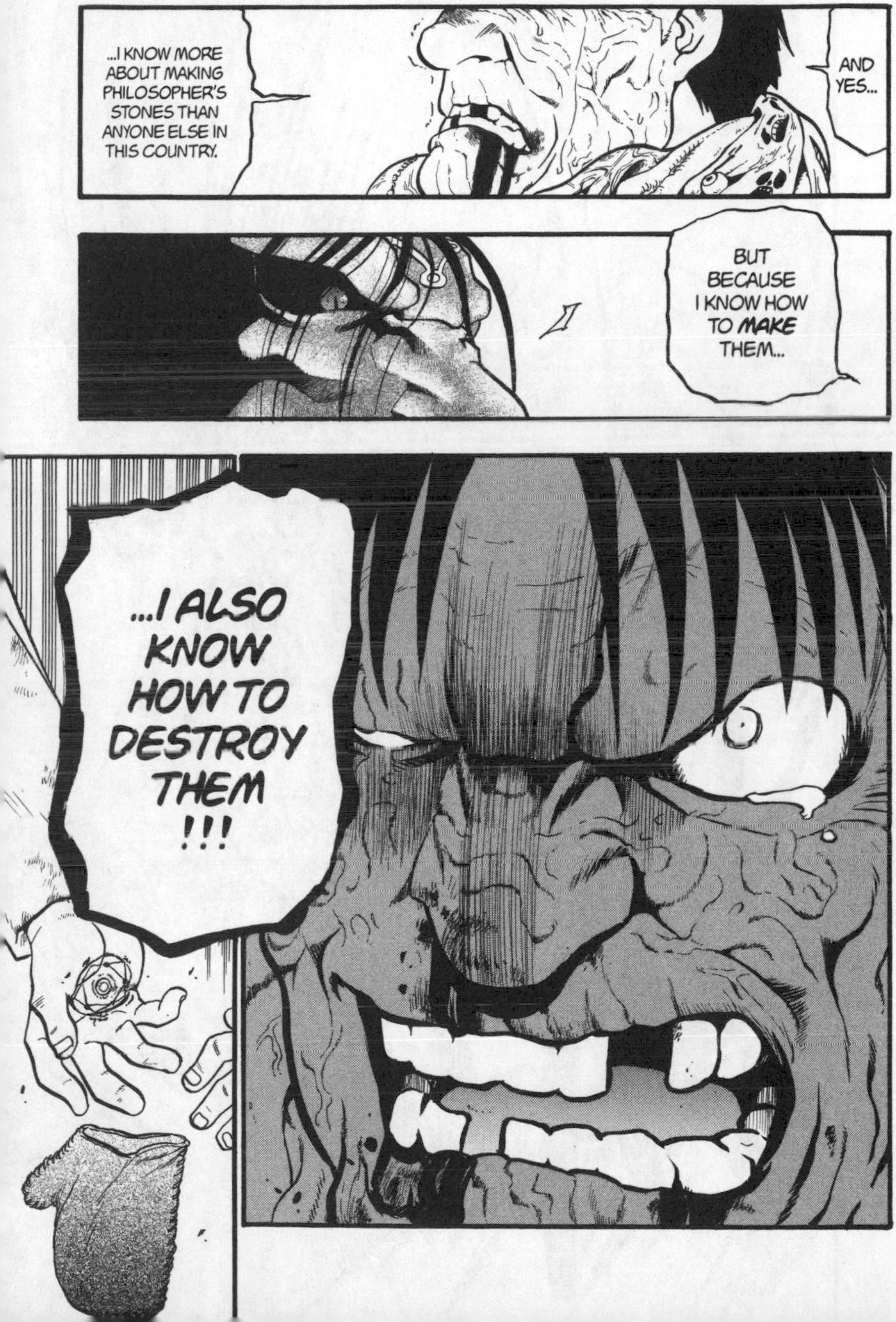
AND YES...
...I KNOW MORE ABOUT MAKING PHILOSOPHER'S STONES THAN ANYONE ELSE IN THIS COUNTRY.
BUT BECAUSE I KNOW HOW TO *MAKE* THEM...
...I ALSO KNOW HOW TO DESTROY THEM!!!

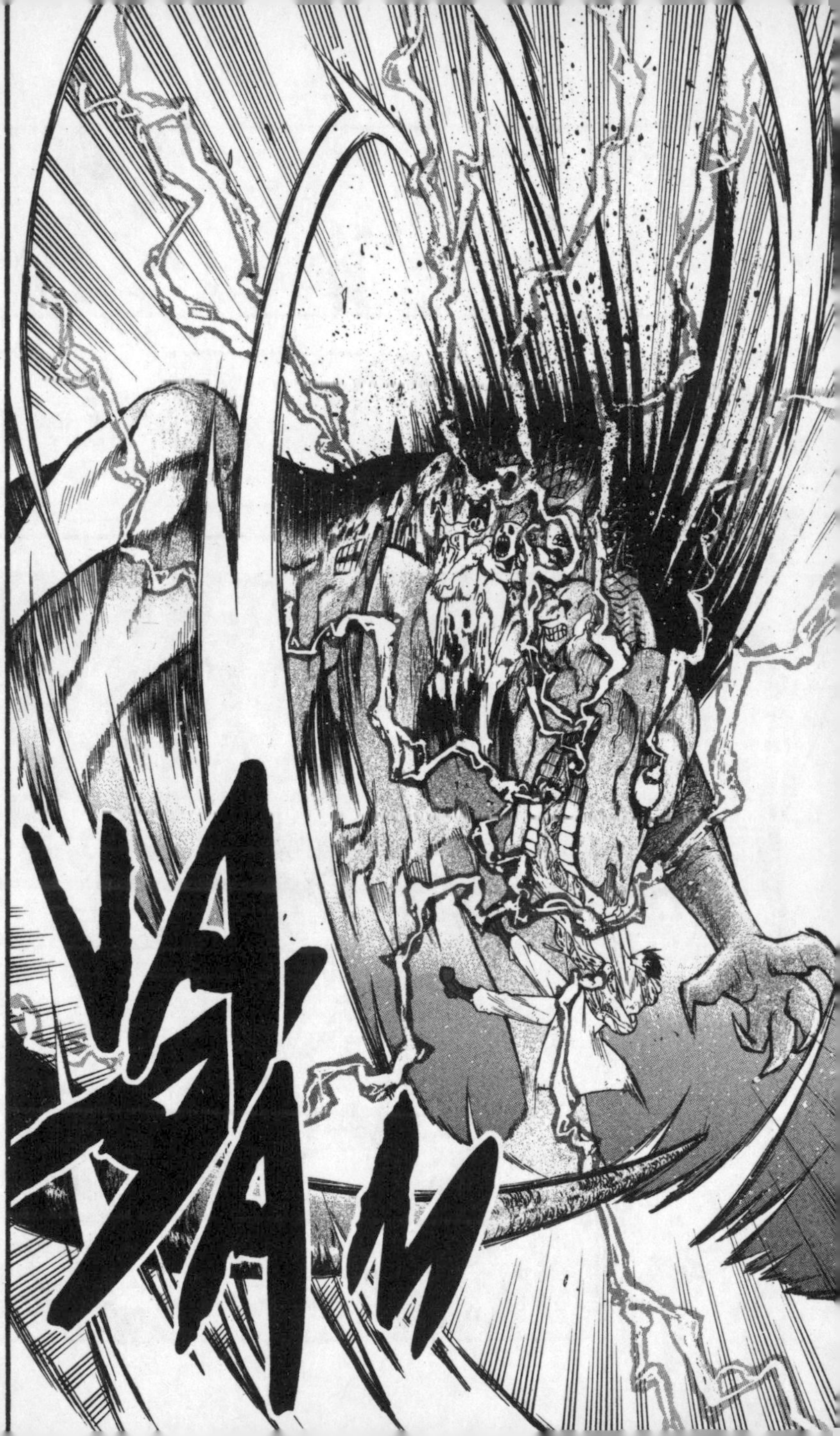
VADAM

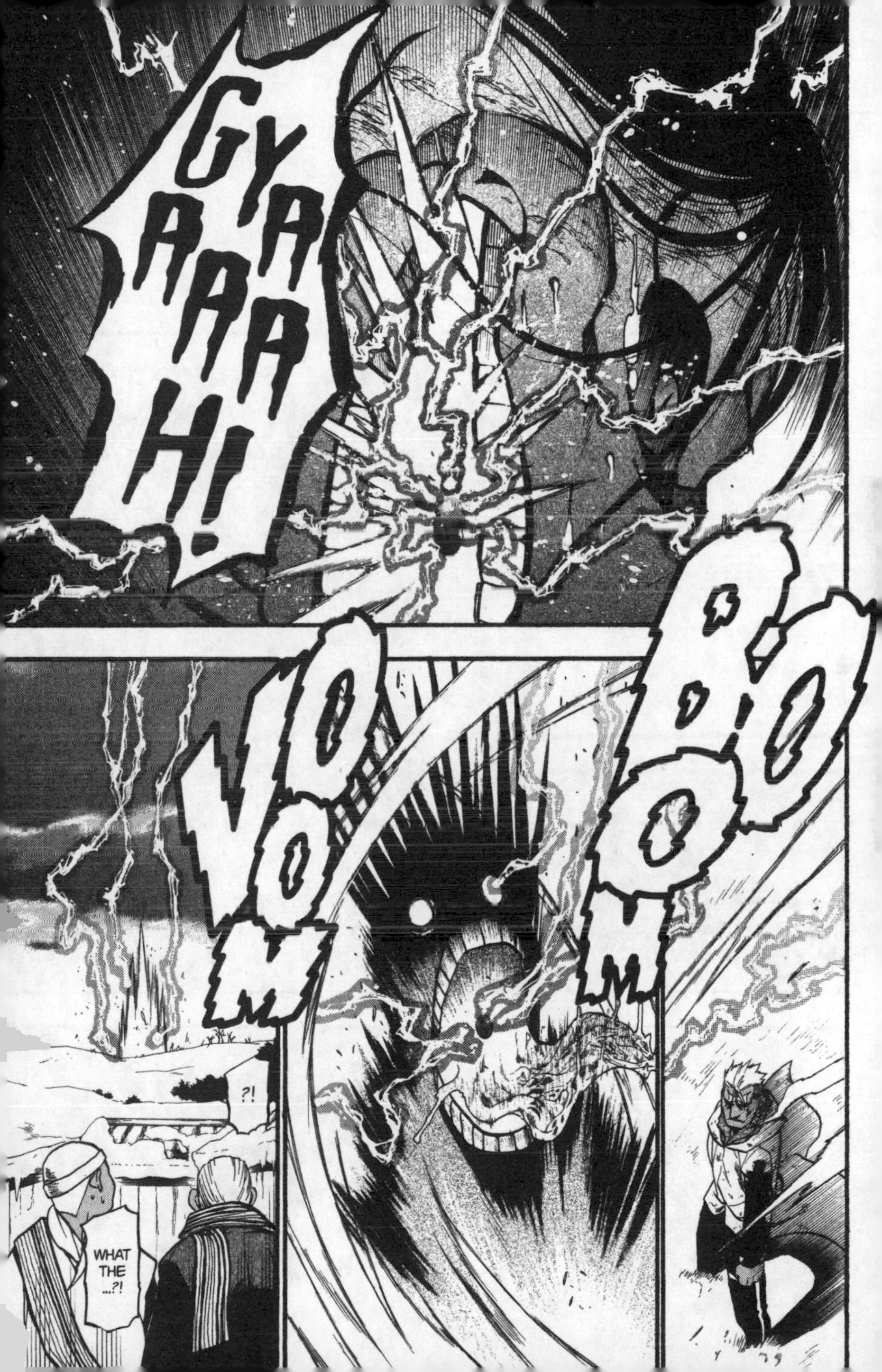
GYAAAAH!
VOOOM
VOOOOOM
?!
WHAT THE ...?!

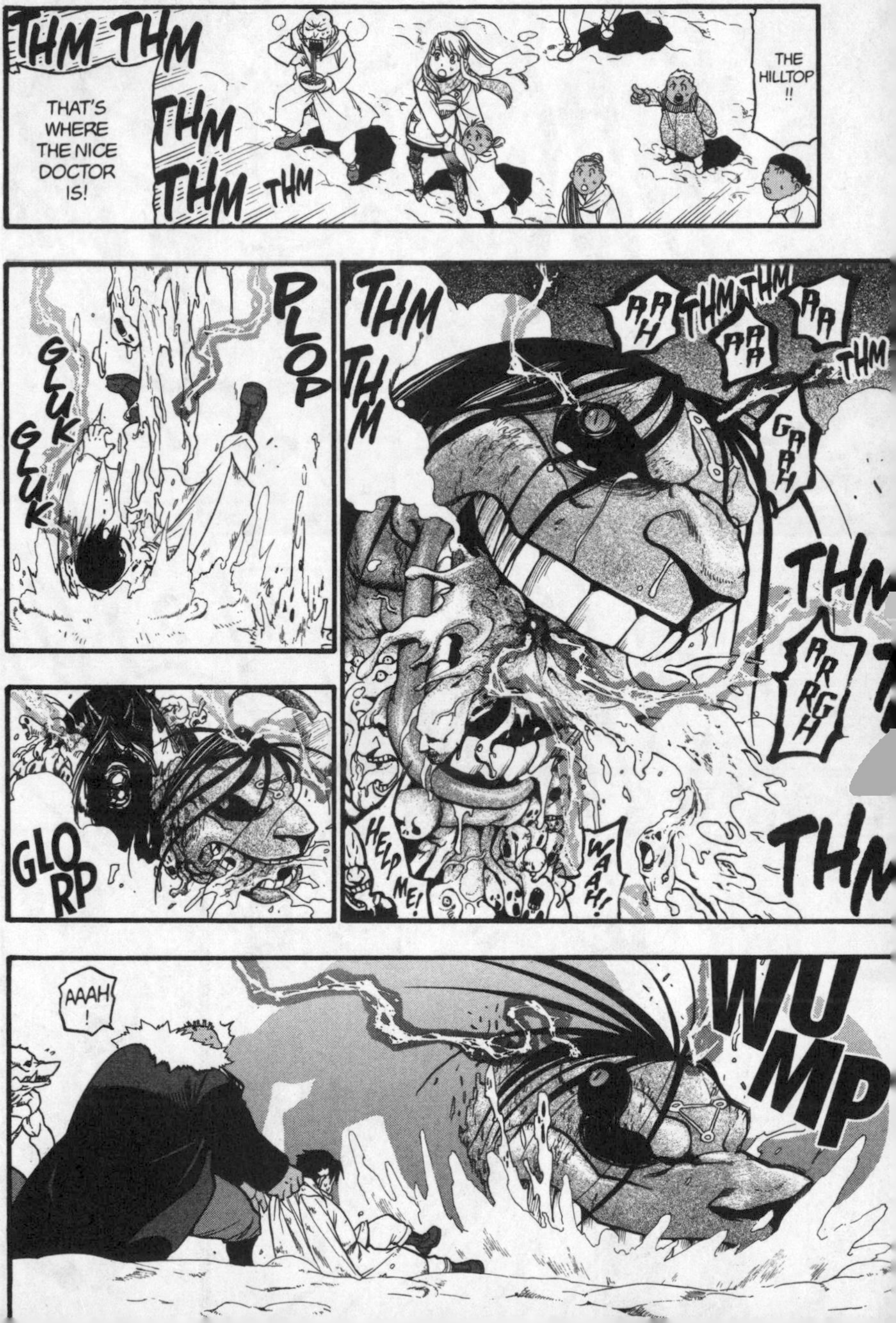
THE HILLTOP !!
THAT'S WHERE THE NICE DOCTOR IS!
THM THM
THM
THM THM
AAH
THM THM
AAA
AA
THM
GAAH
THM
ARRRGH
THM
THM
THM
WAAH!
HELP ME!
THM
PLOP
GLUK GLUK GLUK
GLORP
WUMP
AAAH!

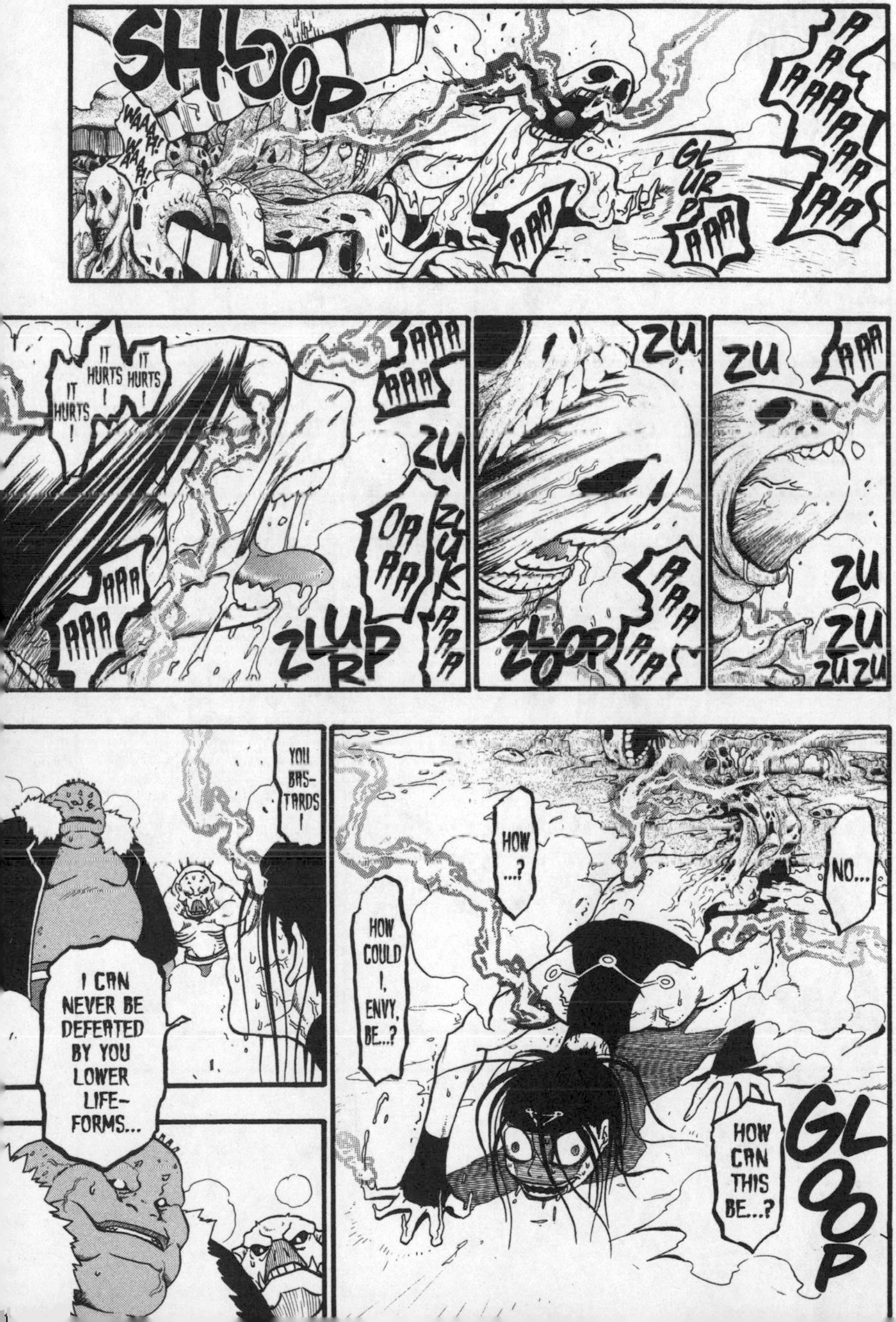

AAAAAAAAAAAA
GLURP
AAA
AAA
SHLOOP
WAAAH! WAAAH! WAAAH!
AAA
ZU
ZU ZU ZUZU
ZU
AAAAAA
ZLOOP
AAAAAA
ZU
ZUZUK AAA
OAAA
IT HURTS! IT HURTS! IT HURTS!
AAAAAA
ZLURP
NO...
HOW...?
HOW COULD I, ENVY, BE...?
GLOOOP
HOW CAN THIS BE...?
YOU BASTARDS!
I CAN NEVER BE DEFEATED BY YOU LOWER LIFE-FORMS...

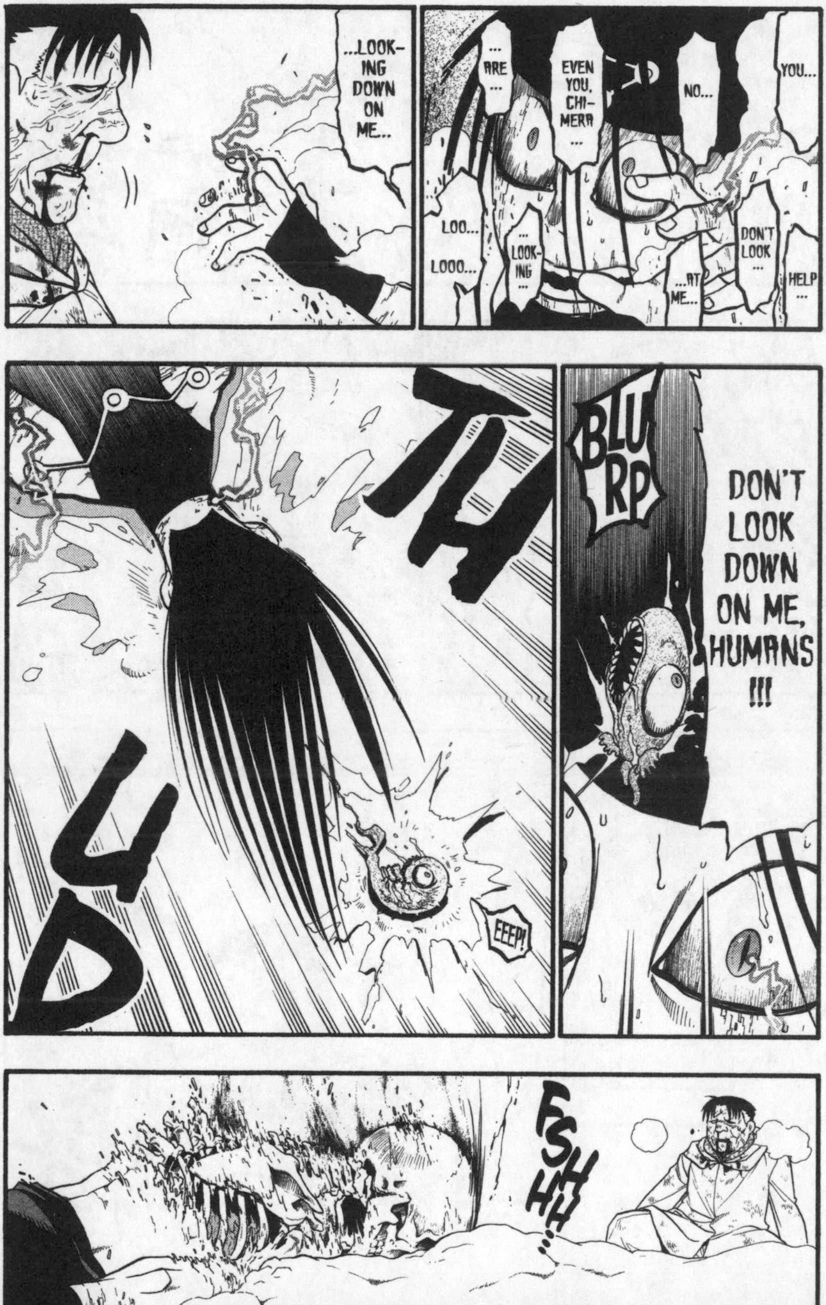
YOU...
NO...
EVEN YOU, CHIMERA...
...ARE...
HELP...
DON'T LOOK...
...AT ME...
...LOOKING...
LOO... LOOO...
...LOOKING DOWN ON ME...
BLURP
DON'T LOOK DOWN ON ME, HUMANS!!!
THUD
EEEP!
FSHHH...

...YOU WORMS...

DON'T LOOK AT ME...

PUNT

WHAT A LAUGH!

NOW *YOU'RE* THE WORM!

HAH!

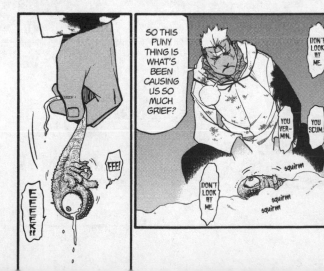

EEEEK!!

FEE!

SO THIS PLINY THING IS WHAT'S BEEN CAUSING US SO MUCH GRIEF?

DON'T LOOK AT ME

YOU VER-MIN.

YOU SCUM.

squirm

squirm squirm

DON'T LOOK AT ME.

DON'T LOOK AT ME.

YOU SCUM.

POF!

FEE!

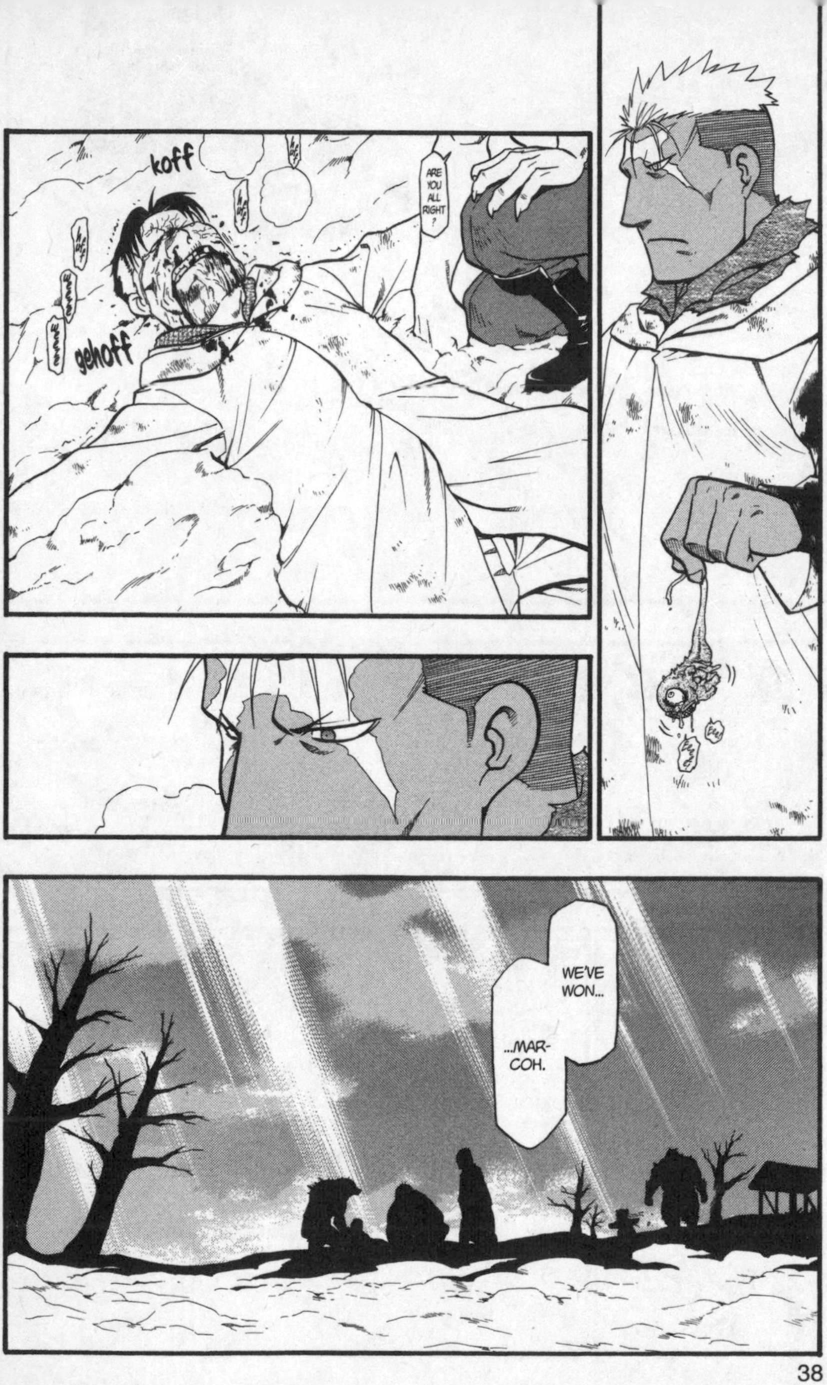
Eee!
Eeee!
ARE YOU ALL RIGHT?
hoff
koff
hoff
hoff
gehoff
WE'VE WON...
...MAR-COH.

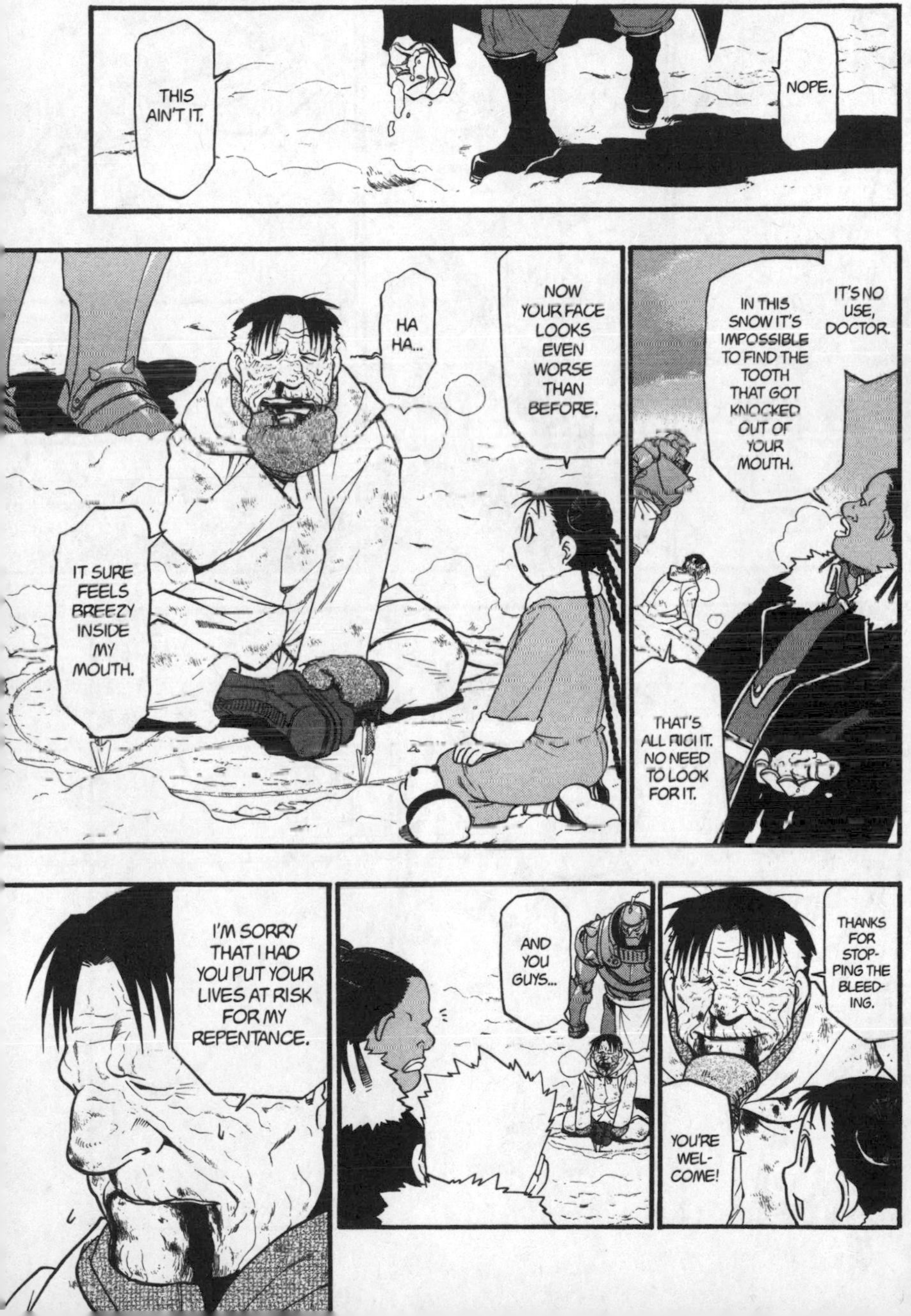
NOPE.
THIS AIN'T IT.
IT'S NO USE, DOCTOR.
IN THIS SNOW IT'S IMPOSSIBLE TO FIND THE TOOTH THAT GOT KNOCKED OUT OF YOUR MOUTH.
THAT'S ALL RIGHT. NO NEED TO LOOK FOR IT.
NOW YOUR FACE LOOKS EVEN WORSE THAN BEFORE.
HA HA...
IT SURE FEELS BREEZY INSIDE MY MOUTH.
THANKS FOR STOPPING THE BLEEDING.
YOU'RE WELCOME!
AND YOU GUYS...
I'M SORRY THAT I HAD YOU PUT YOUR LIVES AT RISK FOR MY REPENTANCE.

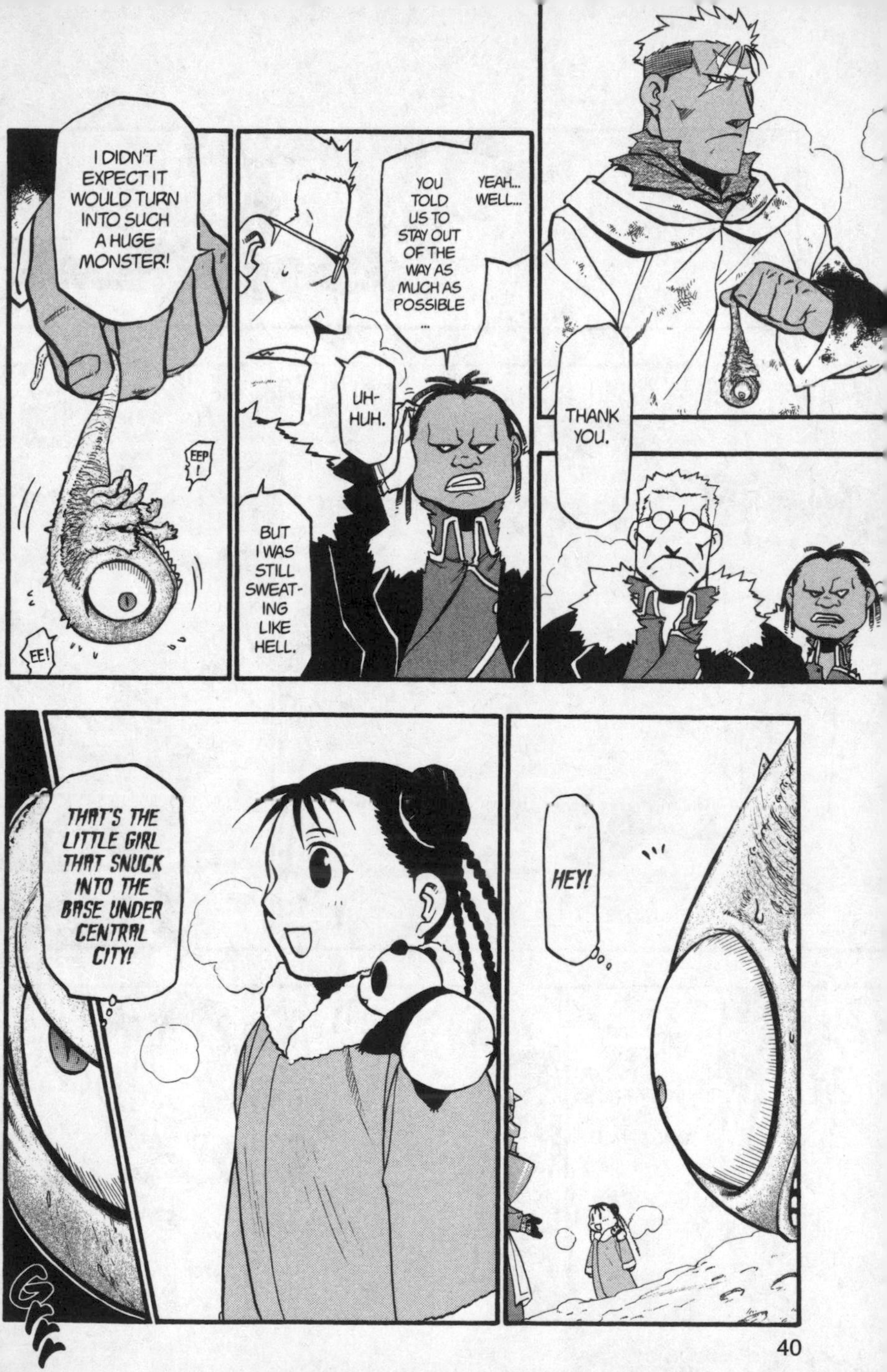
THANK YOU.
YEAH... WELL...
YOU TOLD US TO STAY OUT OF THE WAY AS MUCH AS POSSIBLE...
UH-HUH.
BUT I WAS STILL SWEATING LIKE HELL.
I DIDN'T EXPECT IT WOULD TURN INTO SUCH A HUGE MONSTER!
EEP!
EE!
HEY!
THAT'S THE LITTLE GIRL THAT SNUCK INTO THE BASE UNDER CENTRAL CITY!
GRRR

Chapter 80 The Prodigal Father Returns

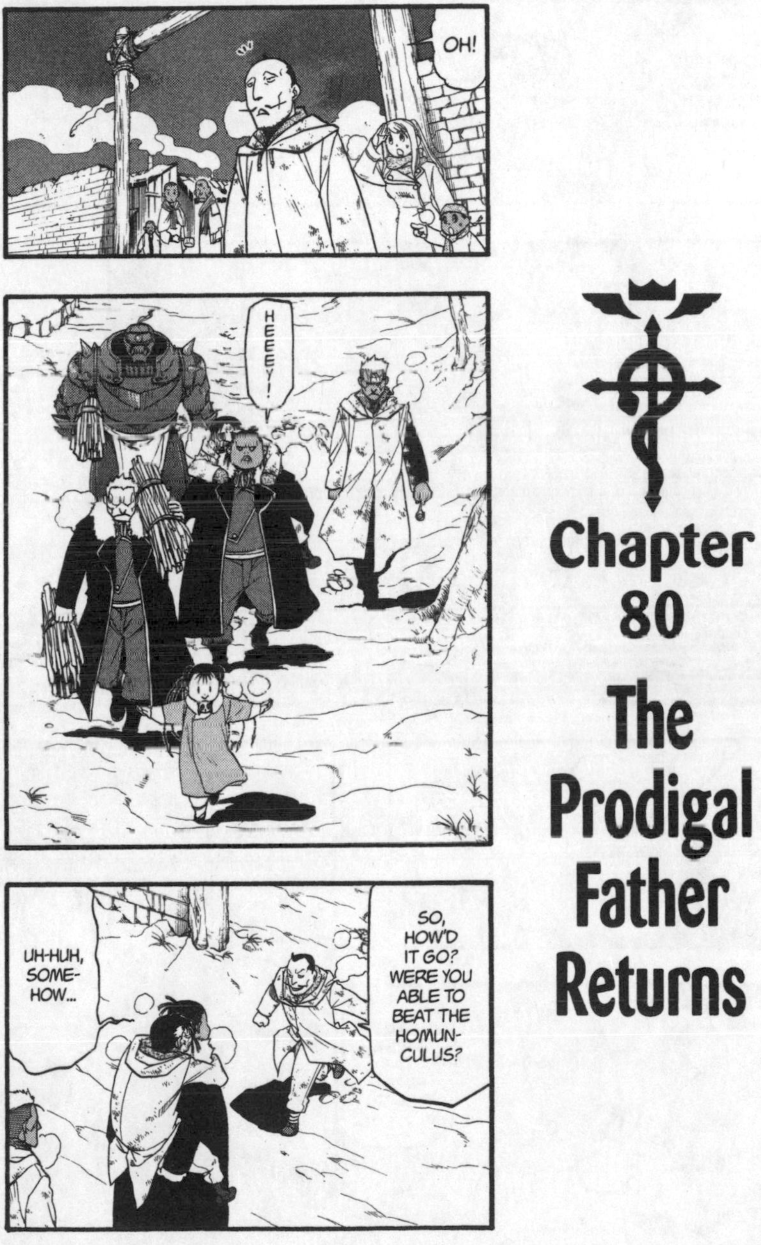
OH!
HEEEY!
SO, HOW'D IT GO? WERE YOU ABLE TO BEAT THE HOMUNCULUS?
UH-HUH, SOMEHOW...

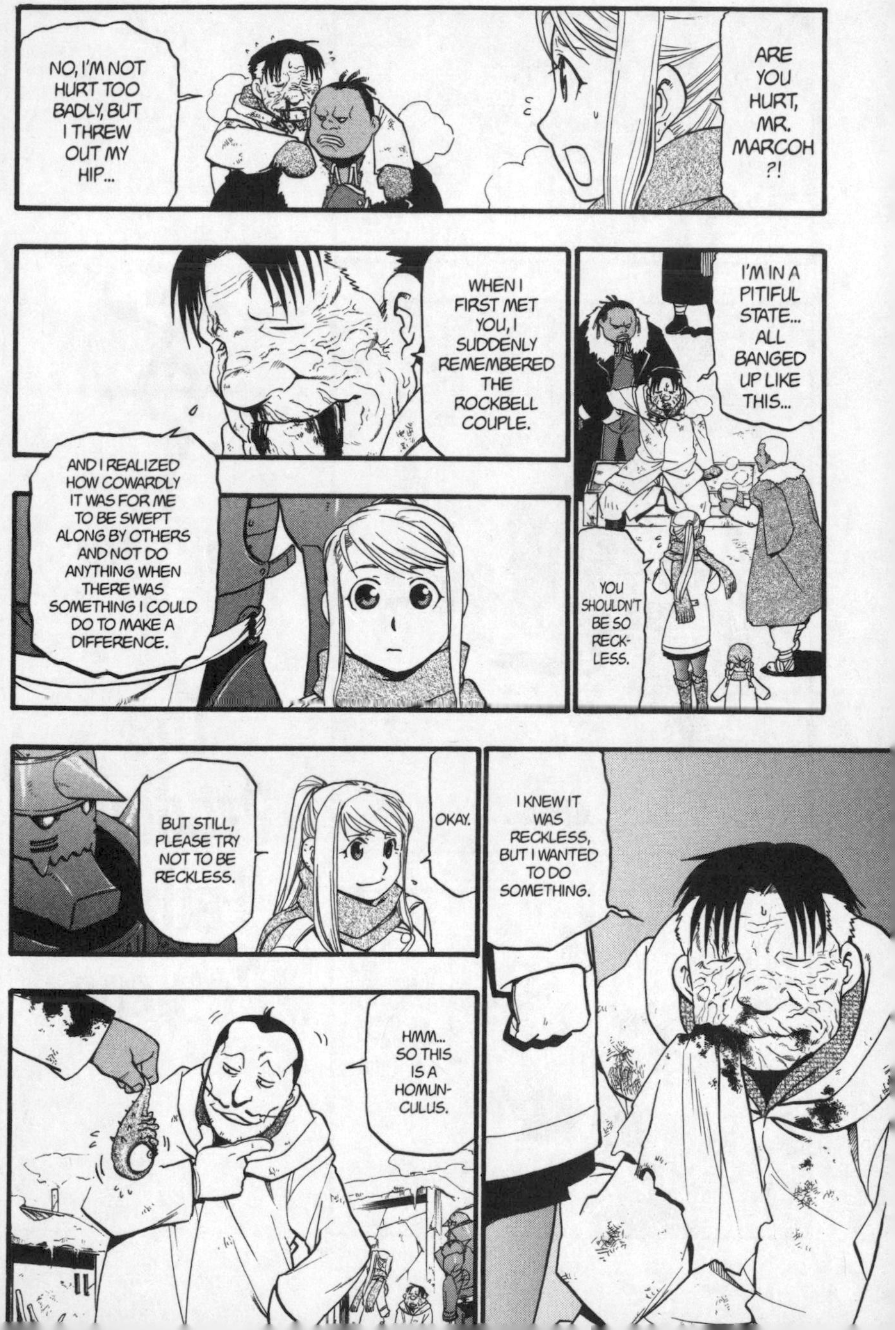
ARE YOU HURT, MR. MARCOH?!
NO, I'M NOT HURT TOO BADLY, BUT I THREW OUT MY HIP...
I'M IN A PITIFUL STATE... ALL BANGED UP LIKE THIS...
YOU SHOULDN'T BE SO RECK-LESS.
WHEN I FIRST MET YOU, I SUDDENLY REMEMBERED THE ROCKBELL COUPLE.
AND I REALIZED HOW COWARDLY IT WAS FOR ME TO BE SWEPT ALONG BY OTHERS AND NOT DO ANYTHING WHEN THERE WAS SOMETHING I COULD DO TO MAKE A DIFFERENCE.
I KNEW IT WAS RECKLESS, BUT I WANTED TO DO SOMETHING.
OKAY.
BUT STILL, PLEASE TRY NOT TO BE RECKLESS.
HMM... SO THIS IS A HOMUN-CULUS.

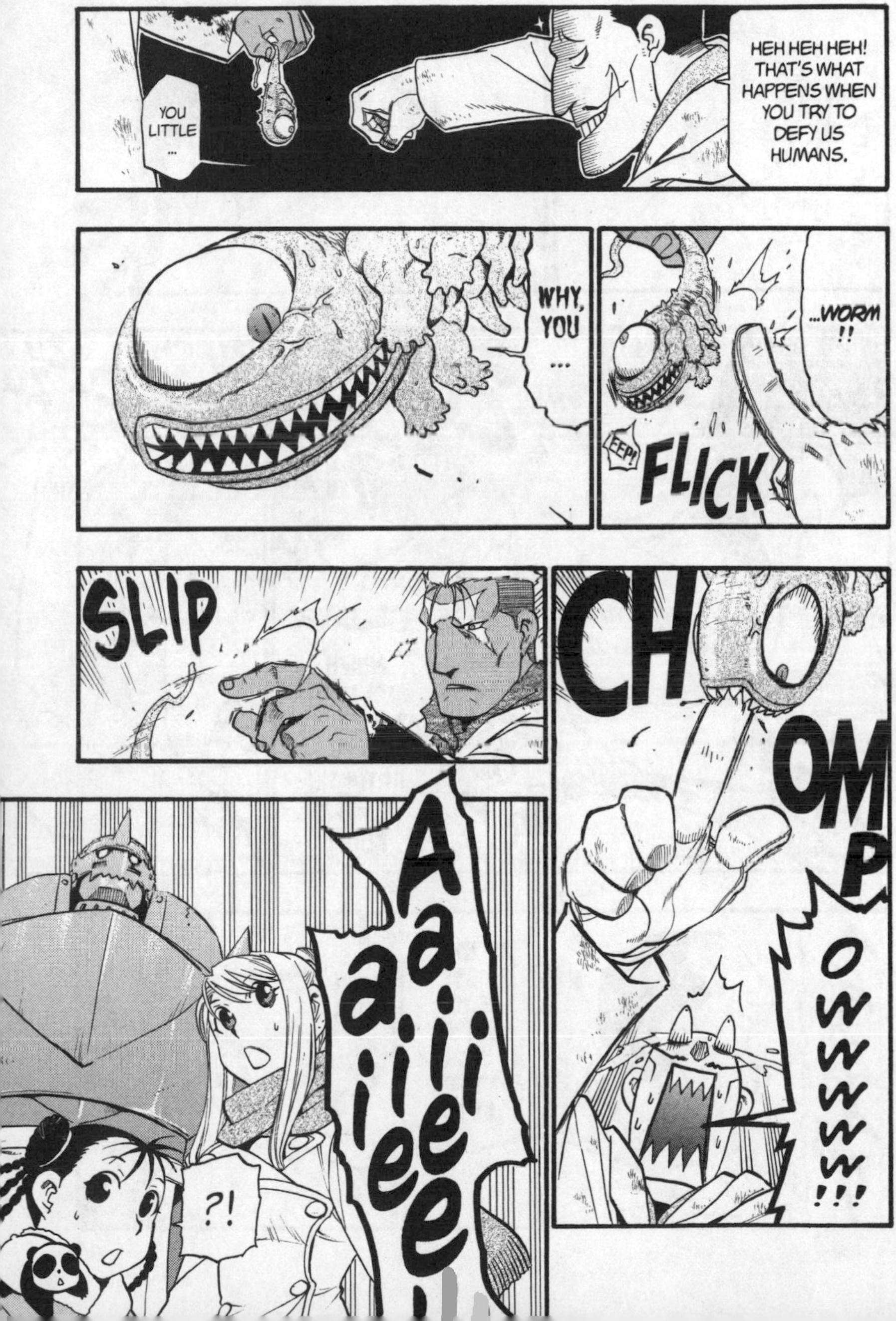
HEH HEH HEH! THAT'S WHAT HAPPENS WHEN YOU TRY TO DEFY US HUMANS.
YOU LITTLE ...
WHY, YOU ...
...WORM !!
EEP!
FLICK
SLIP
CHOMP
OWWWWWW!!!
?!
Aaaiiieeee

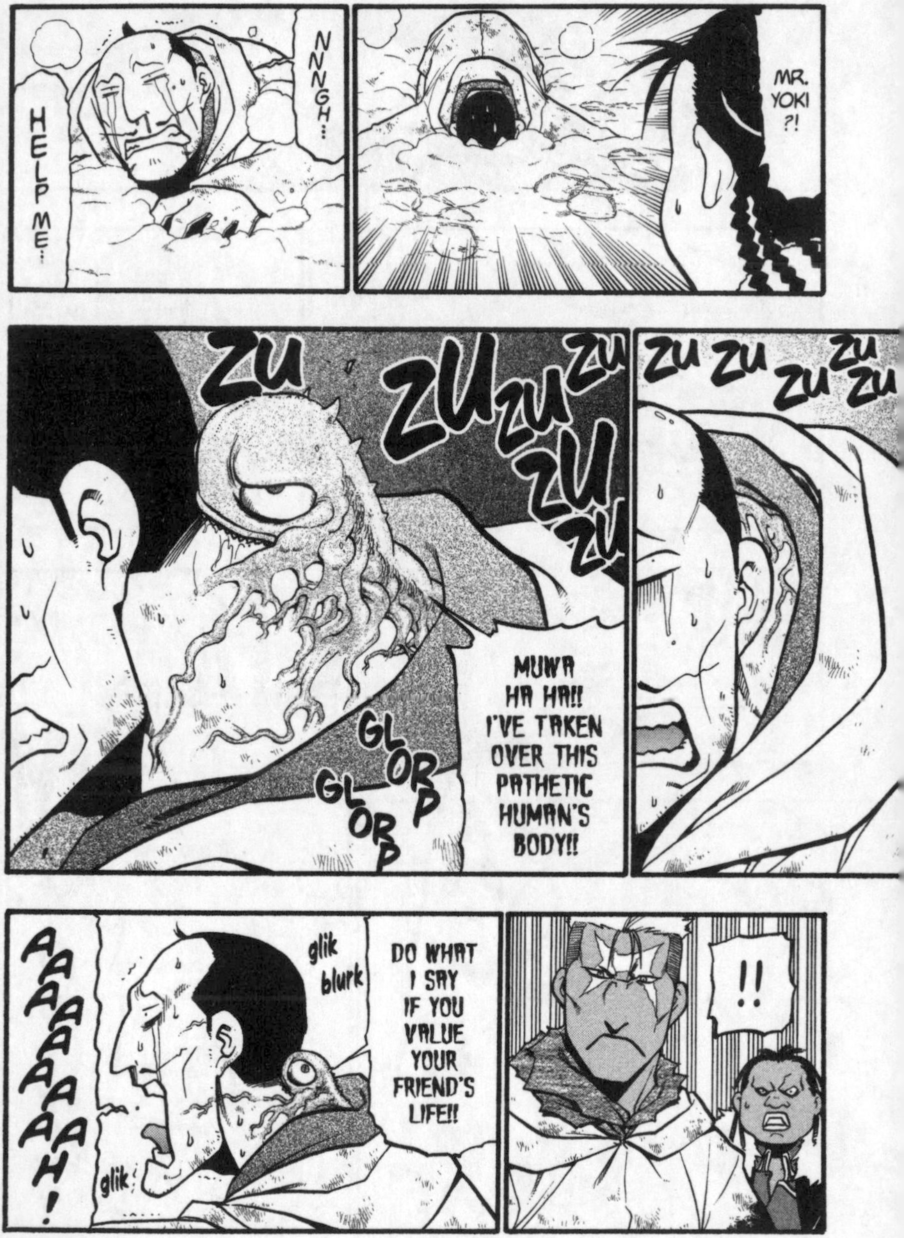

MR. YOKI ?!
NNNGH...
HELP ME...
ZU ZU ZU ZU ZU ZU
ZU ZU ZU ZU ZU ZU ZU
MUWA HA HA!! I'VE TAKEN OVER THIS PATHETIC HUMAN'S BODY!!
GLORP GLORP
!!
DO WHAT I SAY IF YOU VALUE YOUR FRIEND'S LIFE!!
glik blurk
AAAAAAAAAAH!
glik

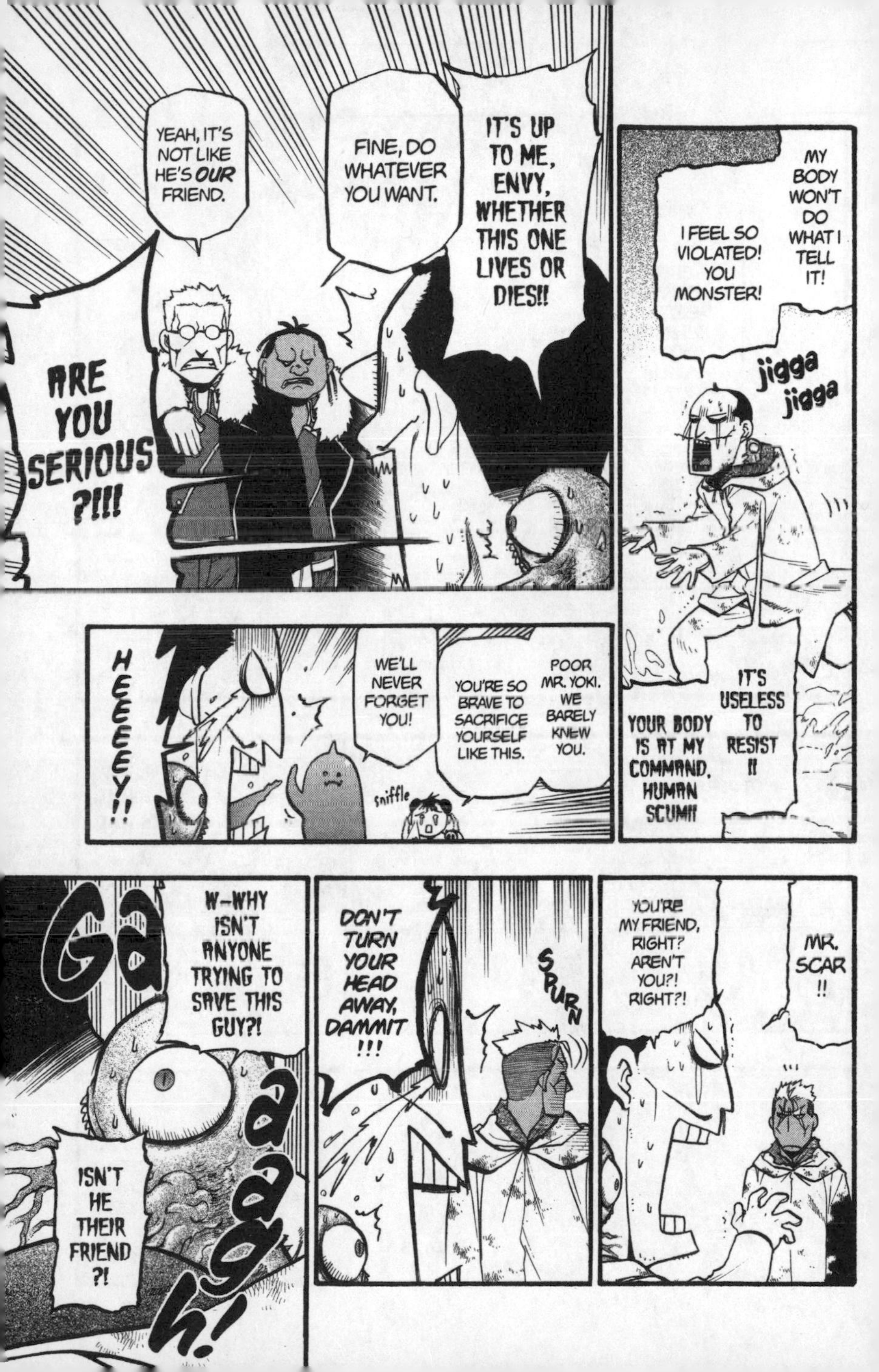
MY BODY WON'T DO WHAT I TELL IT!
I FEEL SO VIOLATED! YOU MONSTER!
jigga jigga
IT'S USELESS TO RESIST!!
YOUR BODY IS AT MY COMMAND, HUMAN SCUM!!
IT'S UP TO ME, ENVY, WHETHER THIS ONE LIVES OR DIES!!
FINE, DO WHATEVER YOU WANT.
YEAH, IT'S NOT LIKE HE'S *OUR* FRIEND.
ARE YOU SERIOUS?!!!
POOR MR. YOKI. WE BARELY KNEW YOU.
YOU'RE SO BRAVE TO SACRIFICE YOURSELF LIKE THIS.
WE'LL NEVER FORGET YOU!
sniffle
HEEEEEY!!
MR. SCAR!!
YOU'RE MY FRIEND, RIGHT? AREN'T YOU?! RIGHT?!
SPURN
DON'T TURN YOUR HEAD AWAY, DAMMIT!!!
W-WHY ISN'T ANYONE TRYING TO SAVE THIS GUY?!
Gaaagh!
ISN'T HE THEIR FRIEND?!

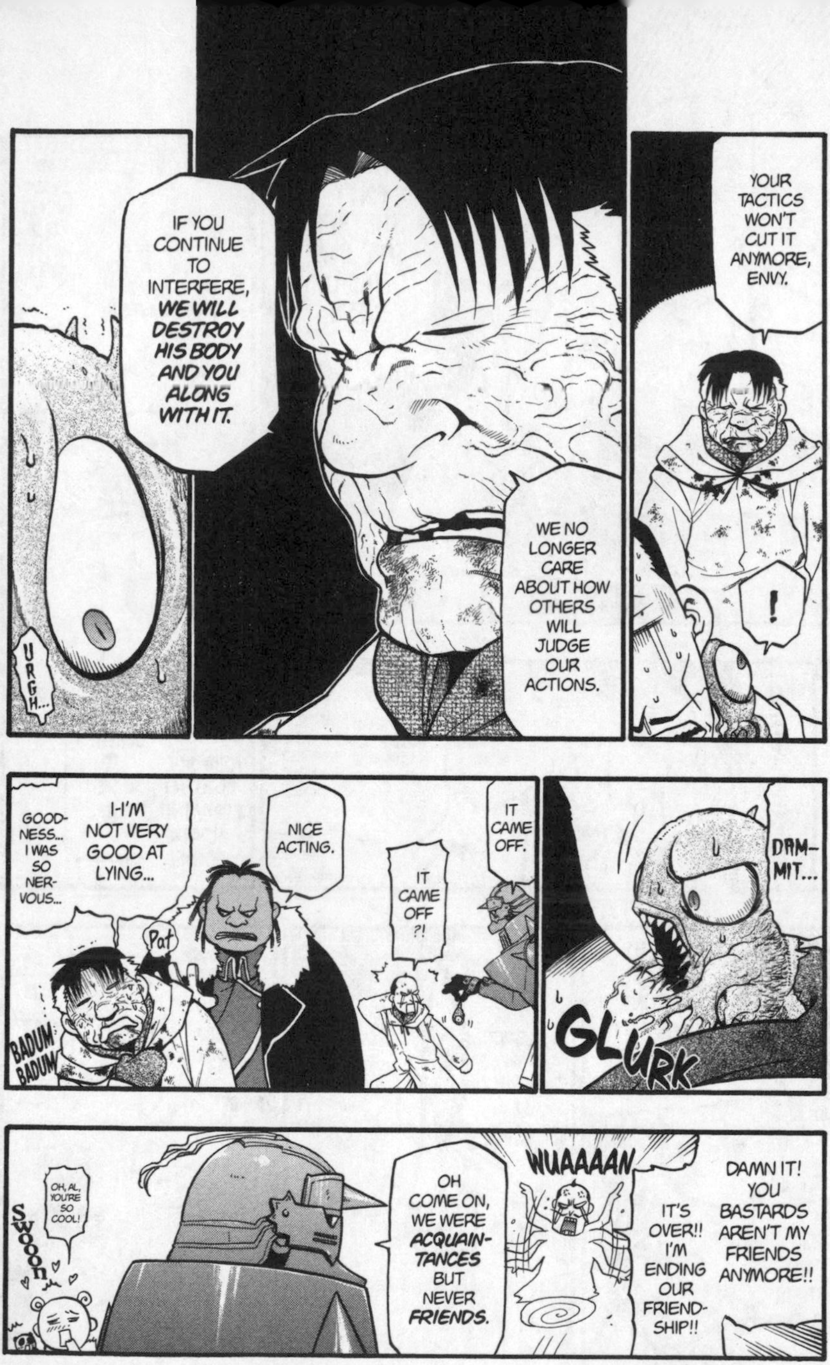
YOUR TACTICS WON'T CUT IT ANYMORE, ENVY.
!
WE NO LONGER CARE ABOUT HOW OTHERS WILL JUDGE OUR ACTIONS.
IF YOU CONTINUE TO INTERFERE, WE WILL DESTROY HIS BODY AND YOU ALONG WITH IT.
URGH...
DAMMIT...
GLURK
IT CAME OFF.
IT CAME OFF ?!
NICE ACTING.
I-I'M NOT VERY GOOD AT LYING...
GOODNESS... I WAS SO NERVOUS...
Pat
BADUM BADUM
DAMN IT! YOU BASTARDS AREN'T MY FRIENDS ANYMORE!!
IT'S OVER!! I'M ENDING OUR FRIENDSHIP!!
WUAAAAN
OH COME ON, WE WERE ACQUAINTANCES BUT NEVER FRIENDS.
OH, AL, YOU'RE SO COOL!
Swooon

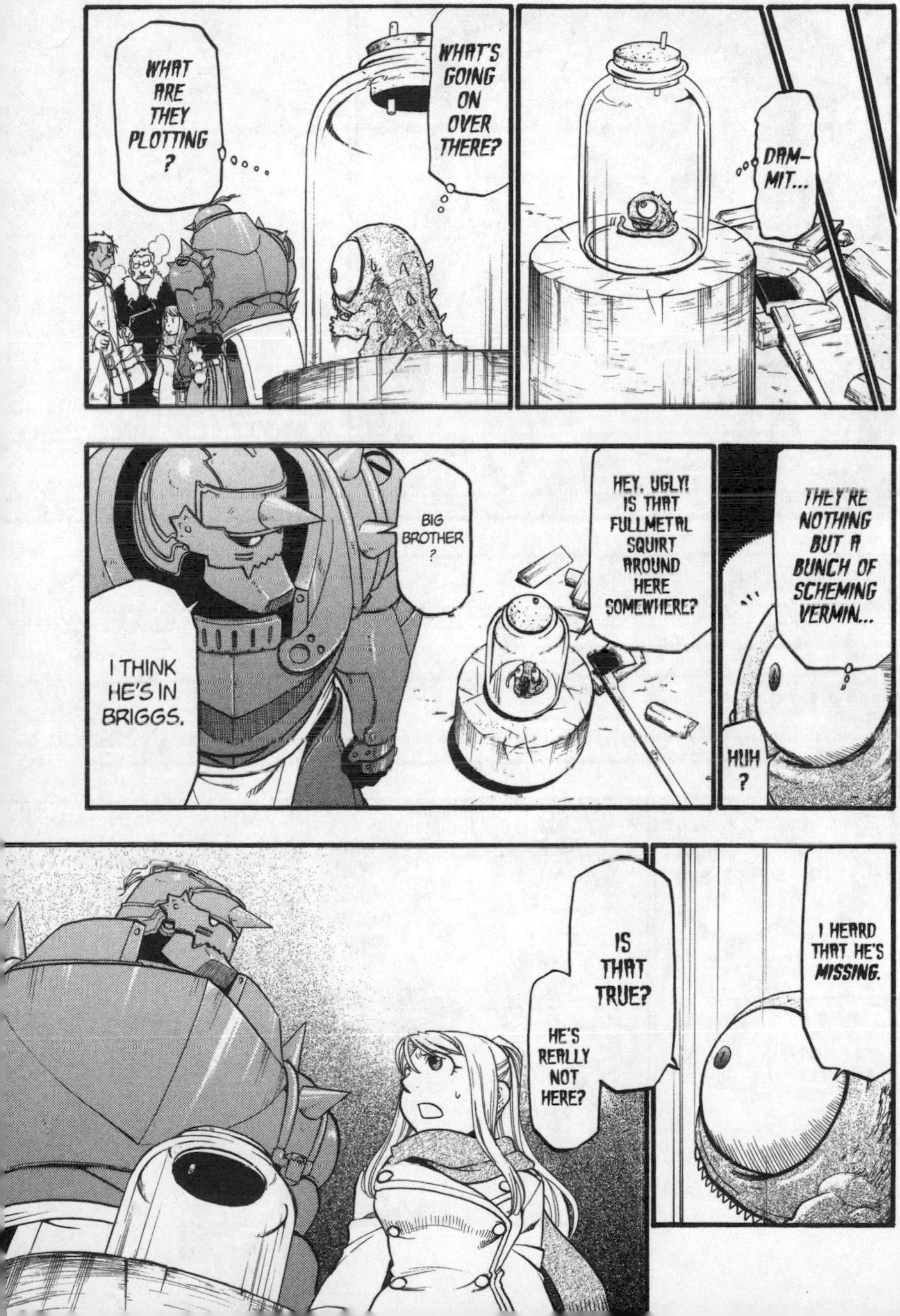
DAM-MIT...
WHAT'S GOING ON OVER THERE?
WHAT ARE THEY PLOTTING?
THEY'RE NOTHING BUT A BUNCH OF SCHEMING VERMIN...
HUH?
HEY, UGLY! IS THAT FULLMETAL SQUIRT AROUND HERE SOMEWHERE?
BIG BROTHER?
I THINK HE'S IN BRIGGS.
I HEARD THAT HE'S MISSING.
IS THAT TRUE?
HE'S REALLY NOT HERE?

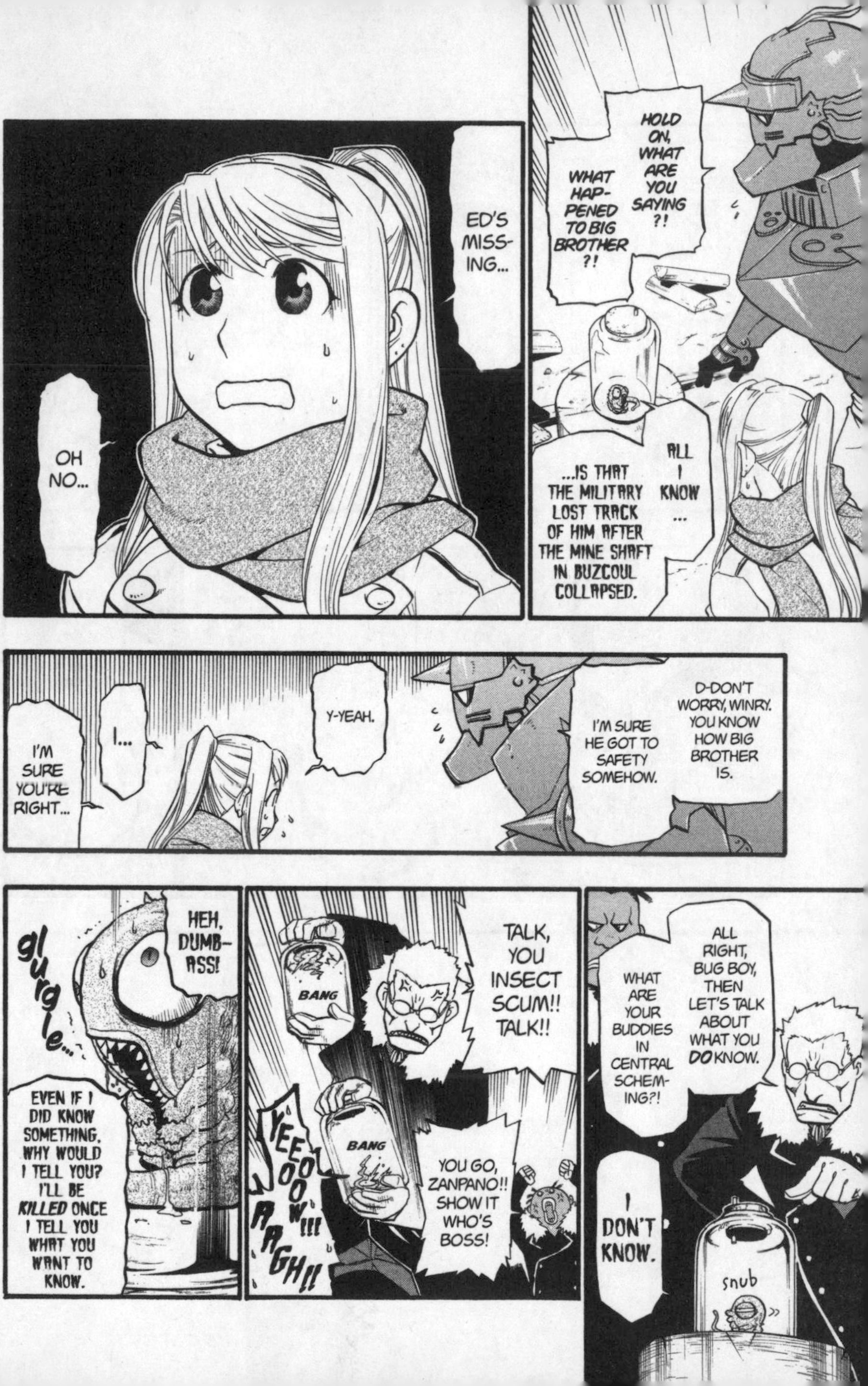
HOLD ON, WHAT ARE YOU SAYING?!
WHAT HAPPENED TO BIG BROTHER?!
ALL I KNOW...
...IS THAT THE MILITARY LOST TRACK OF HIM AFTER THE MINE SHAFT IN BUZCOUL COLLAPSED.
ED'S MISSING...
OH NO...
D-DON'T WORRY, WINRY. YOU KNOW HOW BIG BROTHER IS.
I'M SURE HE GOT TO SAFETY SOMEHOW.
Y-YEAH.
I...
I'M SURE YOU'RE RIGHT...
ALL RIGHT, BUG BOY, THEN LET'S TALK ABOUT WHAT YOU DO KNOW.
WHAT ARE YOUR BUDDIES IN CENTRAL SCHEMING?!
I DON'T KNOW.
snub
TALK, YOU INSECT SCUM!! TALK!!
BANG
BANG
YEEOOOOW!!! ARGH!!
YOU GO, ZANPANO!! SHOW IT WHO'S BOSS!
HEH, DUMBASS!
glurgle...
EVEN IF I DID KNOW SOMETHING, WHY WOULD I TELL YOU? I'LL BE KILLED ONCE I TELL YOU WHAT YOU WANT TO KNOW.

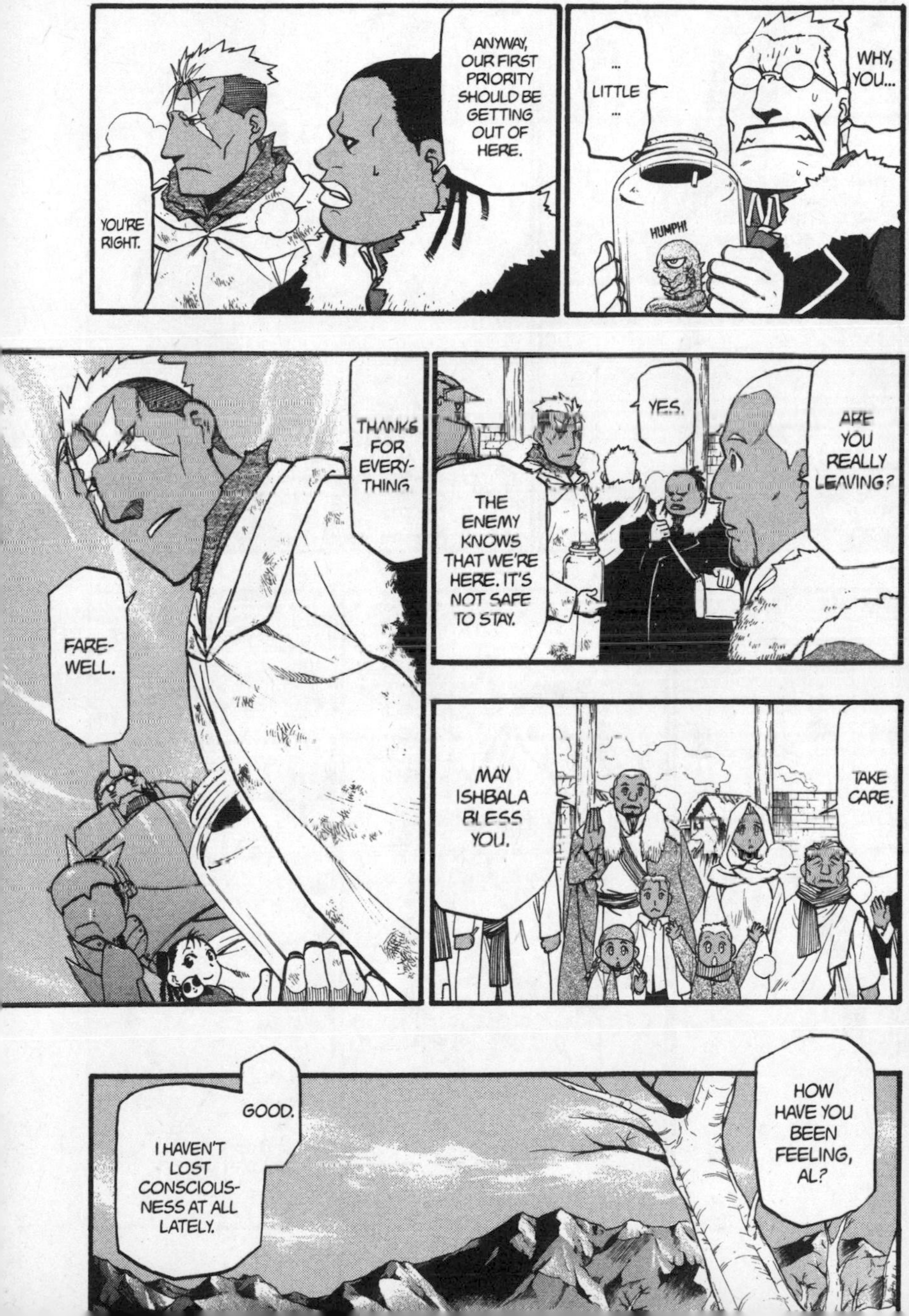
WHY, YOU...
... LITTLE ...
HUMPH!
ANYWAY, OUR FIRST PRIORITY SHOULD BE GETTING OUT OF HERE.
YOU'RE RIGHT.
ARE YOU REALLY LEAVING?
YES.
THE ENEMY KNOWS THAT WE'RE HERE. IT'S NOT SAFE TO STAY.
TAKE CARE.
MAY ISHBALA BLESS YOU.
THANKS FOR EVERY-THING.
FARE-WELL.
HOW HAVE YOU BEEN FEELING, AL?
GOOD.
I HAVEN'T LOST CONSCIOUS-NESS AT ALL LATELY.

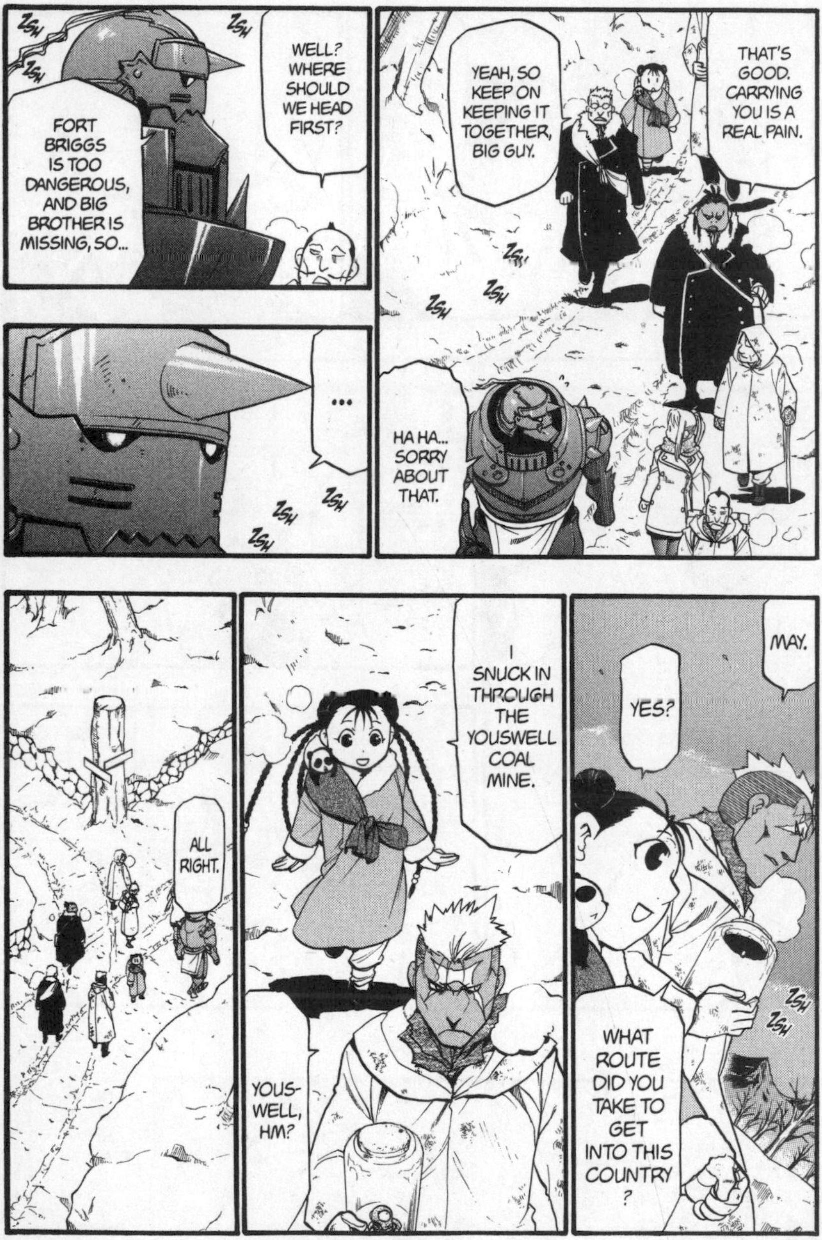
THAT'S GOOD. CARRYING YOU IS A REAL PAIN.
YEAH, SO KEEP ON KEEPING IT TOGETHER, BIG GUY.
ZSH
ZSH
ZSH
HA HA... SORRY ABOUT THAT.
ZSH
WELL? WHERE SHOULD WE HEAD FIRST?
ZSH
ZSH
FORT BRIGGS IS TOO DANGEROUS, AND BIG BROTHER IS MISSING, SO...
...
ZSH
ZSH
ZSH
MAY.
YES?
ZSH
ZSH
WHAT ROUTE DID YOU TAKE TO GET INTO THIS COUNTRY?
I SNUCK IN THROUGH THE YOUSWELL COAL MINE.
YOUS-WELL, HM?
ALL RIGHT.

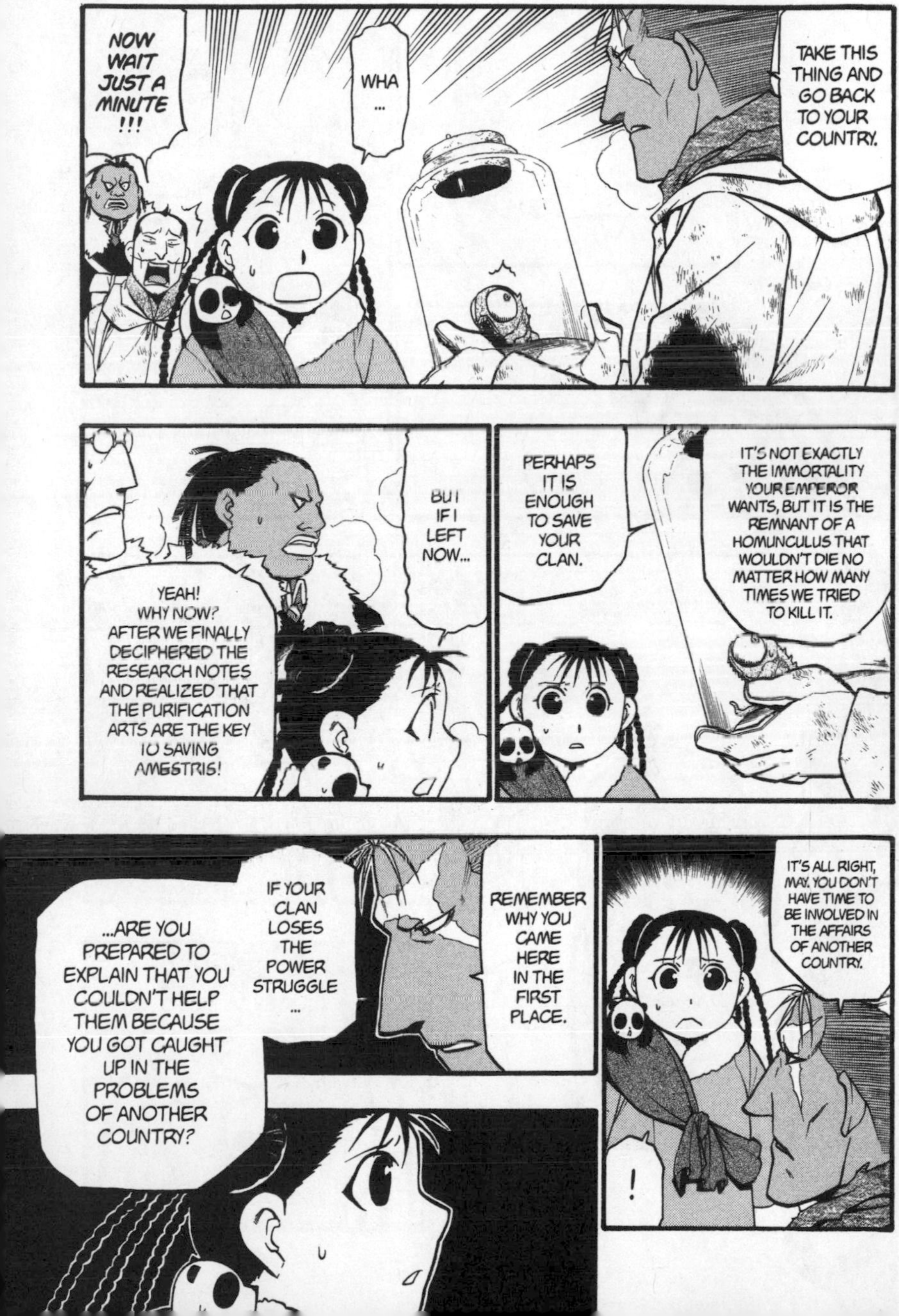
TAKE THIS THING AND GO BACK TO YOUR COUNTRY.
WHA ...
NOW WAIT JUST A MINUTE !!!
IT'S NOT EXACTLY THE IMMORTALITY YOUR EMPEROR WANTS, BUT IT IS THE REMNANT OF A HOMUNCULUS THAT WOULDN'T DIE NO MATTER HOW MANY TIMES WE TRIED TO KILL IT.
PERHAPS IT IS ENOUGH TO SAVE YOUR CLAN.
BUT IF I LEFT NOW...
YEAH! WHY NOW? AFTER WE FINALLY DECIPHERED THE RESEARCH NOTES AND REALIZED THAT THE PURIFICATION ARTS ARE THE KEY TO SAVING AMESTRIS!
IT'S ALL RIGHT, MAY. YOU DON'T HAVE TIME TO BE INVOLVED IN THE AFFAIRS OF ANOTHER COUNTRY.
!
REMEMBER WHY YOU CAME HERE IN THE FIRST PLACE.
IF YOUR CLAN LOSES THE POWER STRUGGLE ...
...ARE YOU PREPARED TO EXPLAIN THAT YOU COULDN'T HELP THEM BECAUSE YOU GOT CAUGHT UP IN THE PROBLEMS OF ANOTHER COUNTRY?

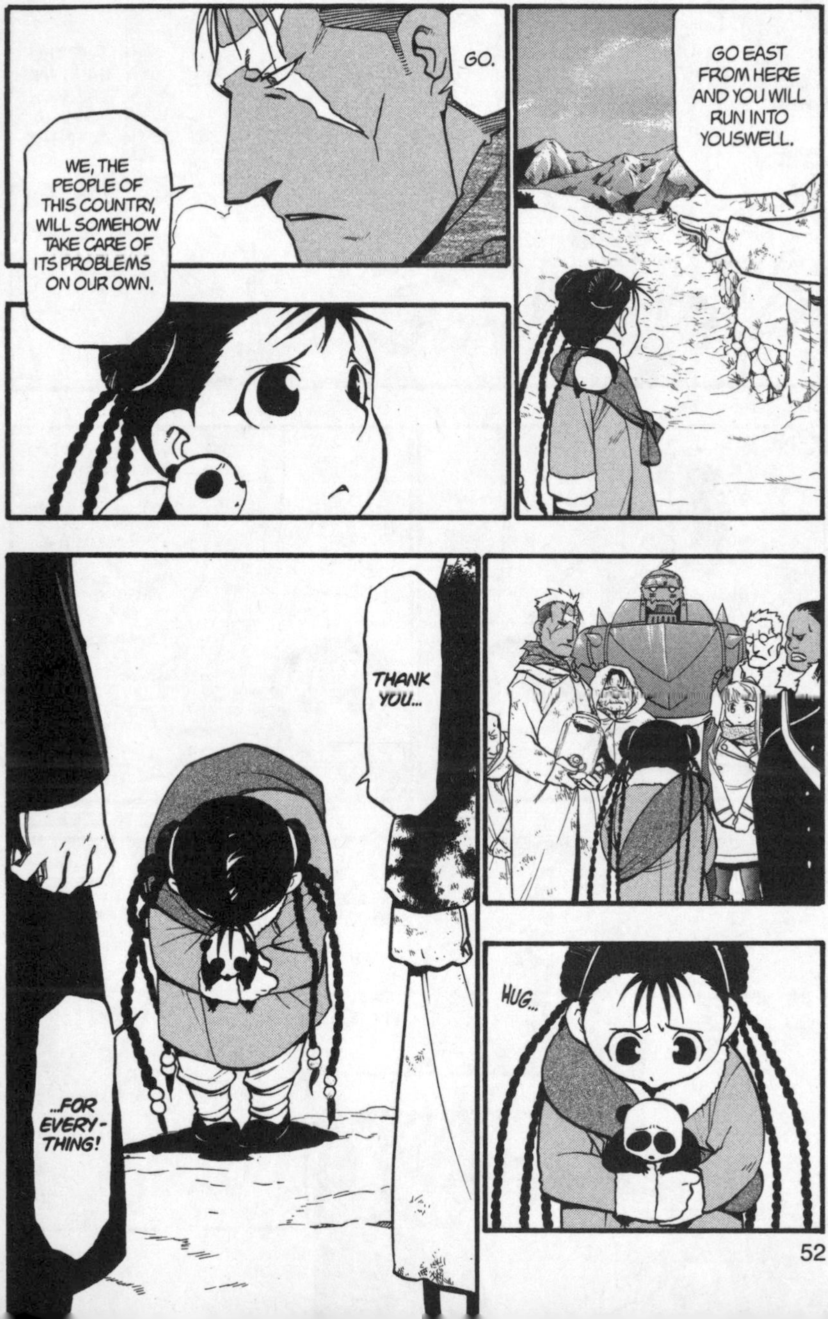
GO EAST FROM HERE AND YOU WILL RUN INTO YOUSWELL.
GO.
WE, THE PEOPLE OF THIS COUNTRY, WILL SOMEHOW TAKE CARE OF ITS PROBLEMS ON OUR OWN.
HUG...
THANK YOU...
...FOR EVERY-THING!

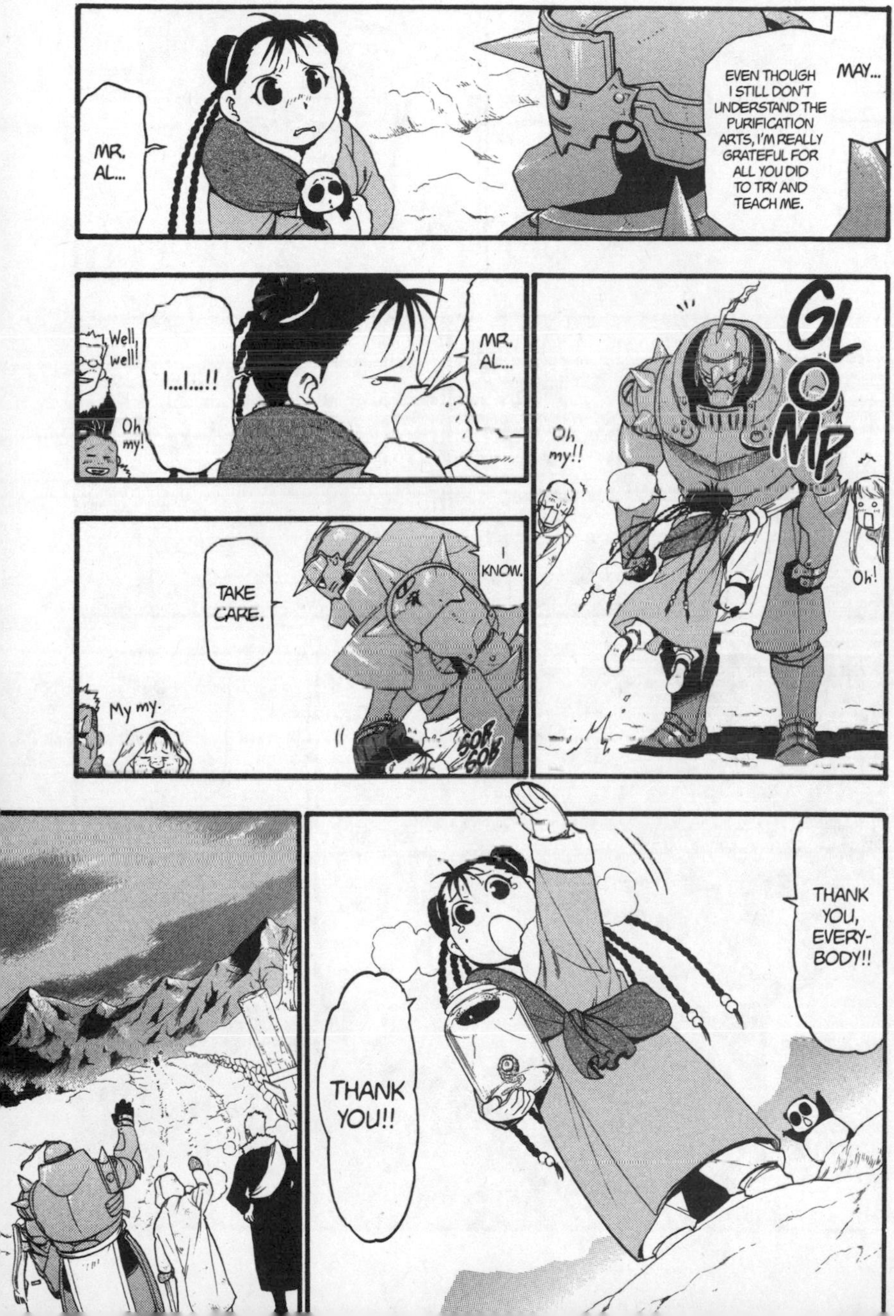
MAY...
EVEN THOUGH I STILL DON'T UNDERSTAND THE PURIFICATION ARTS, I'M REALLY GRATEFUL FOR ALL YOU DID TO TRY AND TEACH ME.
MR. AL...
GLOMP
Oh!
Oh, my!!
MR. AL...
I...I...!!
Well, well!
Oh my!
I KNOW.
TAKE CARE.
SOB SOB
My my.
THANK YOU, EVERY-BODY!!
THANK YOU!!

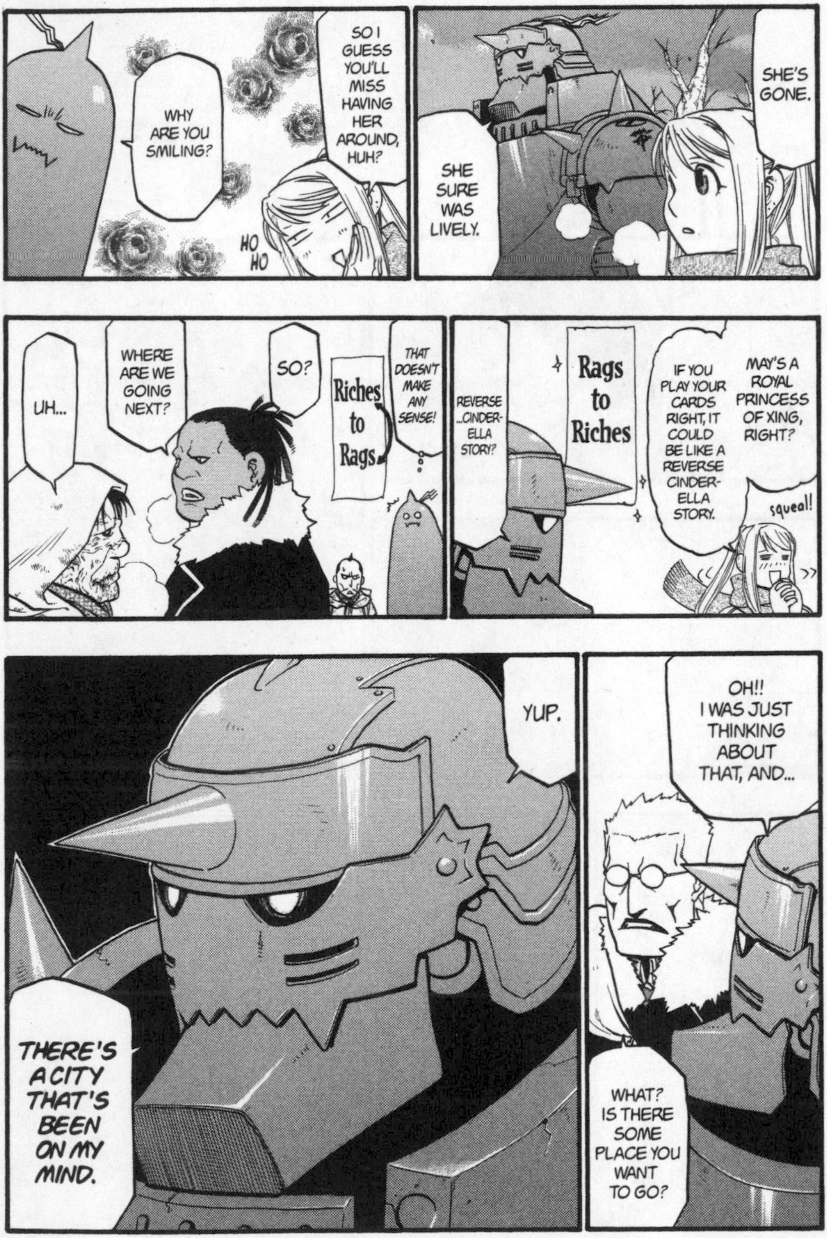
SHE'S GONE.
SHE SURE WAS LIVELY.
SO I GUESS YOU'LL MISS HAVING HER AROUND, HUH?
HO HO
WHY ARE YOU SMILING?
MAY'S A ROYAL PRINCESS OF XING, RIGHT?
IF YOU PLAY YOUR CARDS RIGHT, IT COULD BE LIKE A REVERSE CINDER-ELLA STORY.
squeal!
Rags to Riches
REVERSE ...CINDER-ELLA STORY?
THAT DOESN'T MAKE ANY SENSE!
Riches to Rags
SO?
WHERE ARE WE GOING NEXT?
UH...
OH!! I WAS JUST THINKING ABOUT THAT, AND...
WHAT? IS THERE SOME PLACE YOU WANT TO GO?
YUP.
THERE'S A CITY THAT'S BEEN ON MY MIND.

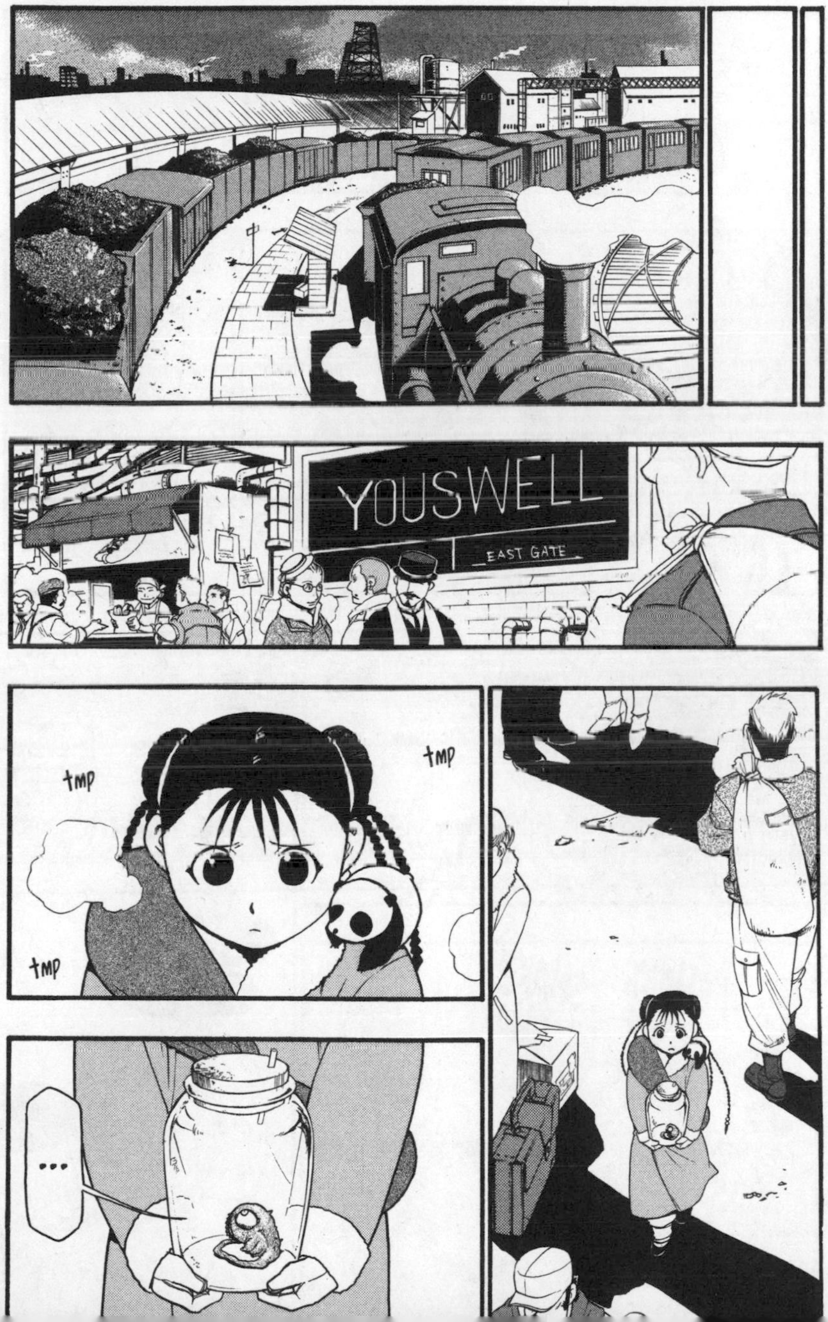
YOUSWELL
EAST GATE
tmp
tmp
tmp
...

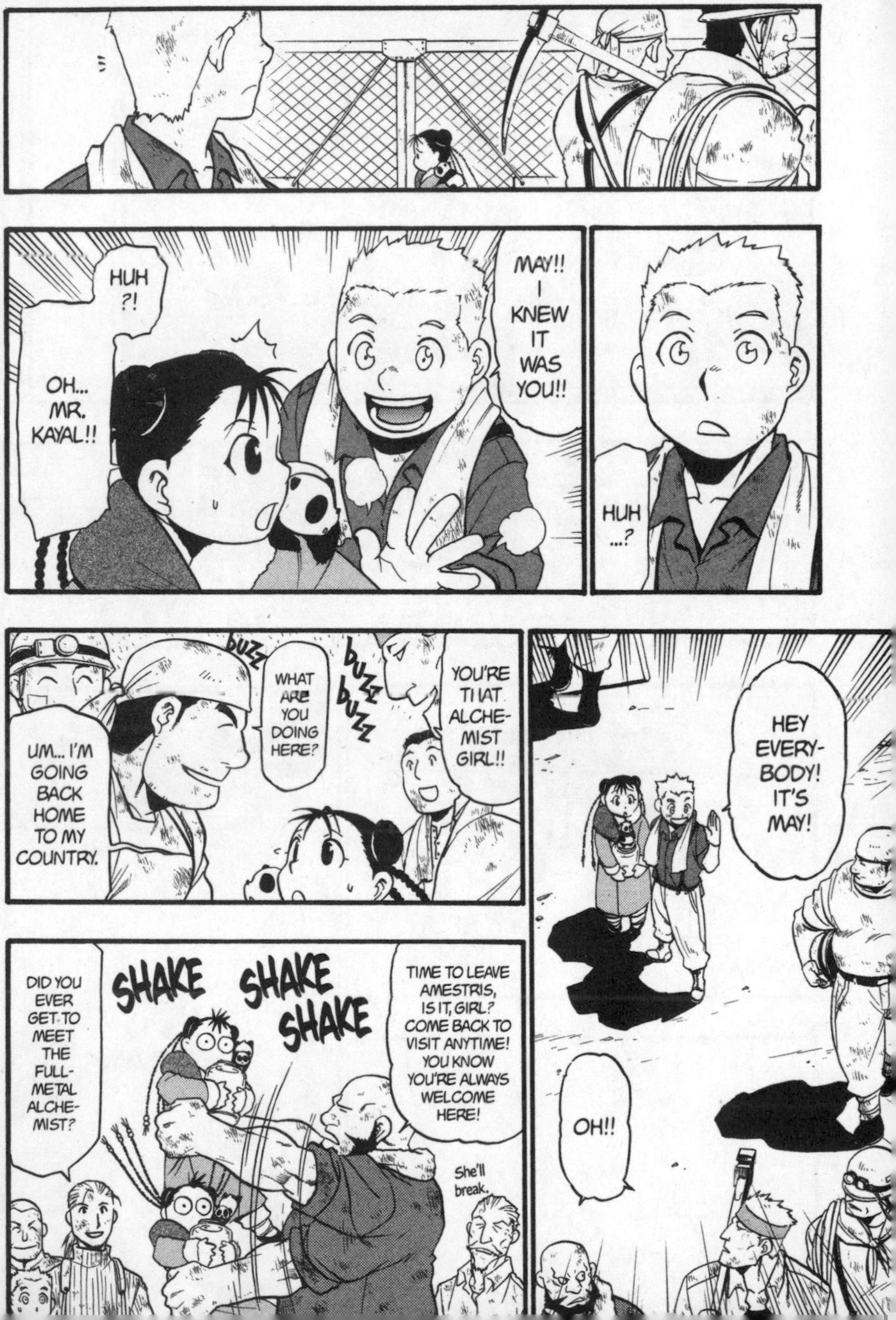
HUH ...?
MAY!! I KNEW IT WAS YOU!!
HUH ?!
OH... MR. KAYAL!!
HEY EVERY-BODY! IT'S MAY!
OH!!
YOU'RE THAT ALCHE-MIST GIRL!!
BUZZ BUZZ BUZZ
WHAT ARE YOU DOING HERE?
UM... I'M GOING BACK HOME TO MY COUNTRY.
TIME TO LEAVE AMESTRIS, IS IT, GIRL? COME BACK TO VISIT ANYTIME! YOU KNOW YOU'RE ALWAYS WELCOME HERE!
SHAKE SHAKE SHAKE
DID YOU EVER GET TO MEET THE FULL-METAL ALCHE-MIST?
She'll break.

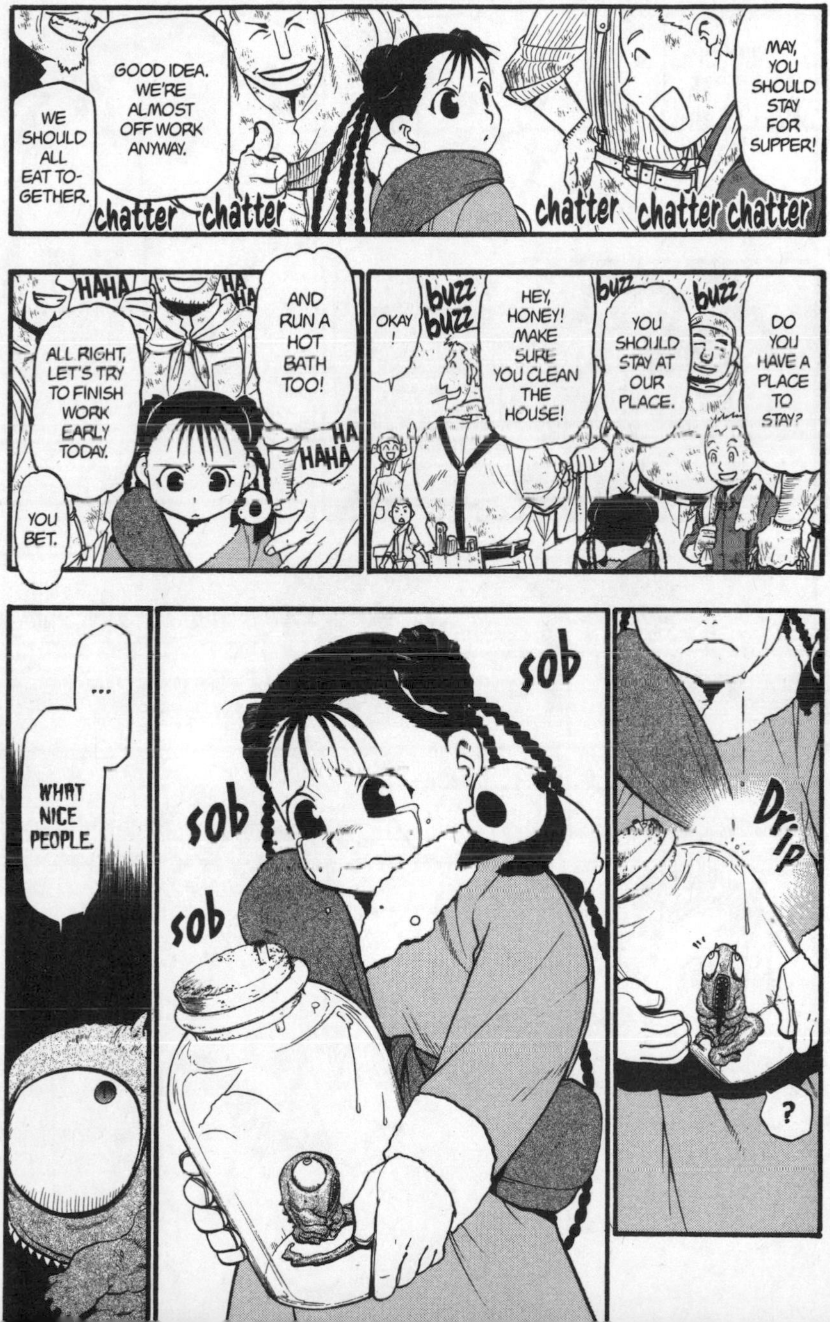
MAY, YOU SHOULD STAY FOR SUPPER!
chatter chatter
chatter
GOOD IDEA. WE'RE ALMOST OFF WORK ANYWAY.
WE SHOULD ALL EAT TO-GETHER.
chatter
chatter
buzz
DO YOU HAVE A PLACE TO STAY?
buzz
YOU SHOULD STAY AT OUR PLACE.
HEY, HONEY! MAKE SURE YOU CLEAN THE HOUSE!
buzz buzz
OKAY!
AND RUN A HOT BATH TOO!
HA HA
HAHA
ALL RIGHT, LET'S TRY TO FINISH WORK EARLY TODAY.
HA HAHA
YOU BET.
Drip
?
sob
sob
sob
...
WHAT NICE PEOPLE.

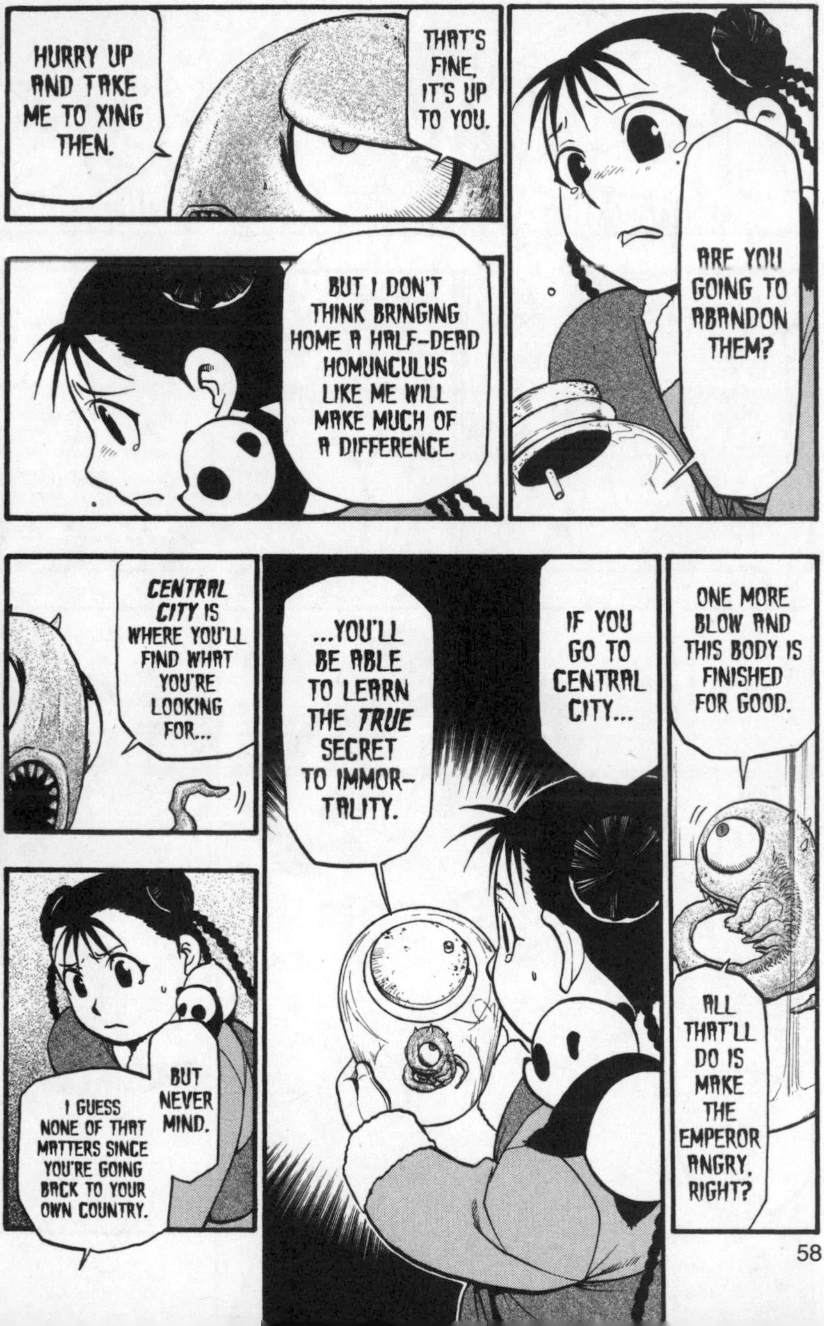
ARE YOU GOING TO ABANDON THEM?
THAT'S FINE, IT'S UP TO YOU.
HURRY UP AND TAKE ME TO XING THEN.
BUT I DON'T THINK BRINGING HOME A HALF-DEAD HOMUNCULUS LIKE ME WILL MAKE MUCH OF A DIFFERENCE.
ONE MORE BLOW AND THIS BODY IS FINISHED FOR GOOD.
ALL THAT'LL DO IS MAKE THE EMPEROR ANGRY, RIGHT?
IF YOU GO TO CENTRAL CITY...
...YOU'LL BE ABLE TO LEARN THE *TRUE* SECRET TO IMMOR-TALITY.
CENTRAL CITY IS WHERE YOU'LL FIND WHAT YOU'RE LOOKING FOR...
BUT NEVER MIND.
I GUESS NONE OF THAT MATTERS SINCE YOU'RE GOING BACK TO YOUR OWN COUNTRY.

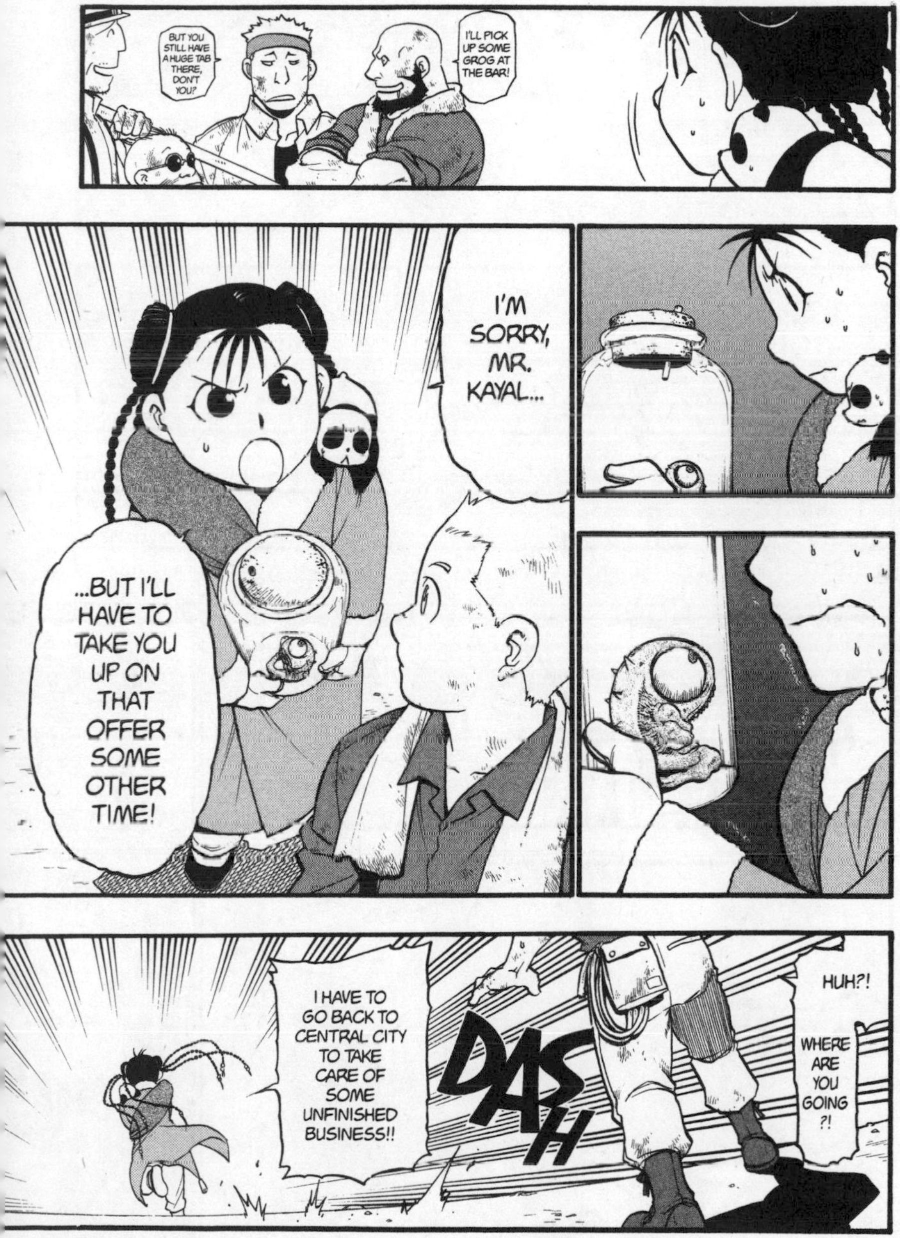
I'LL PICK UP SOME GROG AT THE BAR!
BUT YOU STILL HAVE A HUGE TAB THERE, DON'T YOU?
I'M SORRY, MR. KAYAL...
...BUT I'LL HAVE TO TAKE YOU UP ON THAT OFFER SOME OTHER TIME!
HUH?!
WHERE ARE YOU GOING?!
DASH
I HAVE TO GO BACK TO CENTRAL CITY TO TAKE CARE OF SOME UNFINISHED BUSINESS!!

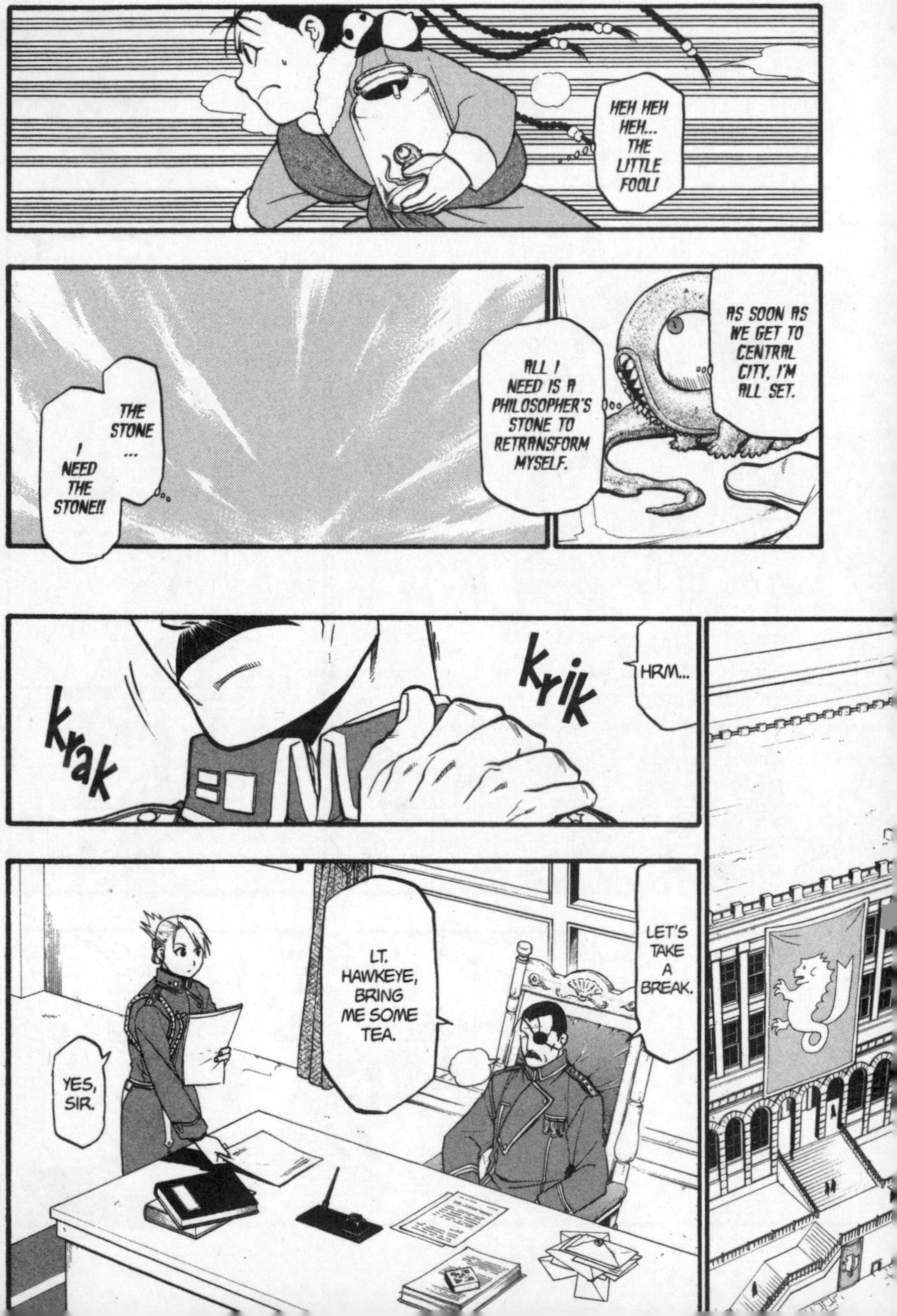
HEH HEH HEH... THE LITTLE FOOL!
AS SOON AS WE GET TO CENTRAL CITY, I'M ALL SET.
ALL I NEED IS A PHILOSOPHER'S STONE TO RETRANSFORM MYSELF.
THE STONE...
I NEED THE STONE!!
HRM...
krik
krak
LET'S TAKE A BREAK.
LT. HAWKEYE, BRING ME SOME TEA.
YES, SIR.

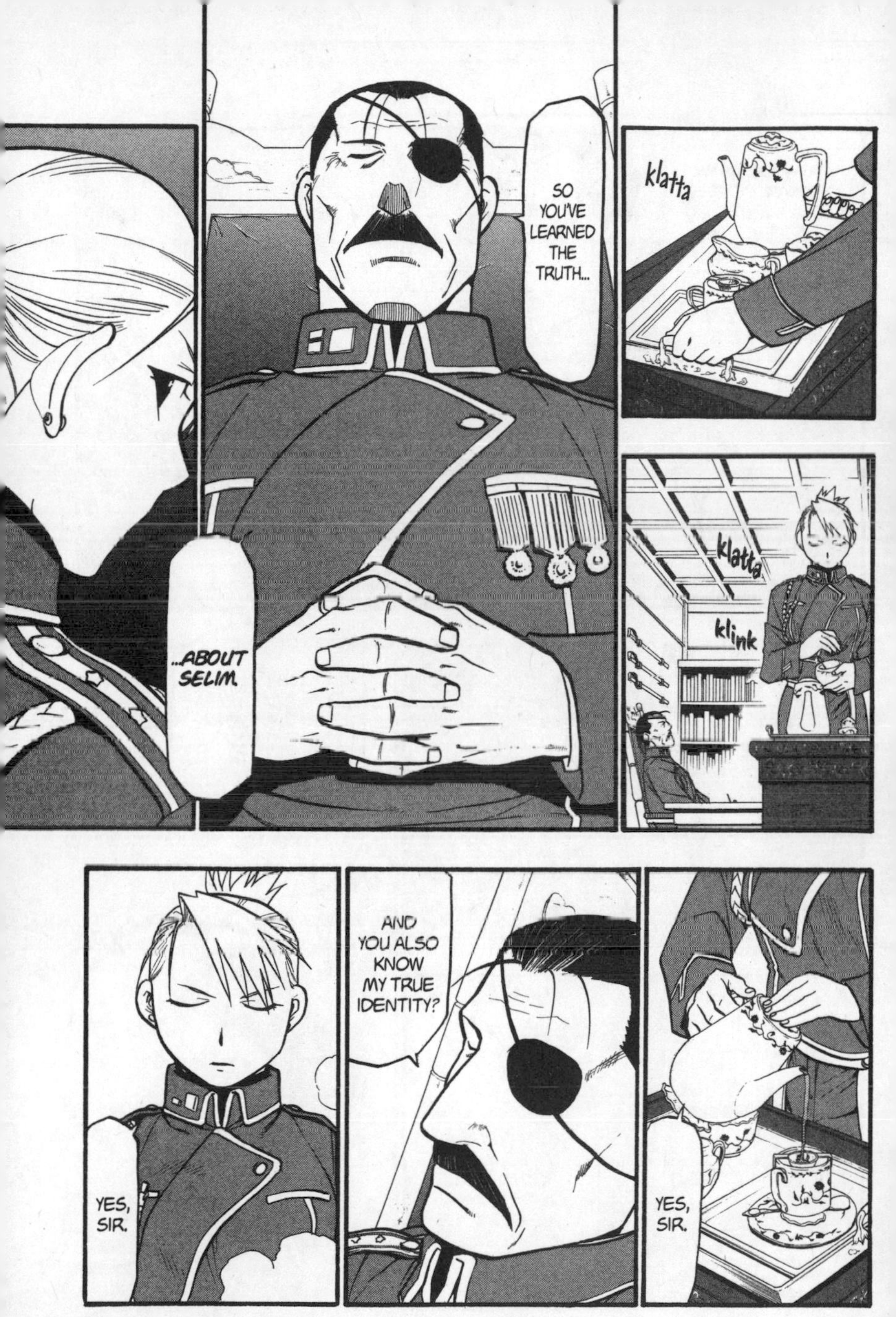
klatta
klatta
klink
SO YOU'VE LEARNED THE TRUTH...
...ABOUT SELIM.
YES, SIR.
AND YOU ALSO KNOW MY TRUE IDENTITY?
YES, SIR.

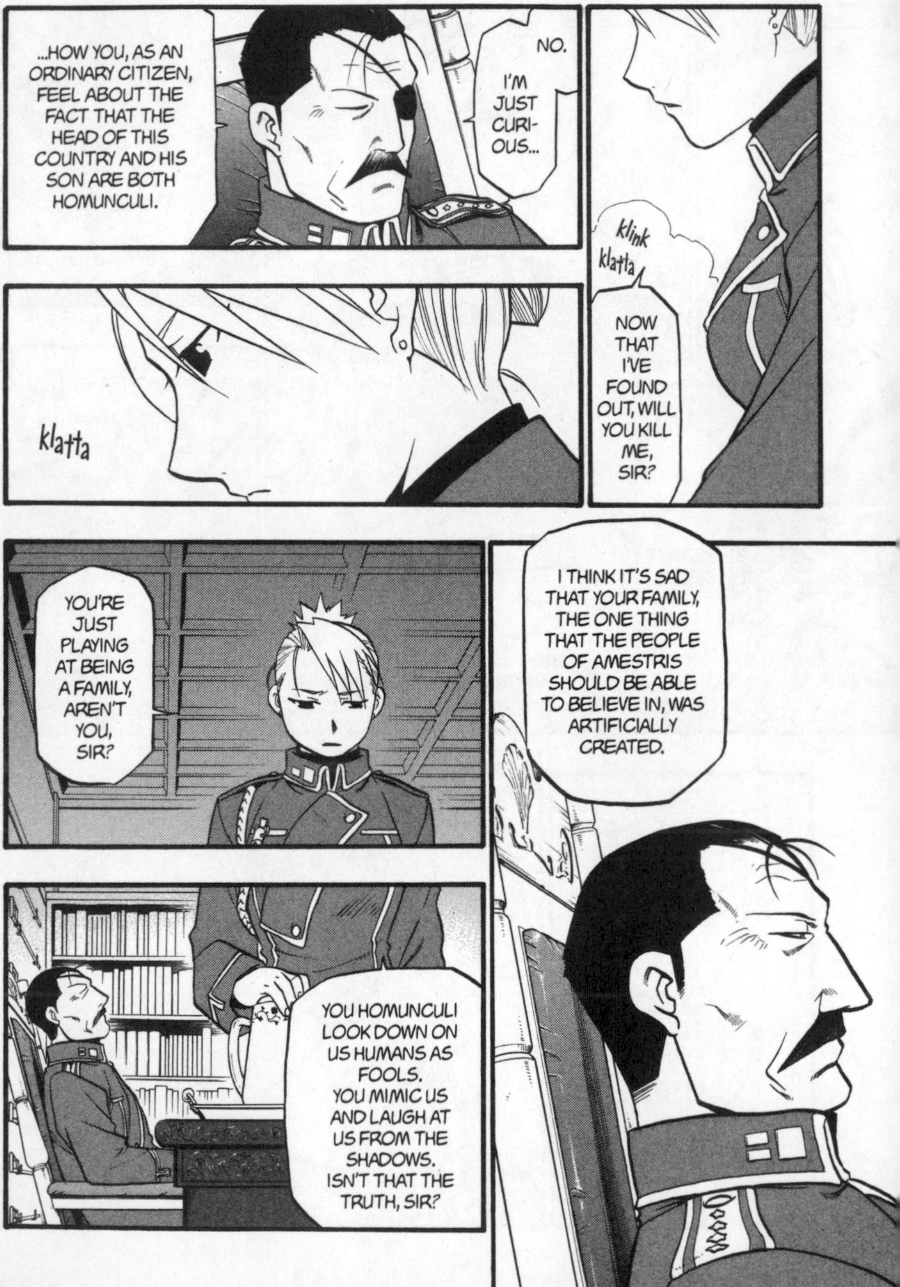
klink
klatta
NOW THAT I'VE FOUND OUT, WILL YOU KILL ME, SIR?
NO.
I'M JUST CURIOUS...
...HOW YOU, AS AN ORDINARY CITIZEN, FEEL ABOUT THE FACT THAT THE HEAD OF THIS COUNTRY AND HIS SON ARE BOTH HOMUNCULI.
klatta
I THINK IT'S SAD THAT YOUR FAMILY, THE ONE THING THAT THE PEOPLE OF AMESTRIS SHOULD BE ABLE TO BELIEVE IN, WAS ARTIFICIALLY CREATED.
YOU'RE JUST PLAYING AT BEING A FAMILY, AREN'T YOU, SIR?
YOU HOMUNCULI LOOK DOWN ON US HUMANS AS FOOLS. YOU MIMIC US AND LAUGH AT US FROM THE SHADOWS. ISN'T THAT THE TRUTH, SIR?

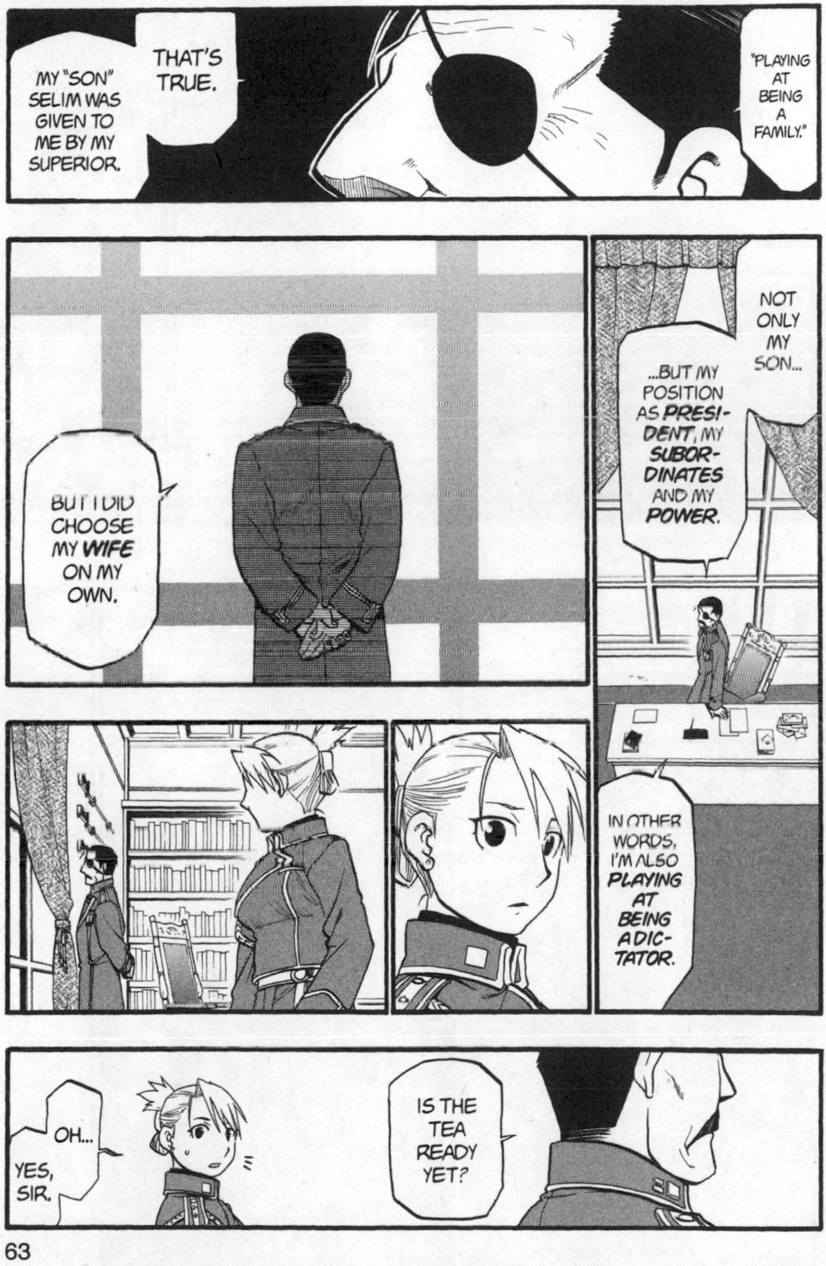
"PLAYING AT BEING A FAMILY."
THAT'S TRUE.
MY "SON" SELIM WAS GIVEN TO ME BY MY SUPERIOR.
NOT ONLY MY SON...
...BUT MY POSITION AS PRESIDENT, MY SUBORDINATES AND MY POWER.
IN OTHER WORDS, I'M ALSO PLAYING AT BEING A DICTATOR.
BUT I DID CHOOSE MY WIFE ON MY OWN.
IS THE TEA READY YET?
OH...
YES, SIR.

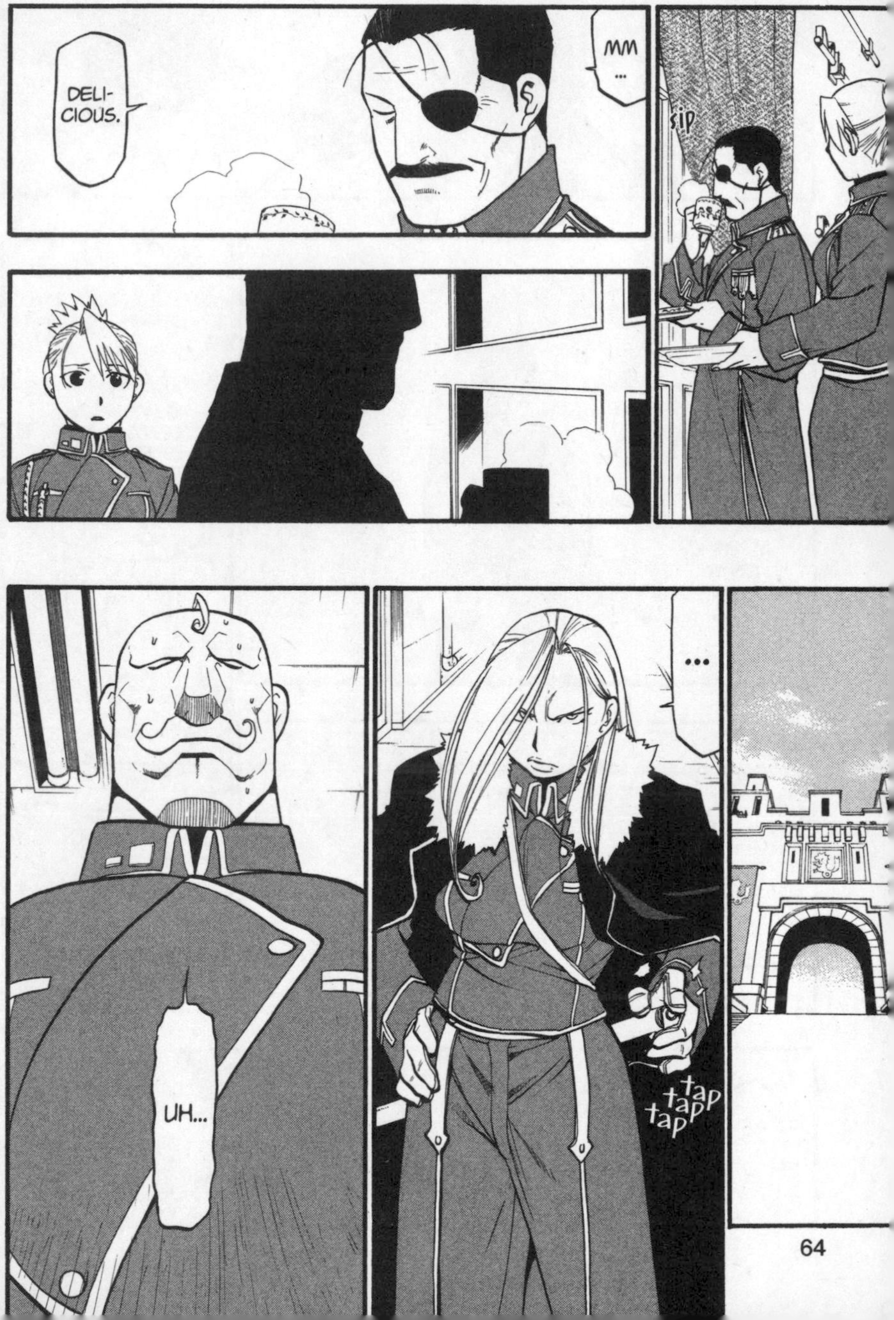
sip
MM...
DELICIOUS.
...
tap tap tap
UH...

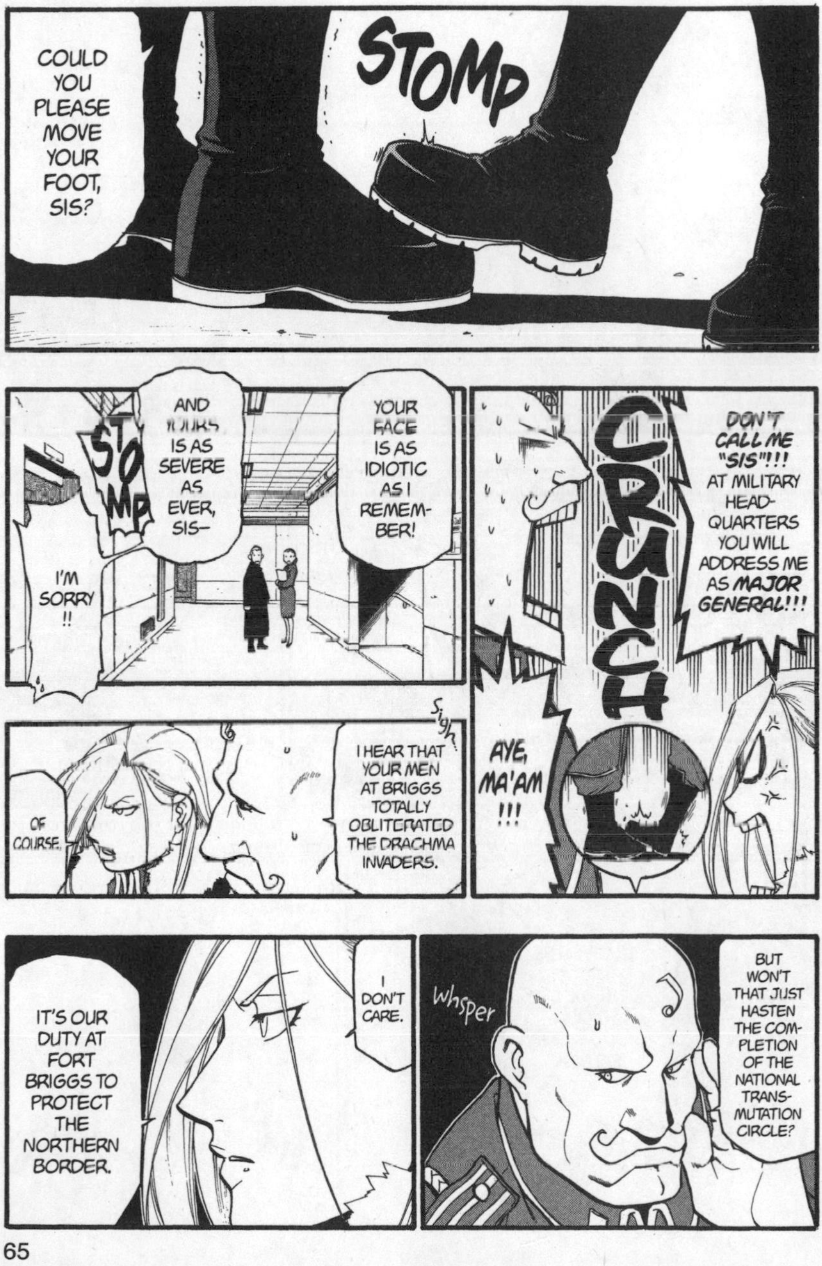
STOMP
COULD YOU PLEASE MOVE YOUR FOOT, SIS?
DON'T CALL ME "SIS"!!! AT MILITARY HEADQUARTERS YOU WILL ADDRESS ME AS MAJOR GENERAL!!!
CRUNCH
AYE, MA'AM !!!
YOUR FACE IS AS IDIOTIC AS I REMEMBER!
AND YOURS IS AS SEVERE AS EVER, SIS—
STOMP
I'M SORRY !!
Sigh
I HEAR THAT YOUR MEN AT BRIGGS TOTALLY OBLITERATED THE DRACHMA INVADERS.
OF COURSE.
BUT WON'T THAT JUST HASTEN THE COMPLETION OF THE NATIONAL TRANSMUTATION CIRCLE?
whsper
I DON'T CARE.
IT'S OUR DUTY AT FORT BRIGGS TO PROTECT THE NORTHERN BORDER.

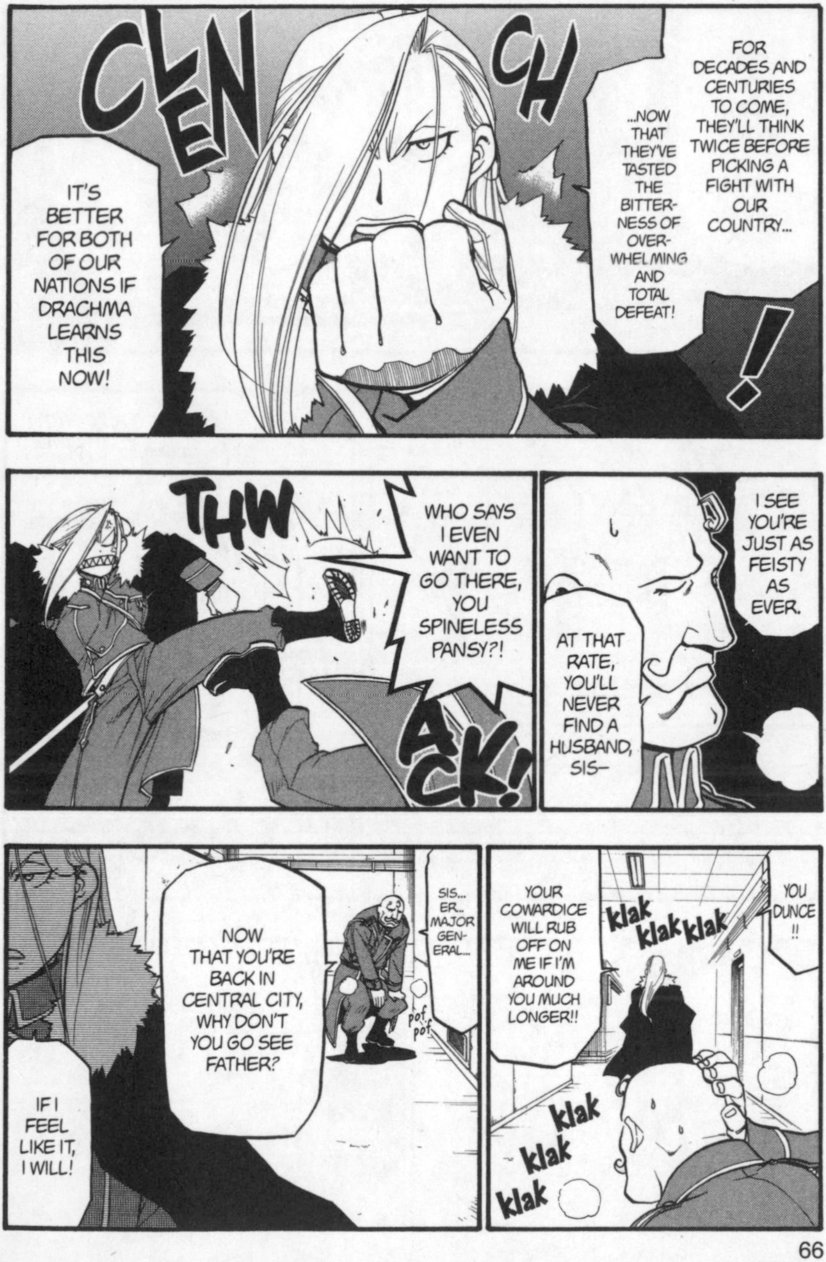
FOR DECADES AND CENTURIES TO COME, THEY'LL THINK TWICE BEFORE PICKING A FIGHT WITH OUR COUNTRY...
...NOW THAT THEY'VE TASTED THE BITTERNESS OF OVERWHELMING AND TOTAL DEFEAT!
CLENCH
!
IT'S BETTER FOR BOTH OF OUR NATIONS IF DRACHMA LEARNS THIS NOW!
I SEE YOU'RE JUST AS FEISTY AS EVER.
AT THAT RATE, YOU'LL NEVER FIND A HUSBAND, SIS–
THWACK!
WHO SAYS I EVEN WANT TO GO THERE, YOU SPINELESS PANSY?!
YOU DUNCE !!
klak klak klak
YOUR COWARDICE WILL RUB OFF ON ME IF I'M AROUND YOU MUCH LONGER!!
klak klak klak
SIS... ER.. MAJOR GENERAL...
pof pof
NOW THAT YOU'RE BACK IN CENTRAL CITY, WHY DON'T YOU GO SEE FATHER?
IF I FEEL LIKE IT, I WILL!

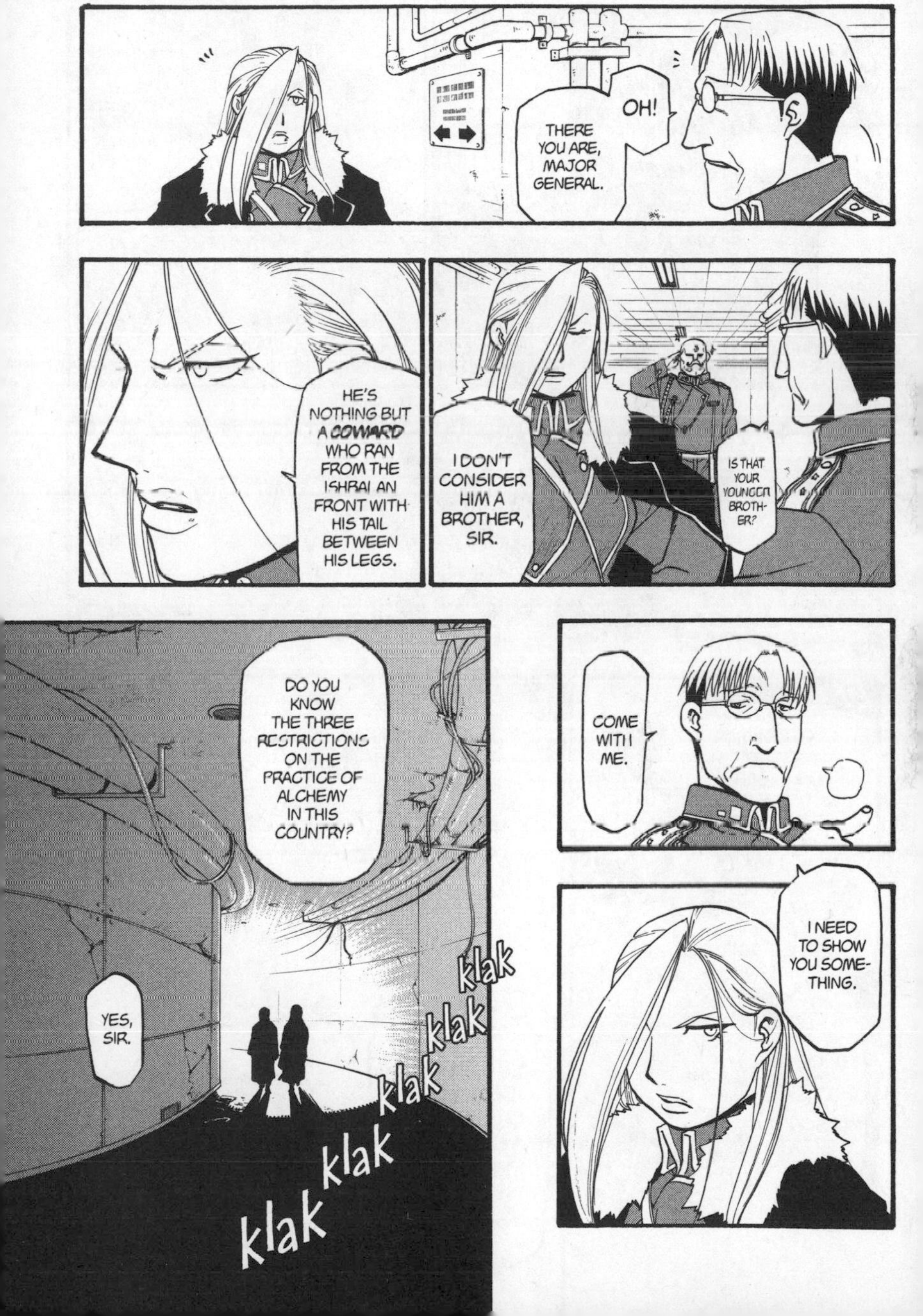
OH!
THERE YOU ARE, MAJOR GENERAL.
IS THAT YOUR YOUNGER BROTHER?
I DON'T CONSIDER HIM A BROTHER, SIR.
HE'S NOTHING BUT A **COWARD** WHO RAN FROM THE ISHBALAN FRONT WITH HIS TAIL BETWEEN HIS LEGS.
COME WITH ME.
I NEED TO SHOW YOU SOMETHING.
DO YOU KNOW THE THREE RESTRICTIONS ON THE PRACTICE OF ALCHEMY IN THIS COUNTRY?
YES, SIR.
klak klak klak klak klak

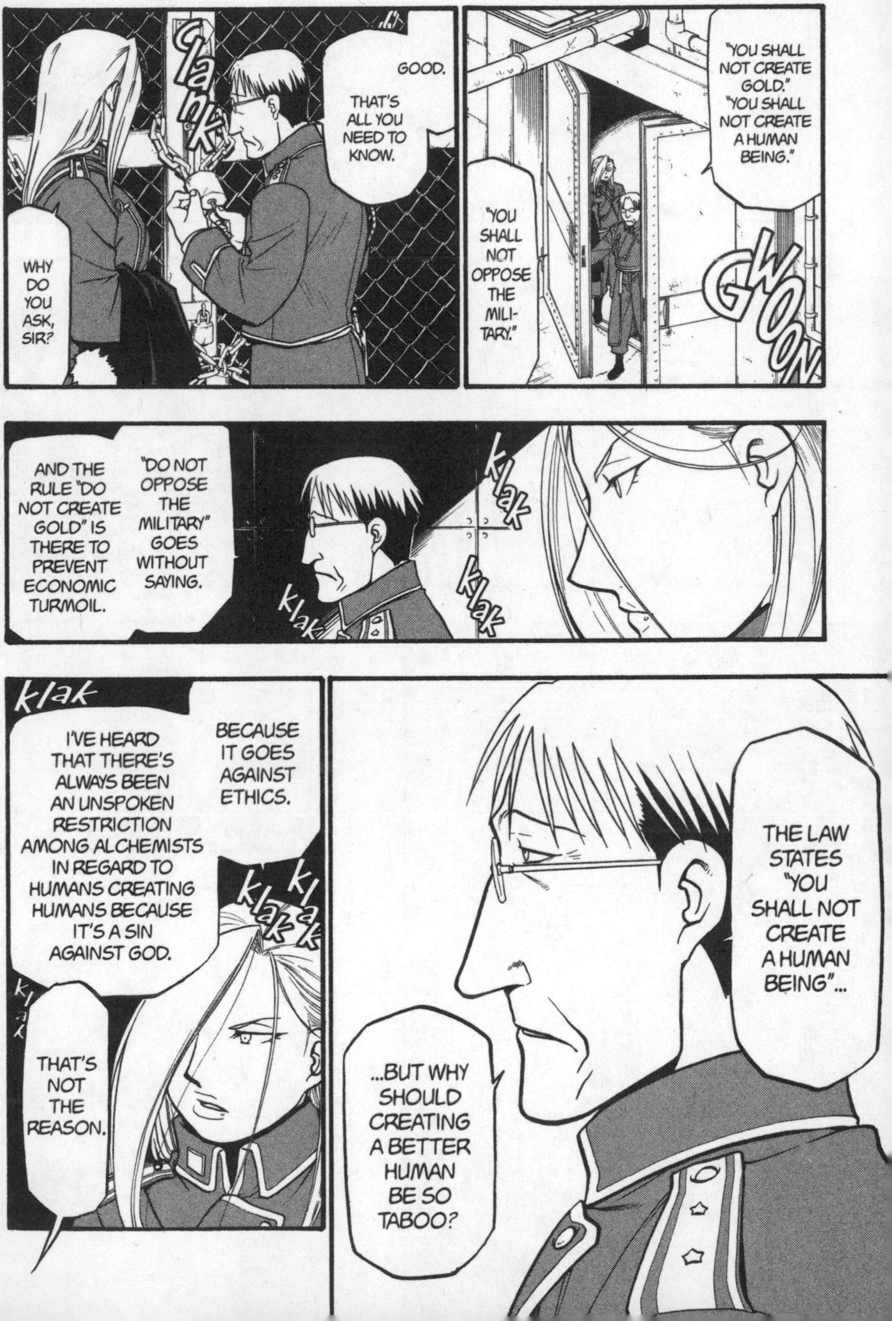
"YOU SHALL NOT CREATE GOLD." "YOU SHALL NOT CREATE A HUMAN BEING."
"YOU SHALL NOT OPPOSE THE MILITARY."
GWOON
GOOD.
THAT'S ALL YOU NEED TO KNOW.
Clank
WHY DO YOU ASK, SIR?
klak
klak
"DO NOT OPPOSE THE MILITARY" GOES WITHOUT SAYING.
AND THE RULE "DO NOT CREATE GOLD" IS THERE TO PREVENT ECONOMIC TURMOIL.
klak
THE LAW STATES "YOU SHALL NOT CREATE A HUMAN BEING"...
...BUT WHY SHOULD CREATING A BETTER HUMAN BE SO TABOO?
klak
BECAUSE IT GOES AGAINST ETHICS.
I'VE HEARD THAT THERE'S ALWAYS BEEN AN UNSPOKEN RESTRICTION AMONG ALCHEMISTS IN REGARD TO HUMANS CREATING HUMANS BECAUSE IT'S A SIN AGAINST GOD.
klak klak
klak
THAT'S NOT THE REASON.

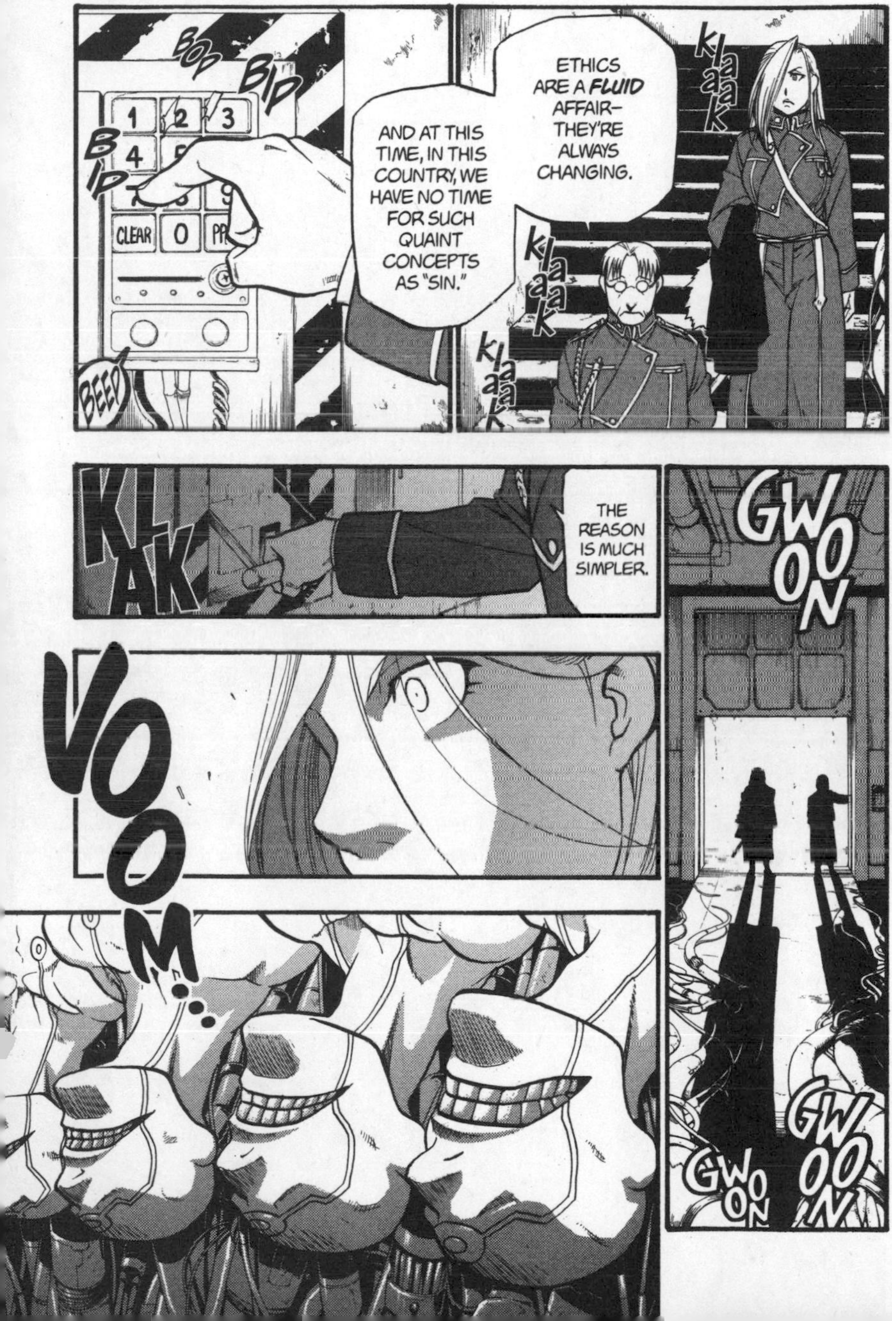

KLAAAK
ETHICS ARE A **FLUID** AFFAIR— THEY'RE ALWAYS CHANGING.
AND AT THIS TIME, IN THIS COUNTRY, WE HAVE NO TIME FOR SUCH QUAINT CONCEPTS AS "SIN."
KLAAAK
KLAAAK
BOP
BIP
BIP
BEED
GWOOON
KLAK
THE REASON IS MUCH SIMPLER.
VOOOM...
GWOOON
GWOON

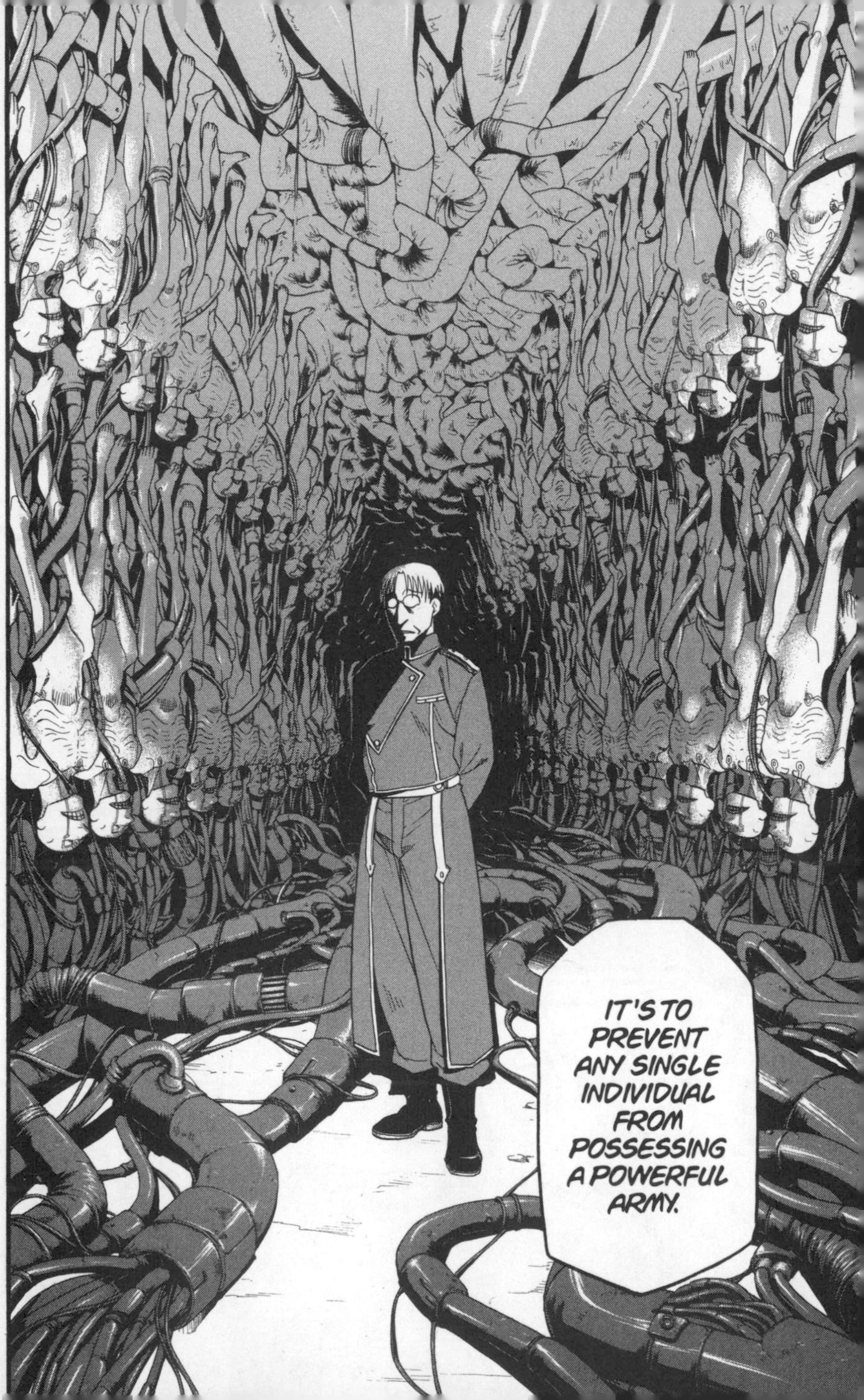
IT'S TO PREVENT ANY SINGLE INDIVIDUAL FROM POSSESSING A POWERFUL ARMY.

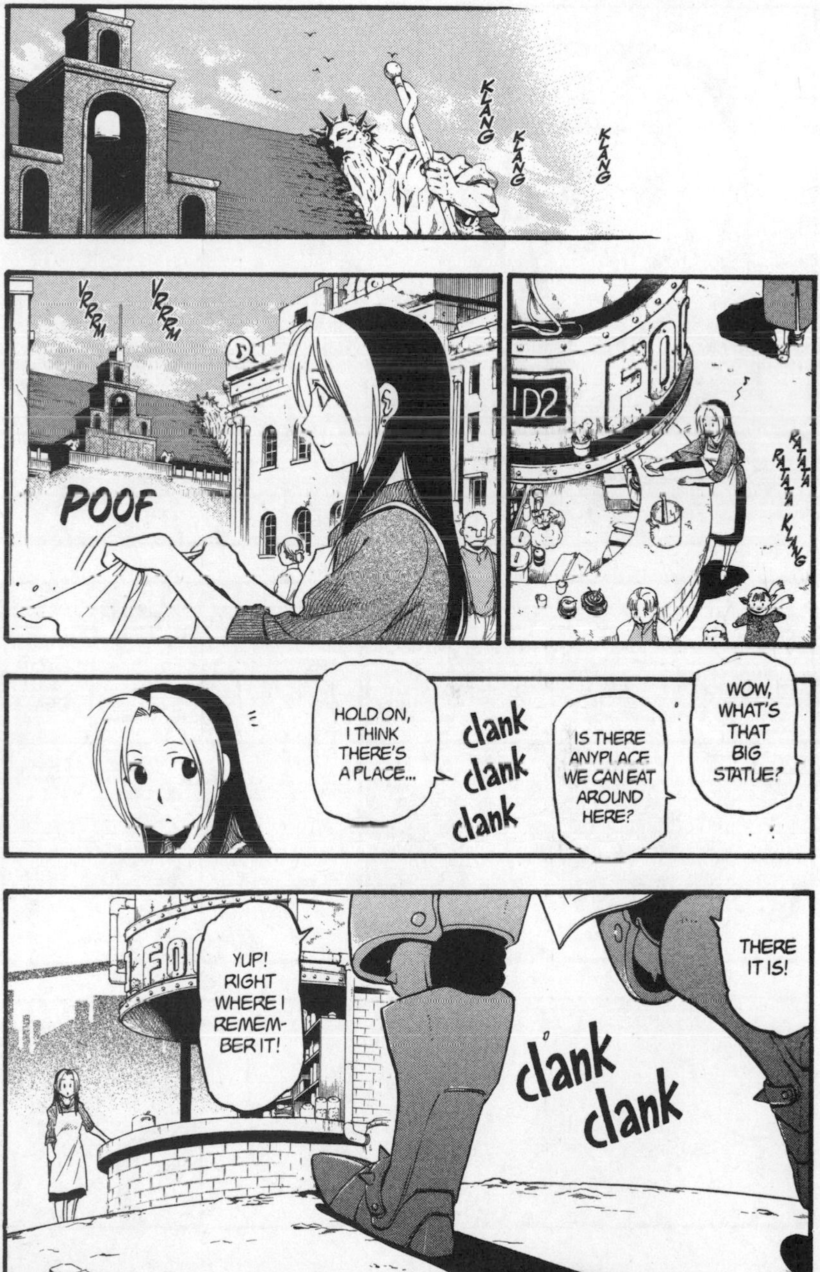
KLANG
KLANG
KLANG
PATATA
PATATA KLANG
VRRRM
VRRRM
POOF
WOW, WHAT'S THAT BIG STATUE?
IS THERE ANYPLACE WE CAN EAT AROUND HERE?
clank clank clank
HOLD ON, I THINK THERE'S A PLACE...
THERE IT IS!
clank clank
YUP! RIGHT WHERE I REMEM-BER IT!

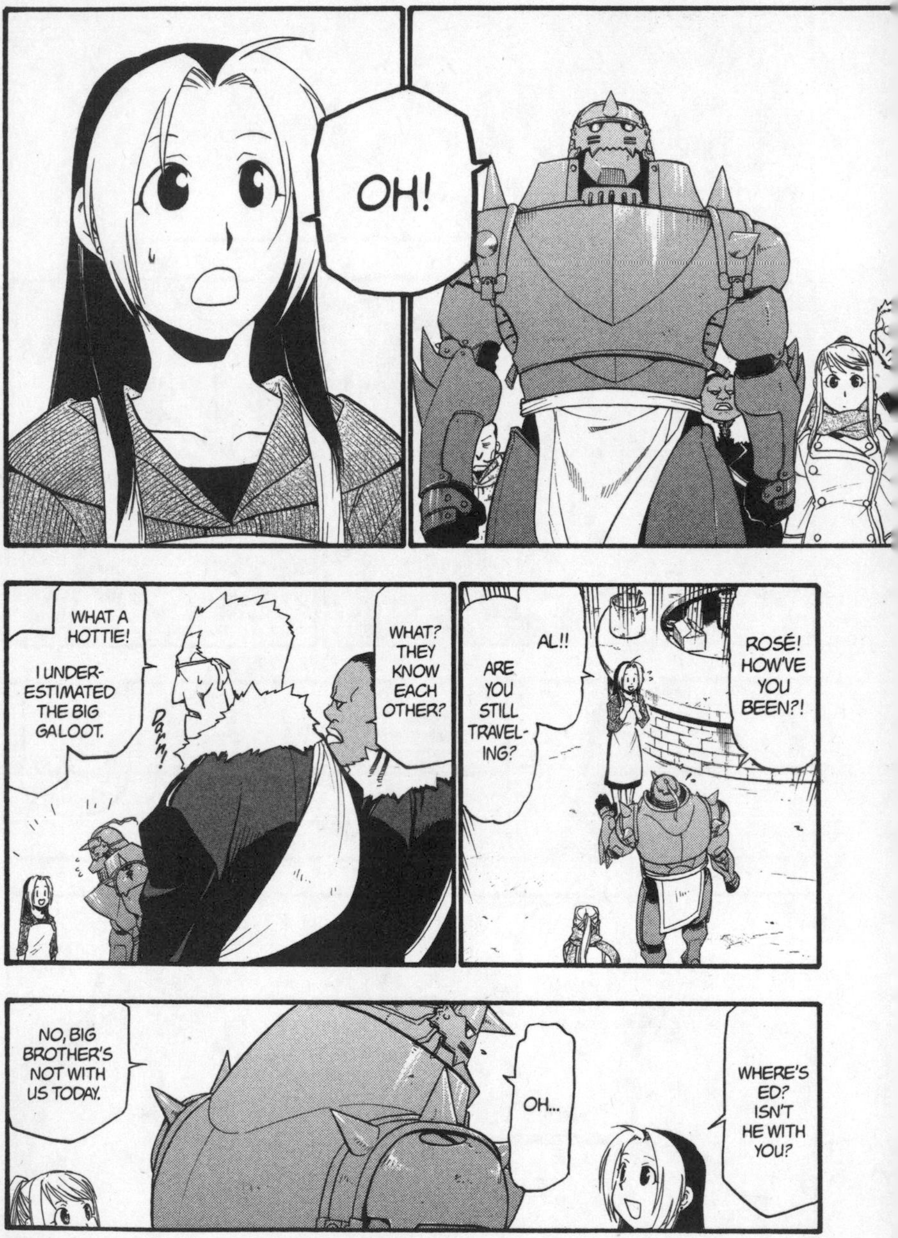
OH!
ROSÉ! HOW'VE YOU BEEN?!
AL!!
ARE YOU STILL TRAVEL-ING?
WHAT? THEY KNOW EACH OTHER?
WHAT A HOTTIE!
I UNDER-ESTIMATED THE BIG GALOOT.
Darn!
WHERE'S ED? ISN'T HE WITH YOU?
OH...
NO, BIG BROTHER'S NOT WITH US TODAY.

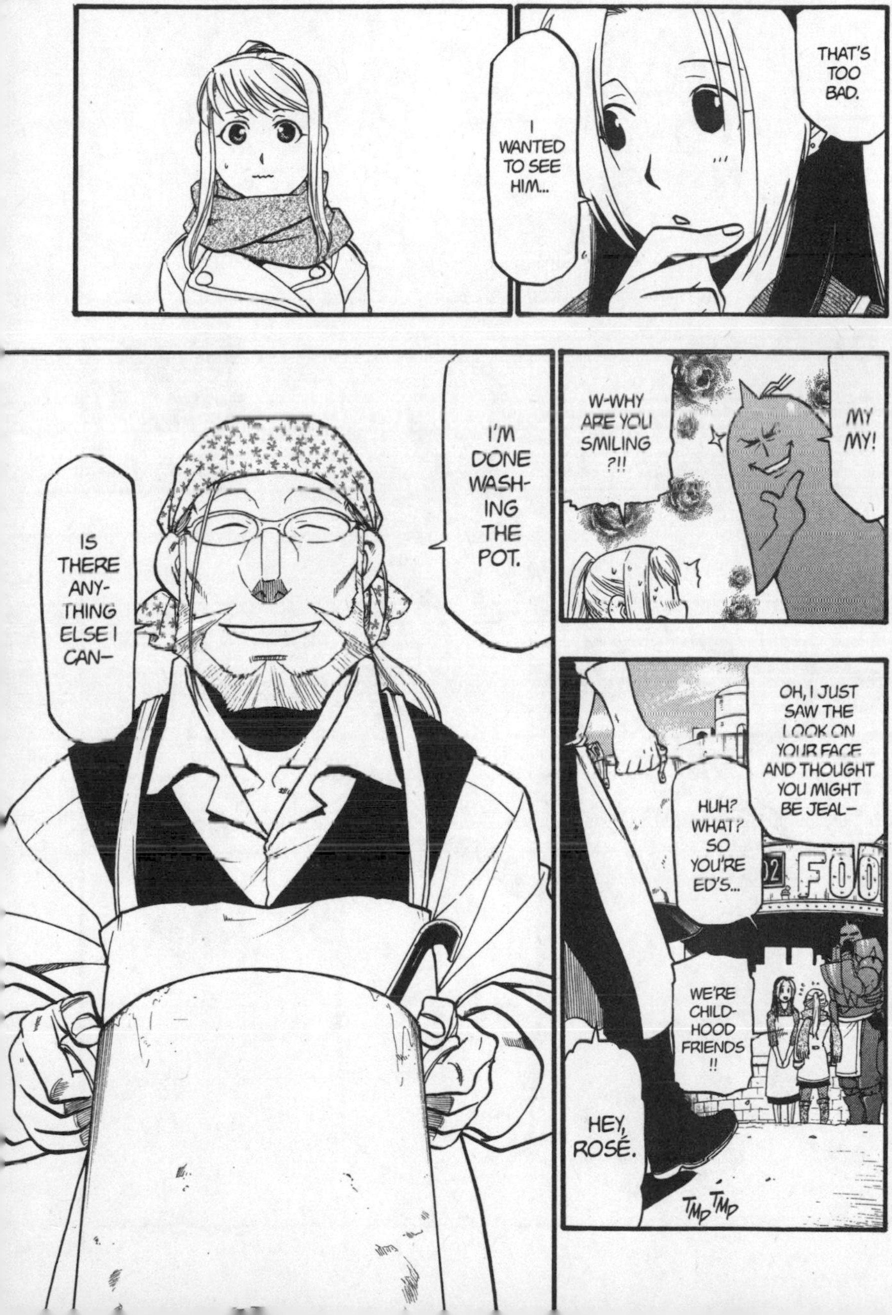
THAT'S TOO BAD.
...
I WANTED TO SEE HIM...
MY MY!
W-WHY ARE YOU SMILING ?!!
OH, I JUST SAW THE LOOK ON YOUR FACE AND THOUGHT YOU MIGHT BE JEAL–
HUH? WHAT? SO YOU'RE ED'S...
WE'RE CHILDHOOD FRIENDS !!
HEY, ROSÉ.
TMP TMP
I'M DONE WASHING THE POT.
IS THERE ANYTHING ELSE I CAN–

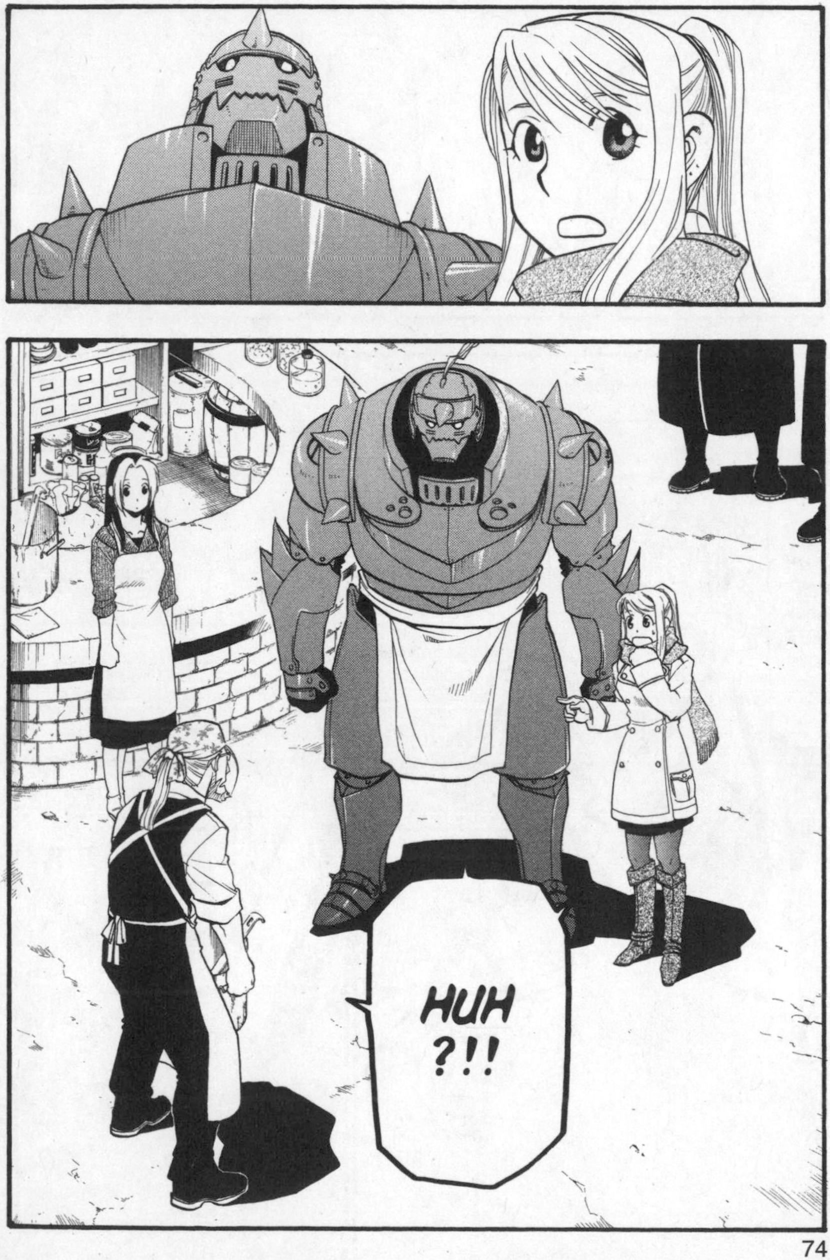
HUH
?!!

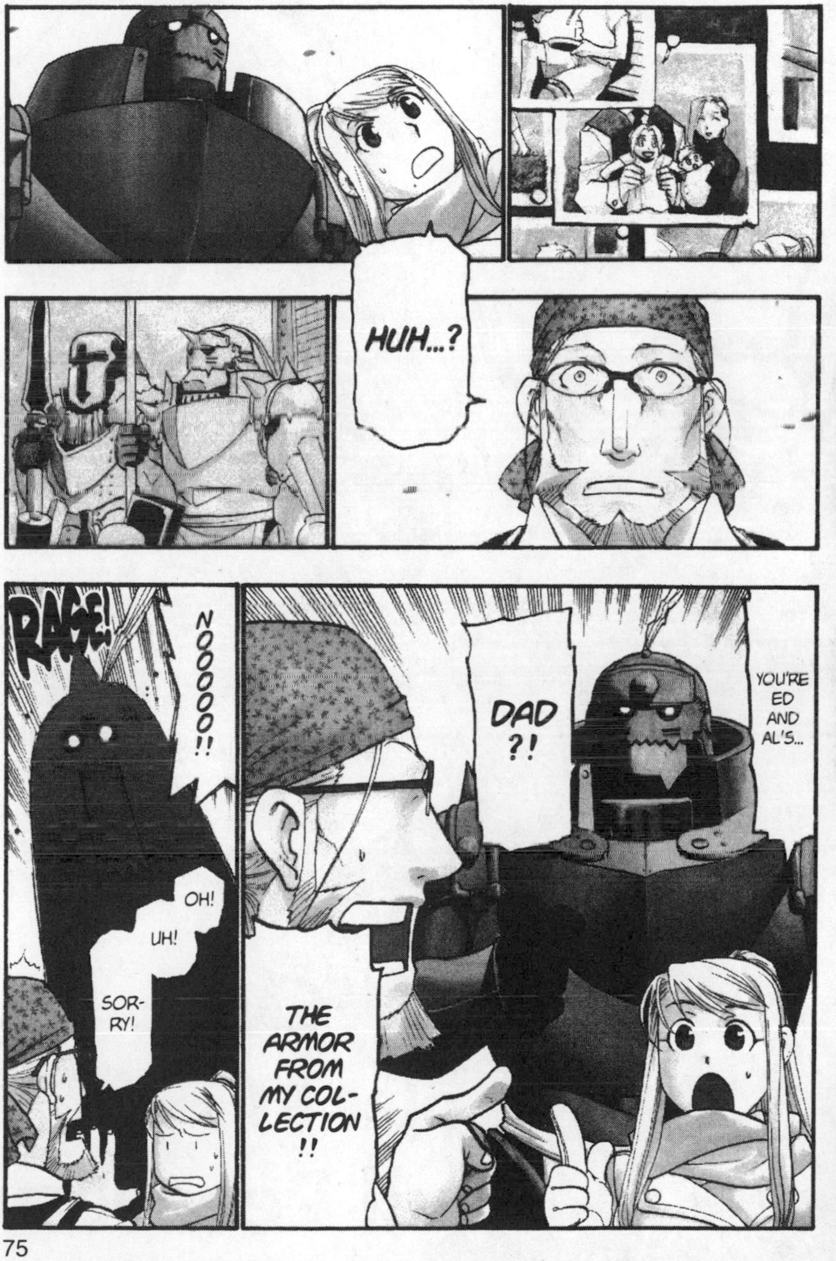
HUH...?
YOU'RE ED AND AL'S...
DAD ?!
THE ARMOR FROM MY COL-LECTION !!
NOOOOOO!!
RAGE!
OH!
UH!
SOR-RY!

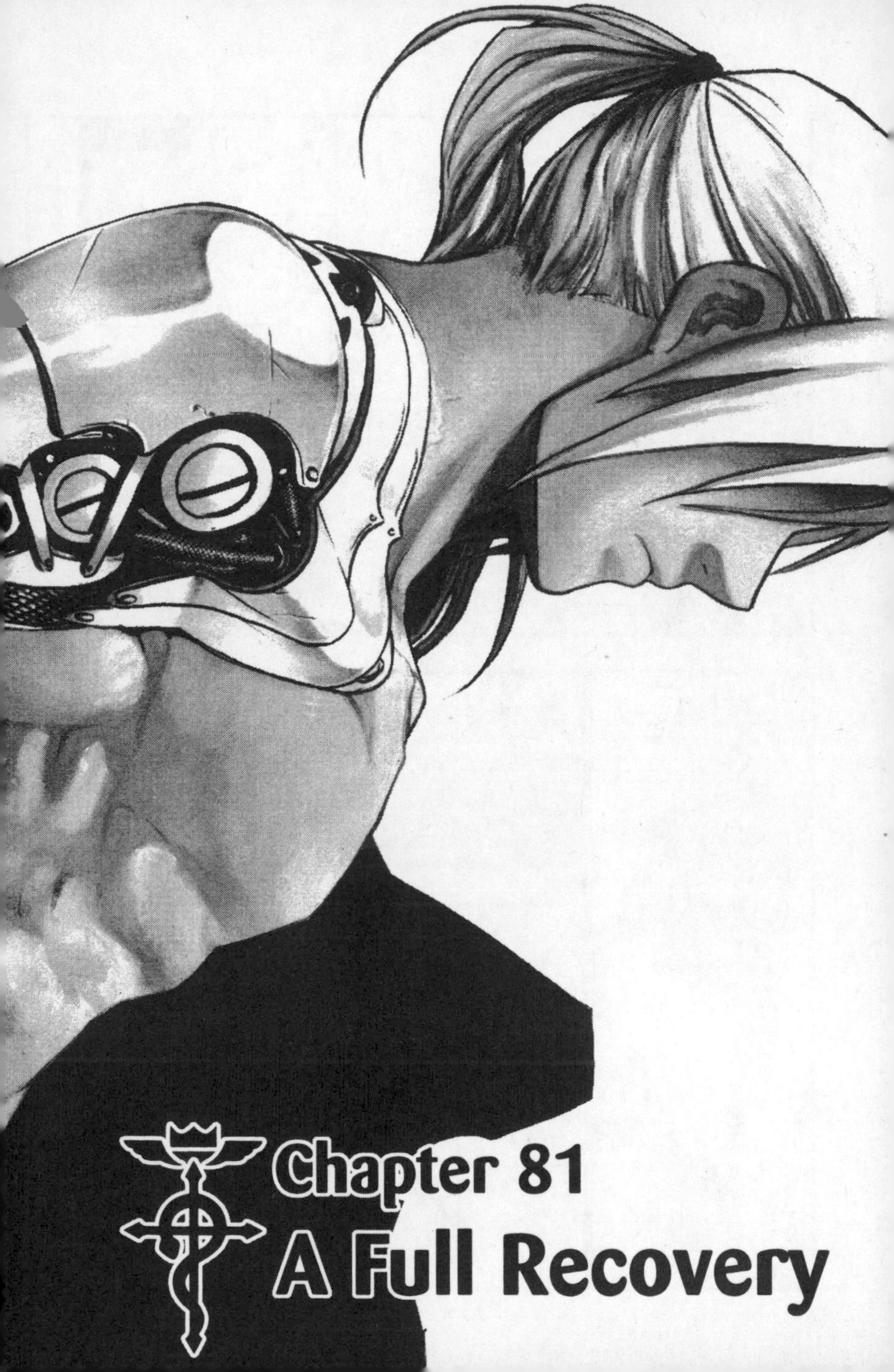

Chapter 81
A Full Recovery

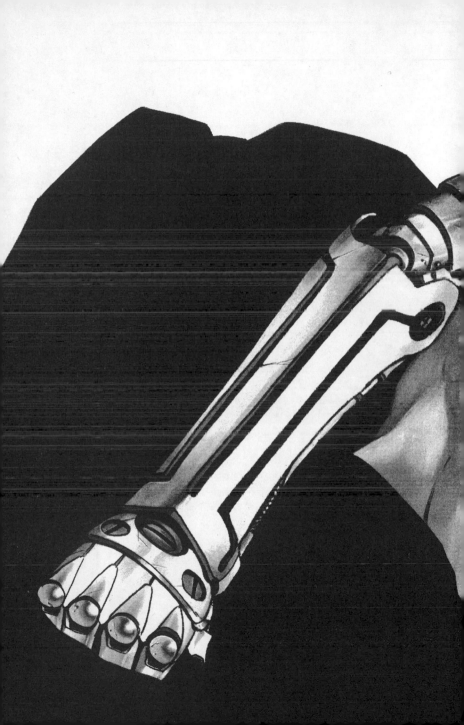

FULLMETAL
ALCHEMIST

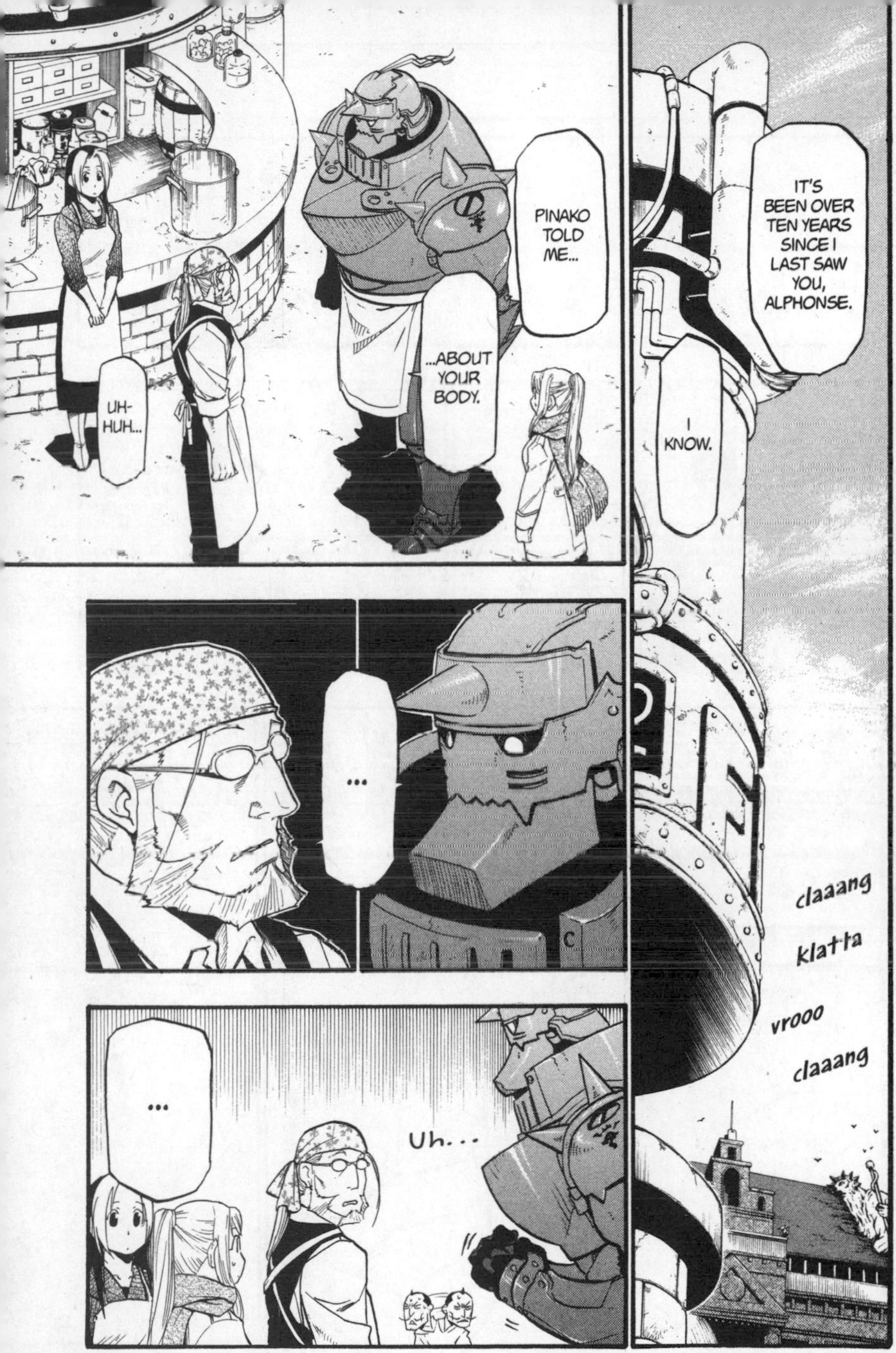
IT'S BEEN OVER TEN YEARS SINCE I LAST SAW YOU, ALPHONSE.
I KNOW.
claaang
klatta
vrooo
claaang
PINAKO TOLD ME...
...ABOUT YOUR BODY.
UH-HUH...
...
...
Uh...

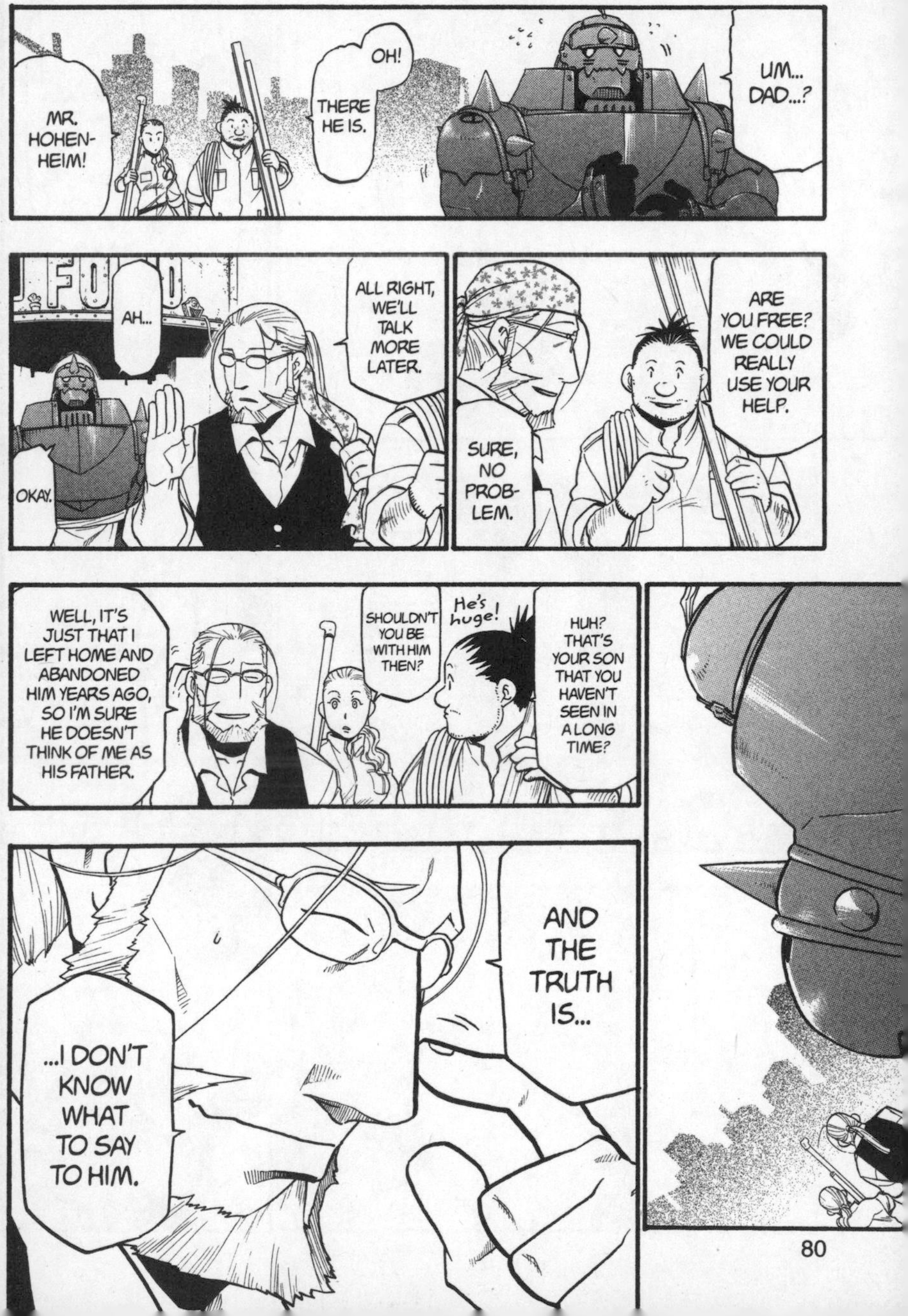
UM... DAD...?
OH! THERE HE IS.
MR. HOHENHEIM!
ARE YOU FREE? WE COULD REALLY USE YOUR HELP.
SURE, NO PROBLEM.
ALL RIGHT, WE'LL TALK MORE LATER.
AH...
OKAY.
HUH? THAT'S YOUR SON THAT YOU HAVEN'T SEEN IN A LONG TIME?
He's huge!
SHOULDN'T YOU BE WITH HIM THEN?
WELL, IT'S JUST THAT I LEFT HOME AND ABANDONED HIM YEARS AGO, SO I'M SURE HE DOESN'T THINK OF ME AS HIS FATHER.
AND THE TRUTH IS...
...I DON'T KNOW WHAT TO SAY TO HIM.

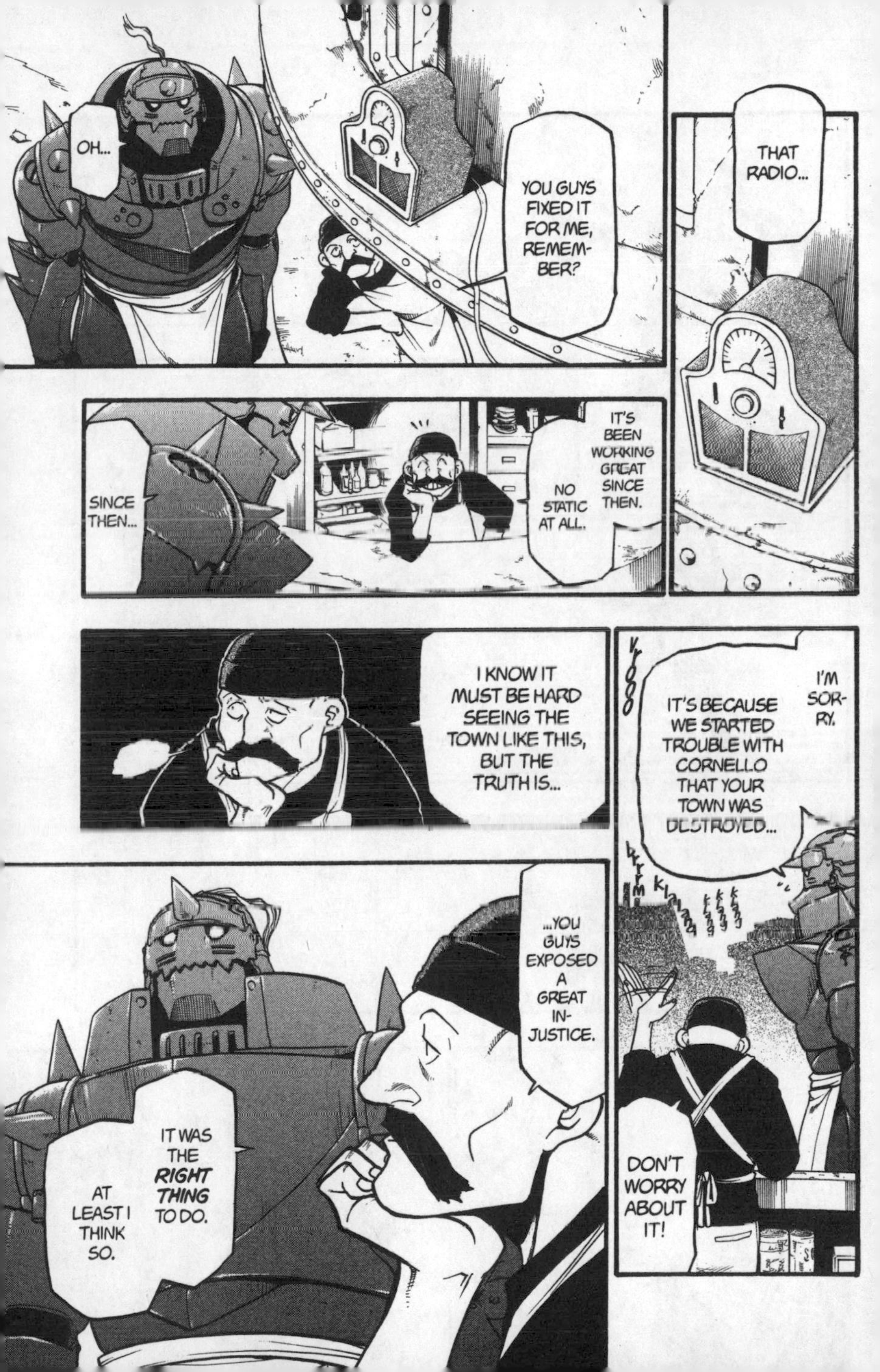

THAT RADIO...
YOU GUYS FIXED IT FOR ME, REMEMBER?
OH...
IT'S BEEN WORKING GREAT SINCE THEN.
NO STATIC AT ALL.
SINCE THEN...
I'M SORRY.
IT'S BECAUSE WE STARTED TROUBLE WITH CORNELLO THAT YOUR TOWN WAS DESTROYED...
DON'T WORRY ABOUT IT!
I KNOW IT MUST BE HARD SEEING THE TOWN LIKE THIS, BUT THE TRUTH IS...
...YOU GUYS EXPOSED A GREAT INJUSTICE.
IT WAS THE ***RIGHT THING*** TO DO.
AT LEAST I THINK SO.

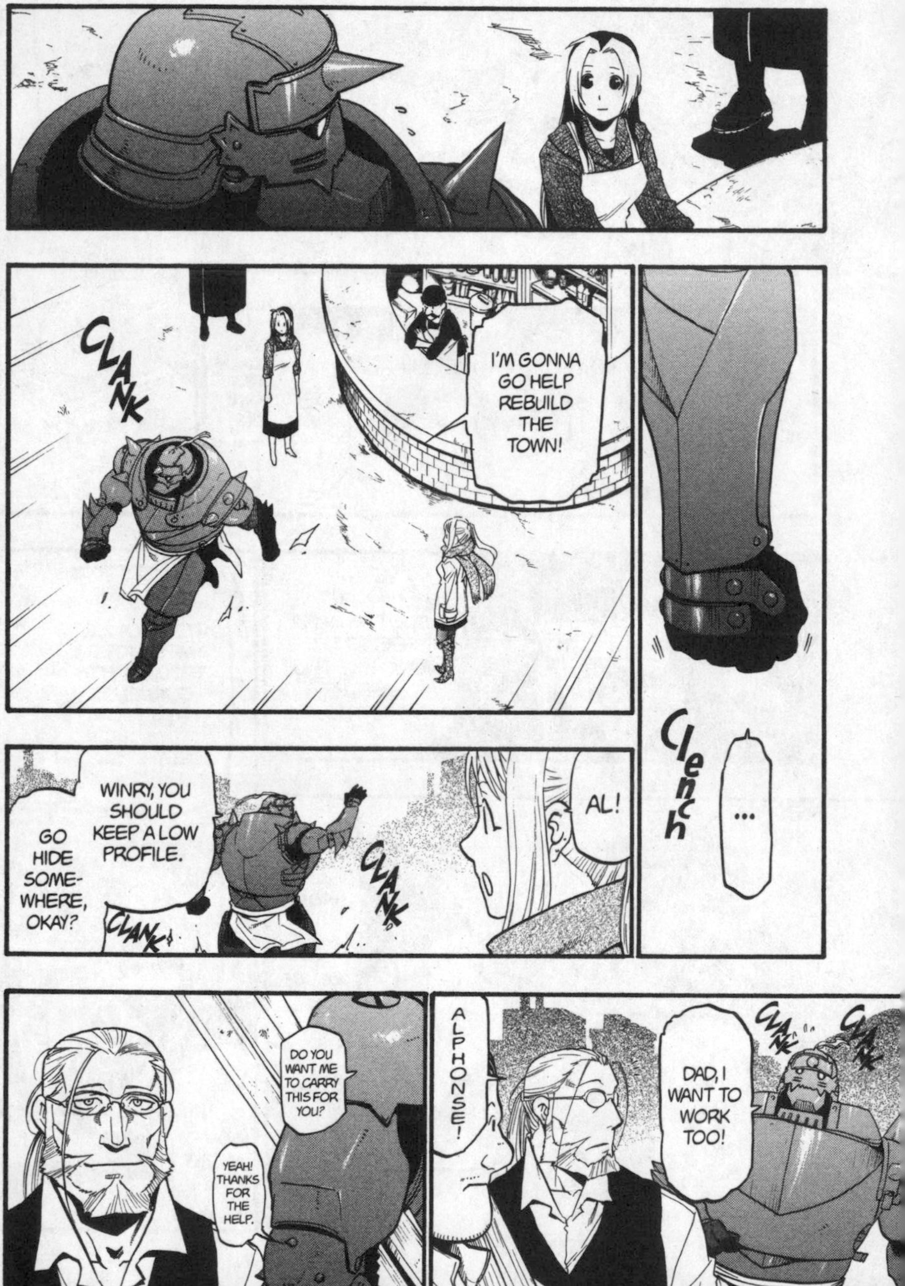
Clench
...
CLANK
I'M GONNA GO HELP REBUILD THE TOWN!
AL!
CLANK
WINRY, YOU SHOULD KEEP A LOW PROFILE.
GO HIDE SOME-WHERE, OKAY?
CLANK
CLANK
CLANK
DAD, I WANT TO WORK TOO!
ALPHONSE!
DO YOU WANT ME TO CARRY THIS FOR YOU?
YEAH! THANKS FOR THE HELP.

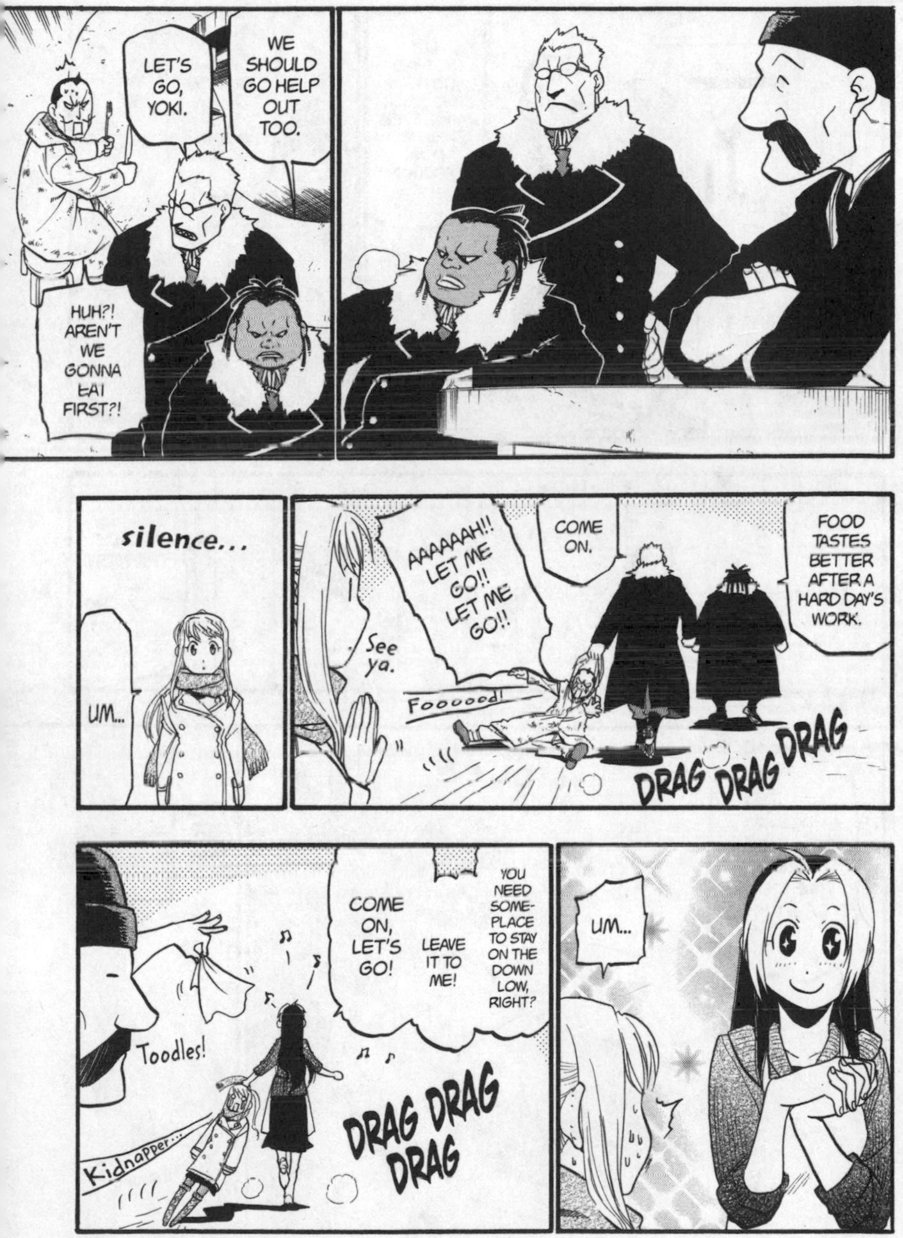
WE SHOULD GO HELP OUT TOO.
LET'S GO, YOKI.
HUH?! AREN'T WE GONNA EAT FIRST?!
FOOD TASTES BETTER AFTER A HARD DAY'S WORK.
COME ON.
AAAAAAH!! LET ME GO!! LET ME GO!!
See ya.
Fooooood!
DRAG DRAG DRAG
silence...
UM...
UM...
YOU NEED SOME-PLACE TO STAY ON THE DOWN LOW, RIGHT?
LEAVE IT TO ME!
COME ON, LET'S GO!
Toodles!
DRAG DRAG DRAG
Kidnapper...

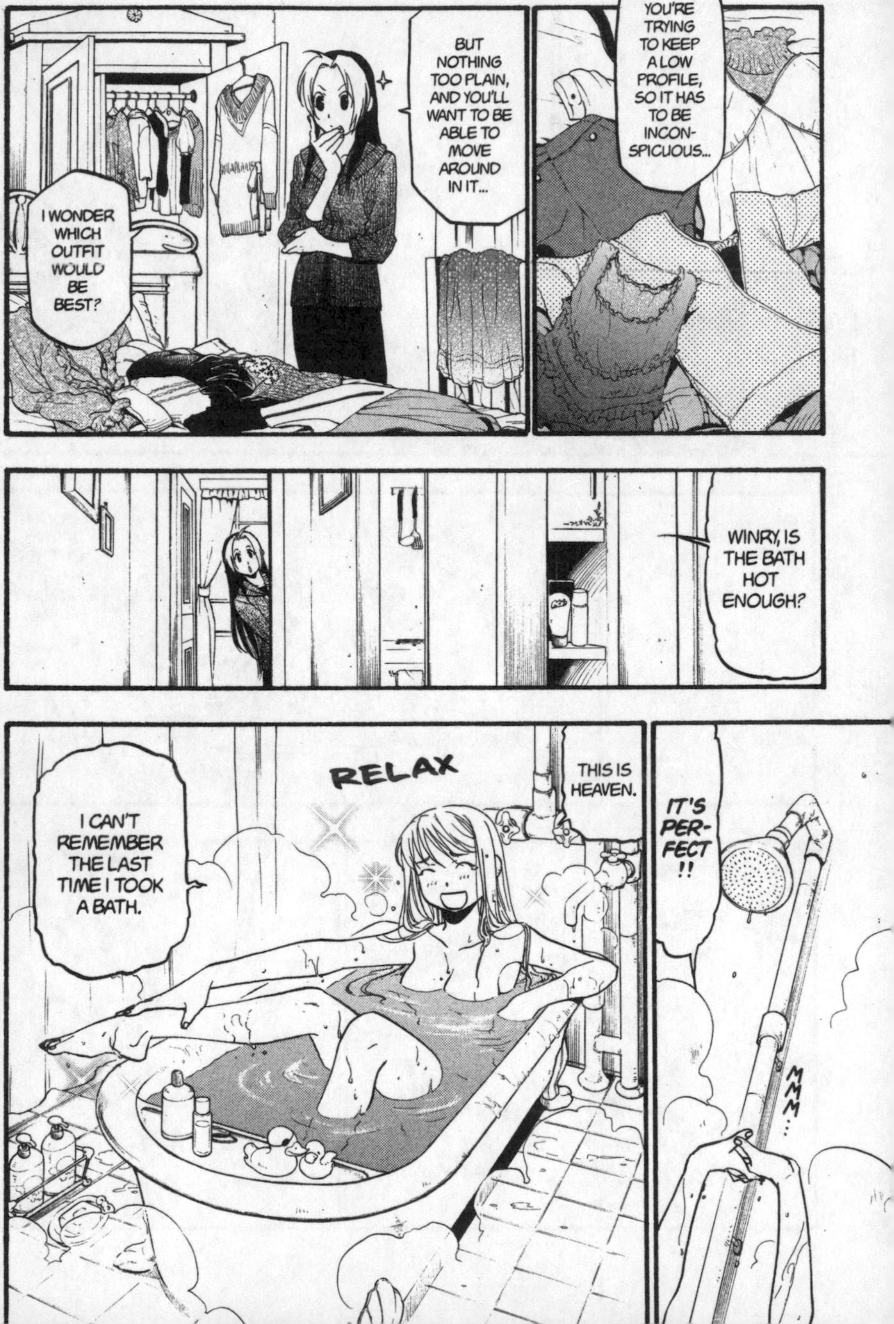
YOU'RE TRYING TO KEEP A LOW PROFILE, SO IT HAS TO BE INCONSPICUOUS...
BUT NOTHING TOO PLAIN, AND YOU'LL WANT TO BE ABLE TO MOVE AROUND IN IT...
I WONDER WHICH OUTFIT WOULD BE BEST?
WINRY, IS THE BATH HOT ENOUGH?
IT'S PERFECT!!
MMM...
THIS IS HEAVEN.
RELAX
I CAN'T REMEMBER THE LAST TIME I TOOK A BATH.

I'M GONNA PUT A CHANGE OF CLOTHES OVER HERE FOR YOU.
OKAY! THANK YOU SO MUCH!
MS. ROSÉ IS SO NICE. ♡
THIS IS GREAT.
Simple needs
YOU KNOW, I REALLY ADMIRE YOU.
BEING ON YOUR OWN AND WORKING AS AN AUTO-MAIL ENGINEER AT SUCH A YOUNG AGE.
SPLISH
YOU MADE ED'S LEG, RIGHT?
YES.
I GUESS I SORT OF DID IT OUT OF FRIENDSHIP...
...
SPLISH
I WONDER IF ED'S ALL RIGHT...
I WONDER IF HE'S STILL MISSING...
I WONDER IF HE'S BEEN ABLE TO TAKE A HOT BATH LATELY...
THAT'S AMAZING.
SO THAT MEANS YOU'RE LITERALLY THE PERSON WHO HELPED ED GET BACK ON HIS FEET.

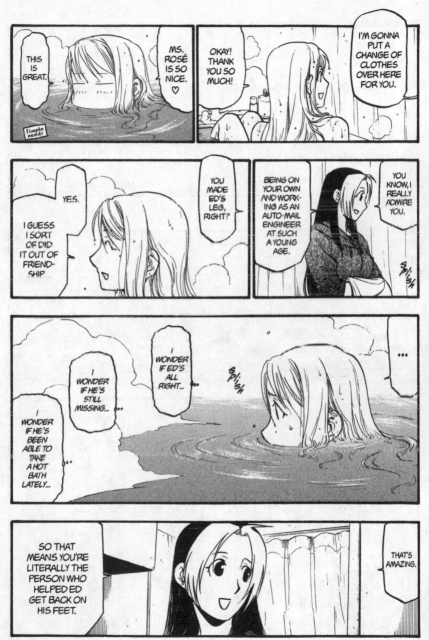

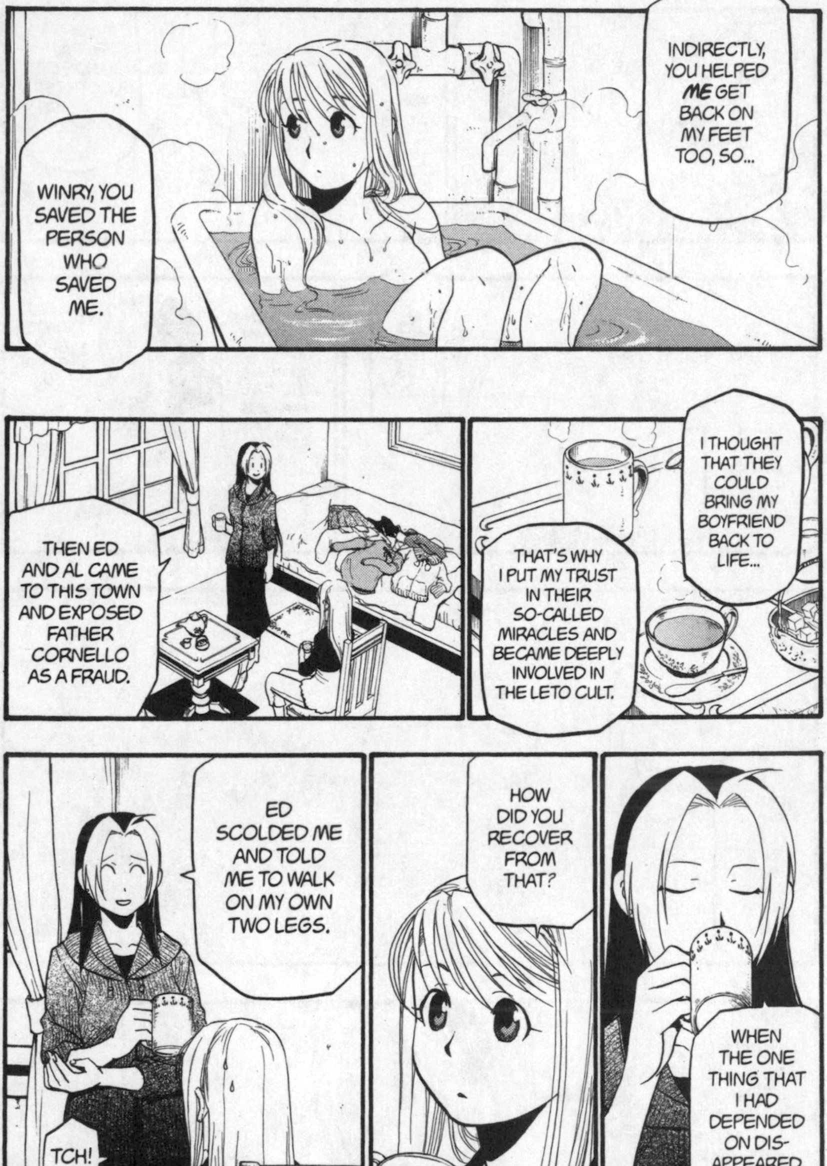
INDIRECTLY, YOU HELPED *ME* GET BACK ON MY FEET TOO, SO...
WINRY, YOU SAVED THE PERSON WHO SAVED ME.
I THOUGHT THAT THEY COULD BRING MY BOYFRIEND BACK TO LIFE...
THAT'S WHY I PUT MY TRUST IN THEIR SO-CALLED MIRACLES AND BECAME DEEPLY INVOLVED IN THE LETO CULT.
THEN ED AND AL CAME TO THIS TOWN AND EXPOSED FATHER CORNELLO AS A FRAUD.
WHEN THE ONE THING THAT I HAD DEPENDED ON DIS-APPEARED, I LOST ALL HOPE.
HOW DID YOU RECOVER FROM THAT?
ED SCOLDED ME AND TOLD ME TO WALK ON MY OWN TWO LEGS.
TCH!

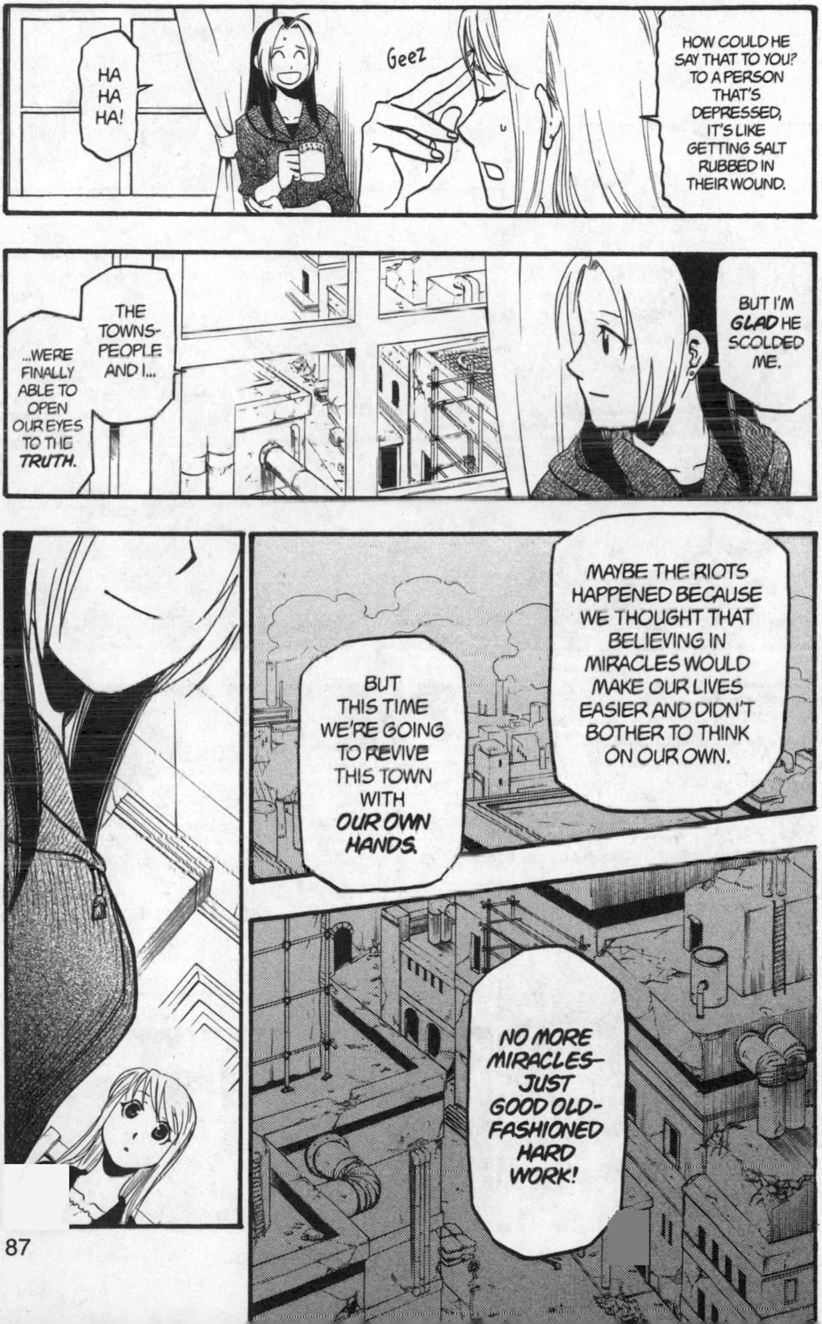
HOW COULD HE SAY THAT TO YOU? TO A PERSON THAT'S DEPRESSED, IT'S LIKE GETTING SALT RUBBED IN THEIR WOUND.
Geez
HA HA HA!
BUT I'M *GLAD* HE SCOLDED ME.
THE TOWNS-PEOPLE AND I...
...WERE FINALLY ABLE TO OPEN OUR EYES TO THE *TRUTH*.
MAYBE THE RIOTS HAPPENED BECAUSE WE THOUGHT THAT BELIEVING IN MIRACLES WOULD MAKE OUR LIVES EASIER AND DIDN'T BOTHER TO THINK ON OUR OWN.
BUT THIS TIME WE'RE GOING TO REVIVE THIS TOWN WITH *OUR OWN HANDS.*
NO MORE MIRACLES- JUST GOOD OLD-FASHIONED HARD WORK!

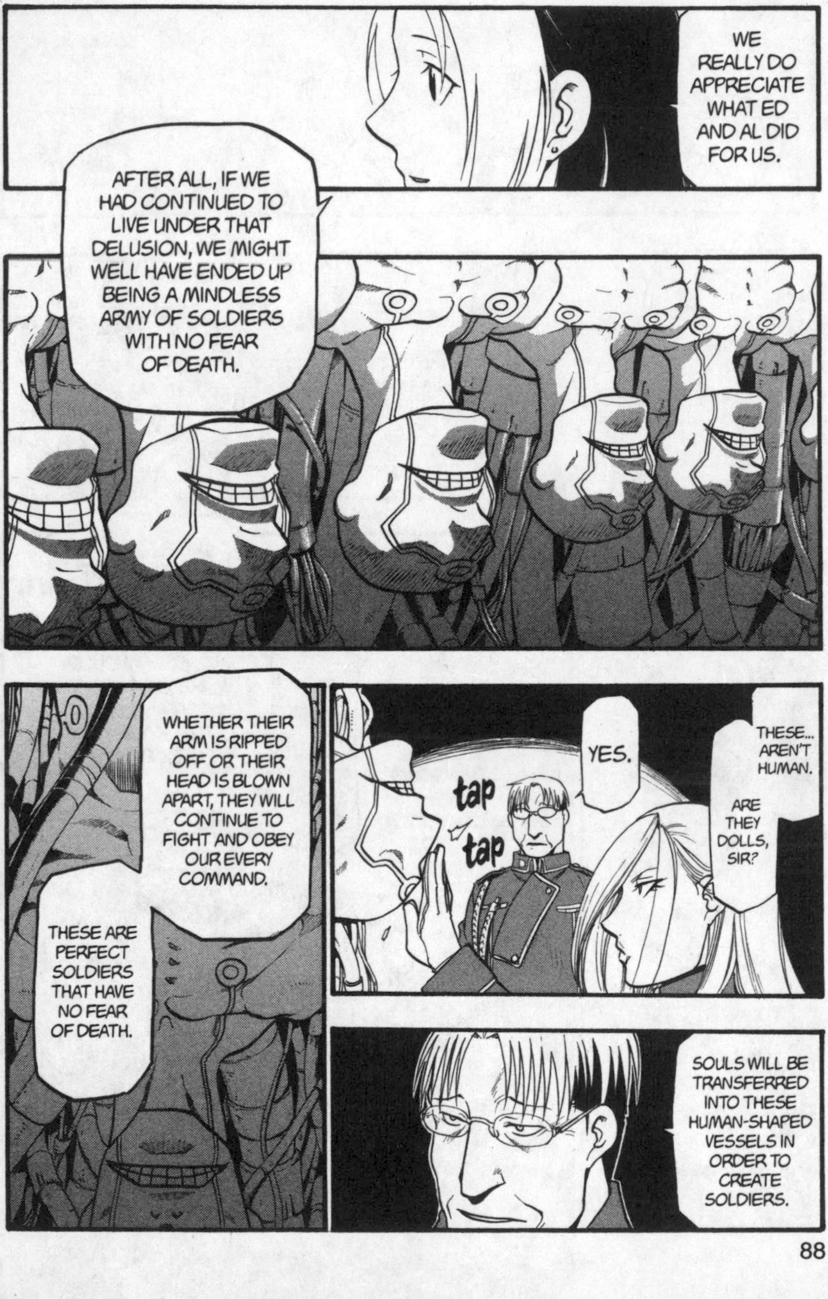
WE REALLY DO APPRECIATE WHAT ED AND AL DID FOR US.
AFTER ALL, IF WE HAD CONTINUED TO LIVE UNDER THAT DELUSION, WE MIGHT WELL HAVE ENDED UP BEING A MINDLESS ARMY OF SOLDIERS WITH NO FEAR OF DEATH.
THESE... AREN'T HUMAN.
ARE THEY DOLLS, SIR?
YES.
tap
tap
SOULS WILL BE TRANSFERRED INTO THESE HUMAN-SHAPED VESSELS IN ORDER TO CREATE SOLDIERS.
WHETHER THEIR ARM IS RIPPED OFF OR THEIR HEAD IS BLOWN APART, THEY WILL CONTINUE TO FIGHT AND OBEY OUR EVERY COMMAND.
THESE ARE PERFECT SOLDIERS THAT HAVE NO FEAR OF DEATH.

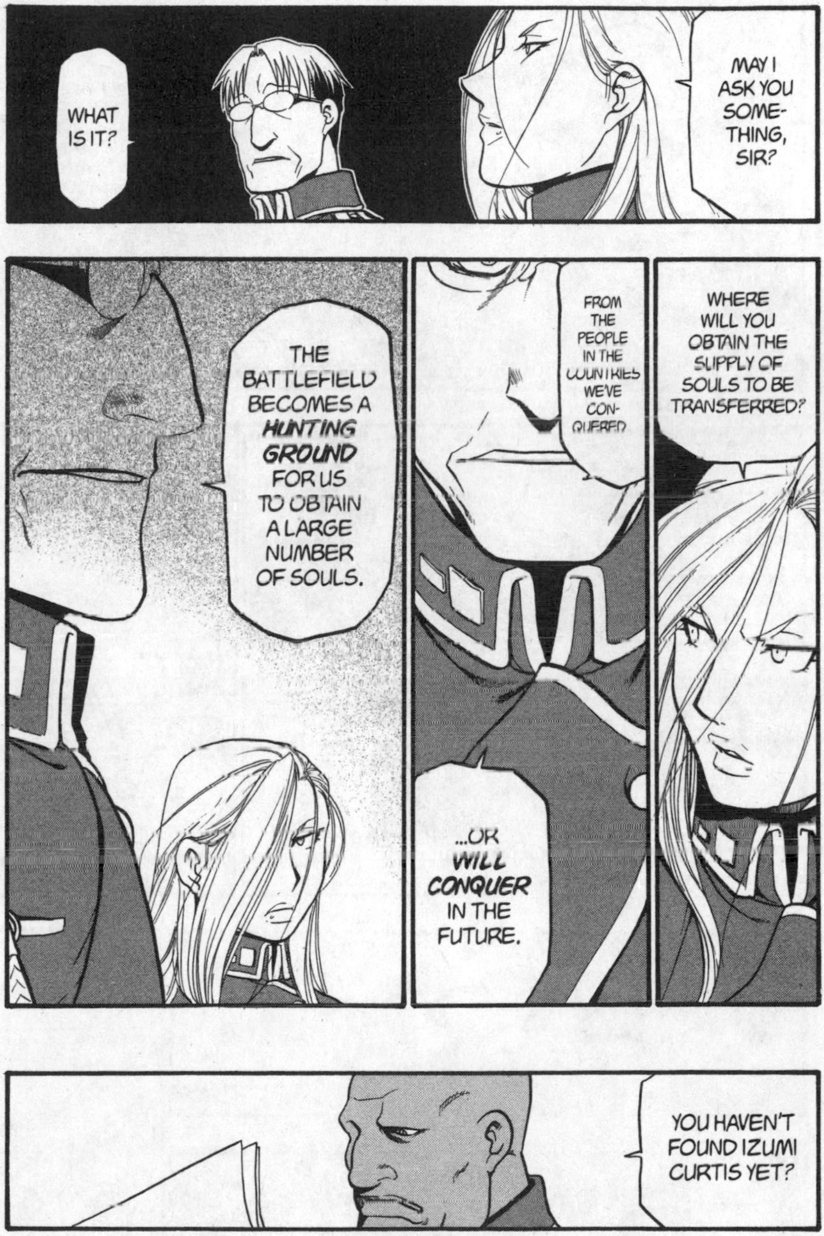
MAY I ASK YOU SOME-THING, SIR?
WHAT IS IT?
WHERE WILL YOU OBTAIN THE SUPPLY OF SOULS TO BE TRANSFERRED?
FROM THE PEOPLE IN THE COUNTRIES WE'VE CON-QUERED
...OR WILL CONQUER IN THE FUTURE.
THE BATTLEFIELD BECOMES A HUNTING GROUND FOR US TO OBTAIN A LARGE NUMBER OF SOULS.
YOU HAVEN'T FOUND IZUMI CURTIS YET?

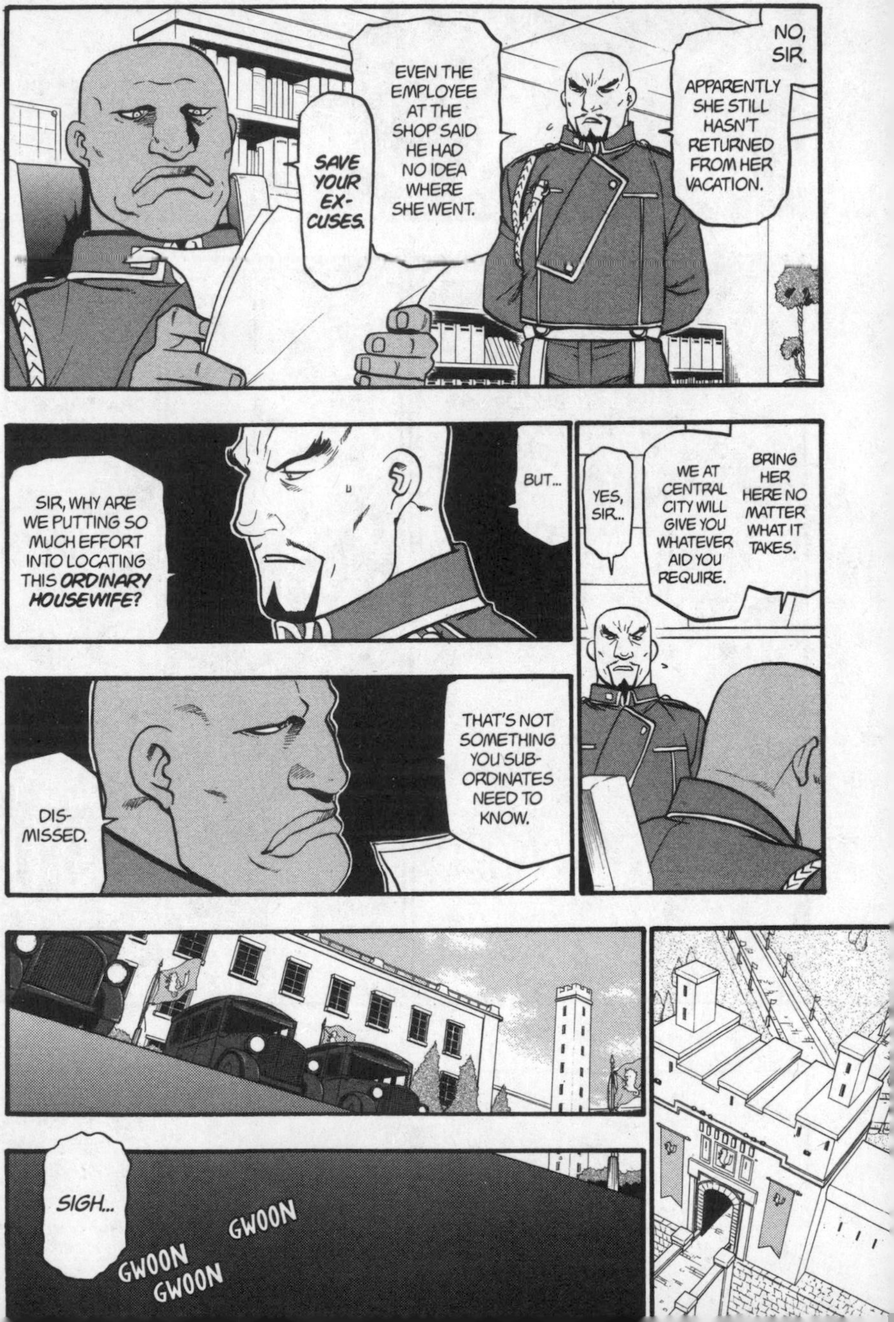
NO, SIR.
APPARENTLY SHE STILL HASN'T RETURNED FROM HER VACATION.
EVEN THE EMPLOYEE AT THE SHOP SAID HE HAD NO IDEA WHERE SHE WENT.
SAVE YOUR EX-CUSES.
BRING HER HERE NO MATTER WHAT IT TAKES.
WE AT CENTRAL CITY WILL GIVE YOU WHATEVER AID YOU REQUIRE.
YES, SIR...
BUT...
SIR, WHY ARE WE PUTTING SO MUCH EFFORT INTO LOCATING THIS ORDINARY HOUSEWIFE?
THAT'S NOT SOMETHING YOU SUB-ORDINATES NEED TO KNOW.
DIS-MISSED.
SIGH...
GWOON
GWOON
GWOON

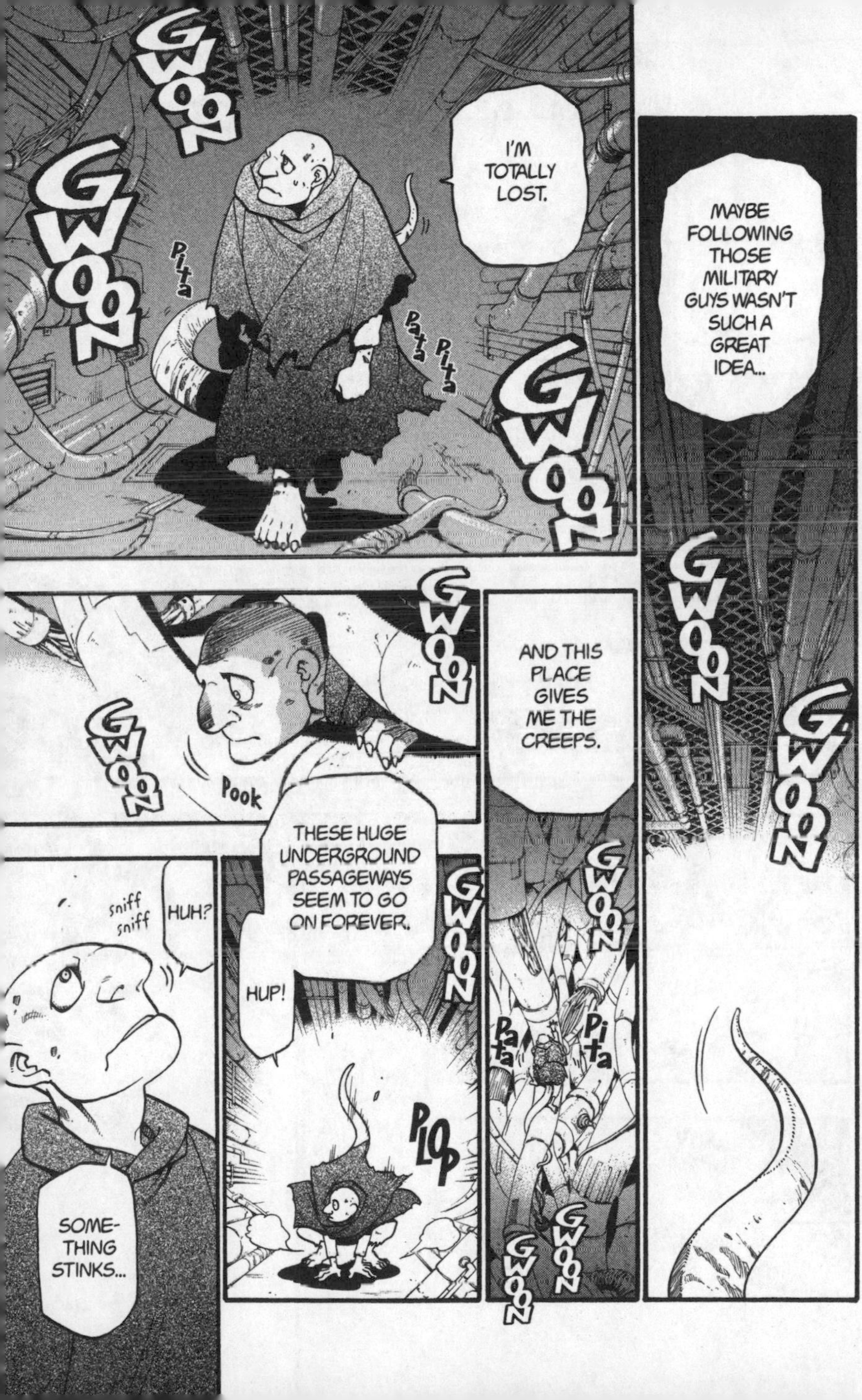
GWOON
GWOON
I'M TOTALLY LOST.
Pita
Pata
Pita
GWOON
MAYBE FOLLOWING THOSE MILITARY GUYS WASN'T SUCH A GREAT IDEA...
GWOON
GWOON
AND THIS PLACE GIVES ME THE CREEPS.
GWOON
Pita
Pata
GWOON
GWOON
GWOON
GWOON
Pook
THESE HUGE UNDERGROUND PASSAGEWAYS SEEM TO GO ON FOREVER.
GWOON
HUP!
PLOP
HUH?
sniff sniff
SOME-THING STINKS...

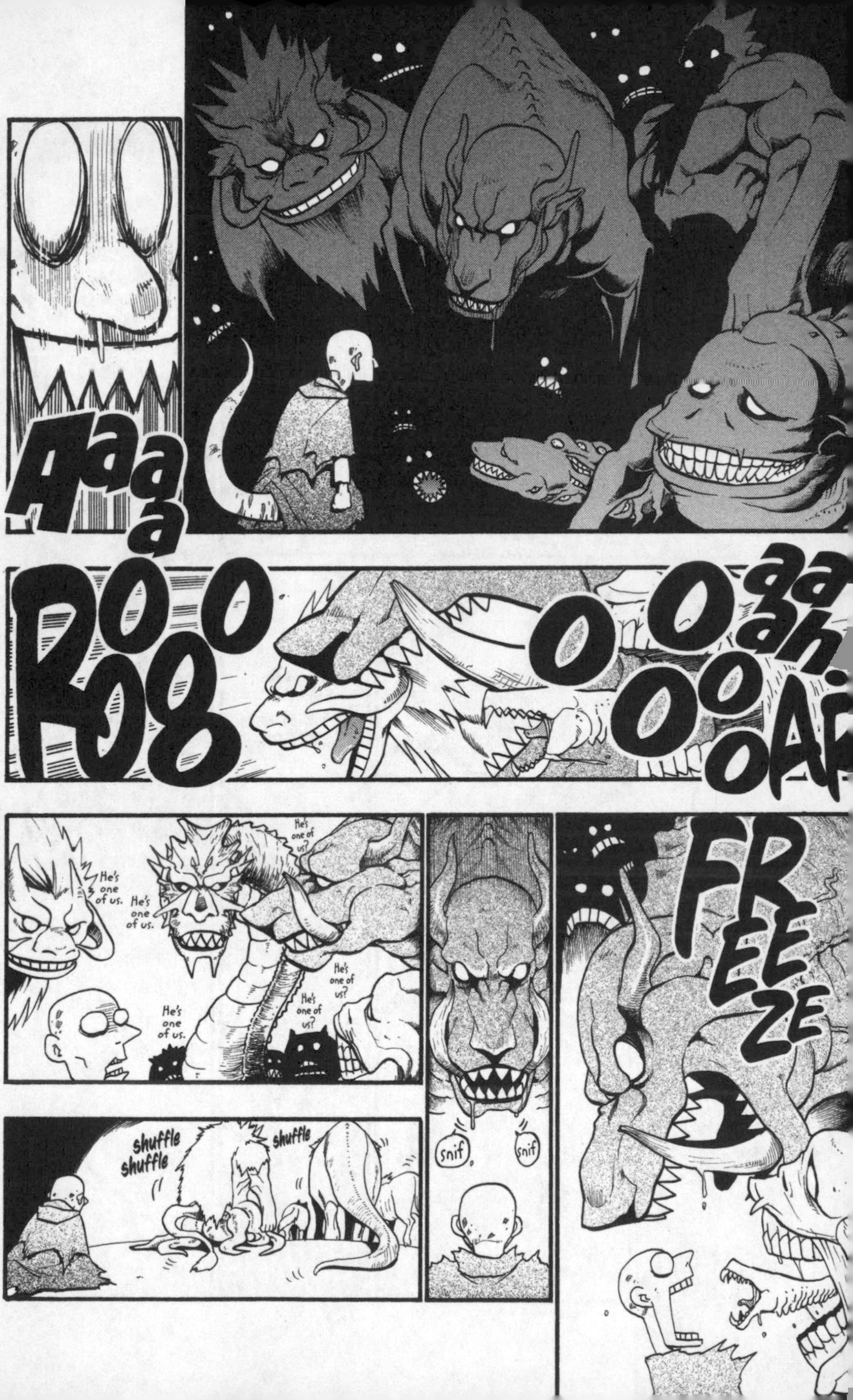
Aaaa
ROOOOO
OOaah OOOOAR!
FREEZE
snif
snif
He's one of us?
He's one of us.
He's one of us.
He's one of us?
He's one of us?
He's one of us.
shuffle
shuffle shuffle

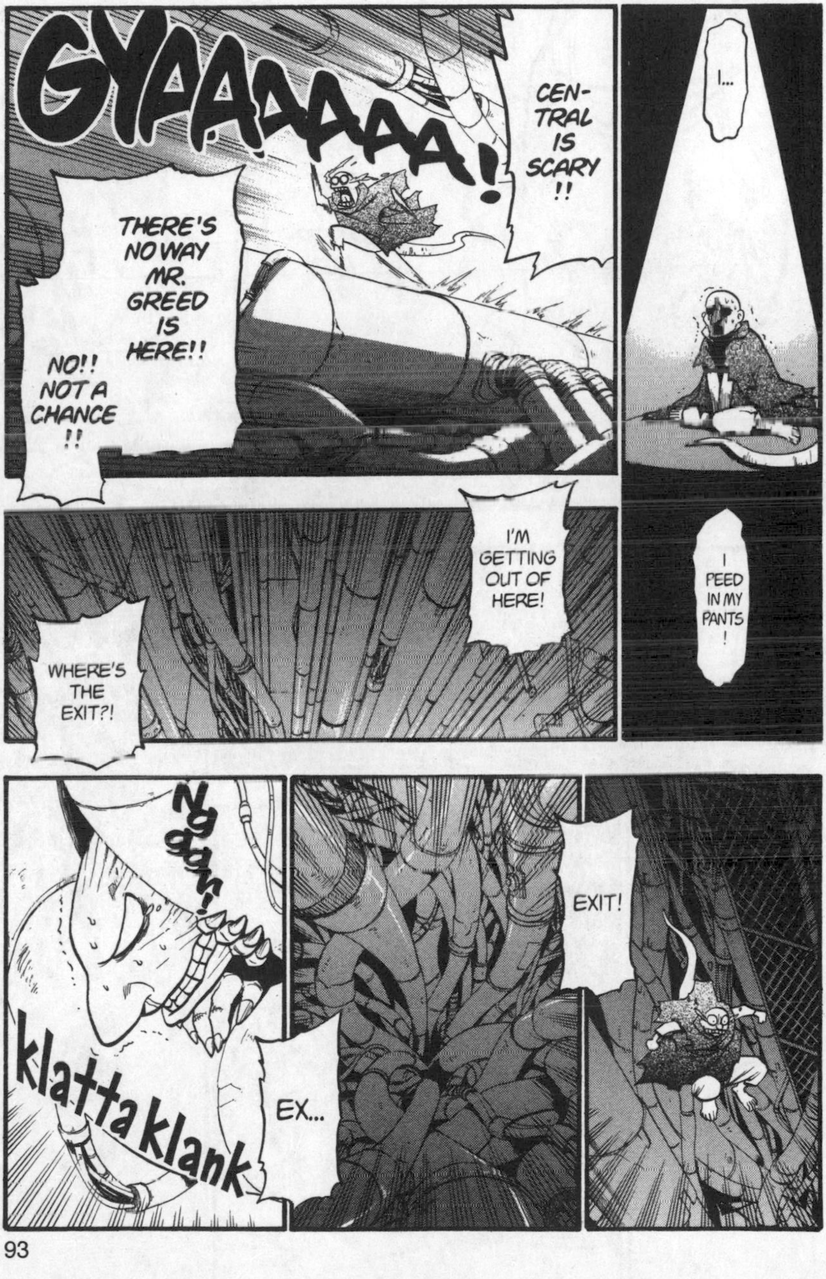
I...
CEN-TRAL IS SCARY!!
GYAAAAAA!
THERE'S NO WAY MR. GREED IS HERE!!
NO!! NOT A CHANCE!!
I PEED IN MY PANTS!
I'M GETTING OUT OF HERE!
WHERE'S THE EXIT?!
EXIT!
Ngaah!
EX...
klattaklank

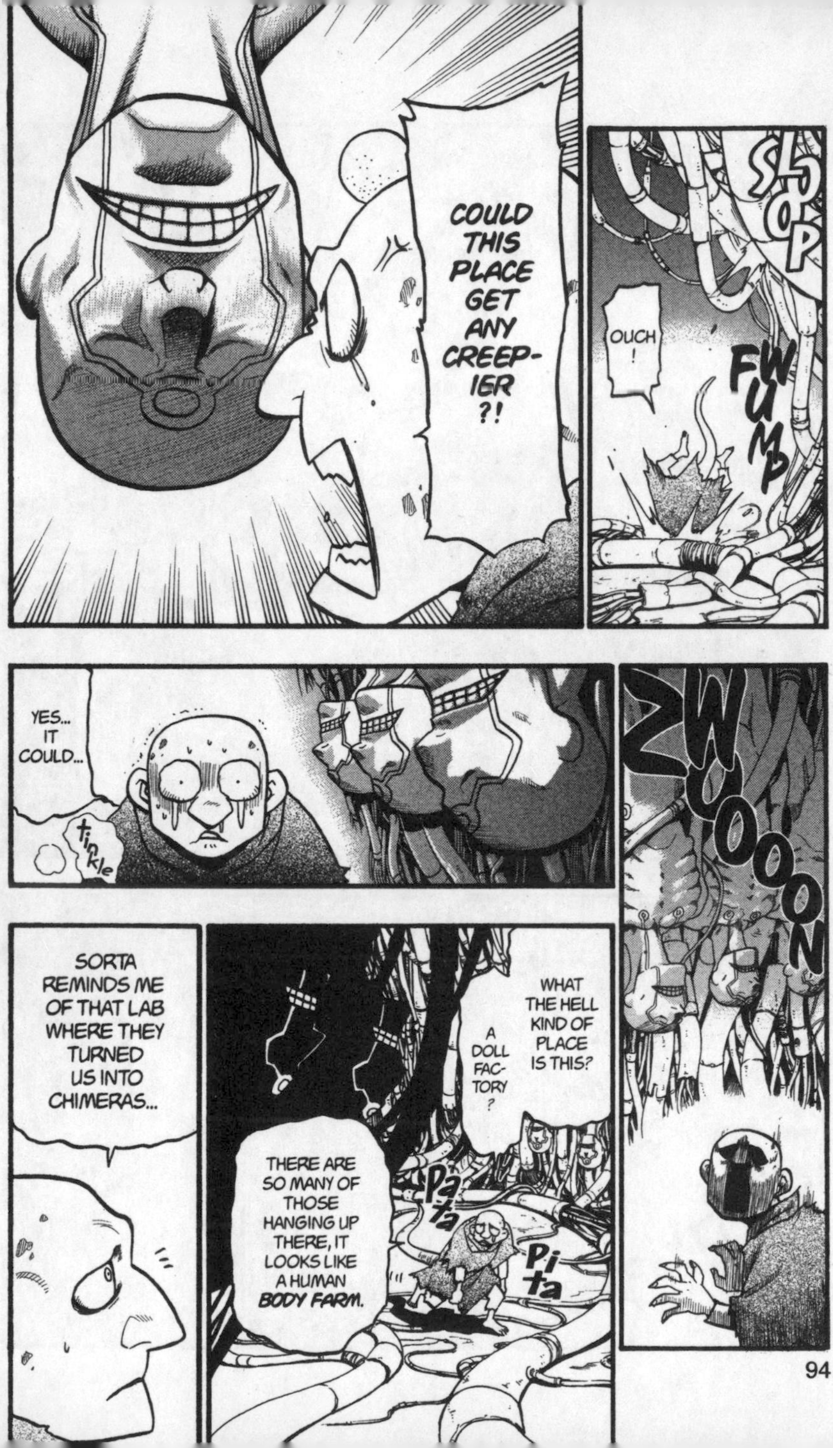
SLOOP
OUCH!
FWUMP
COULD THIS PLACE GET ANY CREEPIER?!
ZWOOOOON
YES... IT COULD...
tinkle
WHAT THE HELL KIND OF PLACE IS THIS?
A DOLL FACTORY?
THERE ARE SO MANY OF THOSE HANGING UP THERE, IT LOOKS LIKE A HUMAN BODY FARM.
Pata
Pita
SORTA REMINDS ME OF THAT LAB WHERE THEY TURNED US INTO CHIMERAS...

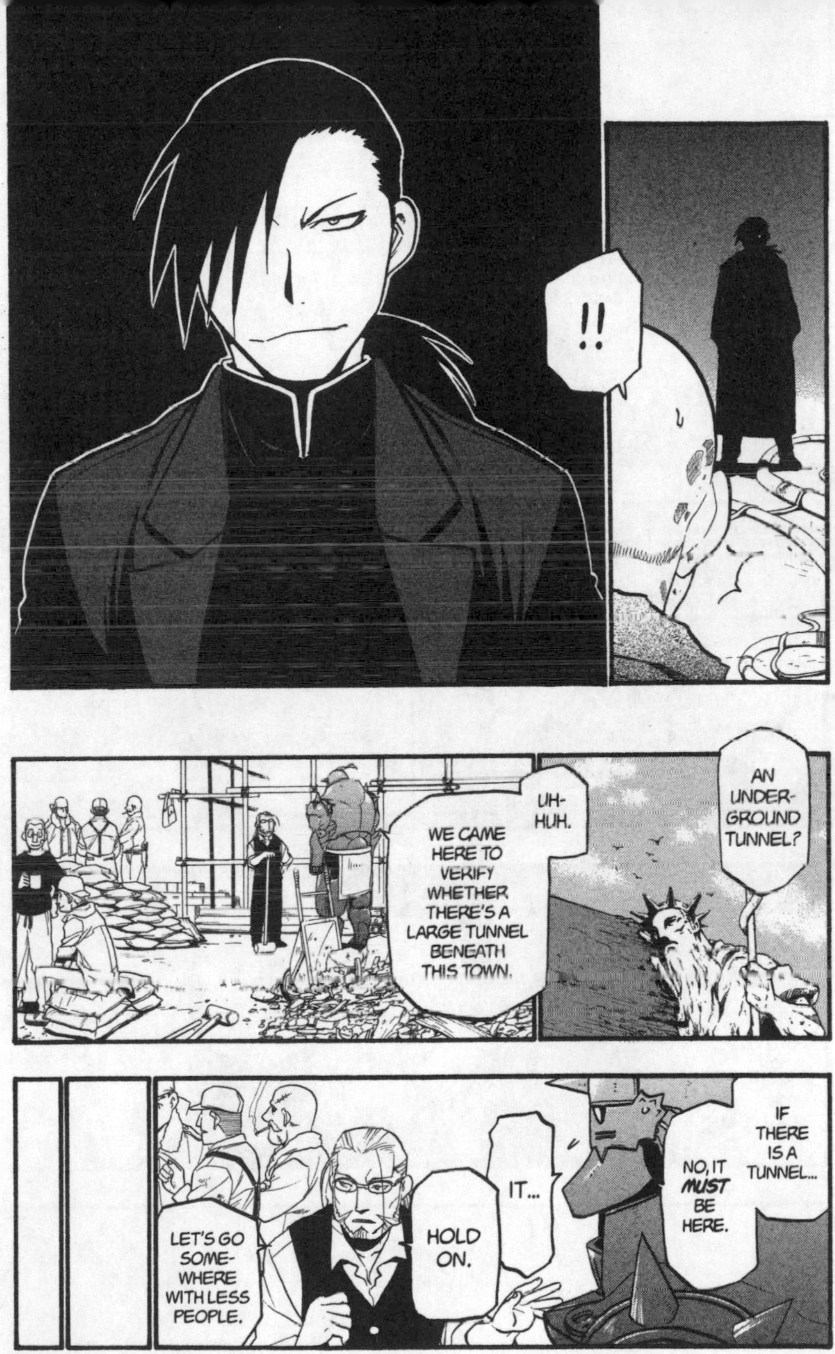
!!
AN UNDER-GROUND TUNNEL?
UH-HUH.
WE CAME HERE TO VERIFY WHETHER THERE'S A LARGE TUNNEL BENEATH THIS TOWN.
IF THERE IS A TUNNEL...
NO, IT *MUST* BE HERE.
IT...
HOLD ON.
LET'S GO SOMEWHERE WITH LESS PEOPLE.

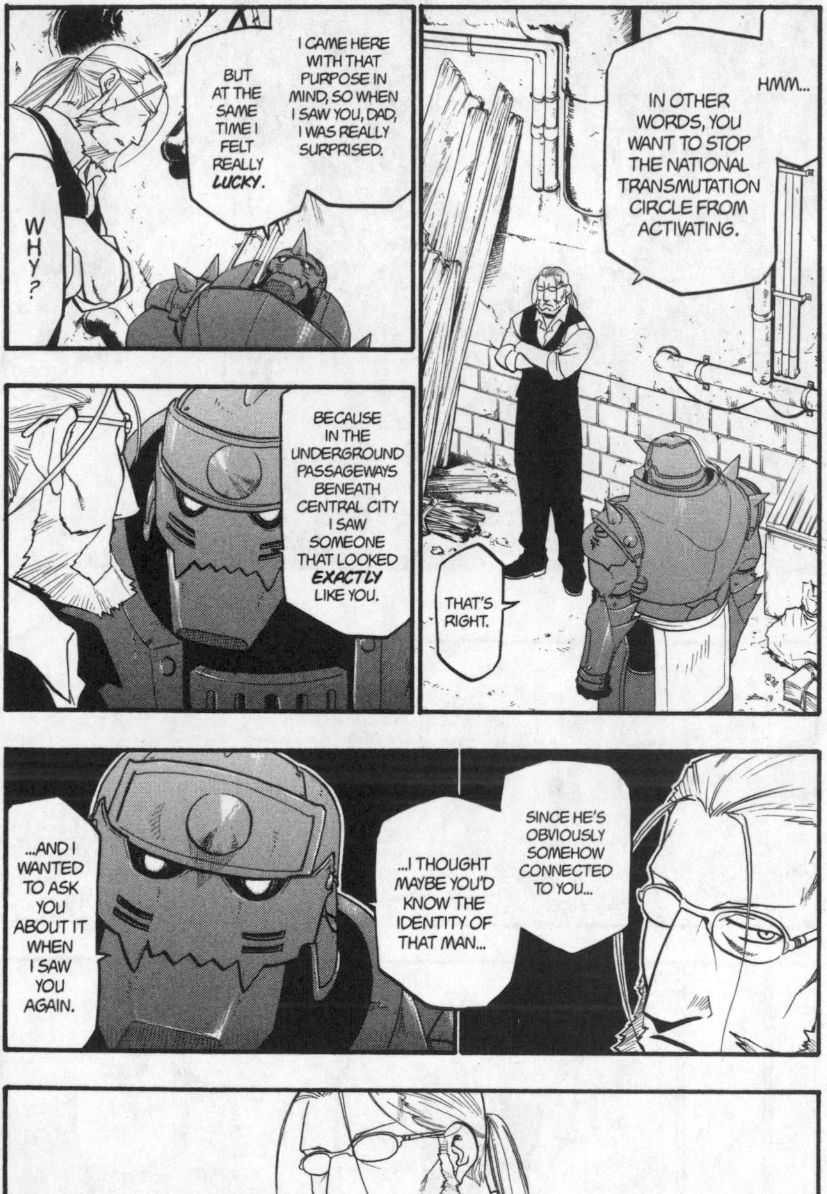
HMM...
IN OTHER WORDS, YOU WANT TO STOP THE NATIONAL TRANSMUTATION CIRCLE FROM ACTIVATING.
THAT'S RIGHT.
I CAME HERE WITH THAT PURPOSE IN MIND, SO WHEN I SAW YOU, DAD, I WAS REALLY SURPRISED.
BUT AT THE SAME TIME I FELT REALLY **LUCKY**.
WHY?
BECAUSE IN THE UNDERGROUND PASSAGEWAYS BENEATH CENTRAL CITY I SAW SOMEONE THAT LOOKED **EXACTLY** LIKE YOU.
SINCE HE'S OBVIOUSLY SOMEHOW CONNECTED TO YOU...
...I THOUGHT MAYBE YOU'D KNOW THE IDENTITY OF THAT MAN...
...AND I WANTED TO ASK YOU ABOUT IT WHEN I SAW YOU AGAIN.

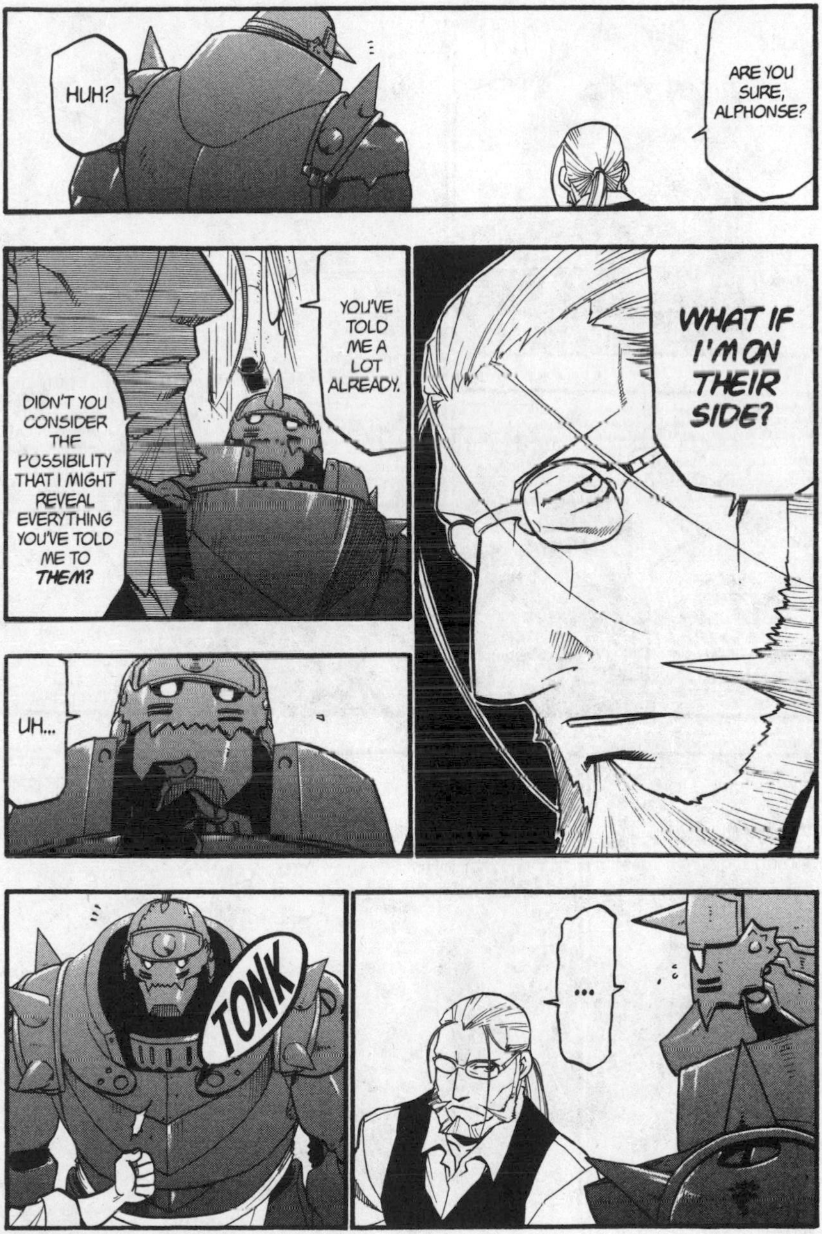
ARE YOU SURE, ALPHONSE?
HUH?
WHAT IF I'M ON THEIR SIDE?
YOU'VE TOLD ME A LOT ALREADY.
DIDN'T YOU CONSIDER THE POSSIBILITY THAT I MIGHT REVEAL EVERYTHING YOU'VE TOLD ME TO *THEM*?
UH...
...
TONK

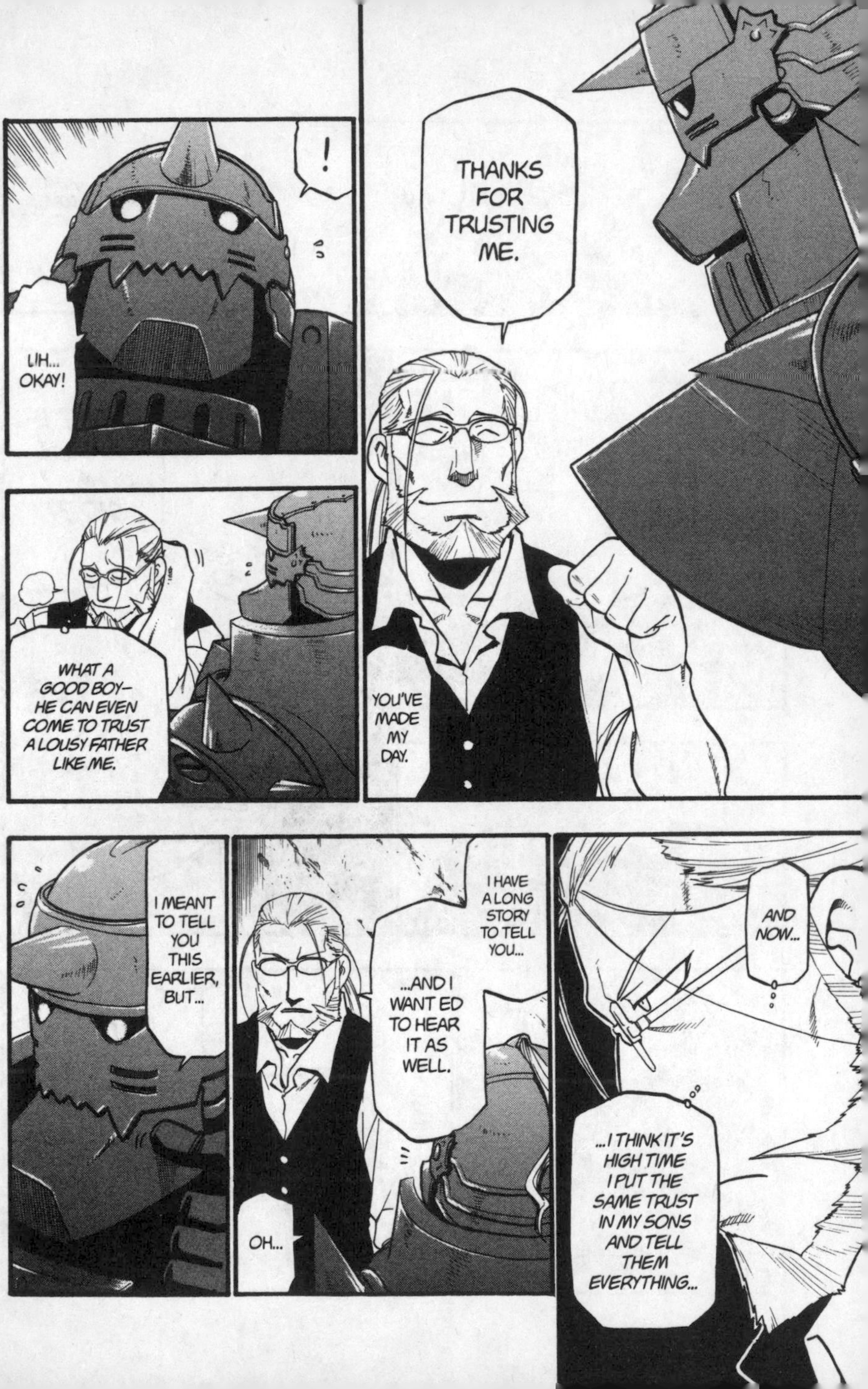
THANKS FOR TRUSTING ME.
YOU'VE MADE MY DAY.
!
UH... OKAY!
WHAT A GOOD BOY— HE CAN EVEN COME TO TRUST A LOUSY FATHER LIKE ME.
AND NOW...
...I THINK IT'S HIGH TIME I PUT THE SAME TRUST IN MY SONS AND TELL THEM EVERYTHING...
I HAVE A LONG STORY TO TELL YOU...
...AND I WANT ED TO HEAR IT AS WELL.
OH...
I MEANT TO TELL YOU THIS EARLIER, BUT...

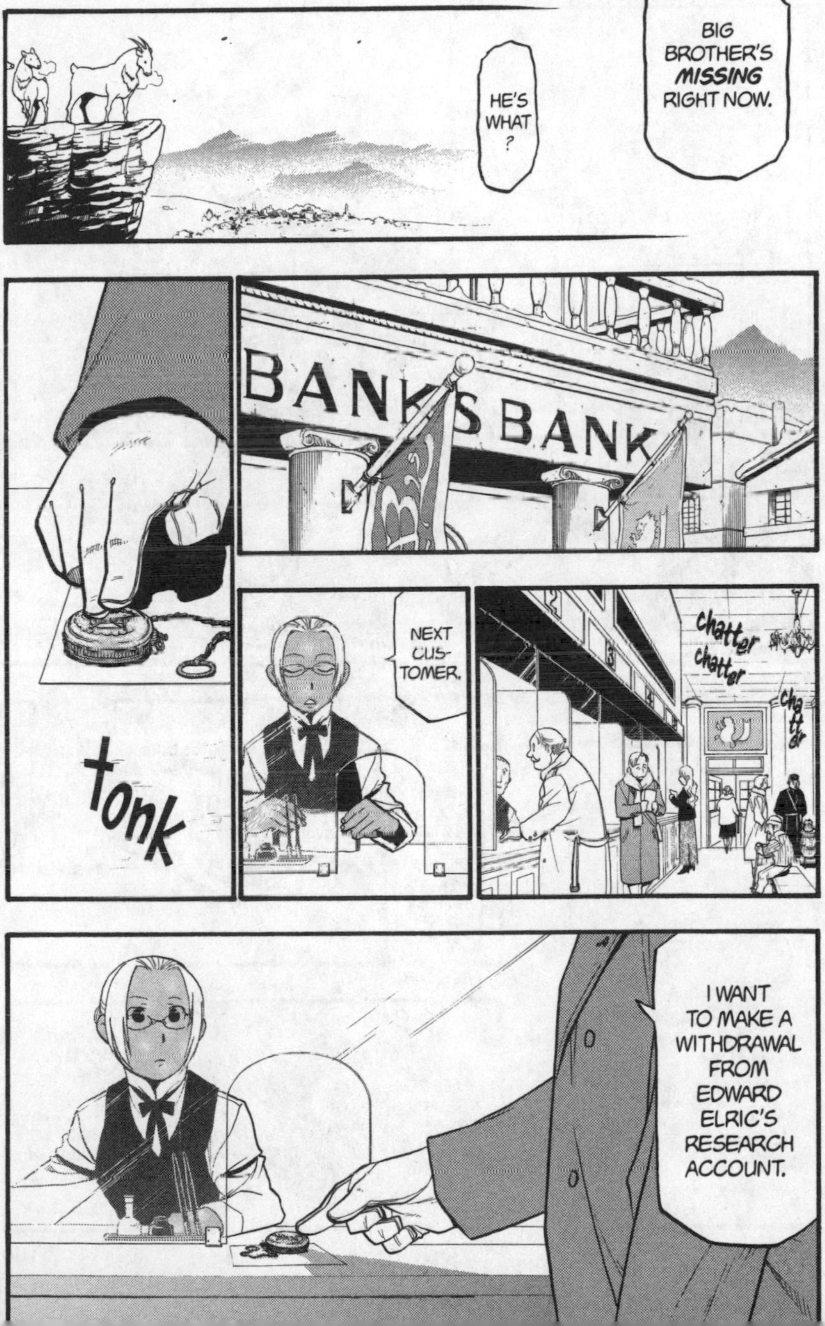
BIG BROTHER'S MISSING RIGHT NOW.
HE'S WHAT?
BANKS BANK
chatter chatter
chatter
NEXT CUS-TOMER.
tonk
I WANT TO MAKE A WITHDRAWAL FROM EDWARD ELRIC'S RESEARCH ACCOUNT.

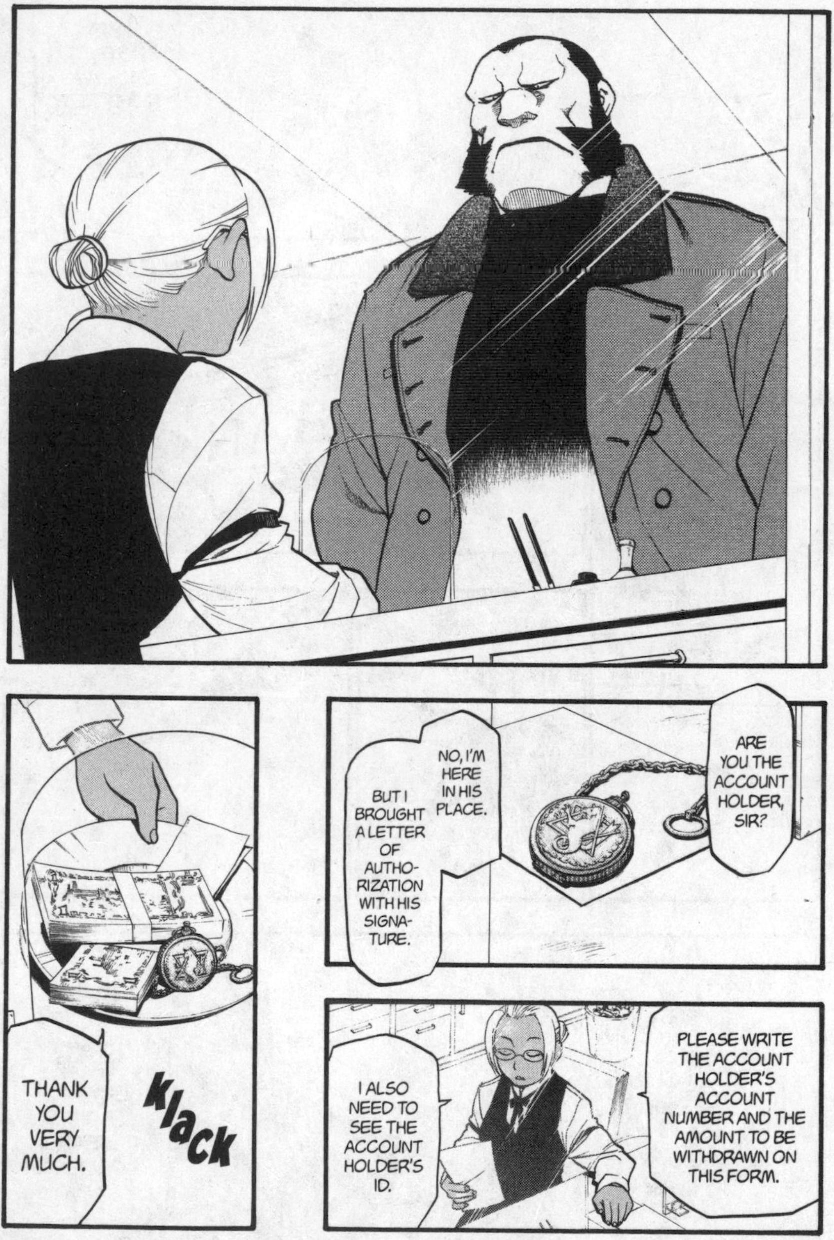
ARE YOU THE ACCOUNT HOLDER, SIR?
NO, I'M HERE IN HIS PLACE.
BUT I BROUGHT A LETTER OF AUTHO-RIZATION WITH HIS SIGNA-TURE.
PLEASE WRITE THE ACCOUNT HOLDER'S ACCOUNT NUMBER AND THE AMOUNT TO BE WITHDRAWN ON THIS FORM.
I ALSO NEED TO SEE THE ACCOUNT HOLDER'S ID.
klack
THANK YOU VERY MUCH.

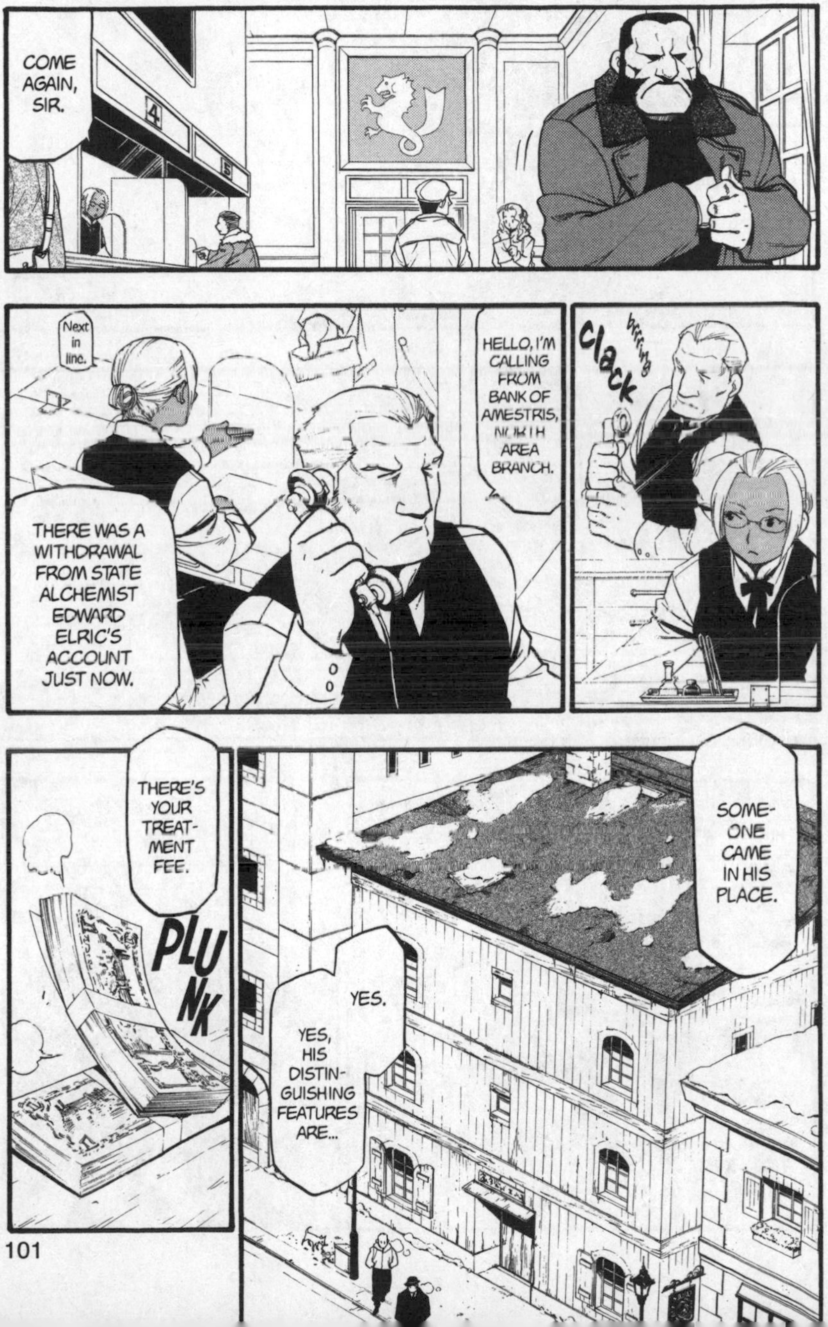
COME AGAIN, SIR.
brrring
CLACK
HELLO, I'M CALLING FROM BANK OF AMESTRIS, NORTH AREA BRANCH.
Next in line.
THERE WAS A WITHDRAWAL FROM STATE ALCHEMIST EDWARD ELRIC'S ACCOUNT JUST NOW.
SOME-ONE CAME IN HIS PLACE.
YES.
YES, HIS DISTIN-GUISHING FEATURES ARE...
THERE'S YOUR TREAT-MENT FEE.
PLUNK

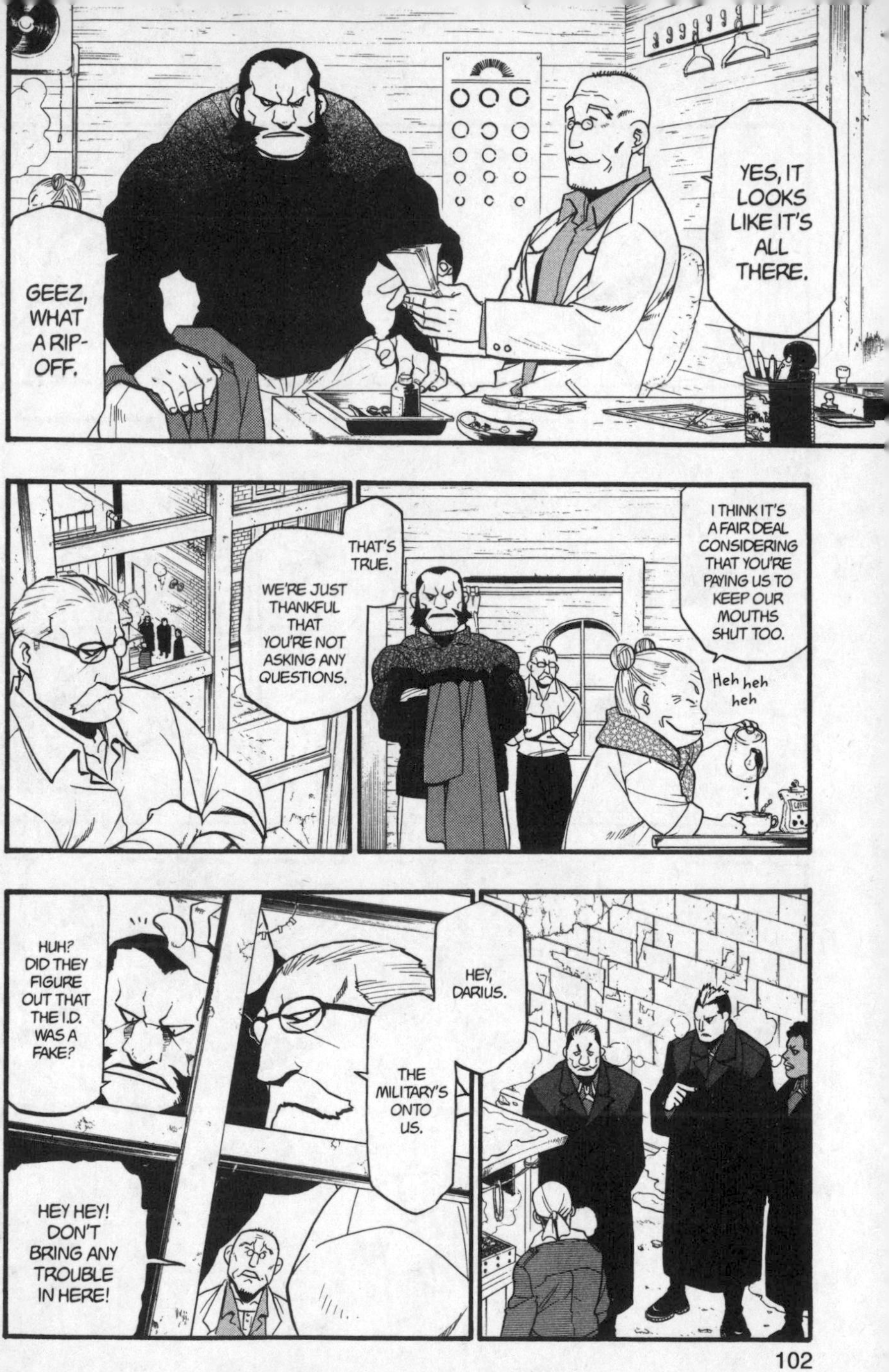
YES, IT LOOKS LIKE IT'S ALL THERE.
GEEZ, WHAT A RIP-OFF.
I THINK IT'S A FAIR DEAL CONSIDERING THAT YOU'RE PAYING US TO KEEP OUR MOUTHS SHUT TOO.
Heh heh heh
THAT'S TRUE.
WE'RE JUST THANKFUL THAT YOU'RE NOT ASKING ANY QUESTIONS.
HEY, DARIUS.
THE MILITARY'S ONTO US.
HUH? DID THEY FIGURE OUT THAT THE I.D. WAS A FAKE?
HEY HEY! DON'T BRING ANY TROUBLE IN HERE!

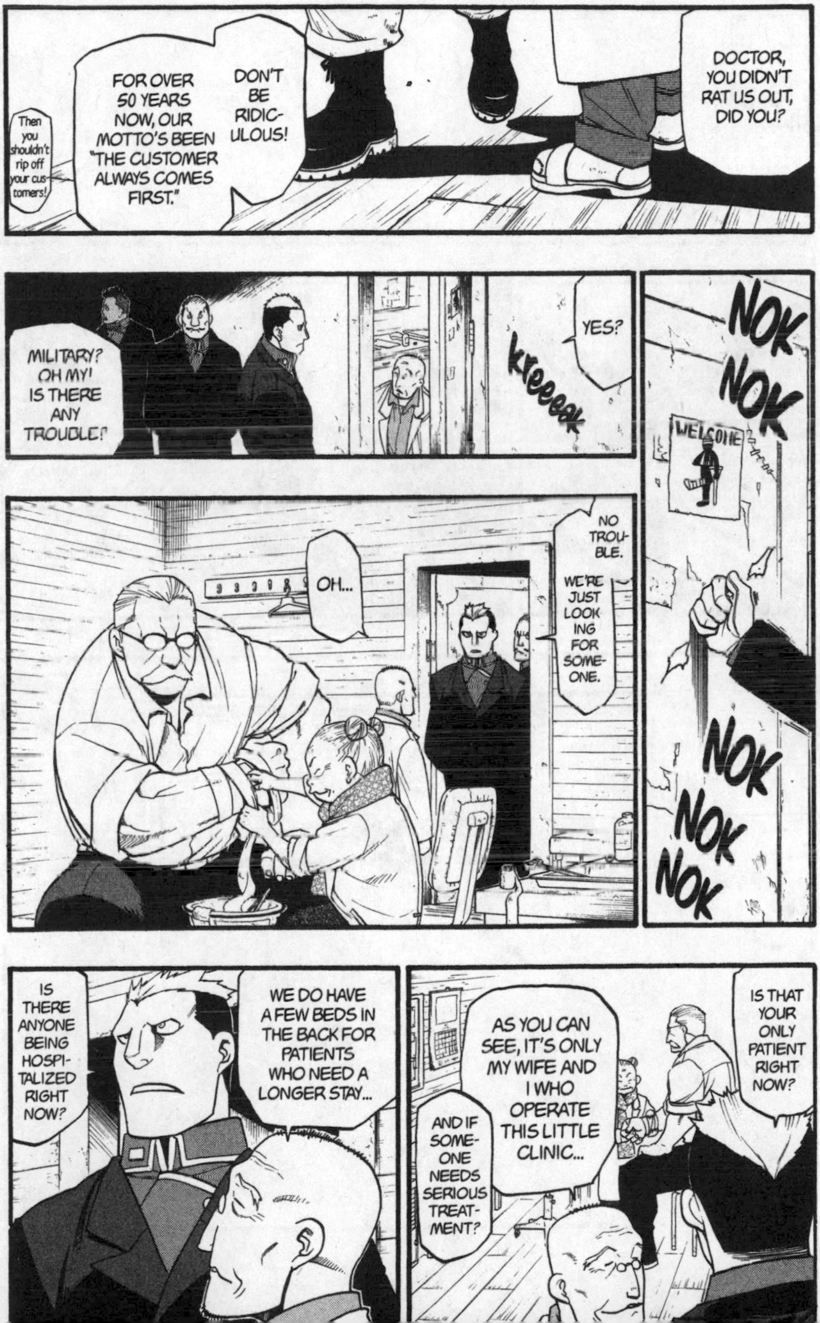
DOCTOR, YOU DIDN'T RAT US OUT, DID YOU?
DON'T BE RIDICULOUS!
FOR OVER 50 YEARS NOW, OUR MOTTO'S BEEN "THE CUSTOMER ALWAYS COMES FIRST."
Then you shouldn't rip off your customers!
NOK NOK
WELCOME
NOK NOK NOK
YES?
kreeeak
MILITARY? OH MY! IS THERE ANY TROUBLE?
NO TROUBLE.
WE'RE JUST LOOKING FOR SOMEONE.
OH...
IS THAT YOUR ONLY PATIENT RIGHT NOW?
AS YOU CAN SEE, IT'S ONLY MY WIFE AND I WHO OPERATE THIS LITTLE CLINIC...
AND IF SOMEONE NEEDS SERIOUS TREATMENT?
WE DO HAVE A FEW BEDS IN THE BACK FOR PATIENTS WHO NEED A LONGER STAY...
IS THERE ANYONE BEING HOSPITALIZED RIGHT NOW?

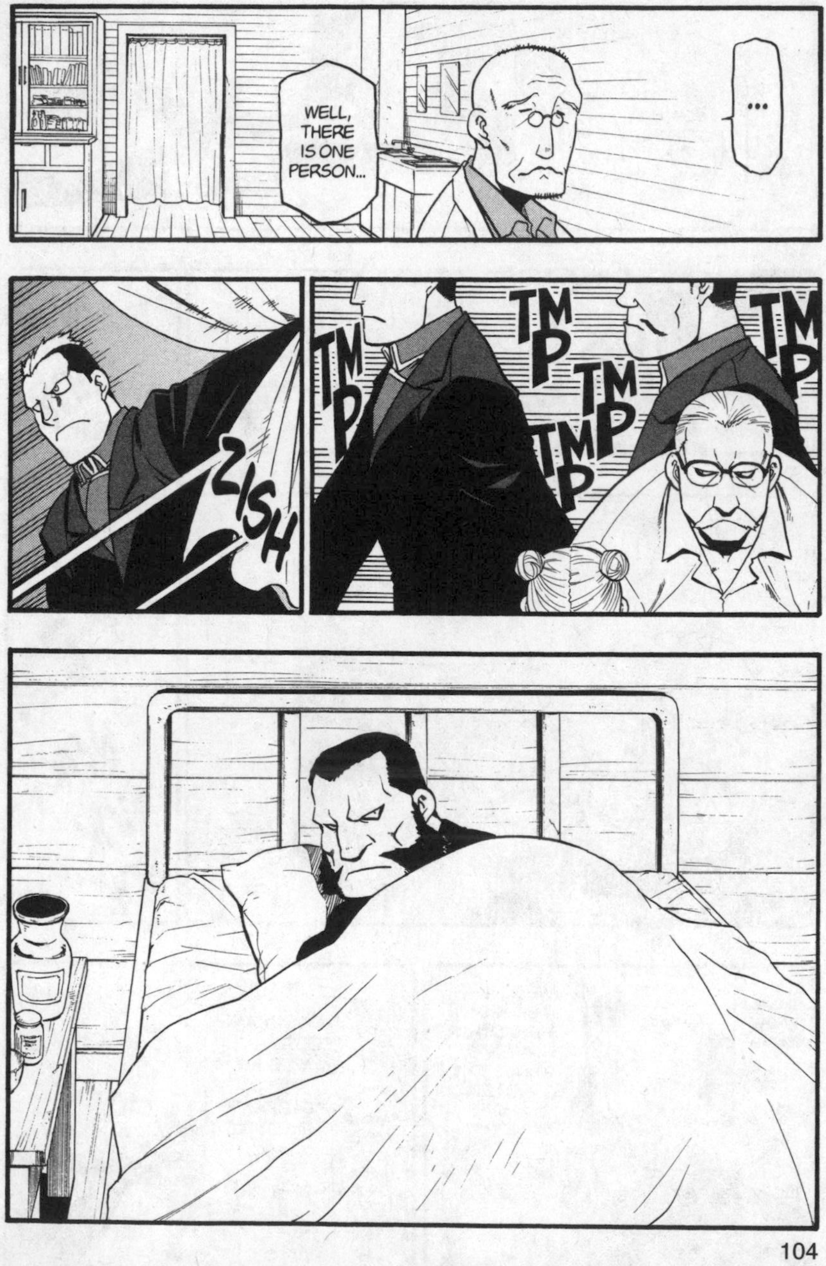
...
WELL, THERE IS ONE PERSON...
TMP
TMP
TMP
TMP
TMP
ZISH

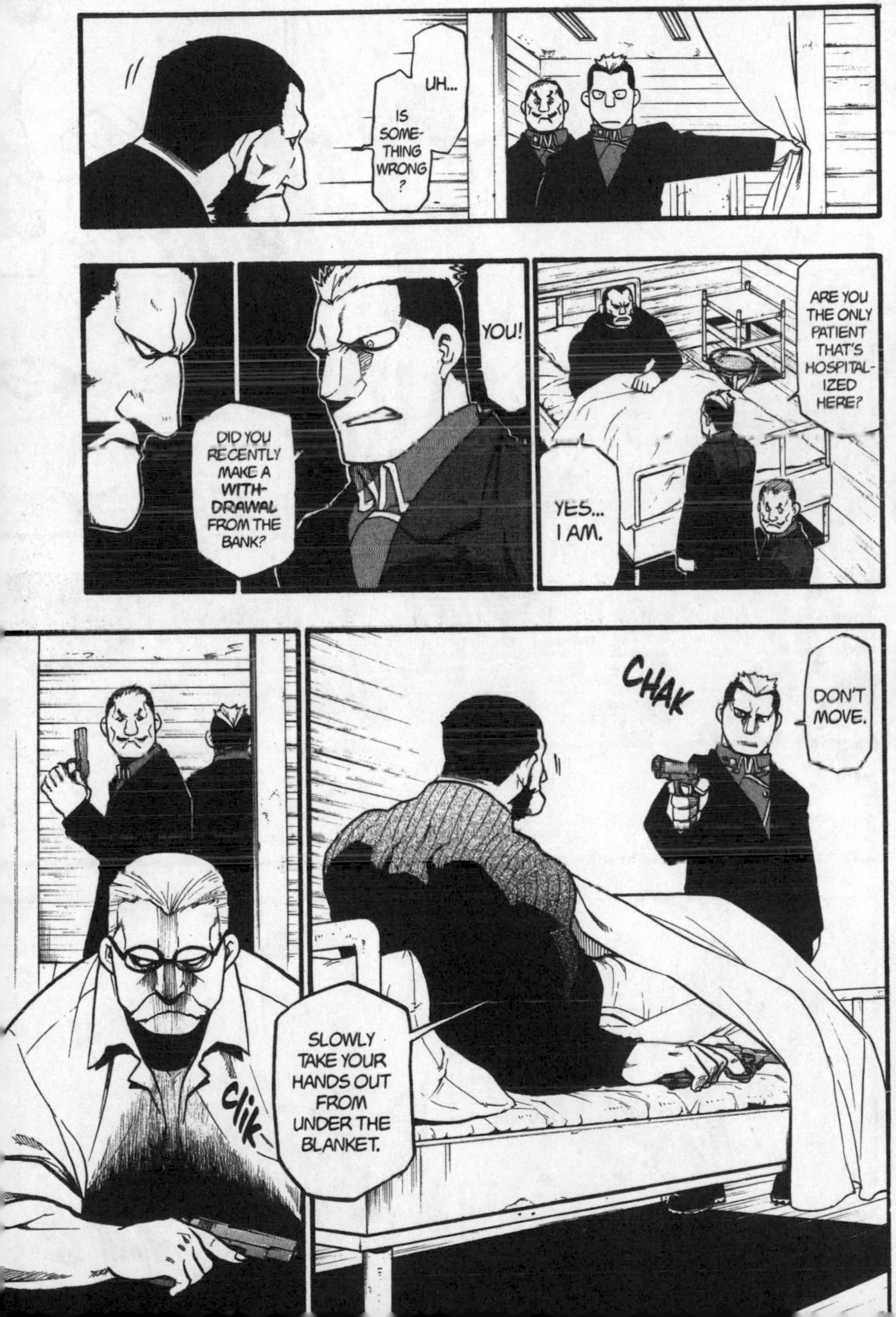
UH...
IS SOMETHING WRONG?
ARE YOU THE ONLY PATIENT THAT'S HOSPITALIZED HERE?
YES... I AM.
YOU!
DID YOU RECENTLY MAKE A WITHDRAWAL FROM THE BANK?
CHAK
DON'T MOVE.
SLOWLY TAKE YOUR HANDS OUT FROM UNDER THE BLANKET.
Clik

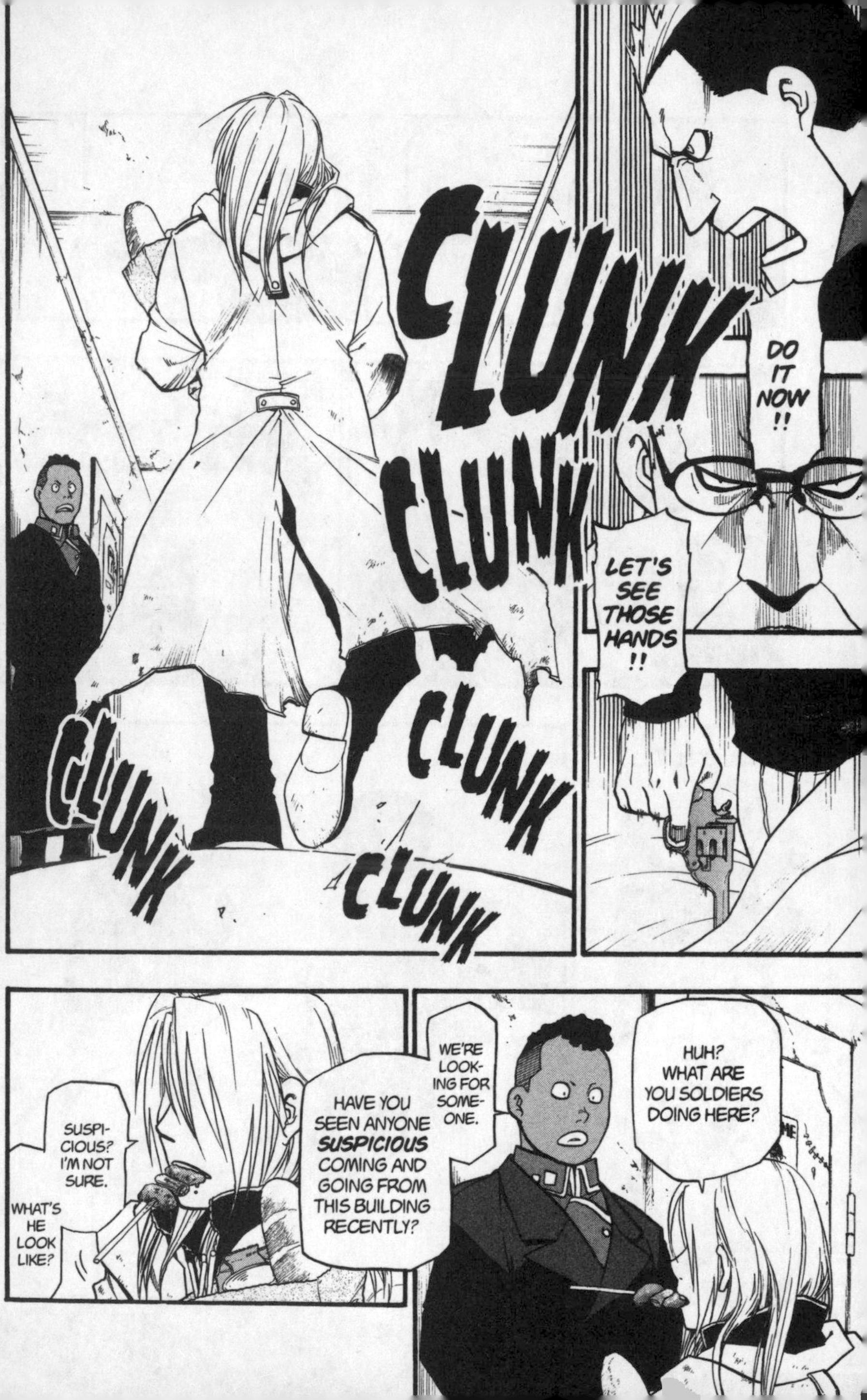
DO IT NOW!!
LET'S SEE THOSE HANDS!!
CLUNK
CLUNK
CLUNK
CLUNK
CLUNK
HUH? WHAT ARE YOU SOLDIERS DOING HERE?
WE'RE LOOKING FOR SOMEONE.
HAVE YOU SEEN ANYONE **SUSPICIOUS** COMING AND GOING FROM THIS BUILDING RECENTLY?
SUSPICIOUS? I'M NOT SURE.
WHAT'S HE LOOK LIKE?

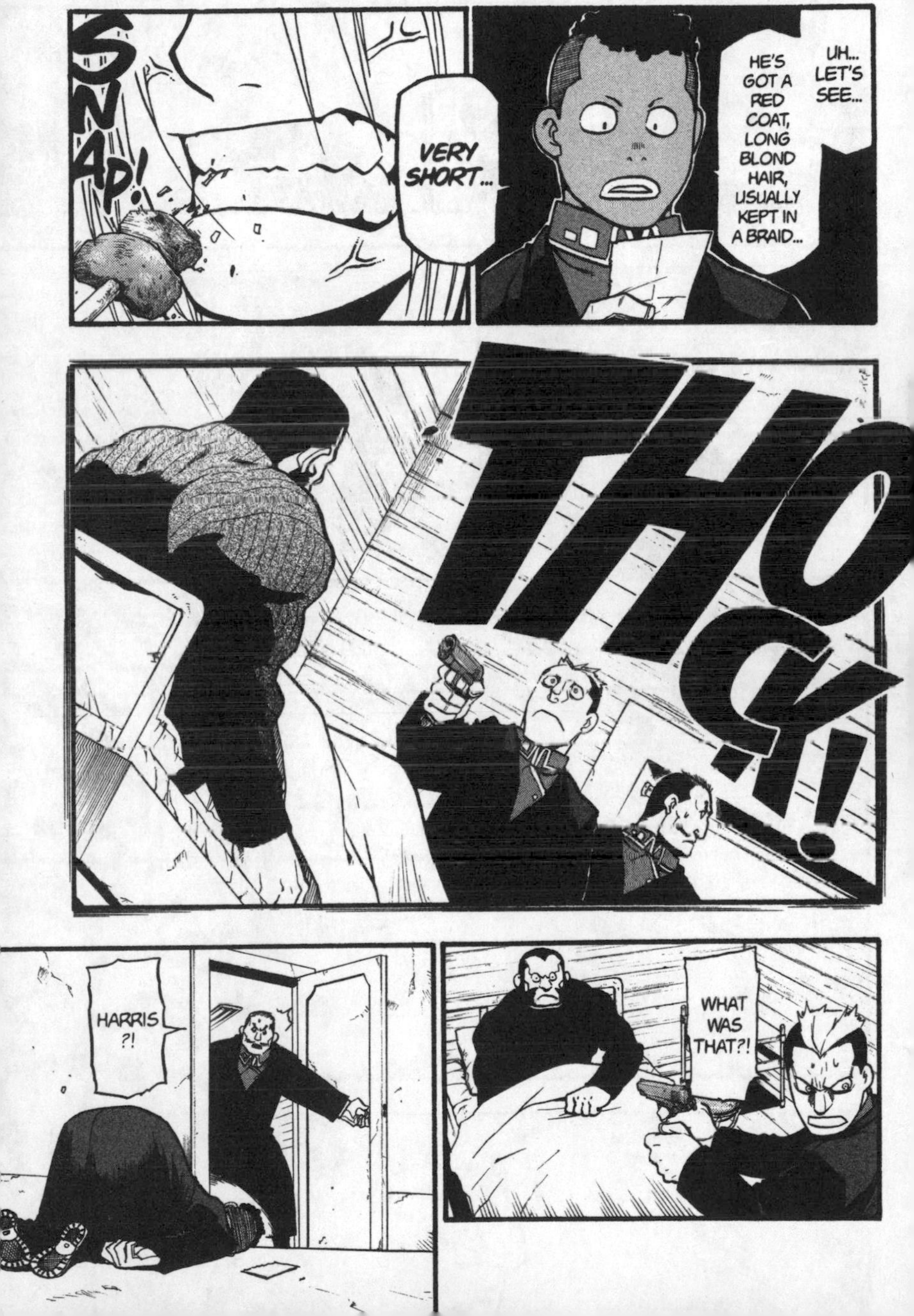
UH... LET'S SEE...
HE'S GOT A RED COAT, LONG BLOND HAIR, USUALLY KEPT IN A BRAID...
VERY SHORT...
SNAP!
THOCK!!
WHAT WAS THAT?!
HARRIS ?!

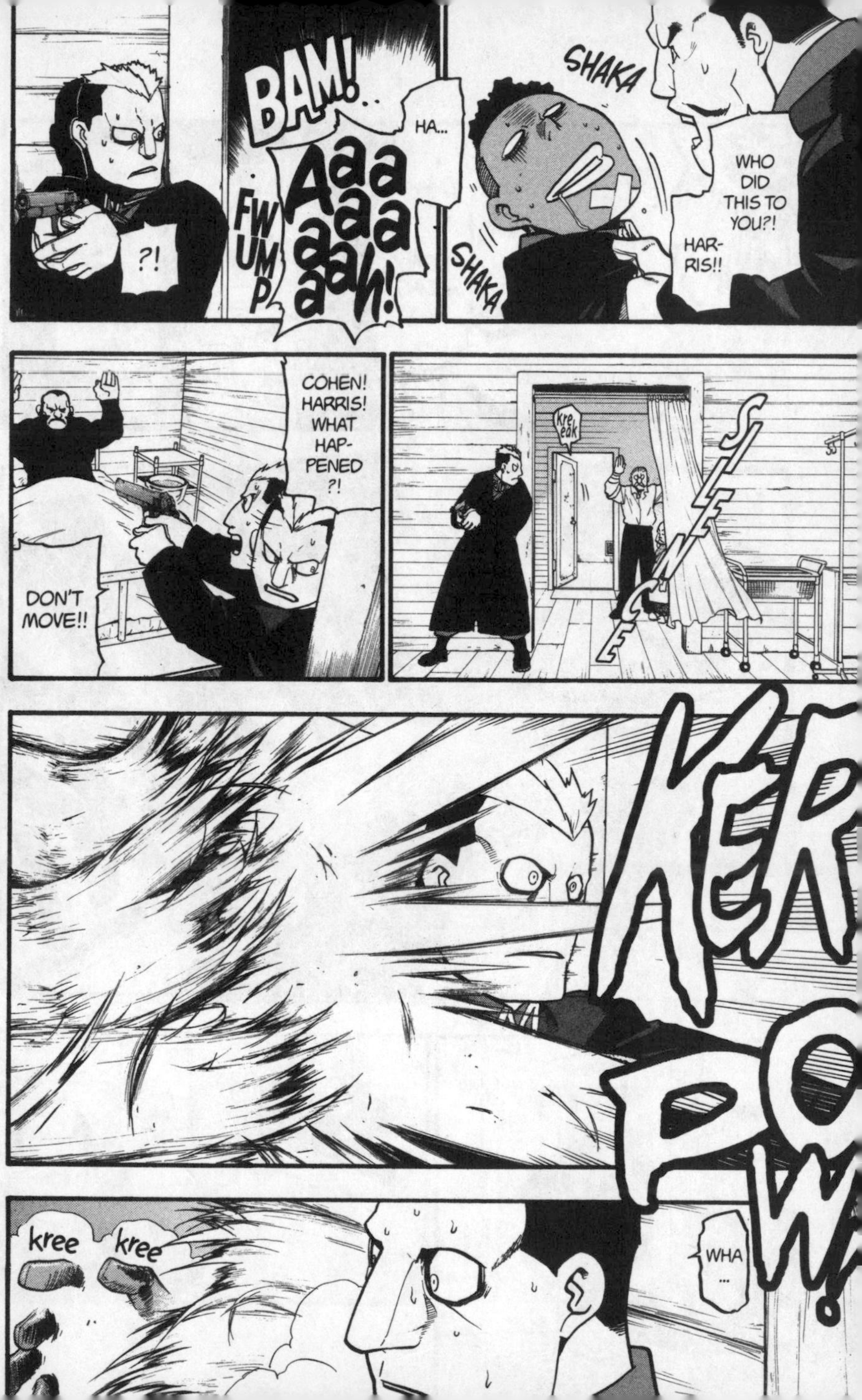
SHAKA
WHO DID THIS TO YOU?!
HARRIS!!
SHAKA
BAM!
HA...
Aaaaaaaaah!
FWUMP
?!
kreeak
SILENCE
COHEN! HARRIS! WHAT HAPPENED?!
DON'T MOVE!!
KERPOW!
WHA...
kree
kree

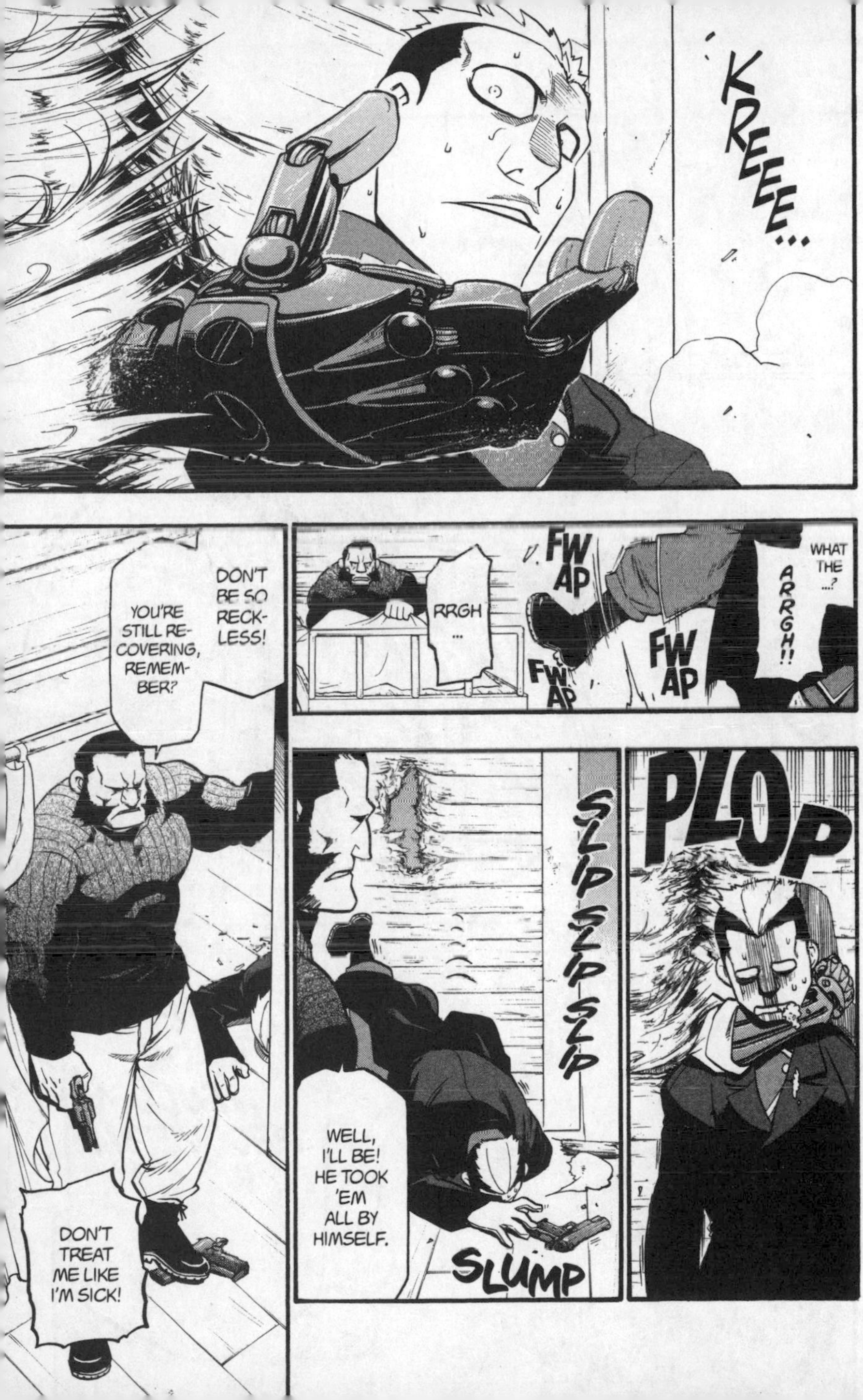
KREEE...
WHAT THE ...?
ARRGH!!
FWAP
FWAP
FWAP
RRGH ...
PLOP
SLIP SLIP SLIP
WELL, I'LL BE! HE TOOK 'EM ALL BY HIMSELF.
SLUMP
DON'T BE SO RECKLESS!
YOU'RE STILL RE-COVERING, REMEM-BER?
DON'T TREAT ME LIKE I'M SICK!

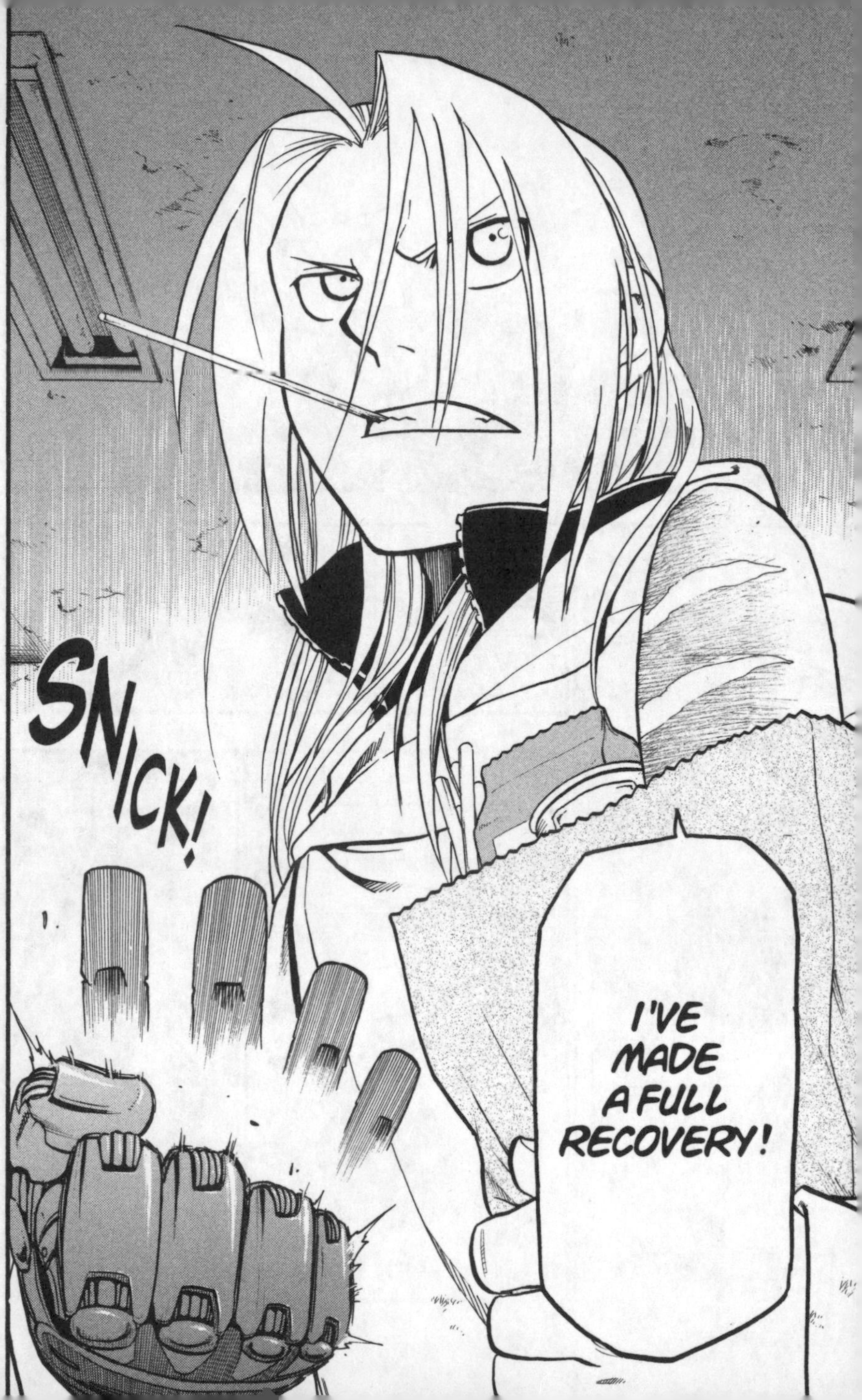

I'VE MADE A FULL RECOVERY!
SNICK!

Chapter 82
Family by Spirit

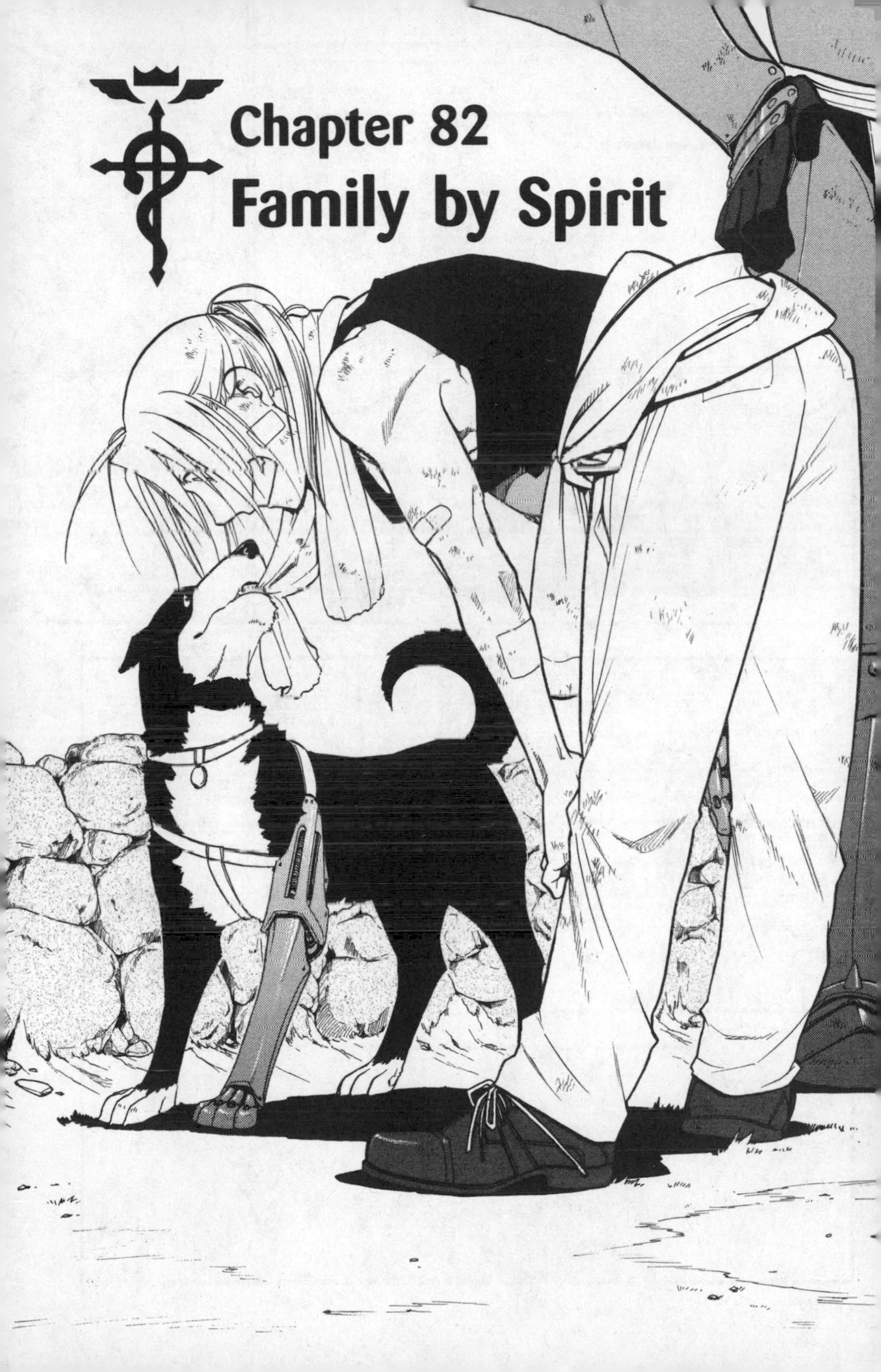

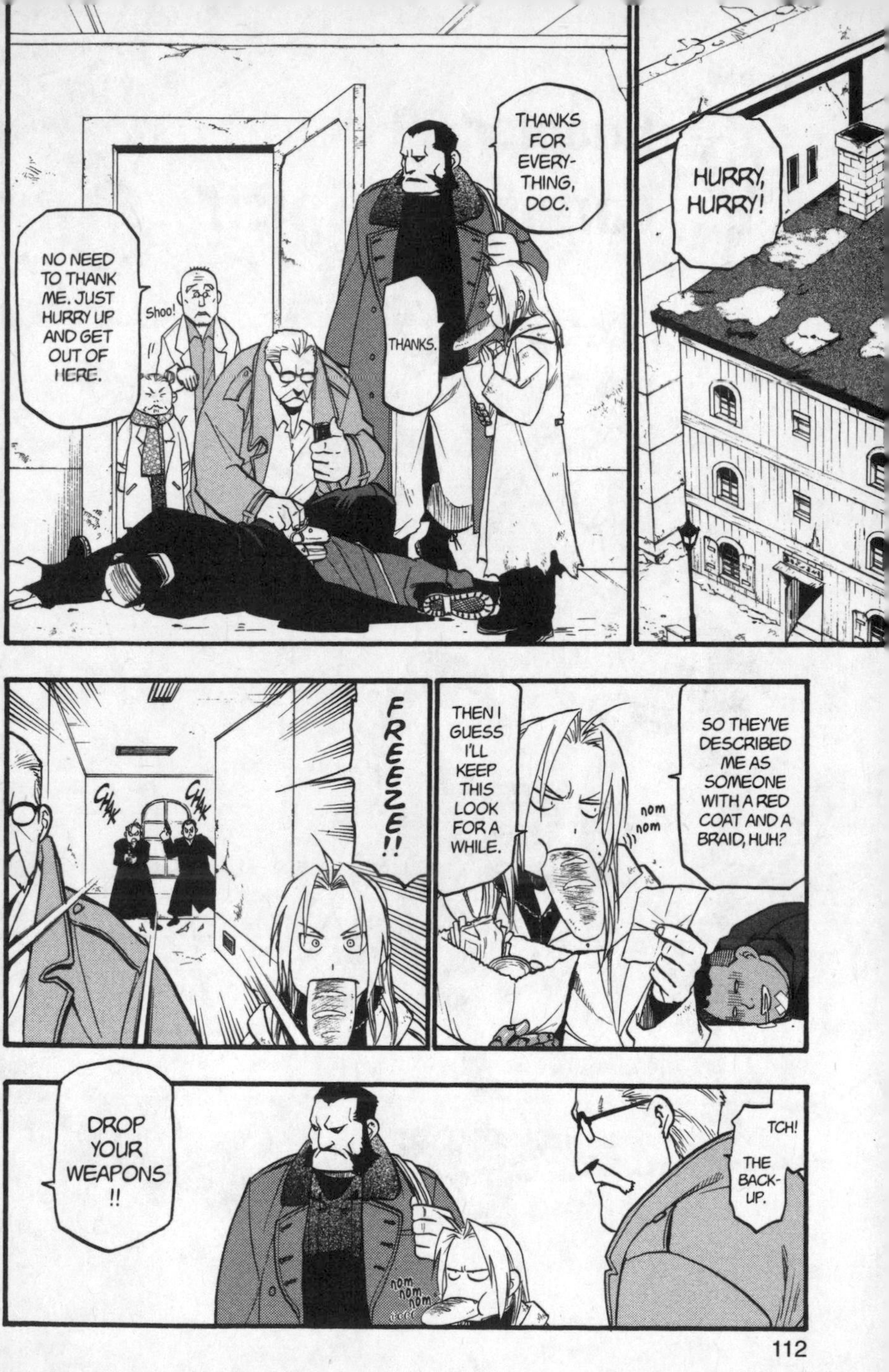
HURRY, HURRY!
THANKS FOR EVERY-THING, DOC.
NO NEED TO THANK ME. JUST HURRY UP AND GET OUT OF HERE.
Shoo!
THANKS.
SO THEY'VE DESCRIBED ME AS SOMEONE WITH A RED COAT AND A BRAID, HUH?
nom nom
THEN I GUESS I'LL KEEP THIS LOOK FOR A WHILE.
FREEZE!!
CHAK
CHAK
TCH!
THE BACK-UP.
DROP YOUR WEAPONS!!
nom nom nom

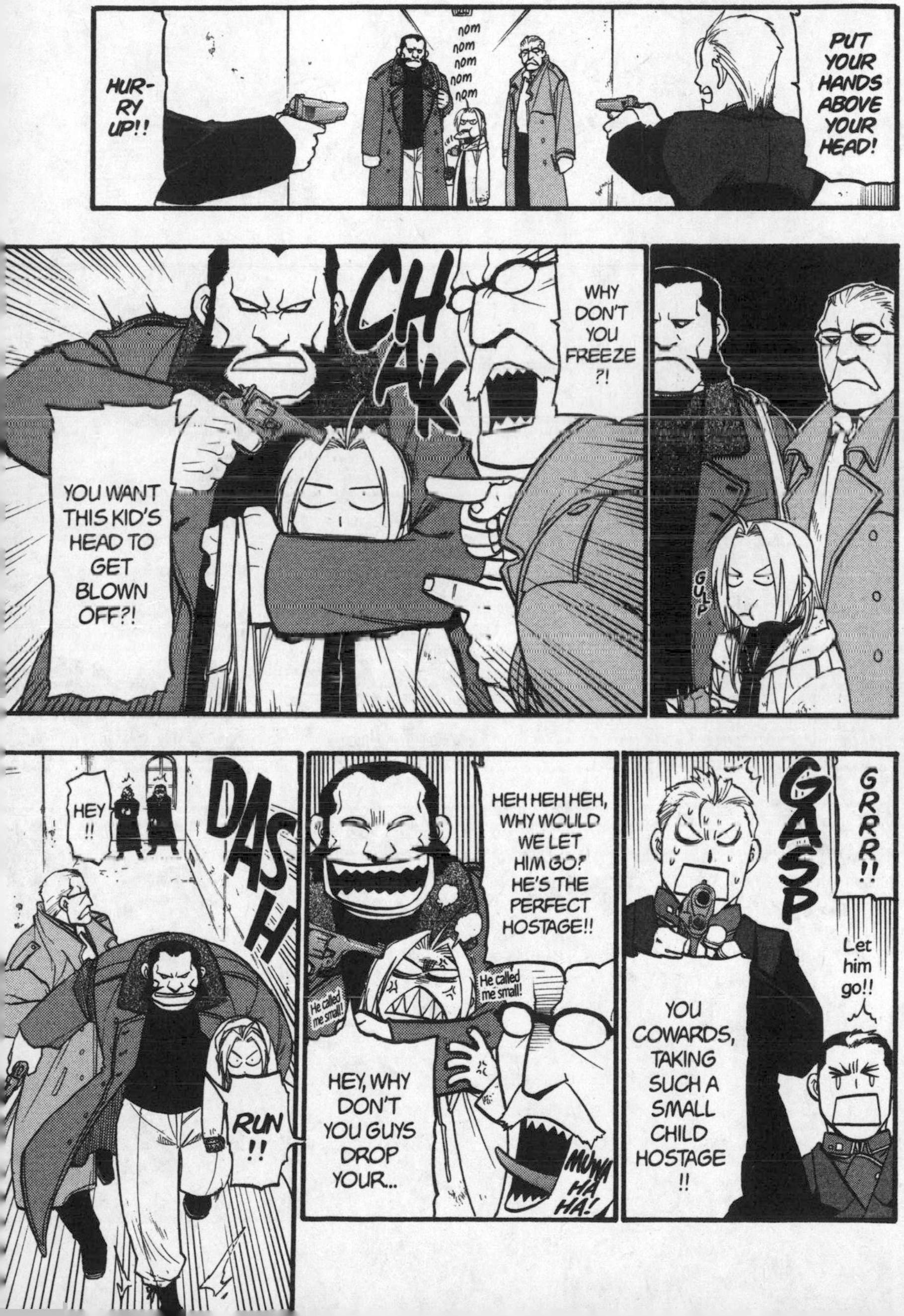
PUT YOUR HANDS ABOVE YOUR HEAD!
nom nom nom nom nom
HURRY UP!!
GULP
WHY DON'T YOU FREEZE?!
CHAK
YOU WANT THIS KID'S HEAD TO GET BLOWN OFF?!
GRRR!!
GASP
Let him go!!
YOU COWARDS, TAKING SUCH A SMALL CHILD HOSTAGE!!
HEH HEH HEH, WHY WOULD WE LET HIM GO? HE'S THE PERFECT HOSTAGE!!
He called me small!
He called me small!
HEY, WHY DON'T YOU GUYS DROP YOUR...
MUWAHAHA!
DASH
HEY!!
RUN!!

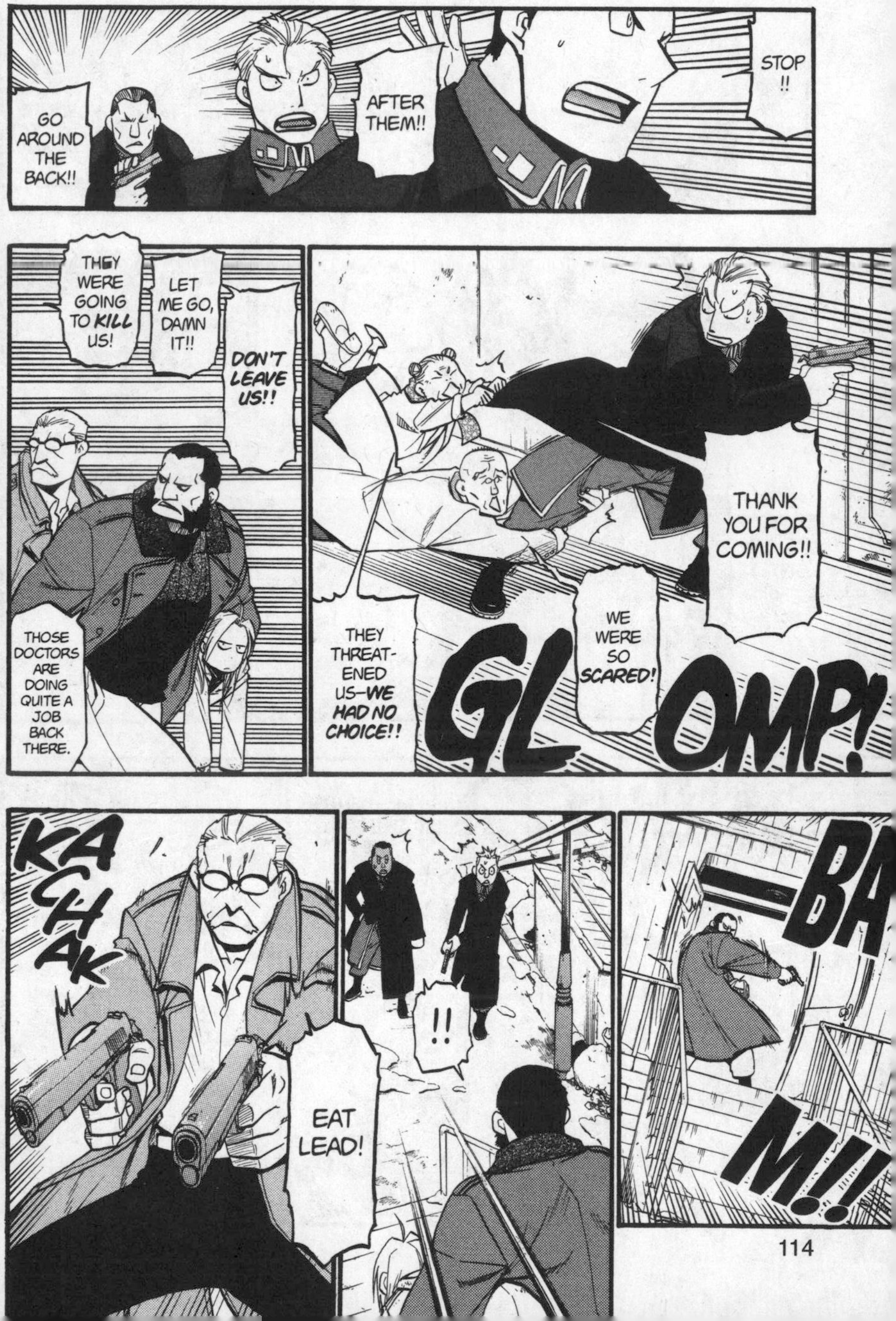
STOP !!
AFTER THEM!!
GO AROUND THE BACK!!
THANK YOU FOR COMING!!
WE WERE SO SCARED!
THEY THREAT-ENED US—WE HAD NO CHOICE!!
GLOMP!
DON'T LEAVE US!!
LET ME GO, DAMN IT!!
THEY WERE GOING TO KILL US!
THOSE DOCTORS ARE DOING QUITE A JOB BACK THERE.
BAM!!
!!
KACHAK
EAT LEAD!

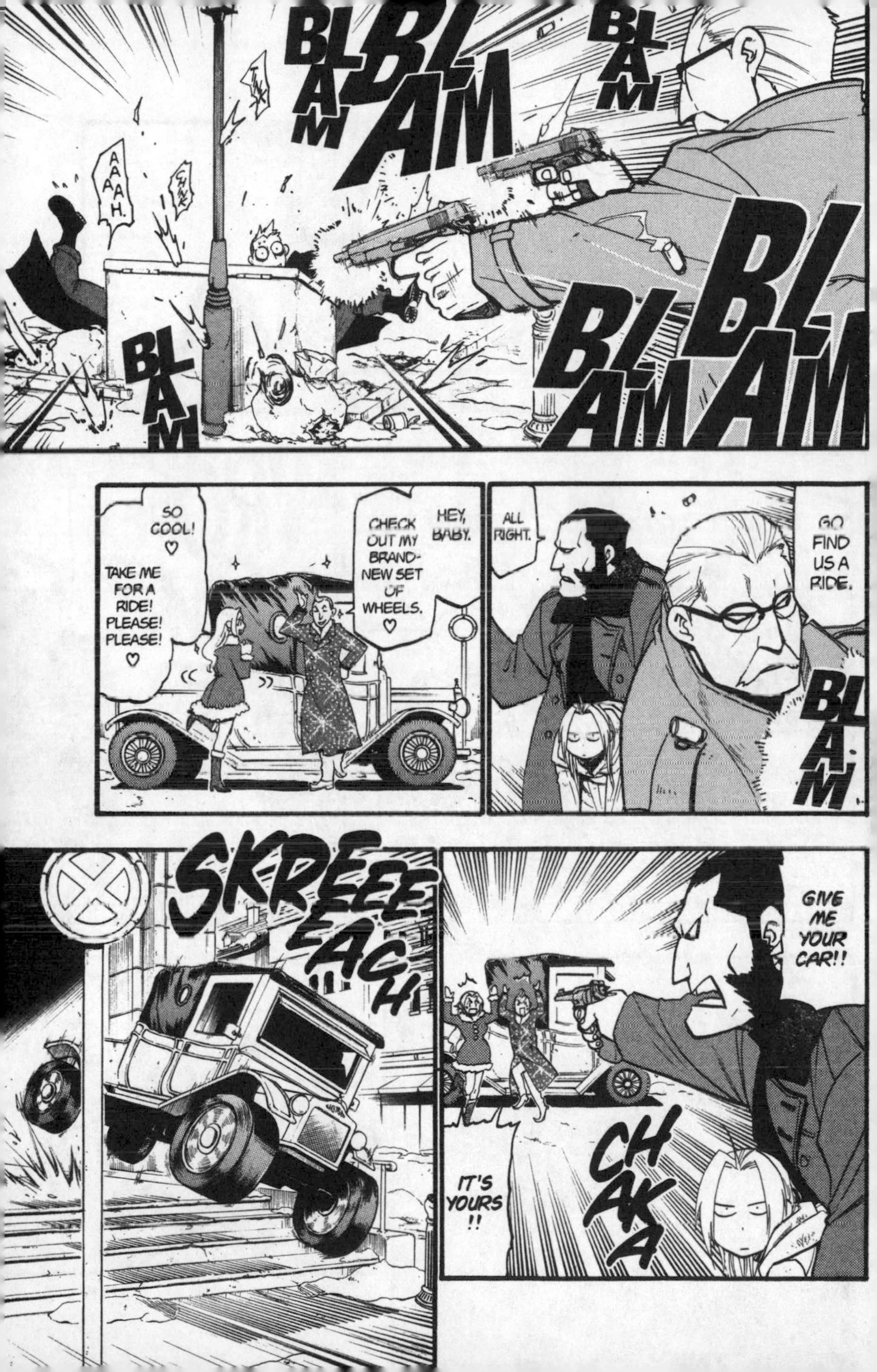
BLAM
BLAM
BLAM
BLAM
BLAM
TINK
CHINK
AAAAH.
BLAM
GO FIND US A RIDE.
ALL RIGHT.
BLAM
HEY, BABY.
CHECK OUT MY BRAND-NEW SET OF WHEELS. ♡
SO COOL! ♡
TAKE ME FOR A RIDE! PLEASE! PLEASE! ♡
GIVE ME YOUR CAR!!
CHAKA
IT'S YOURS!!
SKREEEEACH

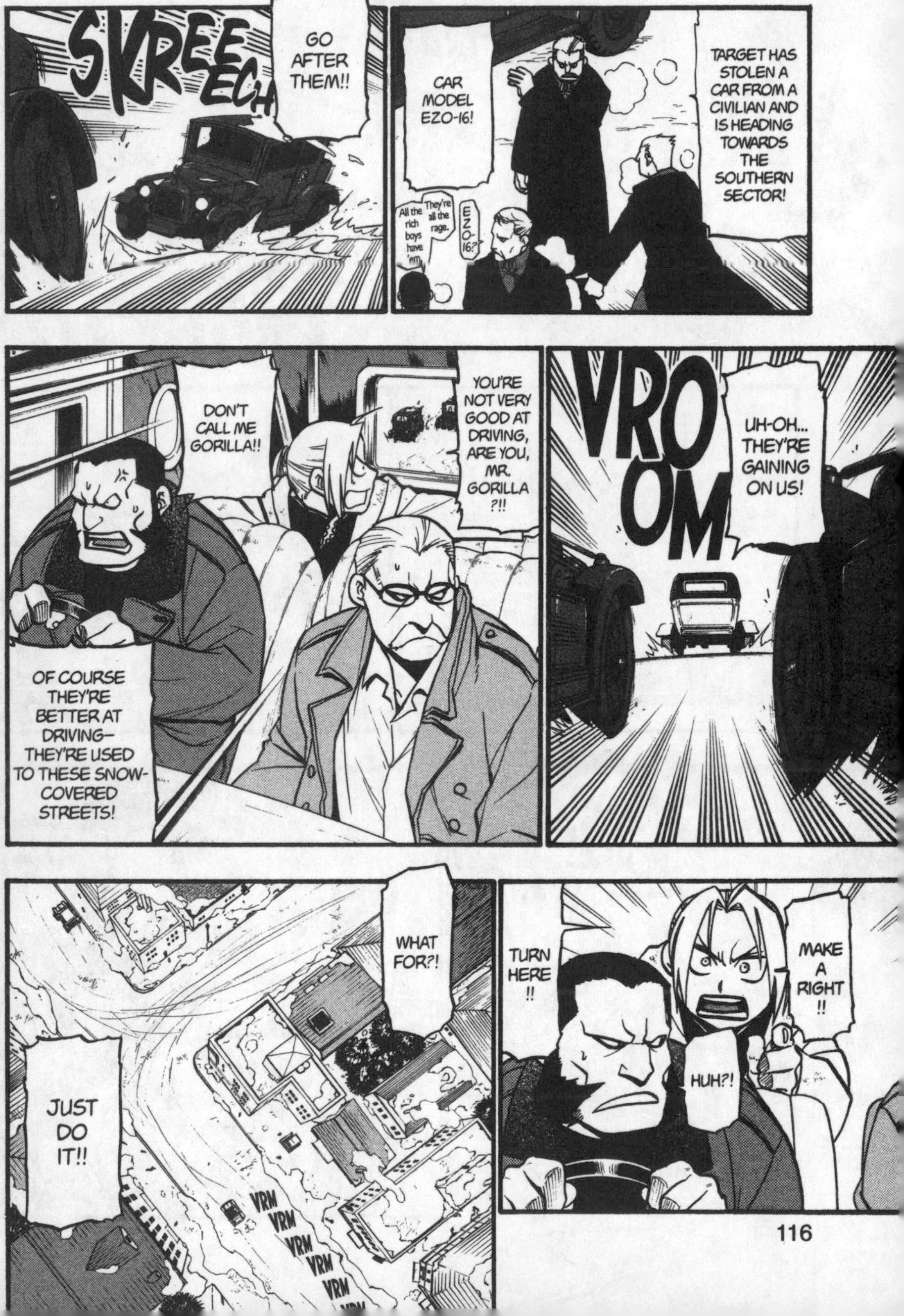
TARGET HAS STOLEN A CAR FROM A CIVILIAN AND IS HEADING TOWARDS THE SOUTHERN SECTOR!
CAR MODEL EZO-16!
EZO-16?
They're all the rage.
All the rich boys have 'em.
SKREEECH
GO AFTER THEM!!
VROOM
UH-OH... THEY'RE GAINING ON US!
YOU'RE NOT VERY GOOD AT DRIVING, ARE YOU, MR. GORILLA?!!
DON'T CALL ME GORILLA!!
OF COURSE THEY'RE BETTER AT DRIVING— THEY'RE USED TO THESE SNOW-COVERED STREETS!
MAKE A RIGHT!!
TURN HERE!!
HUH?!
WHAT FOR?!
JUST DO IT!!
VRM
VRM
VRM
VRM
VRM
VRM

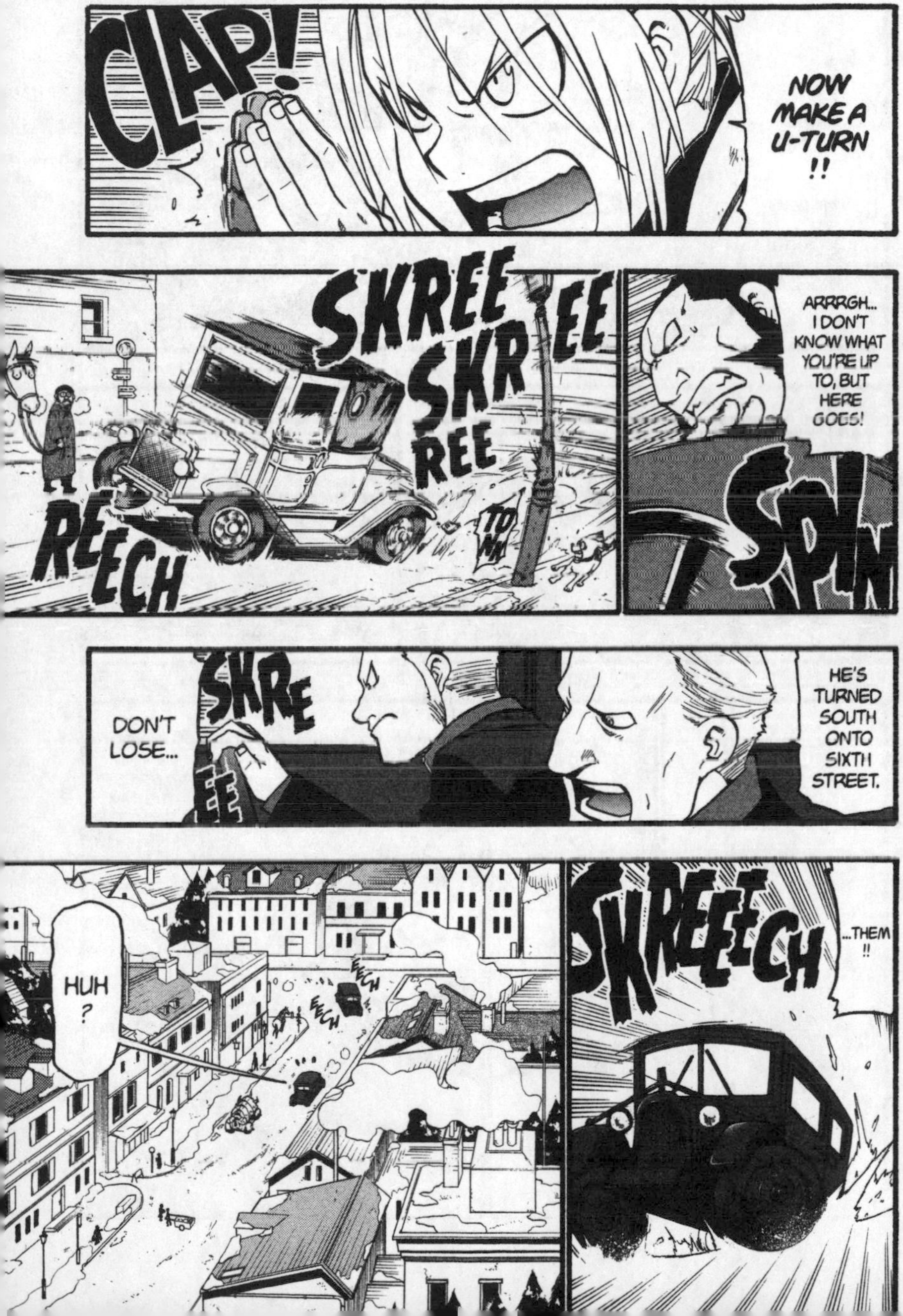
CLAP!
NOW MAKE A U-TURN !!
ARRRGH... I DON'T KNOW WHAT YOU'RE UP TO, BUT HERE GOES!
SPIN
SKREE
SKR
REE
REECH
TONK
HE'S TURNED SOUTH ONTO SIXTH STREET.
SKREE
DON'T LOSE...
SKREEECH
...THEM !!
HUH ?
EECH
EECH

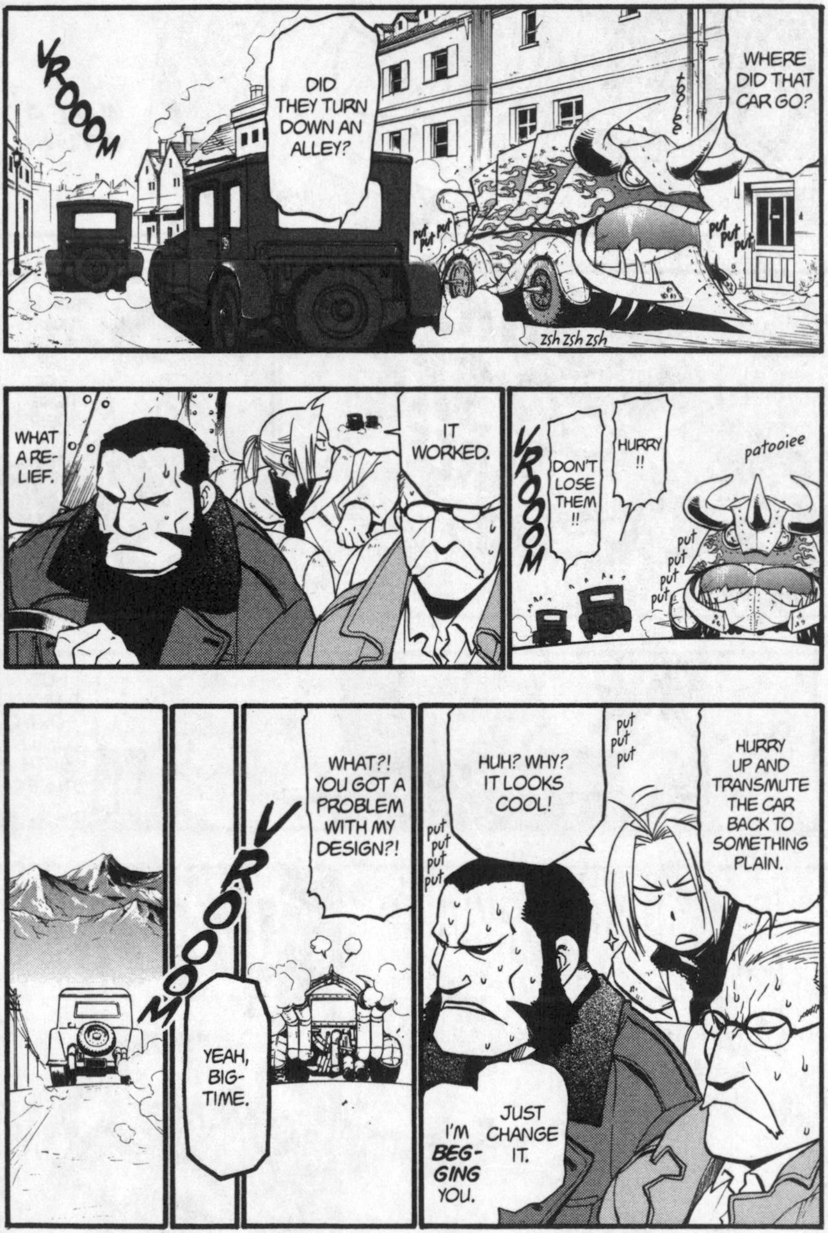
WHERE DID THAT CAR GO?
DID THEY TURN DOWN AN ALLEY?
VROOOOM
put put put
put put put
zsh zsh zsh
patooiee
HURRY !!
DON'T LOSE THEM !!
VROOOOM
put put put put
IT WORKED.
WHAT A RE-LIEF.
HURRY UP AND TRANSMUTE THE CAR BACK TO SOMETHING PLAIN.
put put put
HUH? WHY? IT LOOKS COOL!
put put put put
JUST CHANGE IT.
I'M ***BEG-GING*** YOU.
WHAT?! YOU GOT A PROBLEM WITH MY DESIGN?!
VROOOOM
YEAH, BIG-TIME.

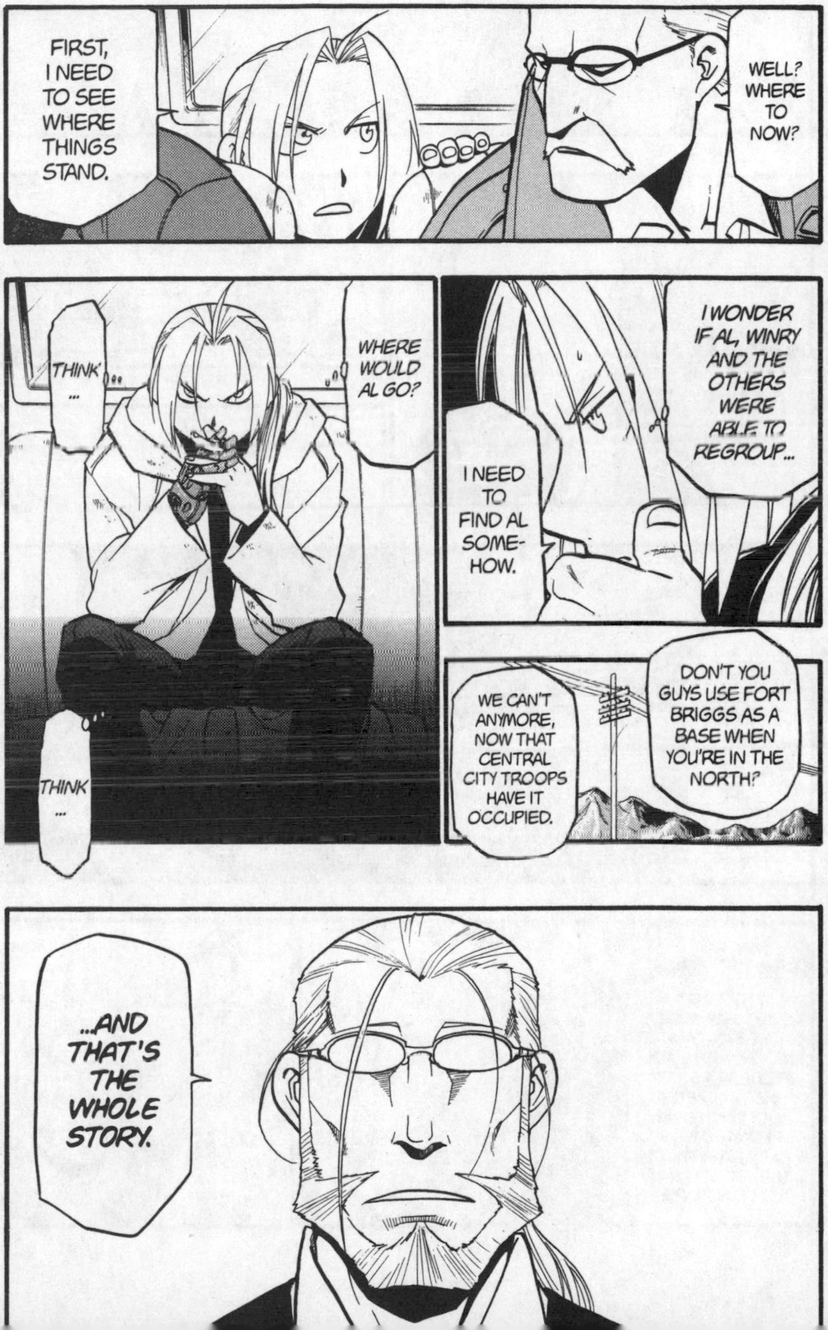
WELL? WHERE TO NOW?
FIRST, I NEED TO SEE WHERE THINGS STAND.
I WONDER IF AL, WINRY AND THE OTHERS WERE ABLE TO REGROUP...
I NEED TO FIND AL SOME-HOW.
DON'T YOU GUYS USE FORT BRIGGS AS A BASE WHEN YOU'RE IN THE NORTH?
WE CAN'T ANYMORE, NOW THAT CENTRAL CITY TROOPS HAVE IT OCCUPIED.
WHERE WOULD AL GO?
THINK...
THINK...
...AND THAT'S THE WHOLE STORY.

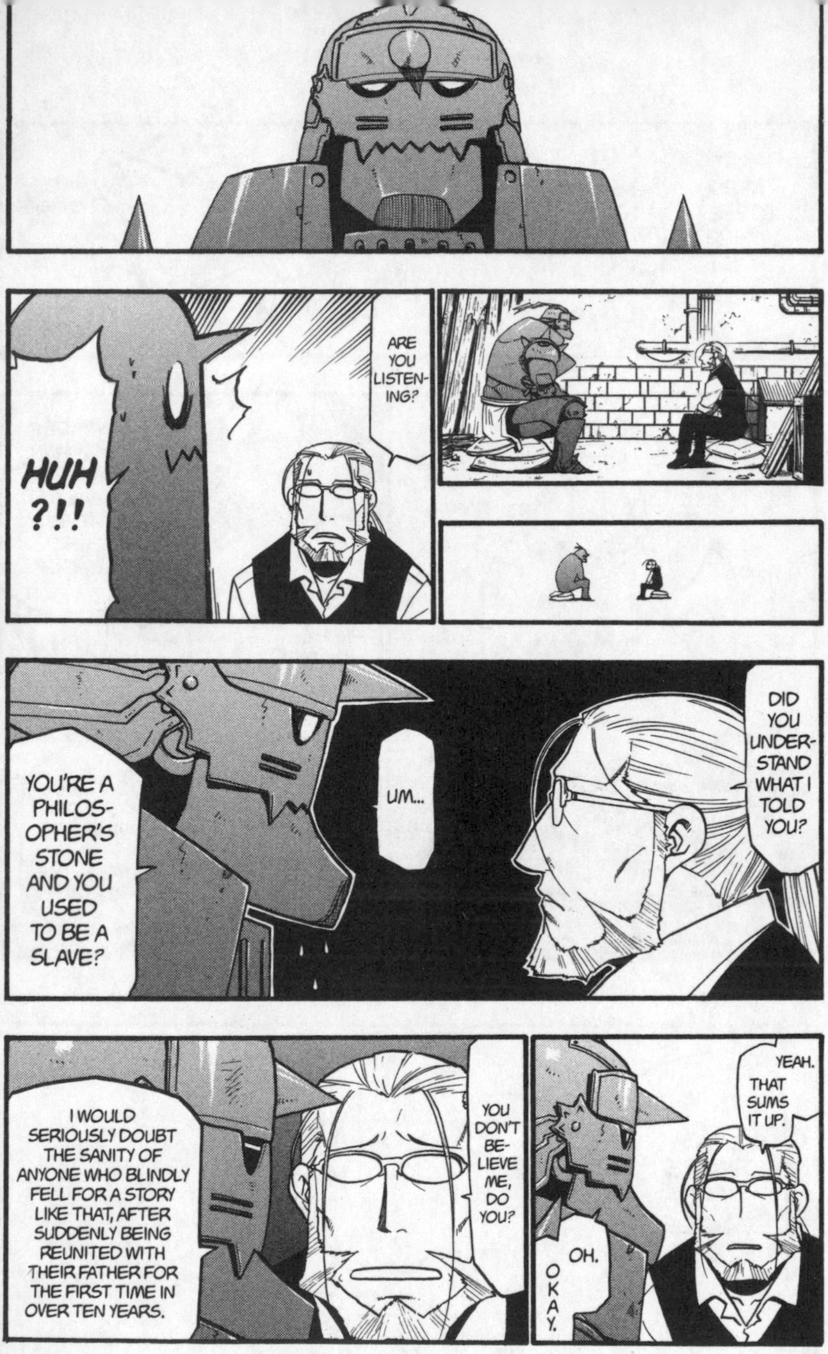
ARE YOU LISTENING?
HUH?!!
DID YOU UNDERSTAND WHAT I TOLD YOU?
UM...
YOU'RE A PHILOSOPHER'S STONE AND YOU USED TO BE A SLAVE?
YEAH. THAT SUMS IT UP.
OH.
OKAY.
YOU DON'T BELIEVE ME, DO YOU?
I WOULD SERIOUSLY DOUBT THE SANITY OF ANYONE WHO BLINDLY FELL FOR A STORY LIKE THAT, AFTER SUDDENLY BEING REUNITED WITH THEIR FATHER FOR THE FIRST TIME IN OVER TEN YEARS.

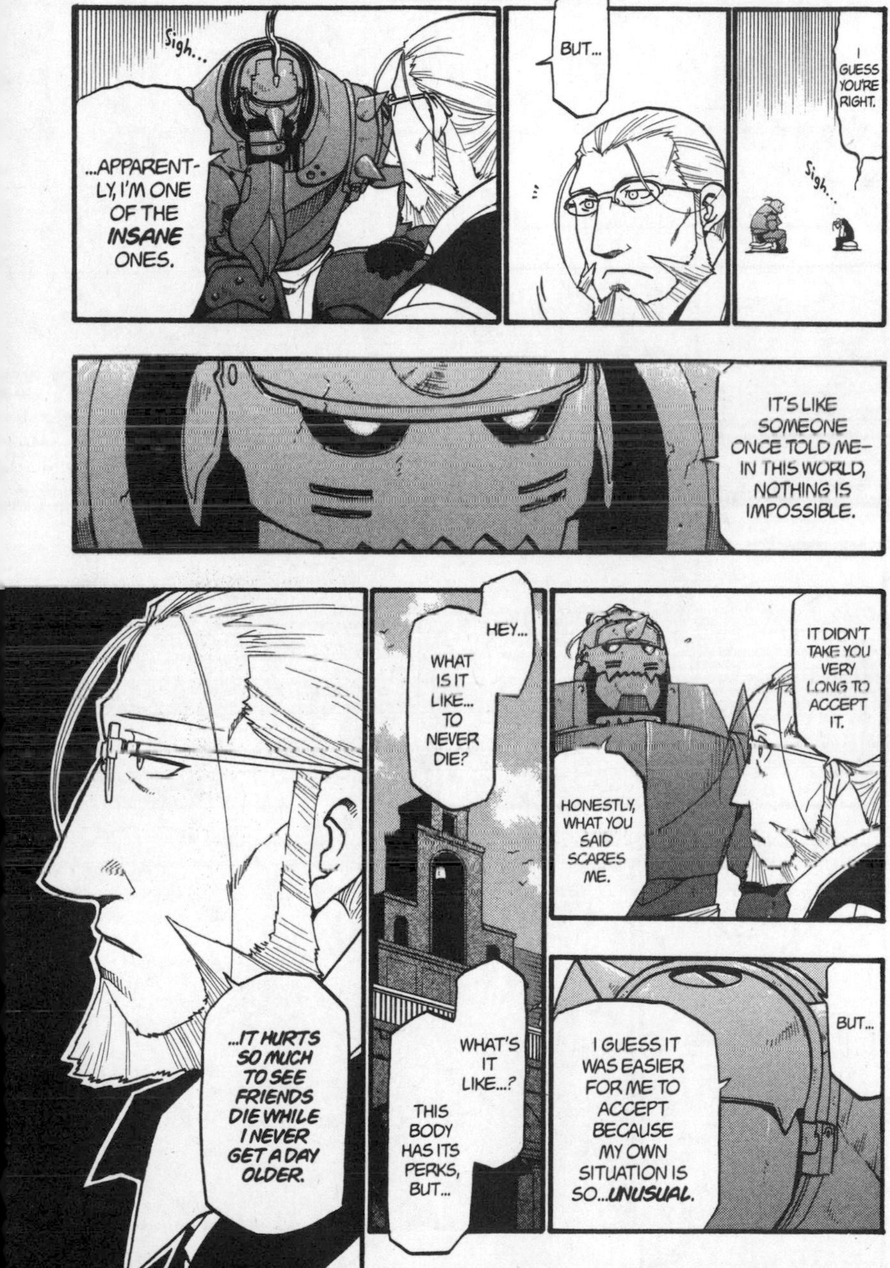
I GUESS YOU'RE RIGHT.
Sigh...
BUT...
Sigh...
...APPARENTLY, I'M ONE OF THE INSANE ONES.
IT'S LIKE SOMEONE ONCE TOLD ME— IN THIS WORLD, NOTHING IS IMPOSSIBLE.
IT DIDN'T TAKE YOU VERY LONG TO ACCEPT IT.
HONESTLY, WHAT YOU SAID SCARES ME.
BUT...
I GUESS IT WAS EASIER FOR ME TO ACCEPT BECAUSE MY OWN SITUATION IS SO...UNUSUAL.
HEY...
WHAT IS IT LIKE... TO NEVER DIE?
WHAT'S IT LIKE...?
THIS BODY HAS ITS PERKS, BUT...
...IT HURTS SO MUCH TO SEE FRIENDS DIE WHILE I NEVER GET A DAY OLDER.

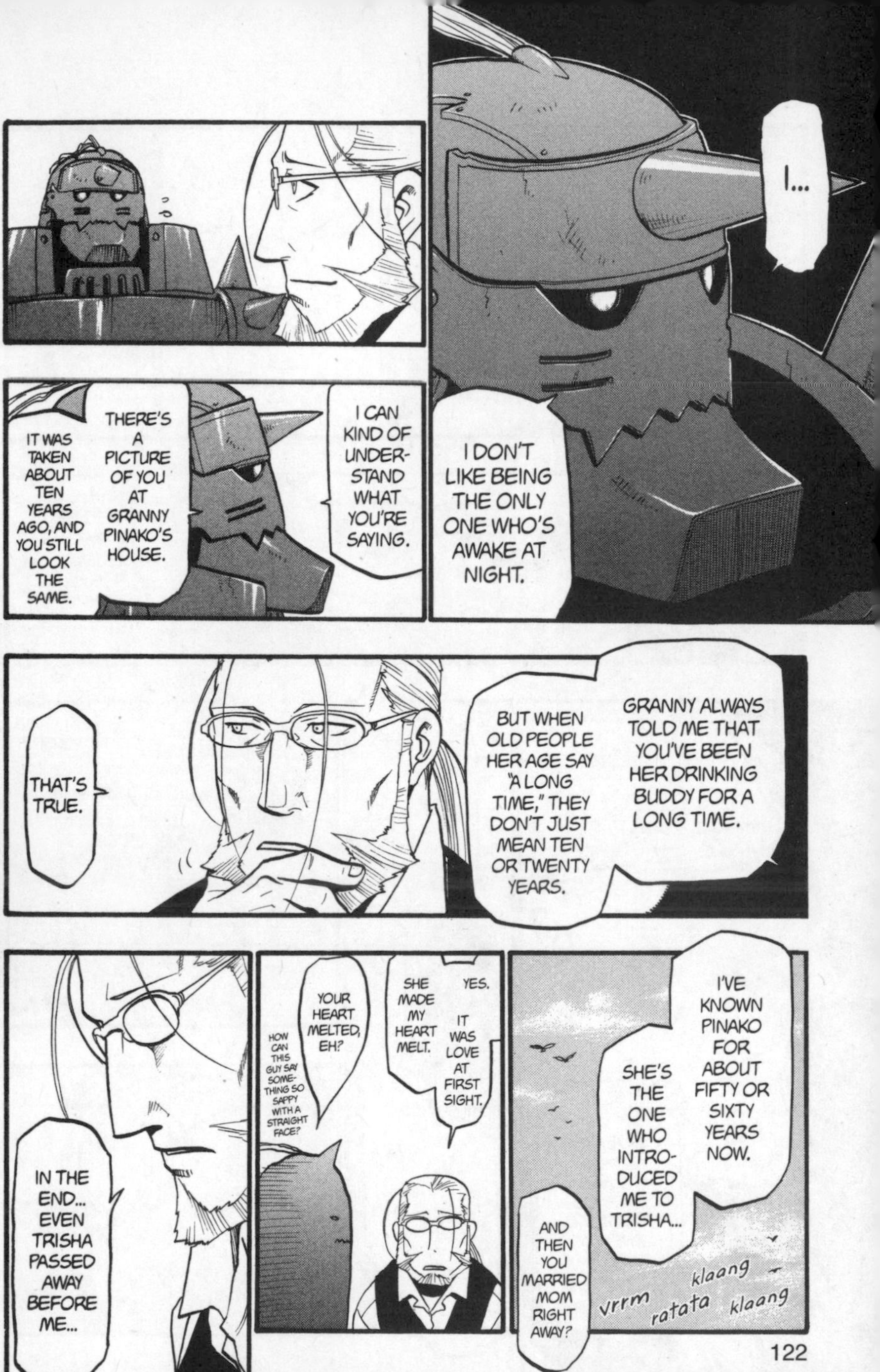
I...
I DON'T LIKE BEING THE ONLY ONE WHO'S AWAKE AT NIGHT.
I CAN KIND OF UNDERSTAND WHAT YOU'RE SAYING.
THERE'S A PICTURE OF YOU AT GRANNY PINAKO'S HOUSE.
IT WAS TAKEN ABOUT TEN YEARS AGO, AND YOU STILL LOOK THE SAME.
GRANNY ALWAYS TOLD ME THAT YOU'VE BEEN HER DRINKING BUDDY FOR A LONG TIME.
BUT WHEN OLD PEOPLE HER AGE SAY "A LONG TIME," THEY DON'T JUST MEAN TEN OR TWENTY YEARS.
THAT'S TRUE.
I'VE KNOWN PINAKO FOR ABOUT FIFTY OR SIXTY YEARS NOW.
SHE'S THE ONE WHO INTRODUCED ME TO TRISHA...
AND THEN YOU MARRIED MOM RIGHT AWAY?
klaang
vrrm
ratata
klaang
YES.
IT WAS LOVE AT FIRST SIGHT.
SHE MADE MY HEART MELT.
YOUR HEART MELTED, EH?
HOW CAN THIS GUY SAY SOMETHING SO SAPPY WITH A STRAIGHT FACE?
IN THE END... EVEN TRISHA PASSED AWAY BEFORE ME...

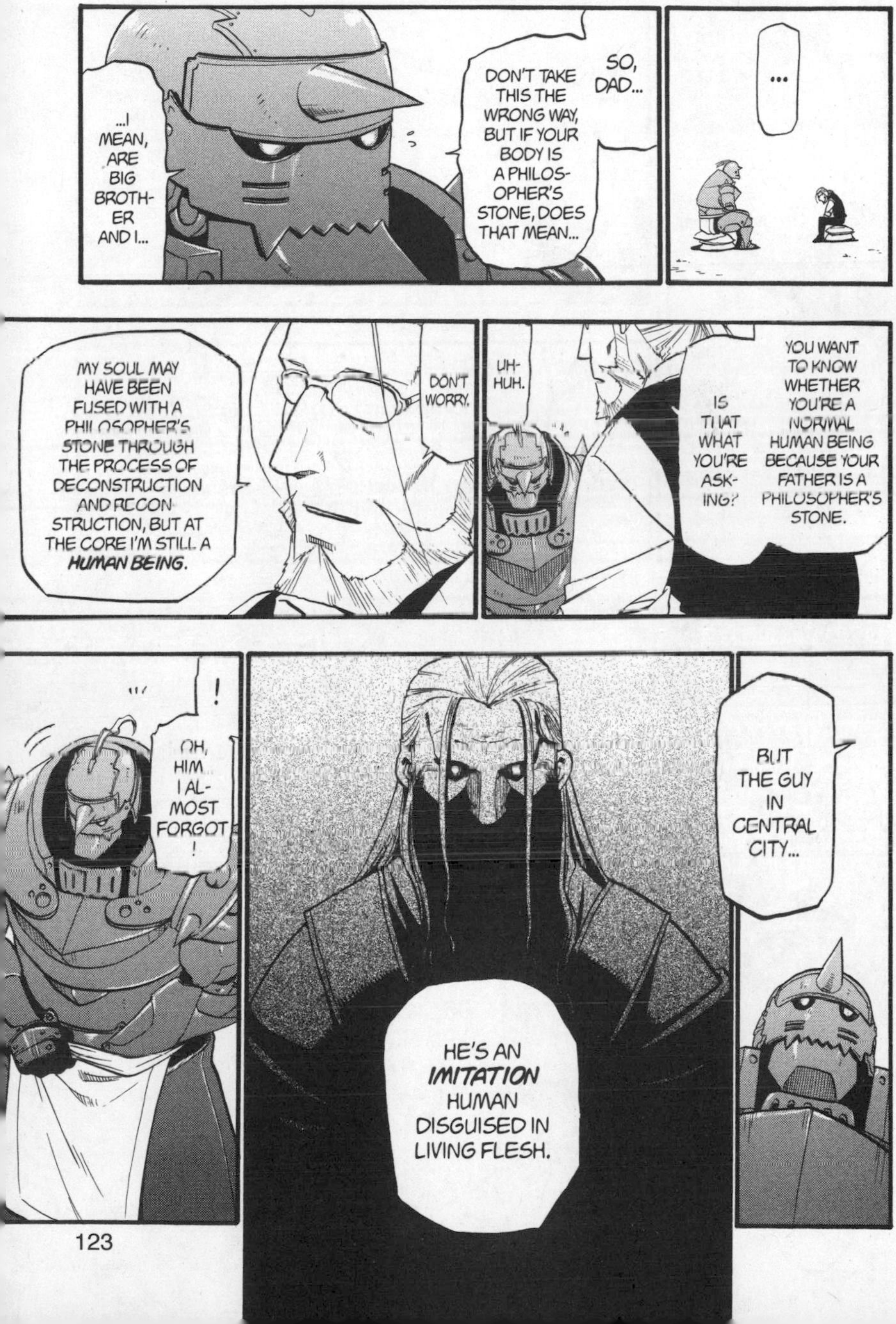
...
SO, DAD...
DON'T TAKE THIS THE WRONG WAY, BUT IF YOUR BODY IS A PHILOSOPHER'S STONE, DOES THAT MEAN...
...I MEAN, ARE BIG BROTHER AND I...
YOU WANT TO KNOW WHETHER YOU'RE A NORMAL HUMAN BEING BECAUSE YOUR FATHER IS A PHILOSOPHER'S STONE.
IS THAT WHAT YOU'RE ASKING?
UH-HUH.
DON'T WORRY.
MY SOUL MAY HAVE BEEN FUSED WITH A PHILOSOPHER'S STONE THROUGH THE PROCESS OF DECONSTRUCTION AND RECONSTRUCTION, BUT AT THE CORE I'M STILL A ***HUMAN BEING***.
BUT THE GUY IN CENTRAL CITY...
HE'S AN ***IMITATION*** HUMAN DISGUISED IN LIVING FLESH.
!
OH, HIM... I ALMOST FORGOT!

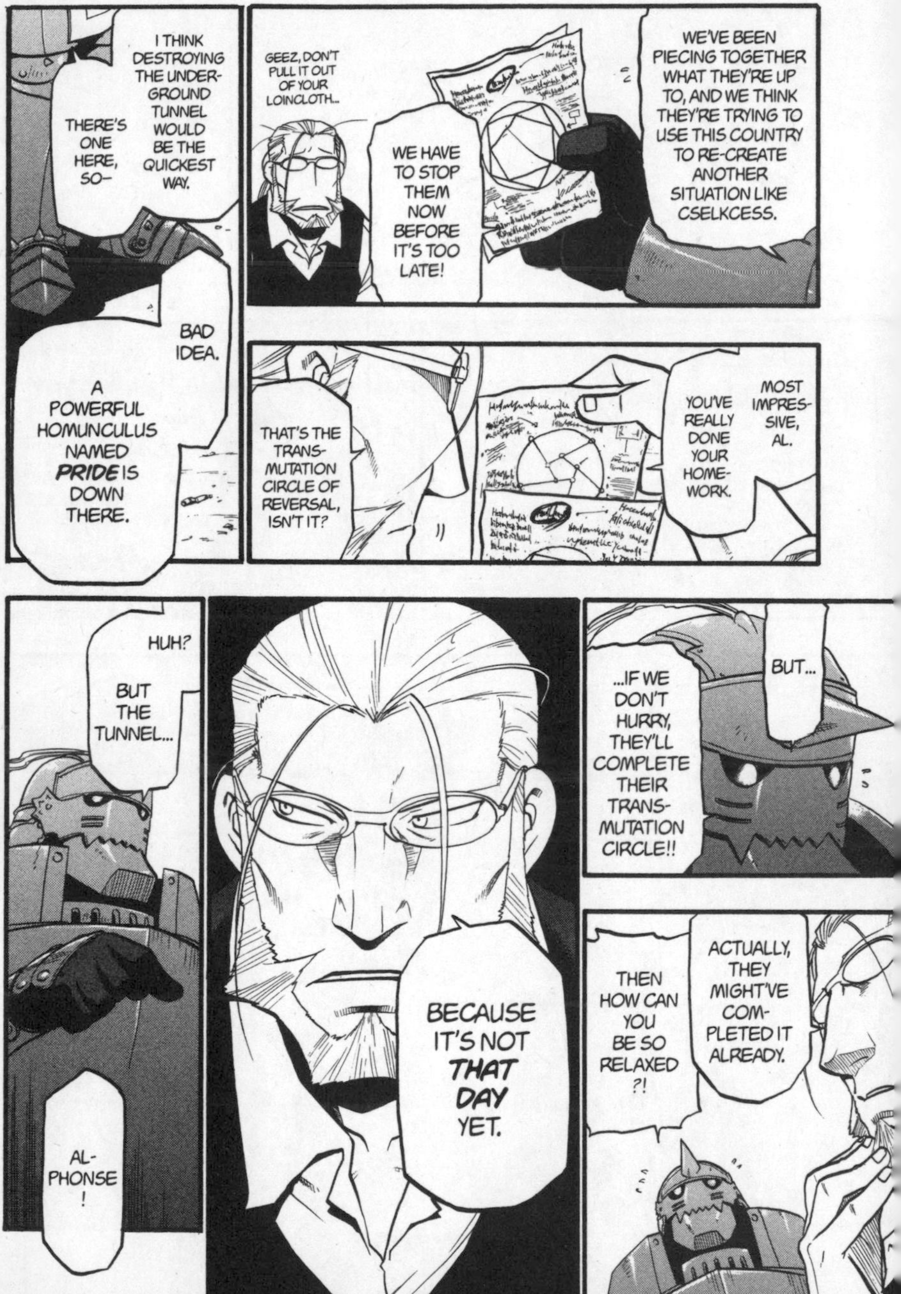
WE'VE BEEN PIECING TOGETHER WHAT THEY'RE UP TO, AND WE THINK THEY'RE TRYING TO USE THIS COUNTRY TO RE-CREATE ANOTHER SITUATION LIKE CSELKCESS.
WE HAVE TO STOP THEM NOW BEFORE IT'S TOO LATE!
GEEZ, DON'T PULL IT OUT OF YOUR LOINCLOTH...
MOST IMPRESSIVE, AL.
YOU'VE REALLY DONE YOUR HOMEWORK.
THAT'S THE TRANSMUTATION CIRCLE OF REVERSAL, ISN'T IT?
I THINK DESTROYING THE UNDERGROUND TUNNEL WOULD BE THE QUICKEST WAY.
THERE'S ONE HERE, SO-
BAD IDEA.
A POWERFUL HOMUNCULUS NAMED PRIDE IS DOWN THERE.
BUT...
...IF WE DON'T HURRY, THEY'LL COMPLETE THEIR TRANSMUTATION CIRCLE!!
ACTUALLY, THEY MIGHT'VE COMPLETED IT ALREADY.
THEN HOW CAN YOU BE SO RELAXED?!
BECAUSE IT'S NOT THAT DAY YET.
HUH?
BUT THE TUNNEL...
ALPHONSE!

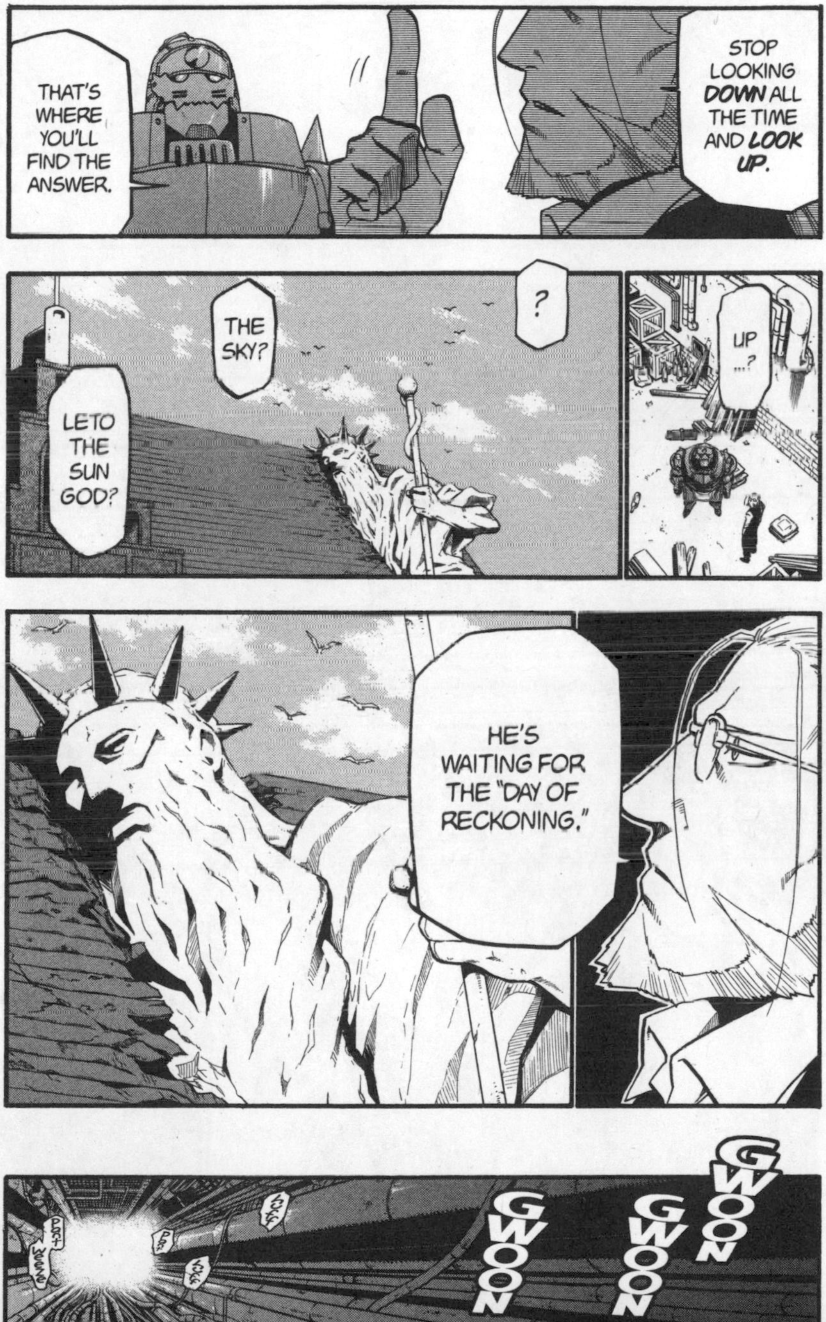
STOP LOOKING DOWN ALL THE TIME AND LOOK UP.
THAT'S WHERE YOU'LL FIND THE ANSWER.
UP ...?
?
THE SKY?
LETO THE SUN GOD?
HE'S WAITING FOR THE "DAY OF RECKONING."
GWOON
GWOON
GWOON
GWOON
huff
pant
huff
pant
wheeze

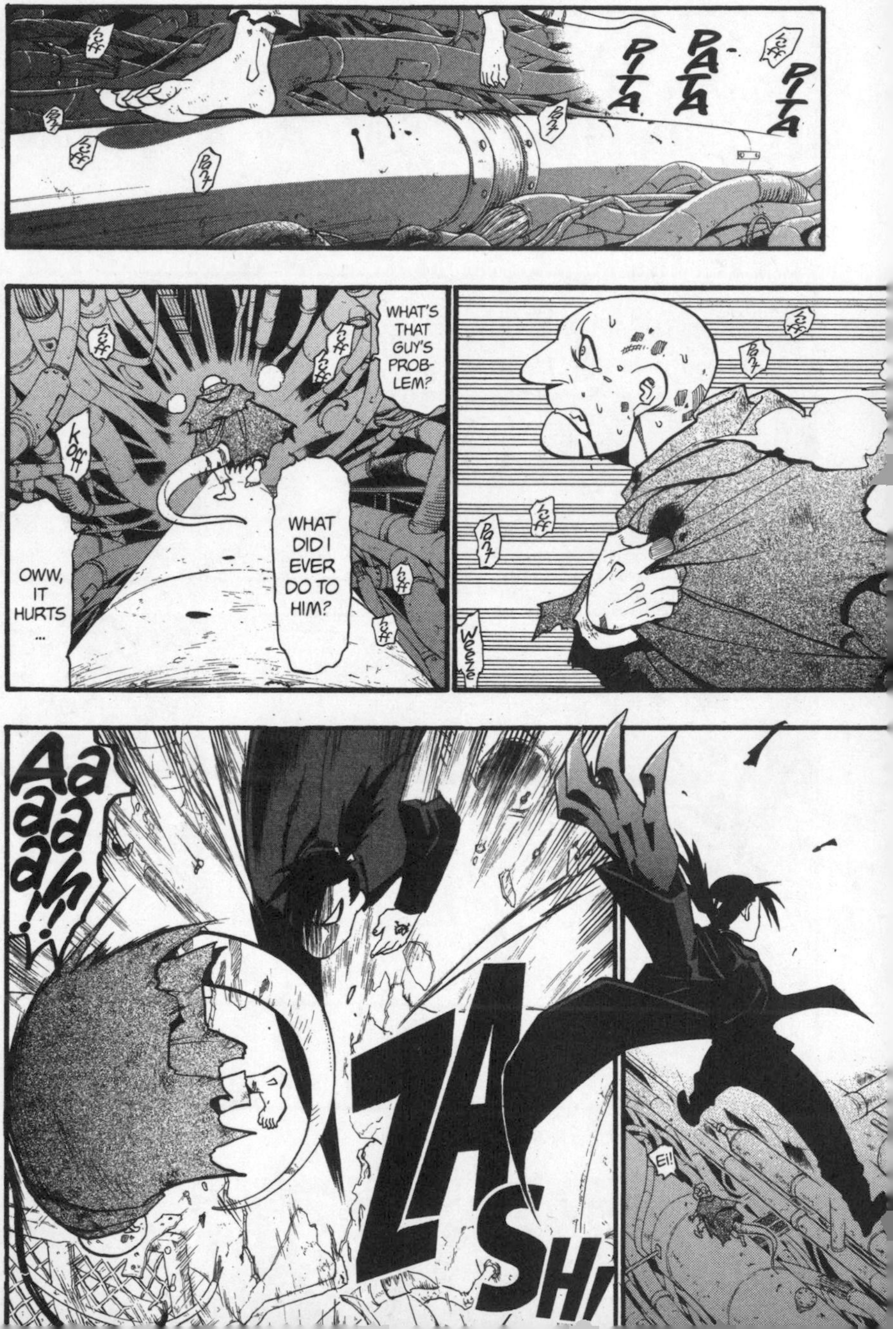
PITA
PA-TA
PITA
Weeze
WHAT'S THAT GUY'S PROB-LEM?
WHAT DID I EVER DO TO HIM?
koff
OWW, IT HURTS ...
Ei!
ZASH!
Aaaaah!!

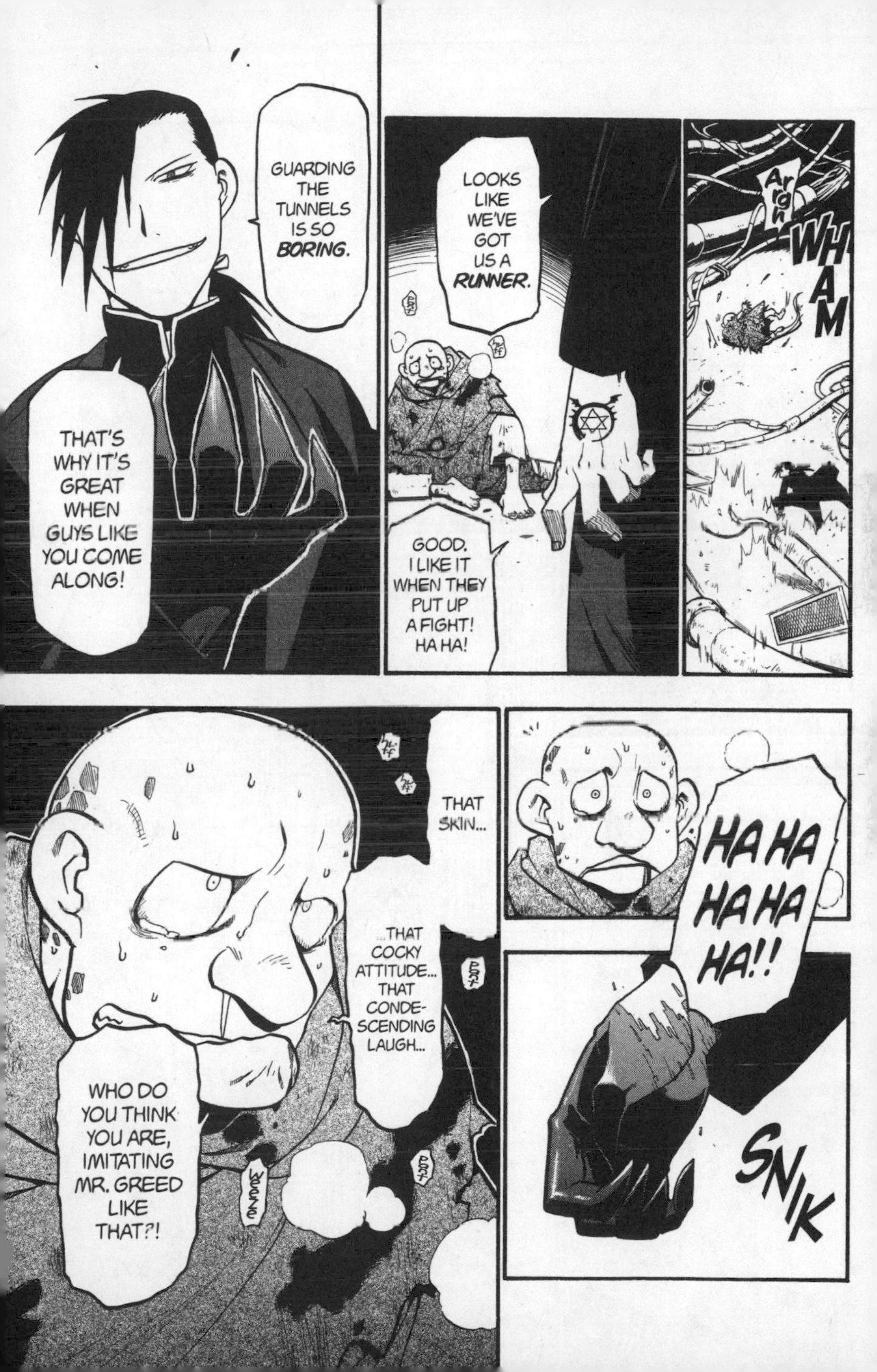
Argh
WHAM
LOOKS LIKE WE'VE GOT US A RUNNER.
GOOD. I LIKE IT WHEN THEY PUT UP A FIGHT! HA HA!
GUARDING THE TUNNELS IS SO BORING.
THAT'S WHY IT'S GREAT WHEN GUYS LIKE YOU COME ALONG!
HA HA HA HA HA!!
SNIK
THAT SKIN...
...THAT COCKY ATTITUDE... THAT CONDESCENDING LAUGH...
WHO DO YOU THINK YOU ARE, IMITATING MR. GREED LIKE THAT?!

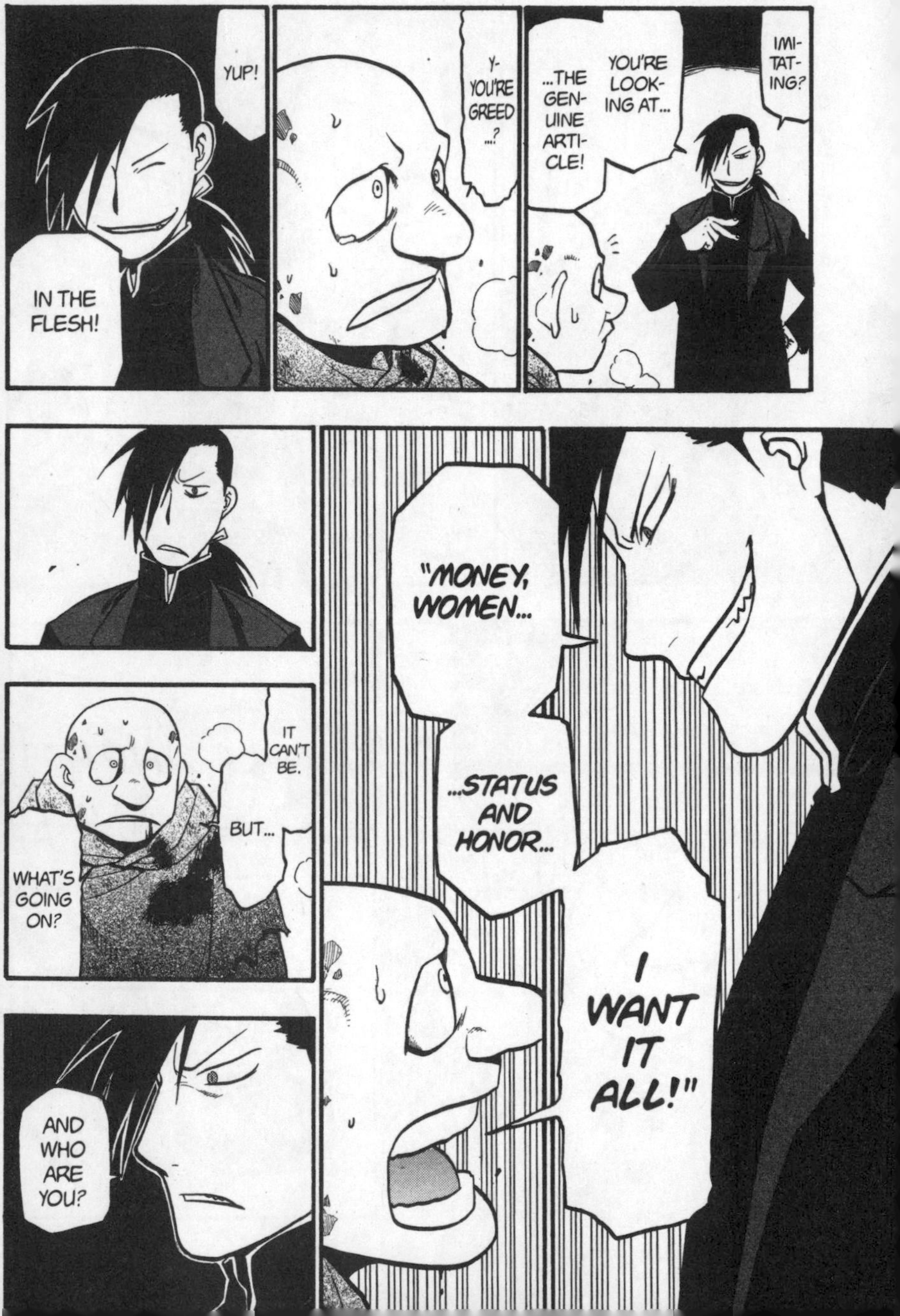
IMI-TAT-ING?
YOU'RE LOOKING AT...
...THE GENUINE ARTICLE!
Y-YOU'RE GREED...?
YUP!
IN THE FLESH!
"MONEY, WOMEN...
...STATUS AND HONOR...
I WANT IT ALL!"
IT CAN'T BE.
BUT...
WHAT'S GOING ON?
AND WHO ARE YOU?

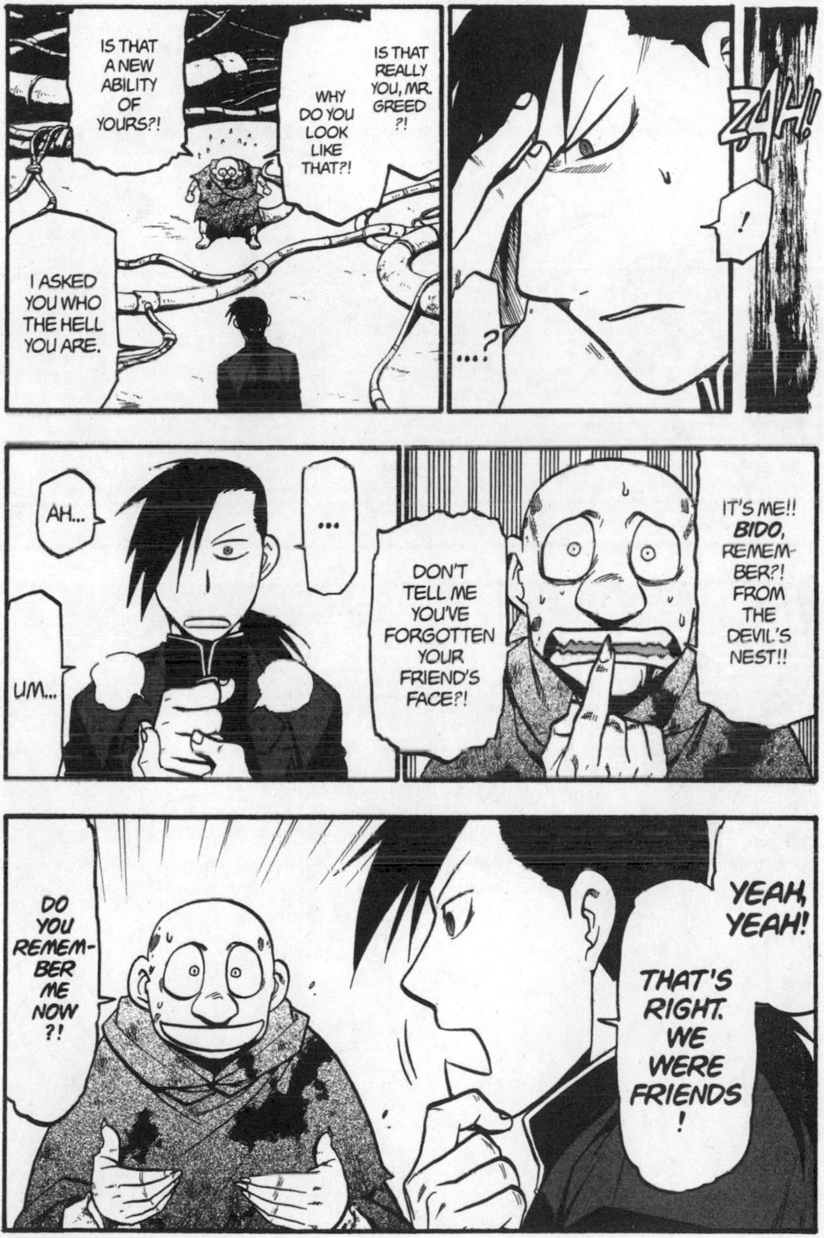
ZAH!
!
...?
IS THAT REALLY YOU, MR. GREED?!
WHY DO YOU LOOK LIKE THAT?!
IS THAT A NEW ABILITY OF YOURS?!
I ASKED YOU WHO THE HELL YOU ARE.
IT'S ME!! BIDO, REMEMBER?! FROM THE DEVIL'S NEST!!
DON'T TELL ME YOU'VE FORGOTTEN YOUR FRIEND'S FACE?!
...
AH...
UM...
YEAH, YEAH!
THAT'S RIGHT. WE WERE FRIENDS!
DO YOU REMEMBER ME NOW?!

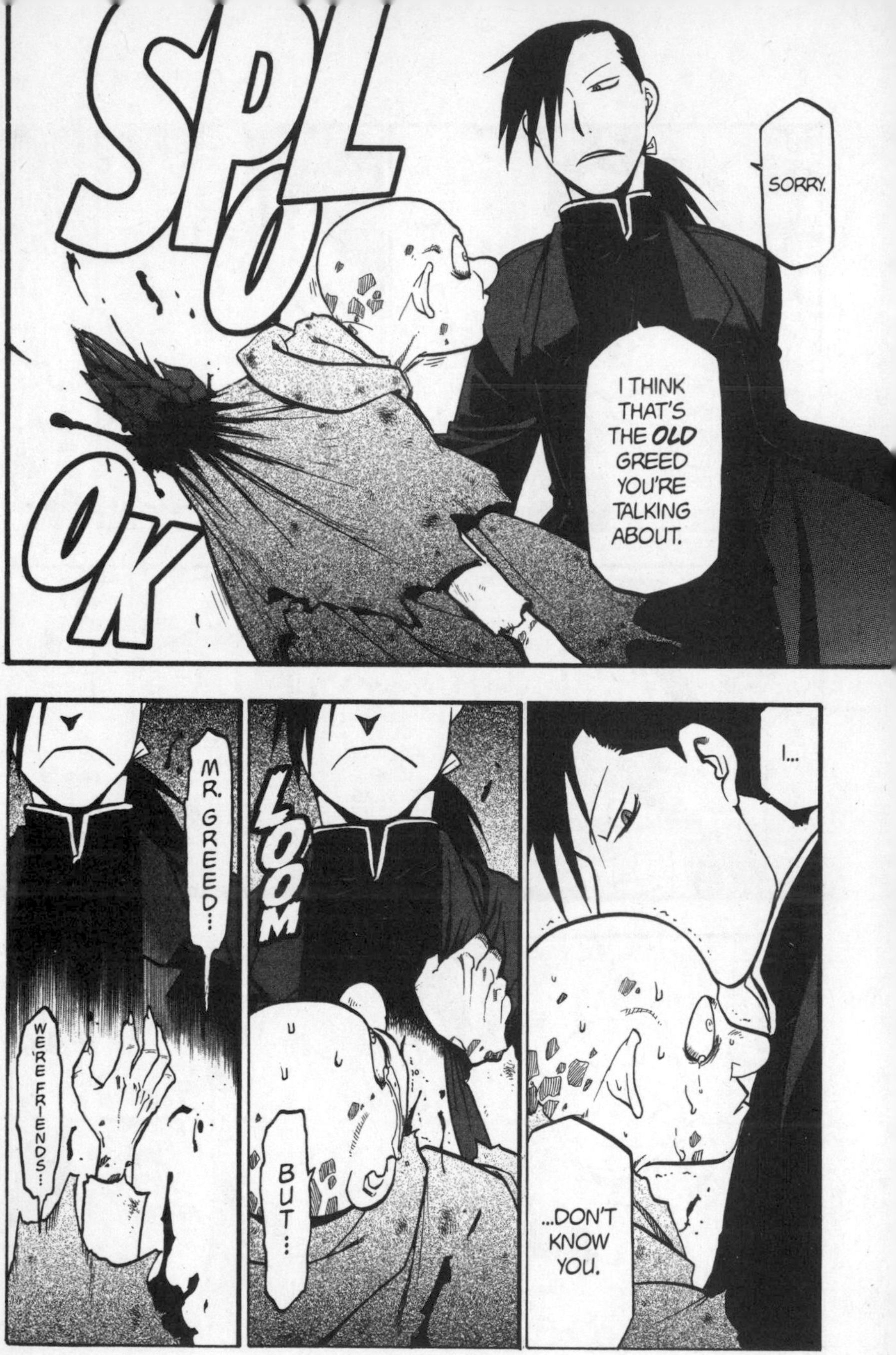
SPLOOK
SORRY.
I THINK THAT'S THE OLD GREED YOU'RE TALKING ABOUT.
I...
...DON'T KNOW YOU.
LOOM
BUT...
MR. GREED...
WE'RE FRIENDS...

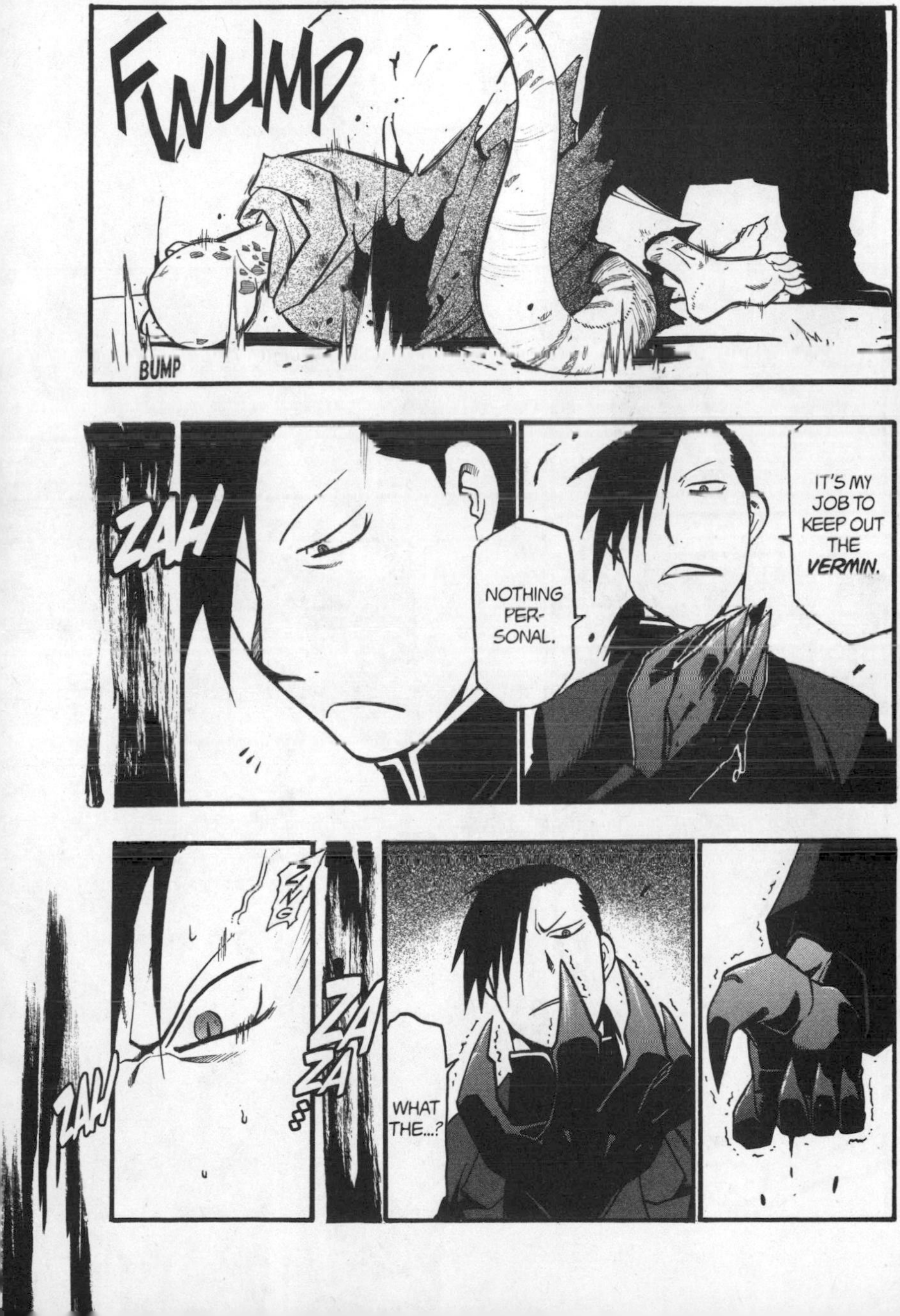
FWUMP
BUMP
IT'S MY JOB TO KEEP OUT THE *VERMIN*.
ZAH
NOTHING PERSONAL.
ZA ZA
WHAT THE...?
ZING
ZAH

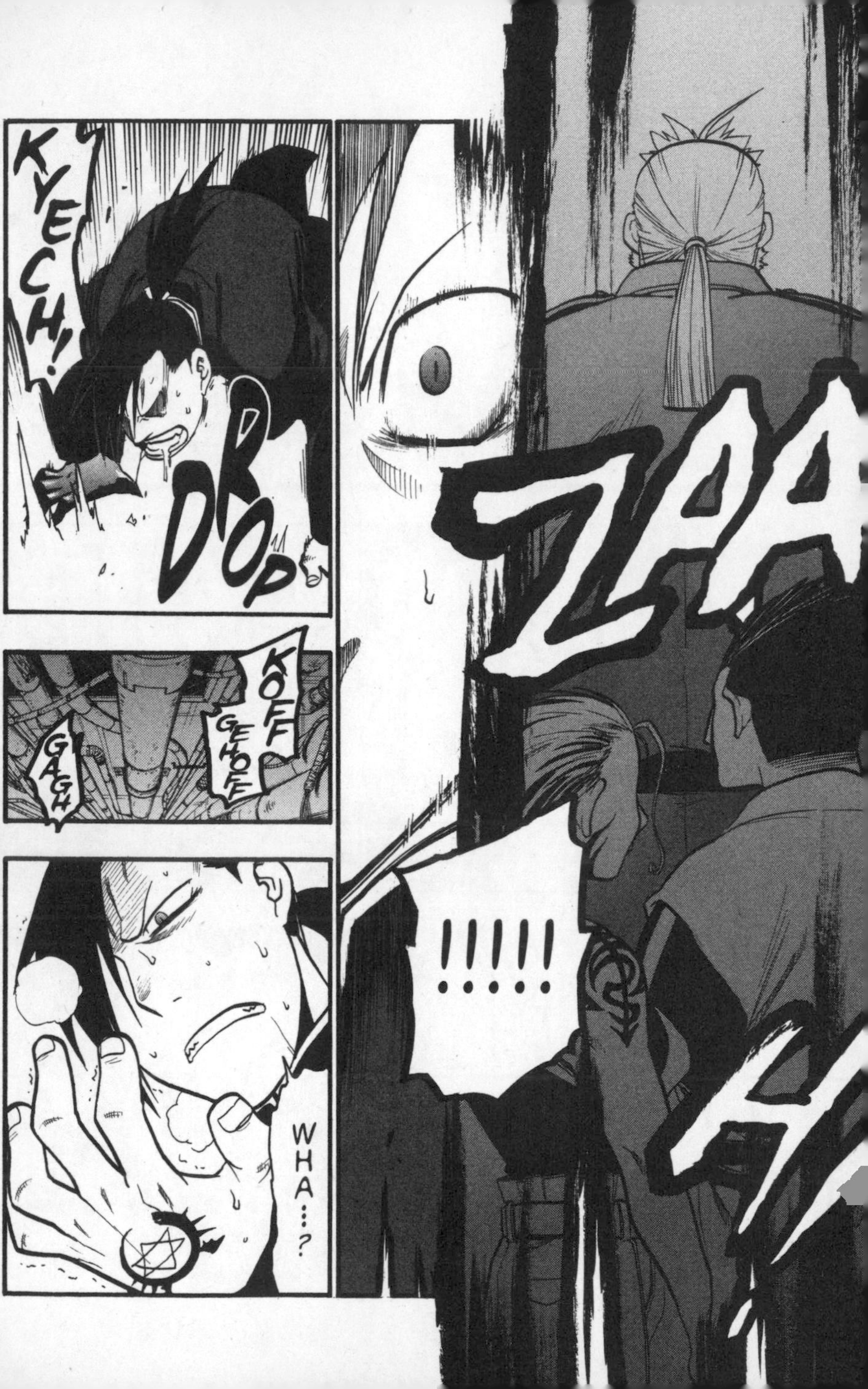
!!!!!
KYECH!
DROP
KOFF
GEHOFF
GAGH
WHA...?

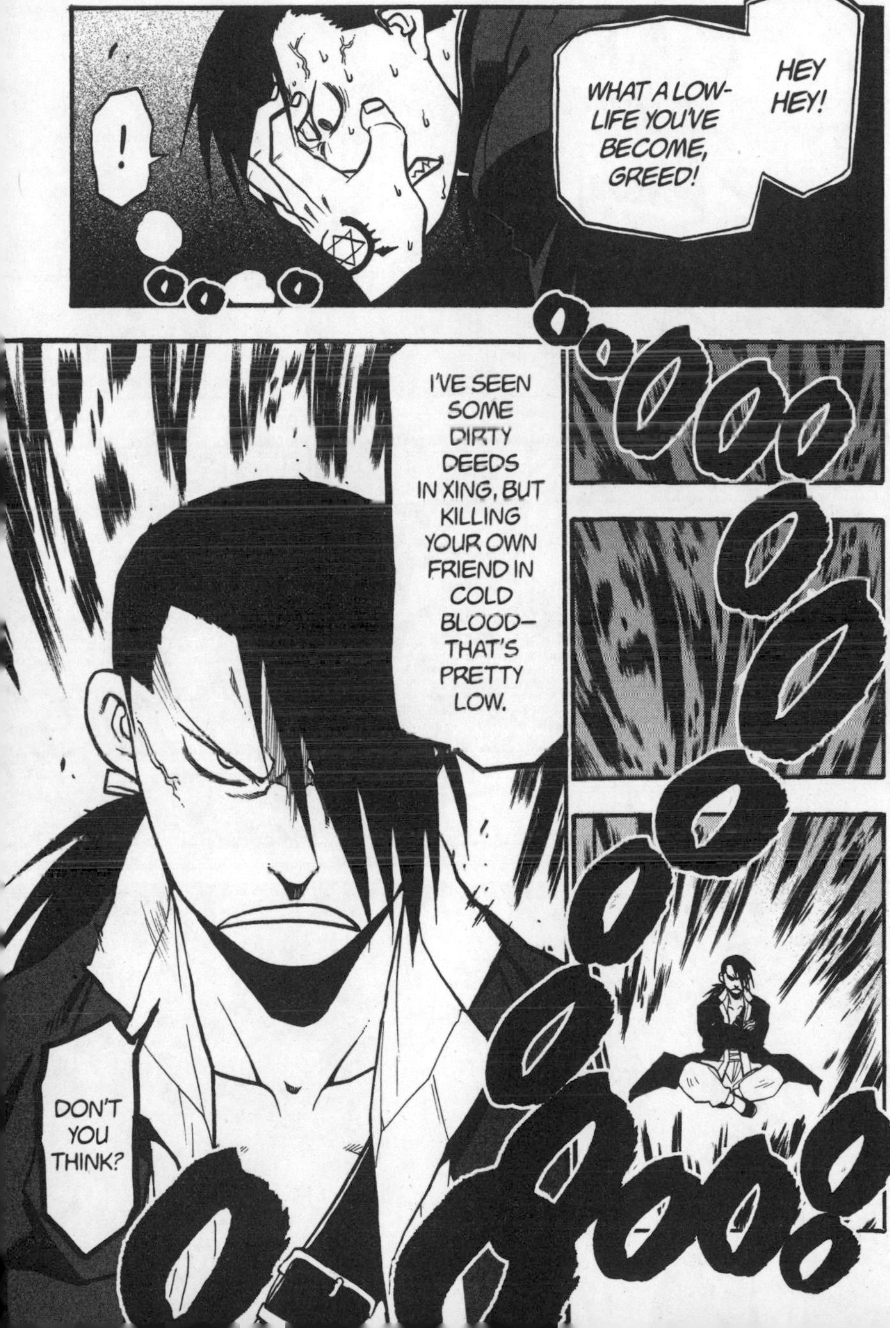
HEY HEY!
WHAT A LOW-LIFE YOU'VE BECOME, GREED!
!
I'VE SEEN SOME DIRTY DEEDS IN XING, BUT KILLING YOUR OWN FRIEND IN COLD BLOOD—THAT'S PRETTY LOW.
DON'T YOU THINK?

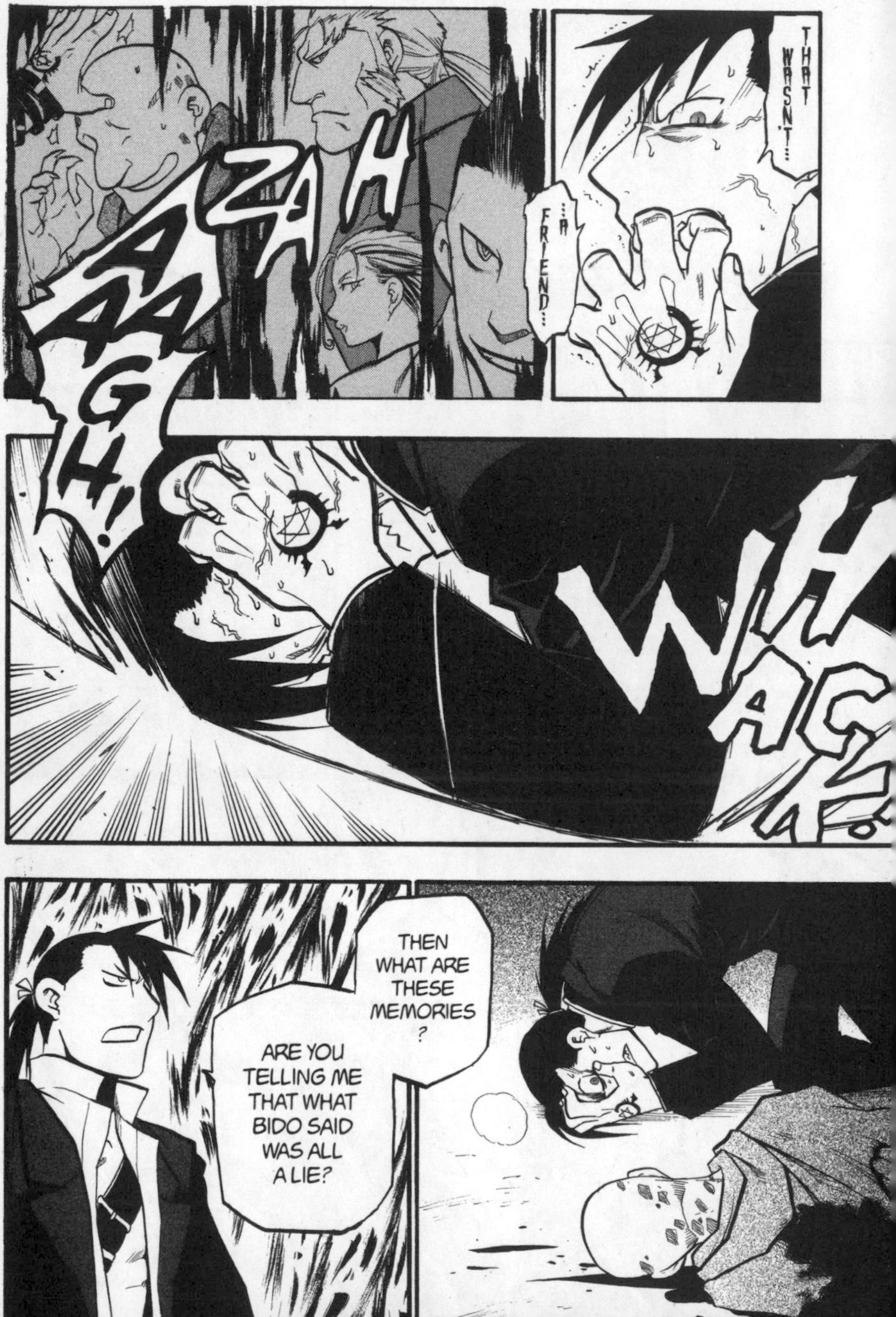
THAT WASN'T...
...A FRIEND...
ZAH
AAAGH!
WHACK
THEN WHAT ARE THESE MEMORIES?
ARE YOU TELLING ME THAT WHAT BIDO SAID WAS ALL A LIE?

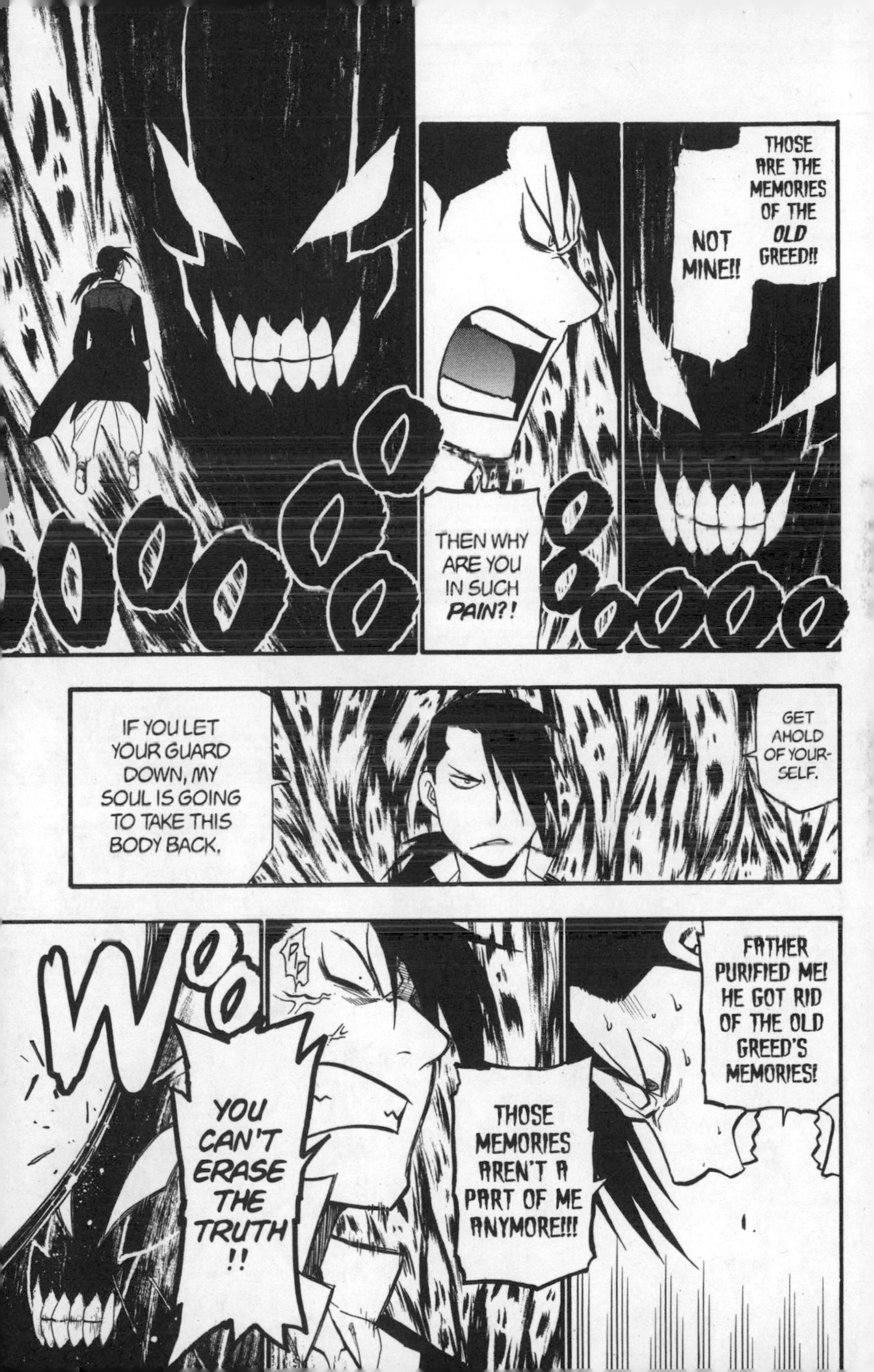
THOSE ARE THE MEMORIES OF THE OLD GREED!!
NOT MINE!!
THEN WHY ARE YOU IN SUCH PAIN?!
GET AHOLD OF YOUR-SELF.
IF YOU LET YOUR GUARD DOWN, MY SOUL IS GOING TO TAKE THIS BODY BACK.
FATHER PURIFIED ME! HE GOT RID OF THE OLD GREED'S MEMORIES!
THOSE MEMORIES AREN'T A PART OF ME ANYMORE!!!
YOU CAN'T ERASE THE TRUTH!!

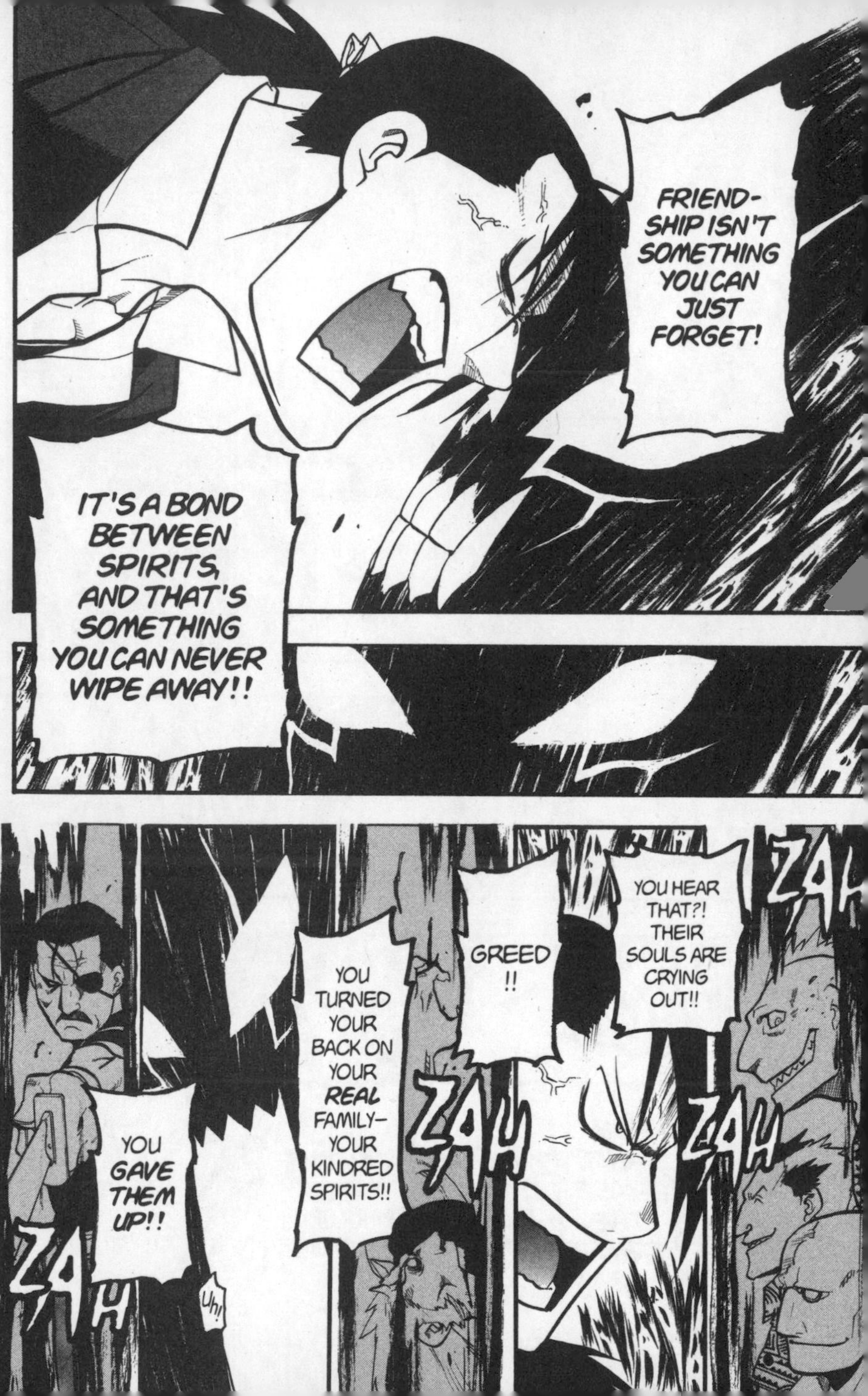
FRIEND-SHIP ISN'T SOMETHING YOU CAN JUST FORGET!
IT'S A BOND BETWEEN SPIRITS, AND THAT'S SOMETHING YOU CAN NEVER WIPE AWAY!!
ZAH
YOU HEAR THAT?! THEIR SOULS ARE CRYING OUT!!
ZAH
GREED !!
ZAH
YOU TURNED YOUR BACK ON YOUR ***REAL*** FAMILY— YOUR KINDRED SPIRITS!!
YOU GAVE THEM UP!!
ZAH
Uh!

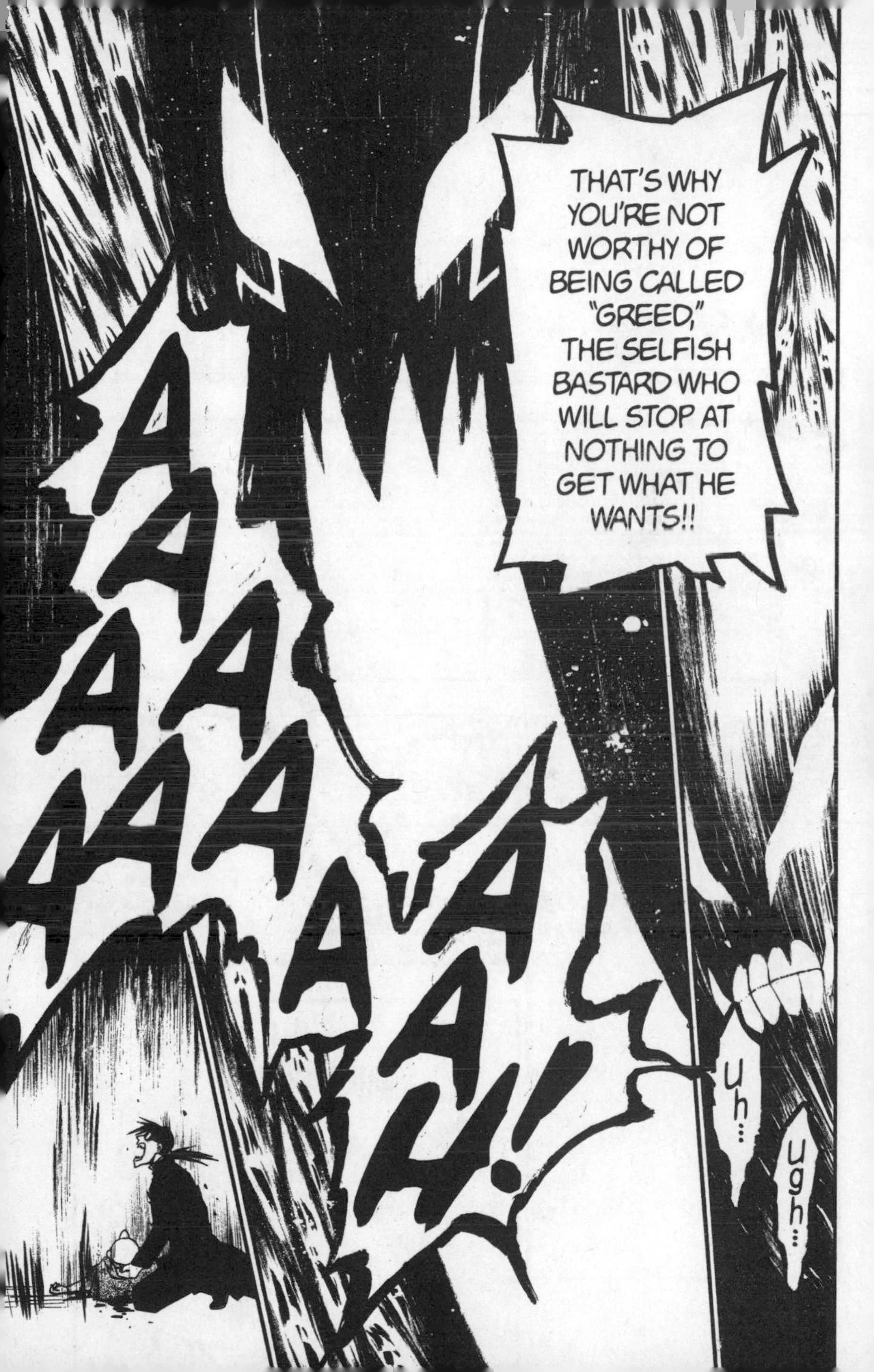
THAT'S WHY YOU'RE NOT WORTHY OF BEING CALLED "GREED," THE SELFISH BASTARD WHO WILL STOP AT NOTHING TO GET WHAT HE WANTS!!
AAAAAAAAAAAH!!
Uh...
Ugh...

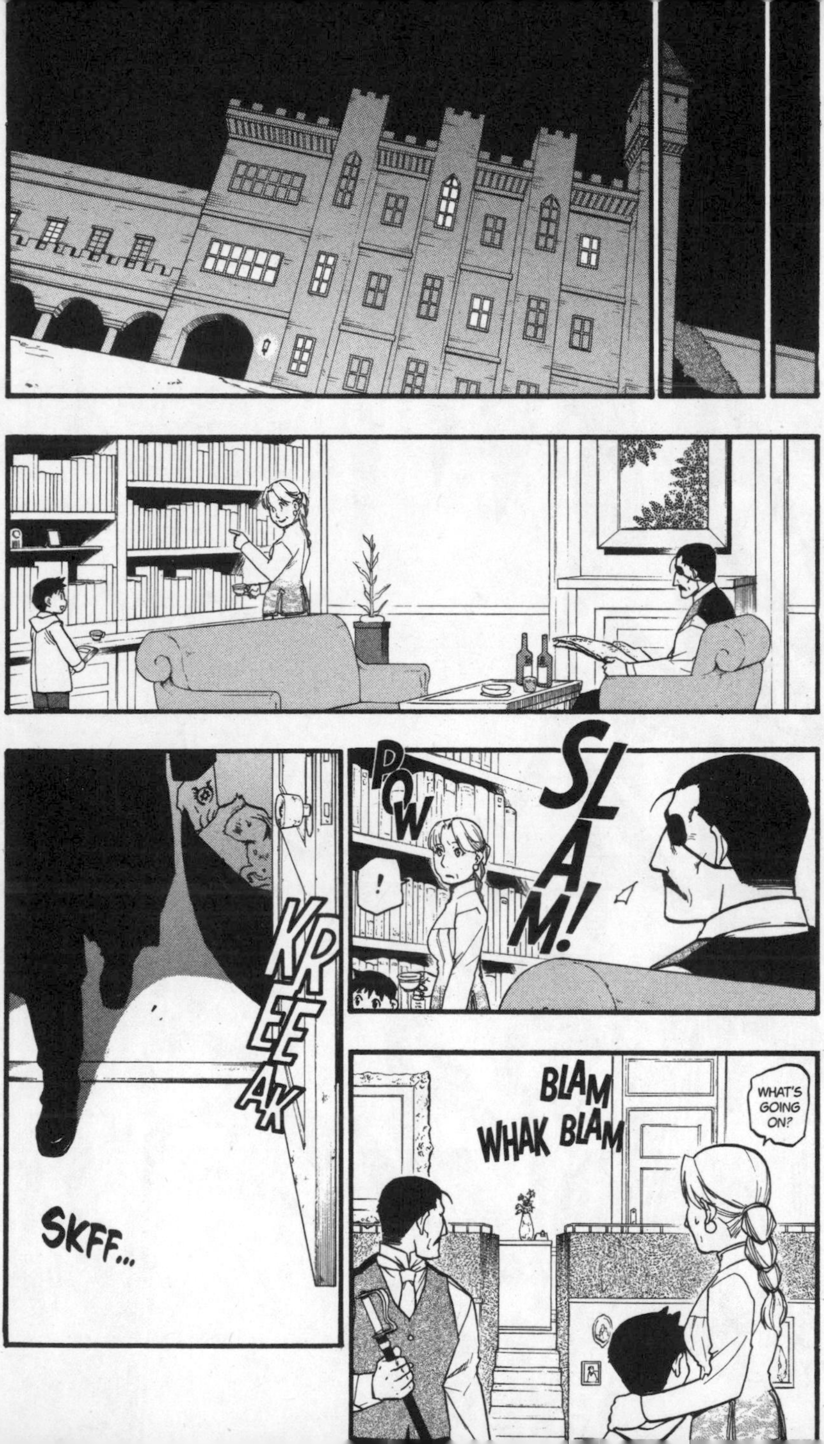
SLAM!
POW
!
WHAT'S GOING ON?
BLAM
WHAK BLAM
KREEAK
SKFF...

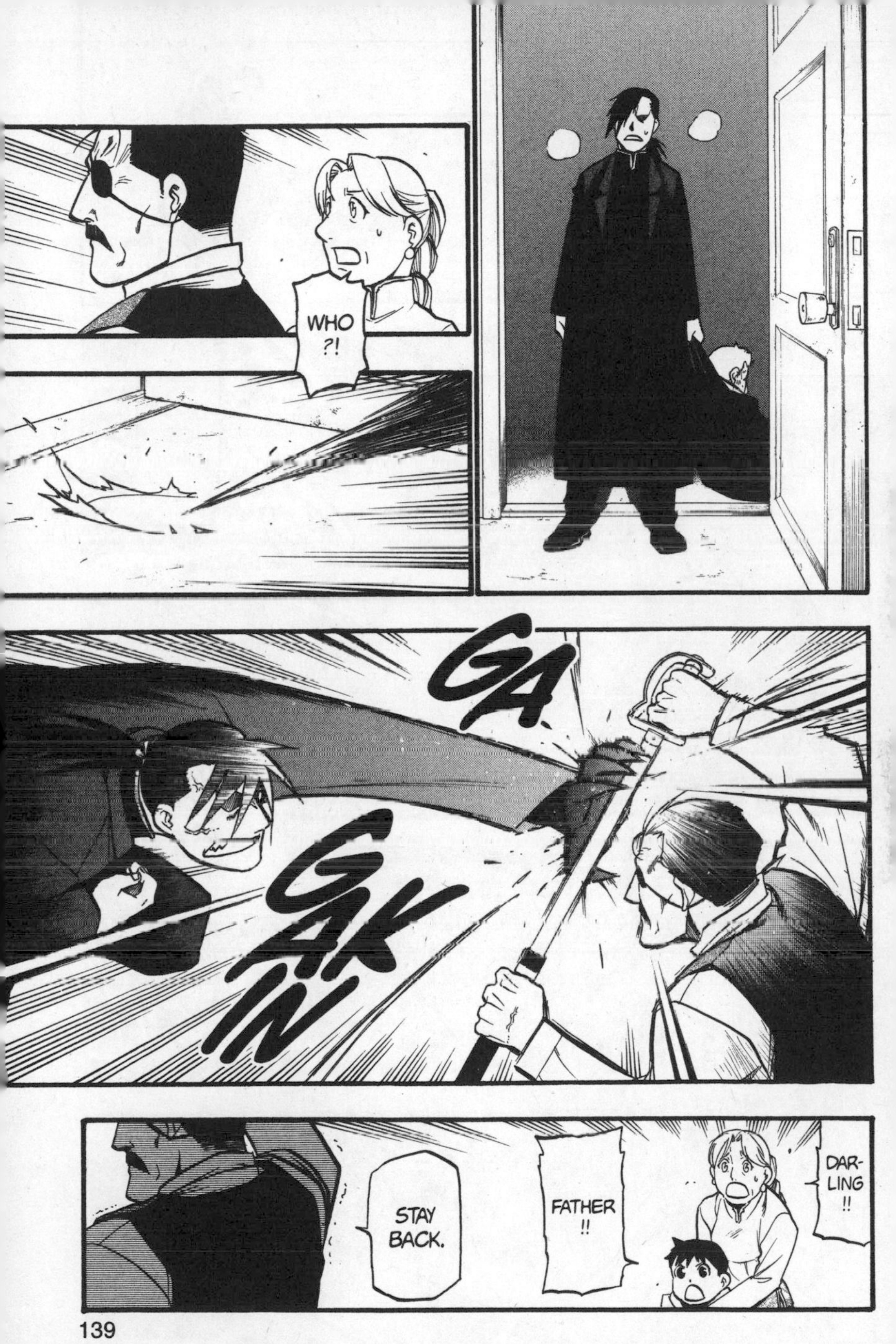
WHO ?!
GA
GAKIN
DAR-LING !!
FATHER !!
STAY BACK.

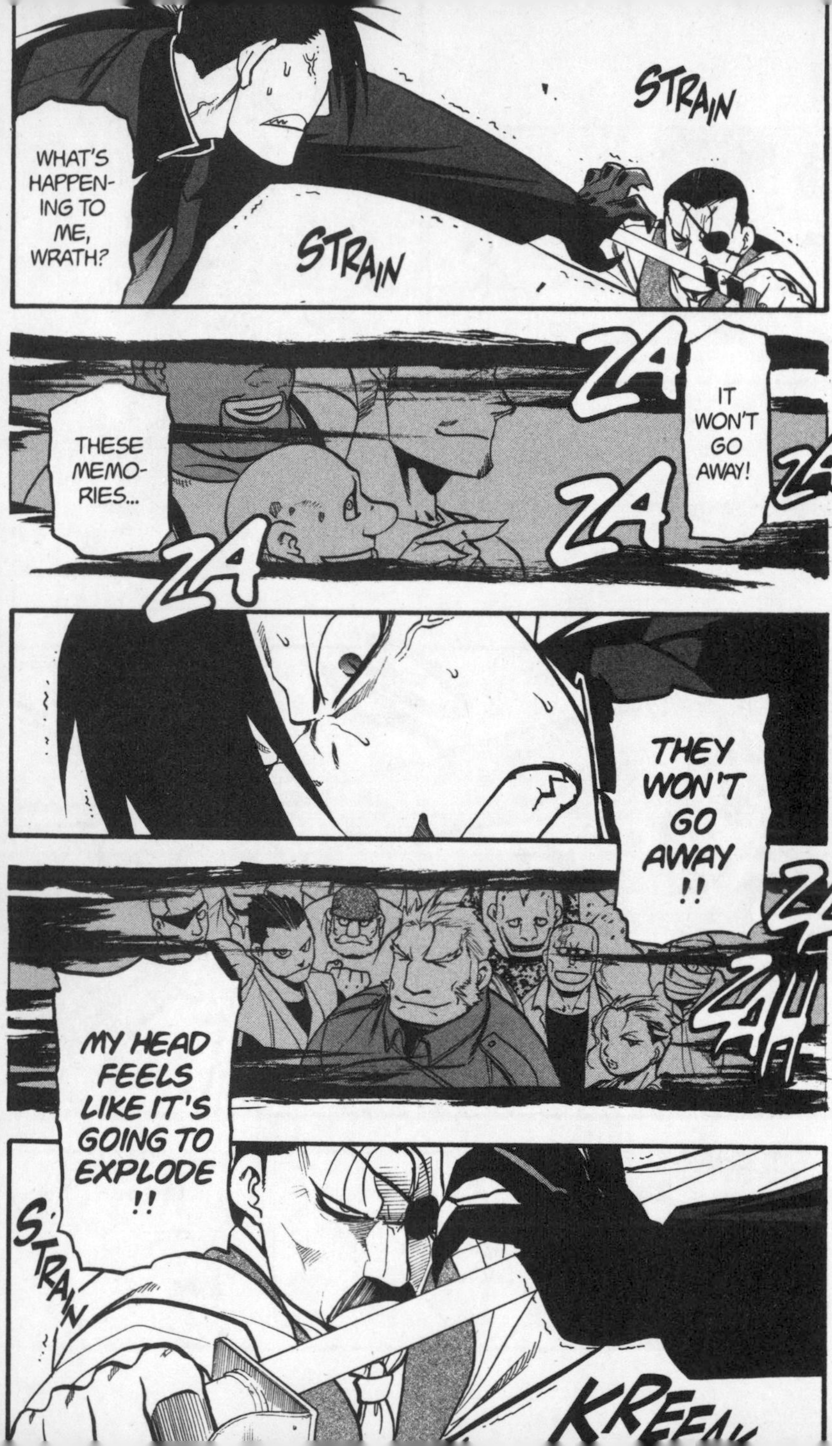
STRAIN
WHAT'S HAPPEN-ING TO ME, WRATH?
STRAIN
ZA
IT WON'T GO AWAY!
ZA
ZA
THESE MEMO-RIES...
ZA
THEY WON'T GO AWAY!!
ZA
ZAH
MY HEAD FEELS LIKE IT'S GOING TO EXPLODE!!
STRAIN
KREEAK

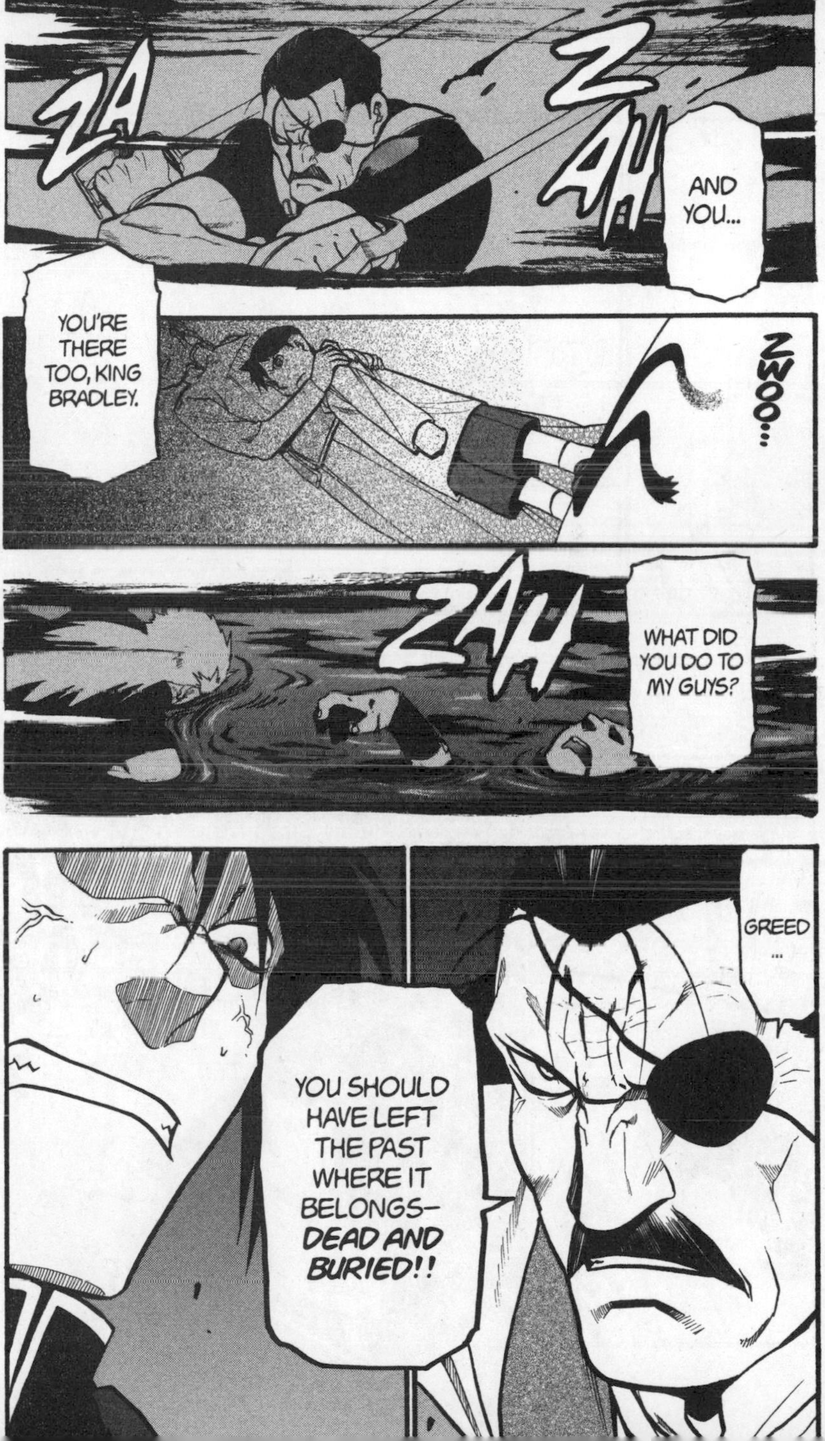
ZAH
AND YOU...
ZA
YOU'RE THERE TOO, KING BRADLEY.
ZWOO...
WHAT DID YOU DO TO MY GUYS?
ZAH
GREED...
YOU SHOULD HAVE LEFT THE PAST WHERE IT BELONGS— *DEAD AND BURIED!!*

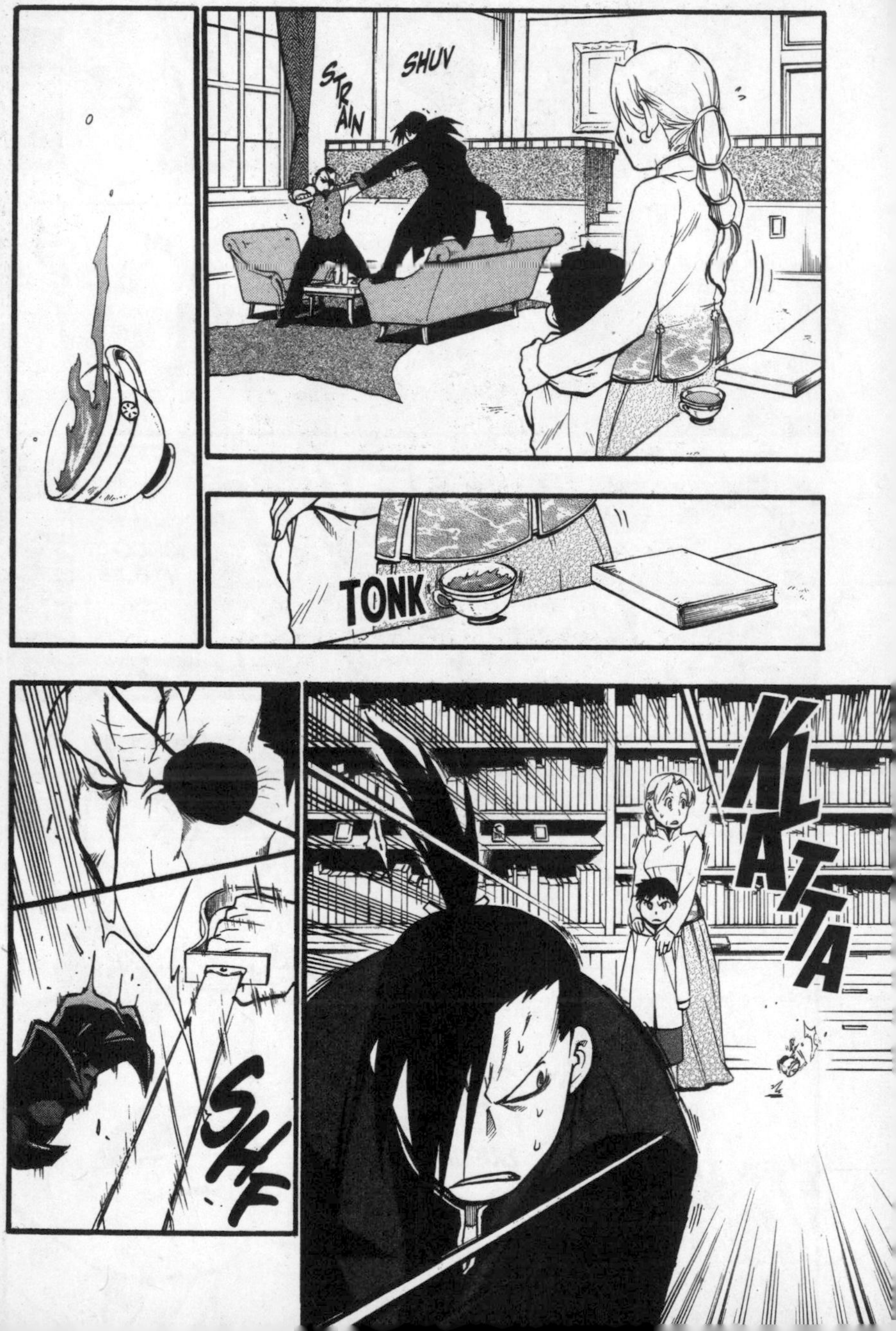
SHUV
STRAIN
TONK
KLATTA
SHF

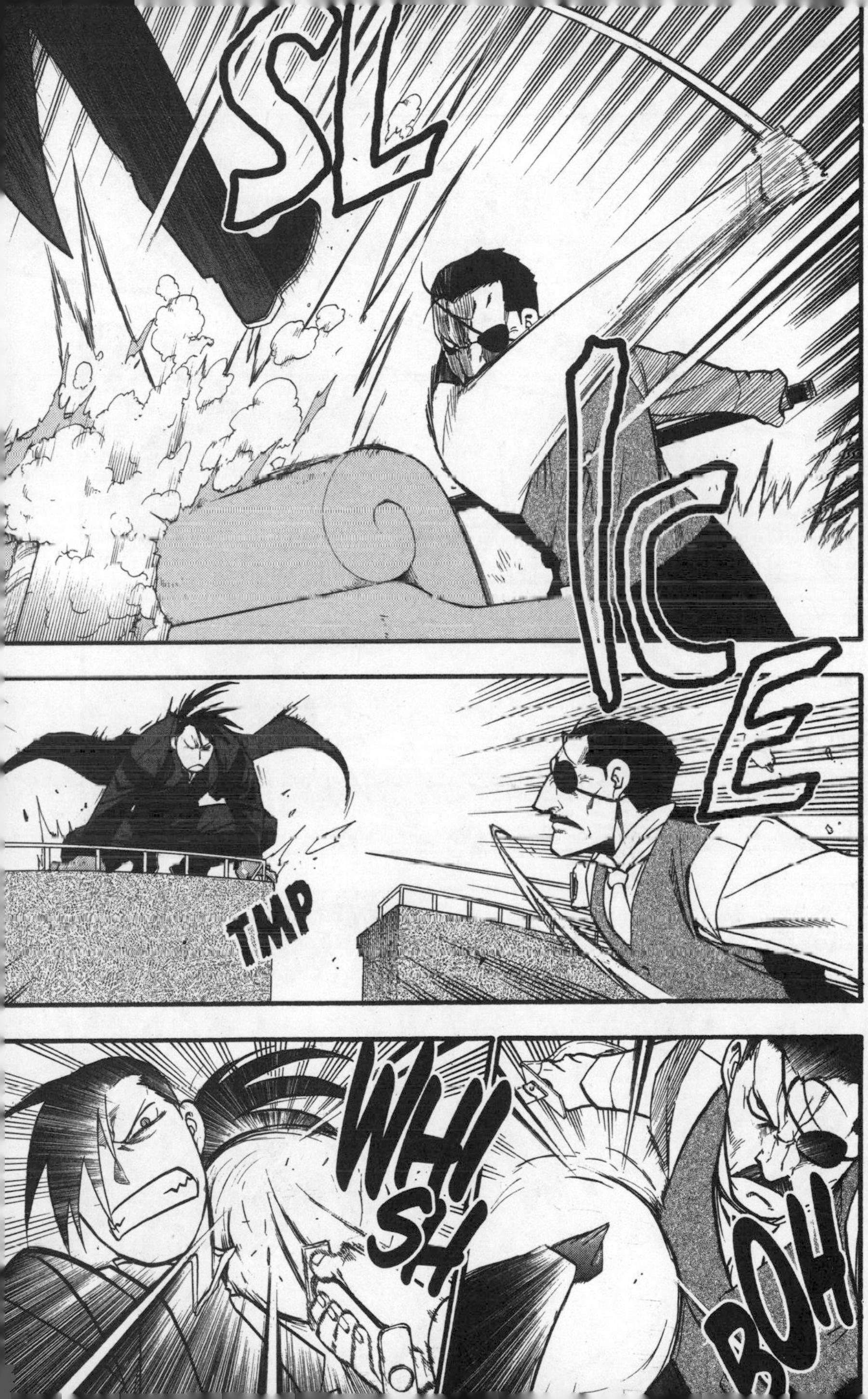
SLICE
TMP
BOH
WHISH

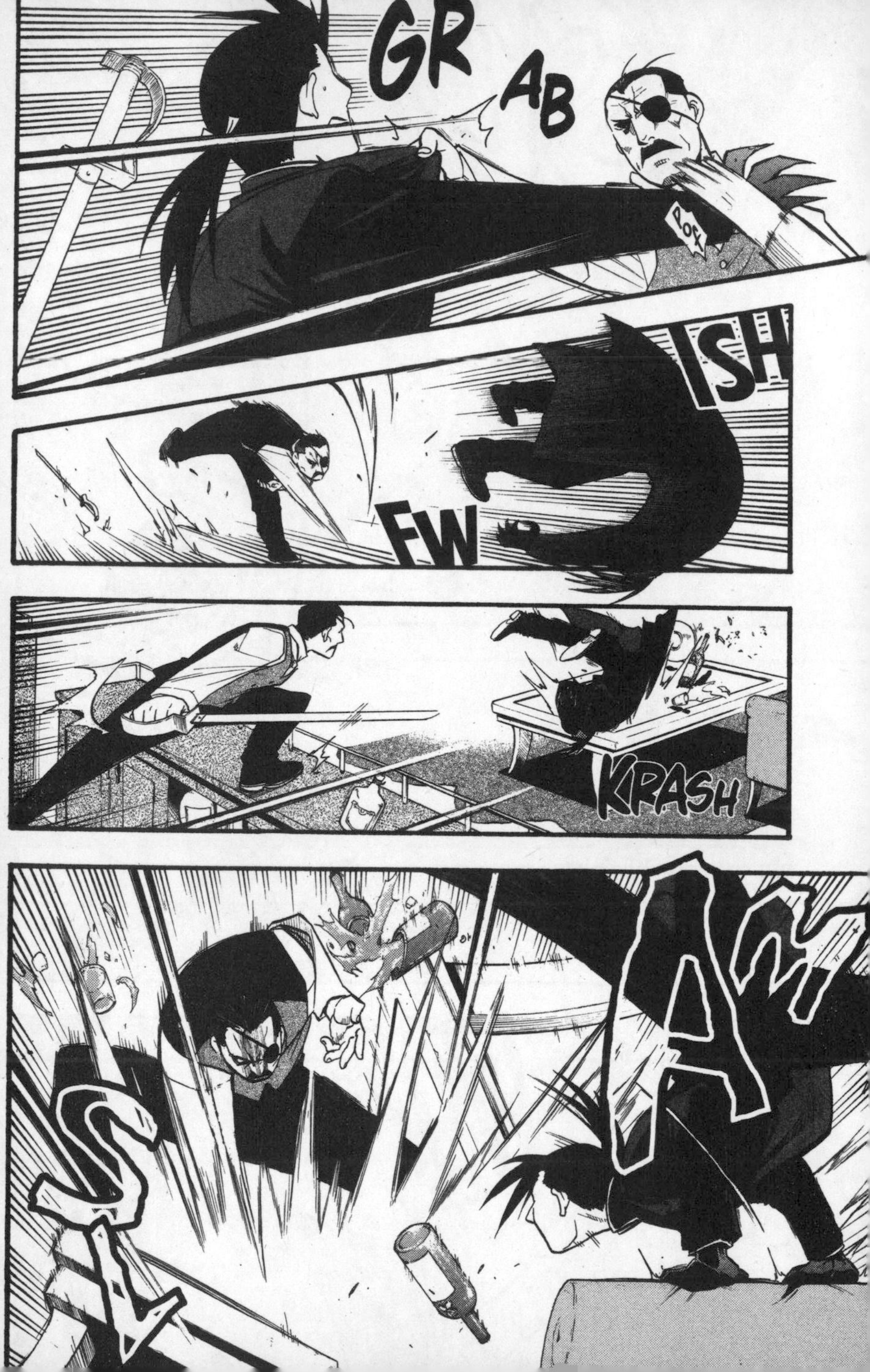
GRAB
POK
FWISH
KRASH

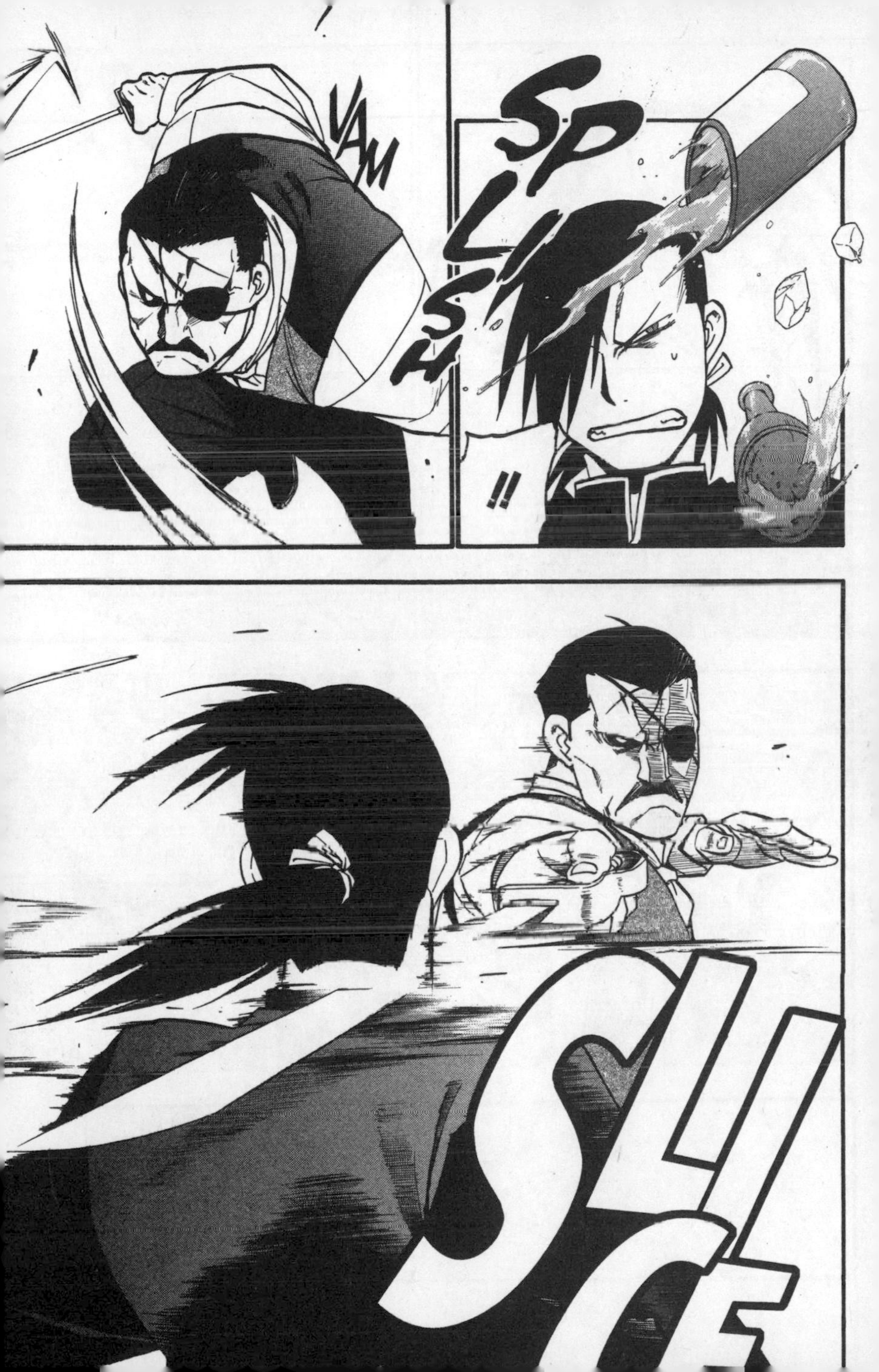
SPLISH
!!
VAM
SLICE

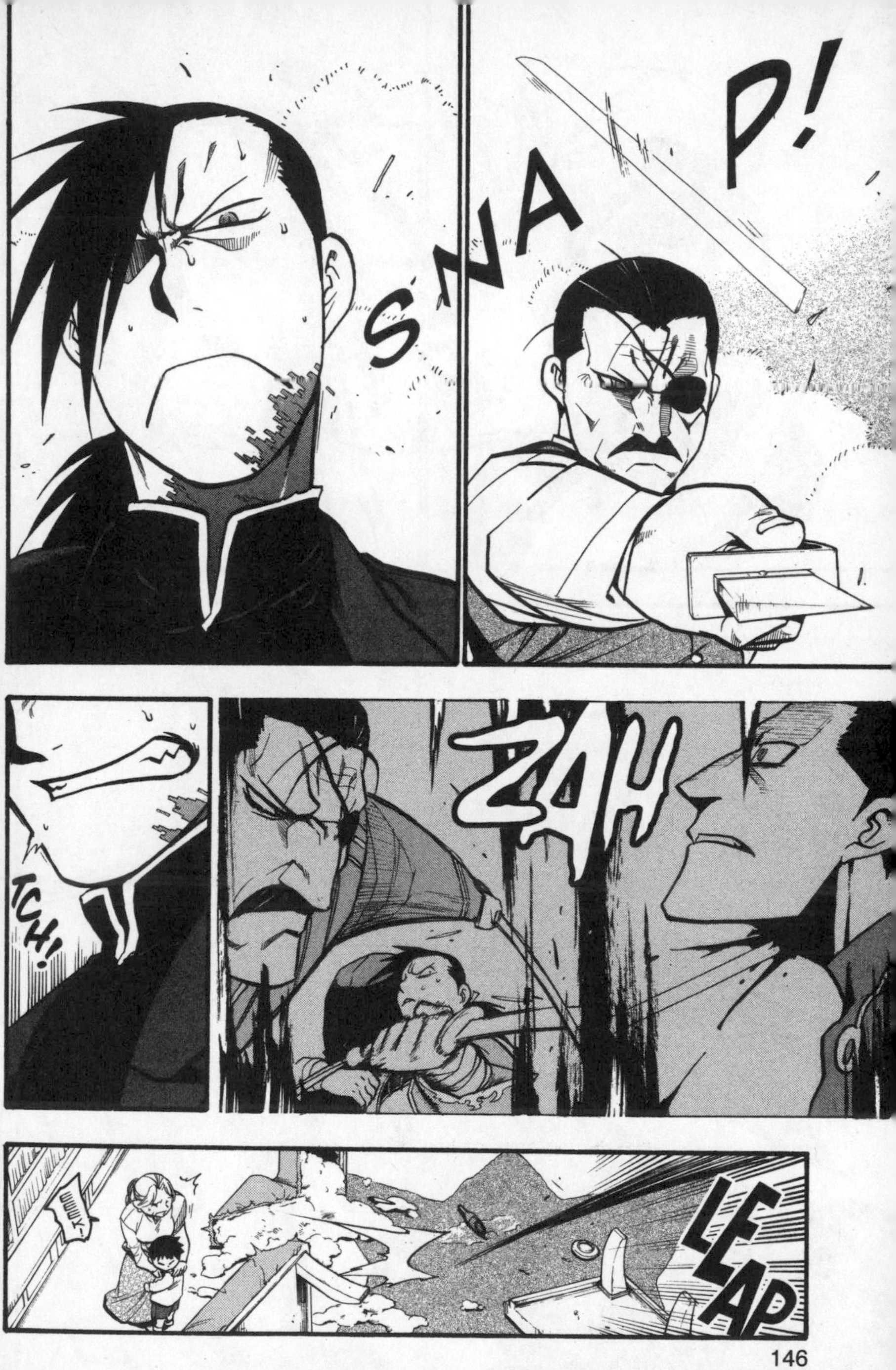
SNAP!
ZAH
TCH!
LEAP
EEEEK!

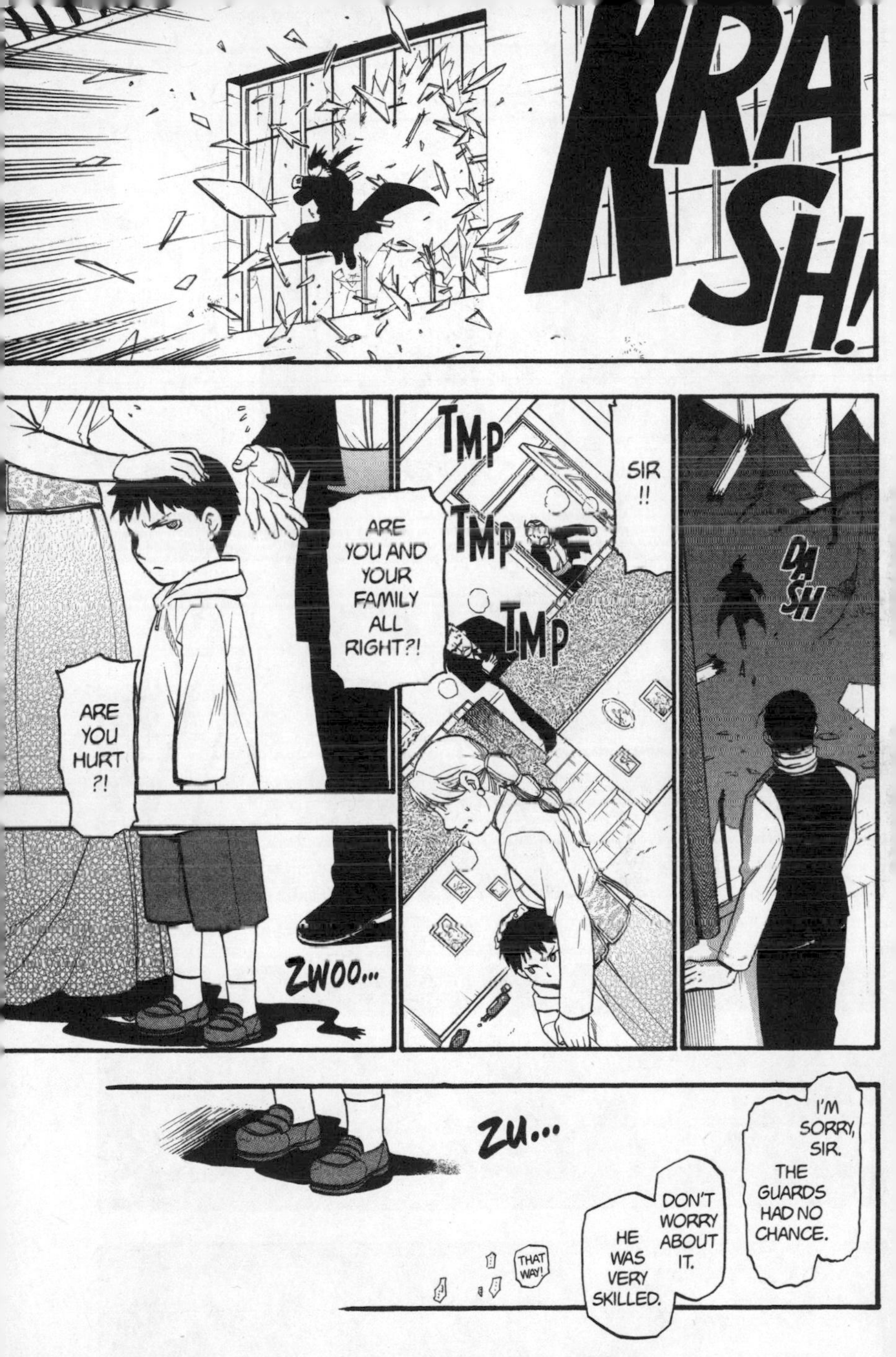
KRAASH!
DASH
SIR!!
TMP
TMP
TMP
ARE YOU AND YOUR FAMILY ALL RIGHT?!
ARE YOU HURT?!
ZWOO...
I'M SORRY, SIR. THE GUARDS HAD NO CHANCE.
DON'T WORRY ABOUT IT. HE WAS VERY SKILLED.
THAT WAY!
ZU...

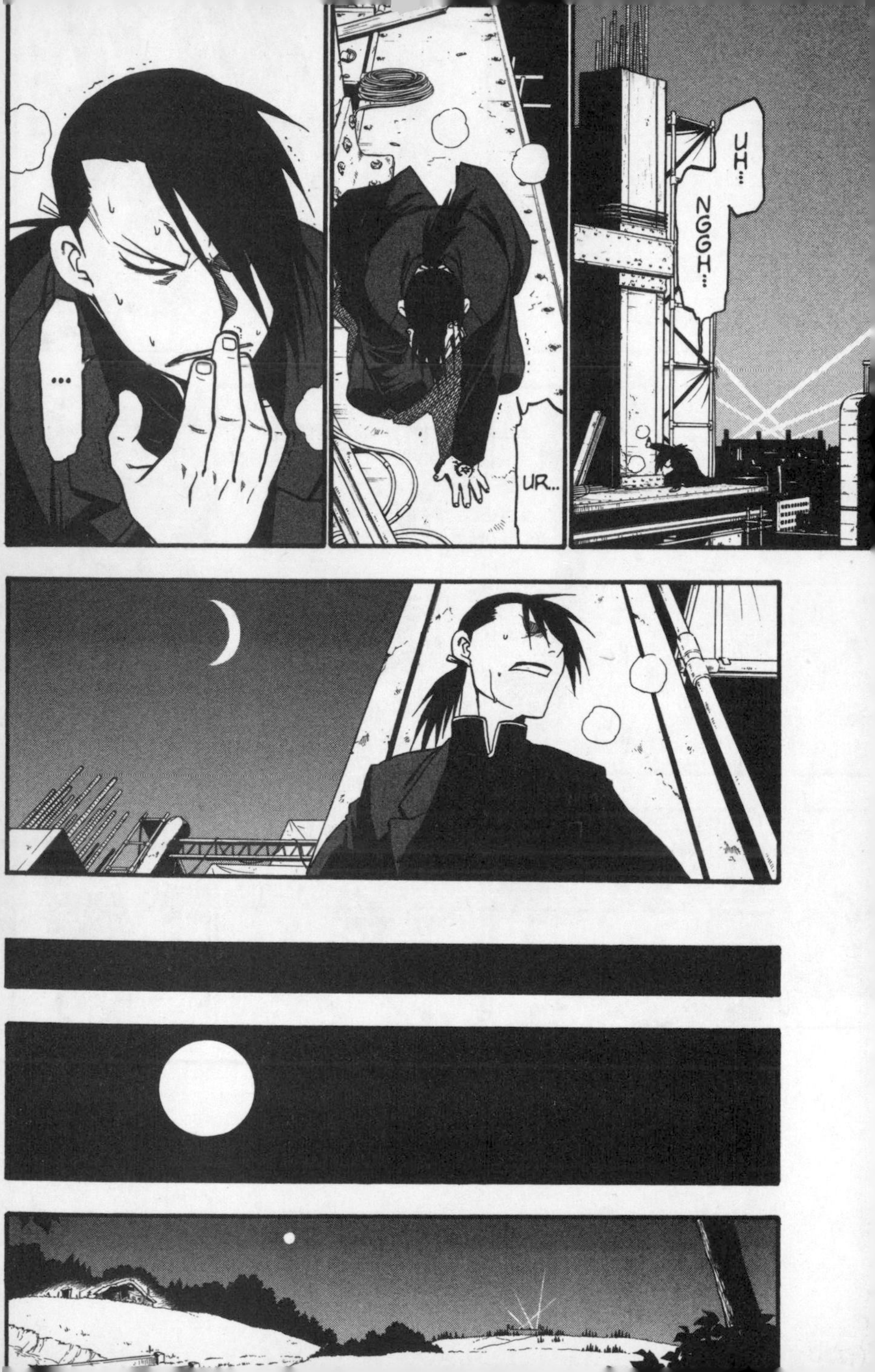
UH... NGGH...
UR...
...

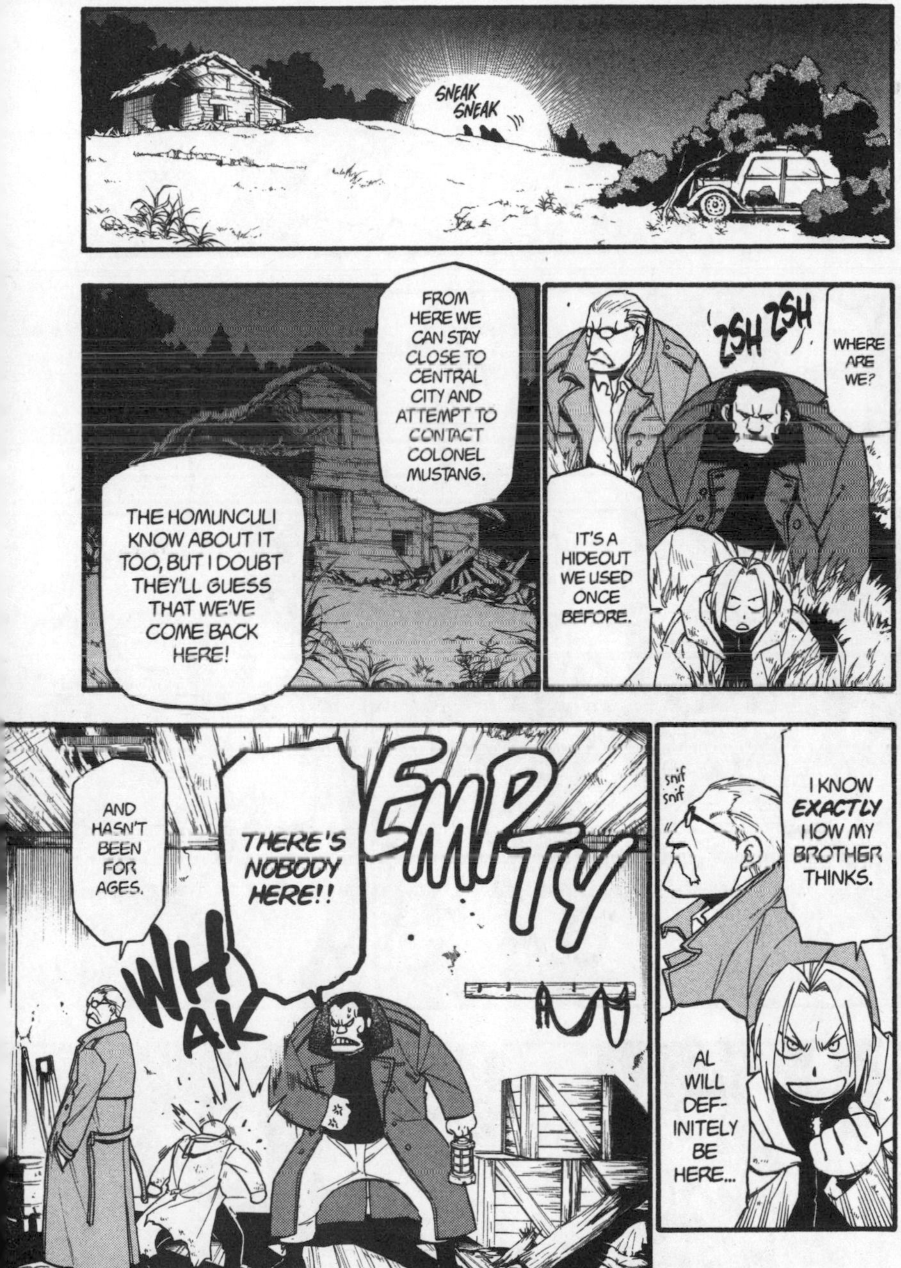
SNEAK SNEAK
WHERE ARE WE?
ZSH ZSH
IT'S A HIDEOUT WE USED ONCE BEFORE.
FROM HERE WE CAN STAY CLOSE TO CENTRAL CITY AND ATTEMPT TO CONTACT COLONEL MUSTANG.
THE HOMUNCULI KNOW ABOUT IT TOO, BUT I DOUBT THEY'LL GUESS THAT WE'VE COME BACK HERE!
snif snif
I KNOW *EXACTLY* HOW MY BROTHER THINKS.
AL WILL DEF-INITELY BE HERE...
EMPTY
THERE'S NOBODY HERE!!
AND HASN'T BEEN FOR AGES.
WHAK

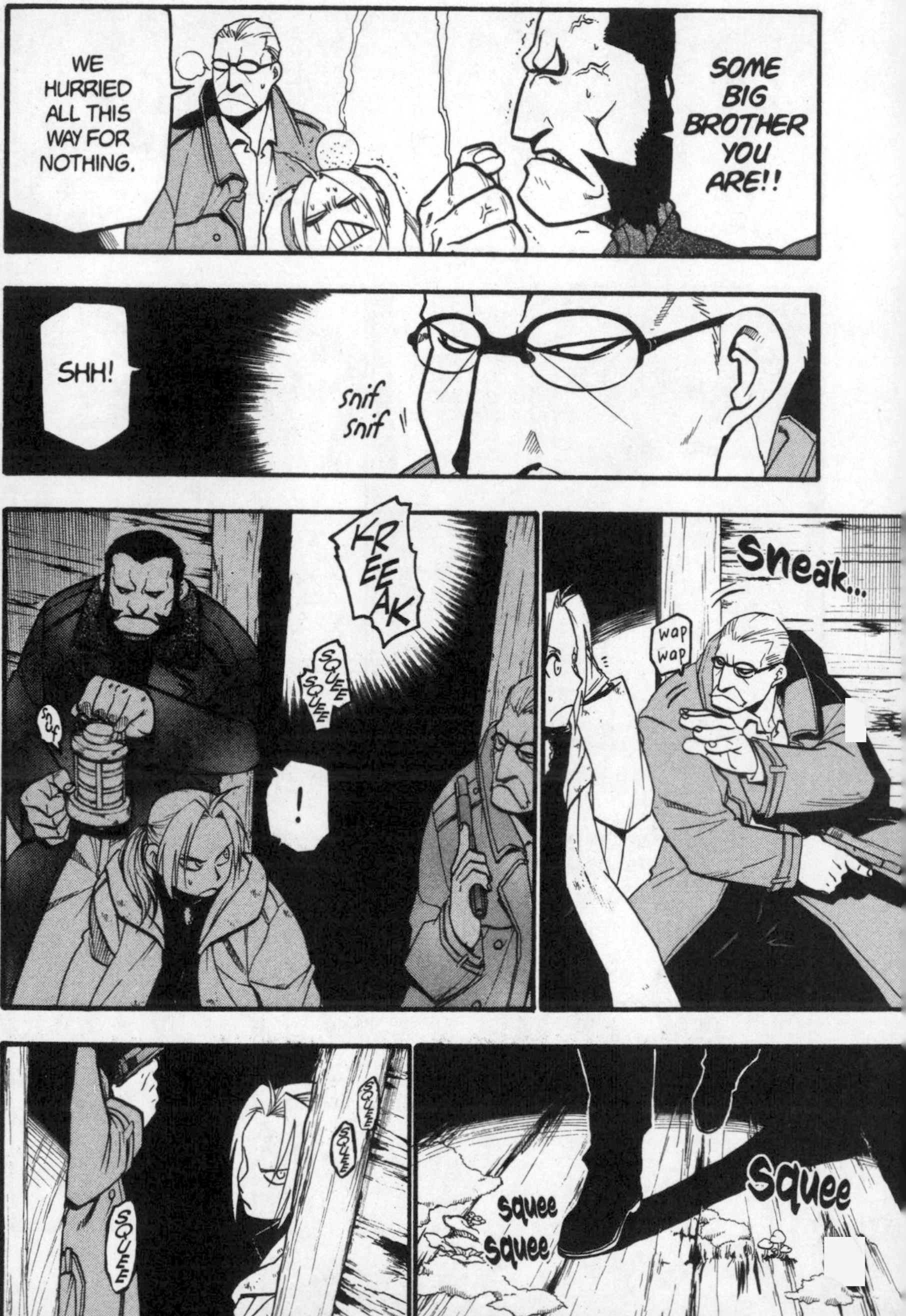
SOME BIG BROTHER YOU ARE!!
WE HURRIED ALL THIS WAY FOR NOTHING.
snif snif
SHH!
Sneak...
wap wap
KREEEAK
SQUEE SQUEE
snif
!
squee
squee squee
SQUEE SQUEE
SQUEE

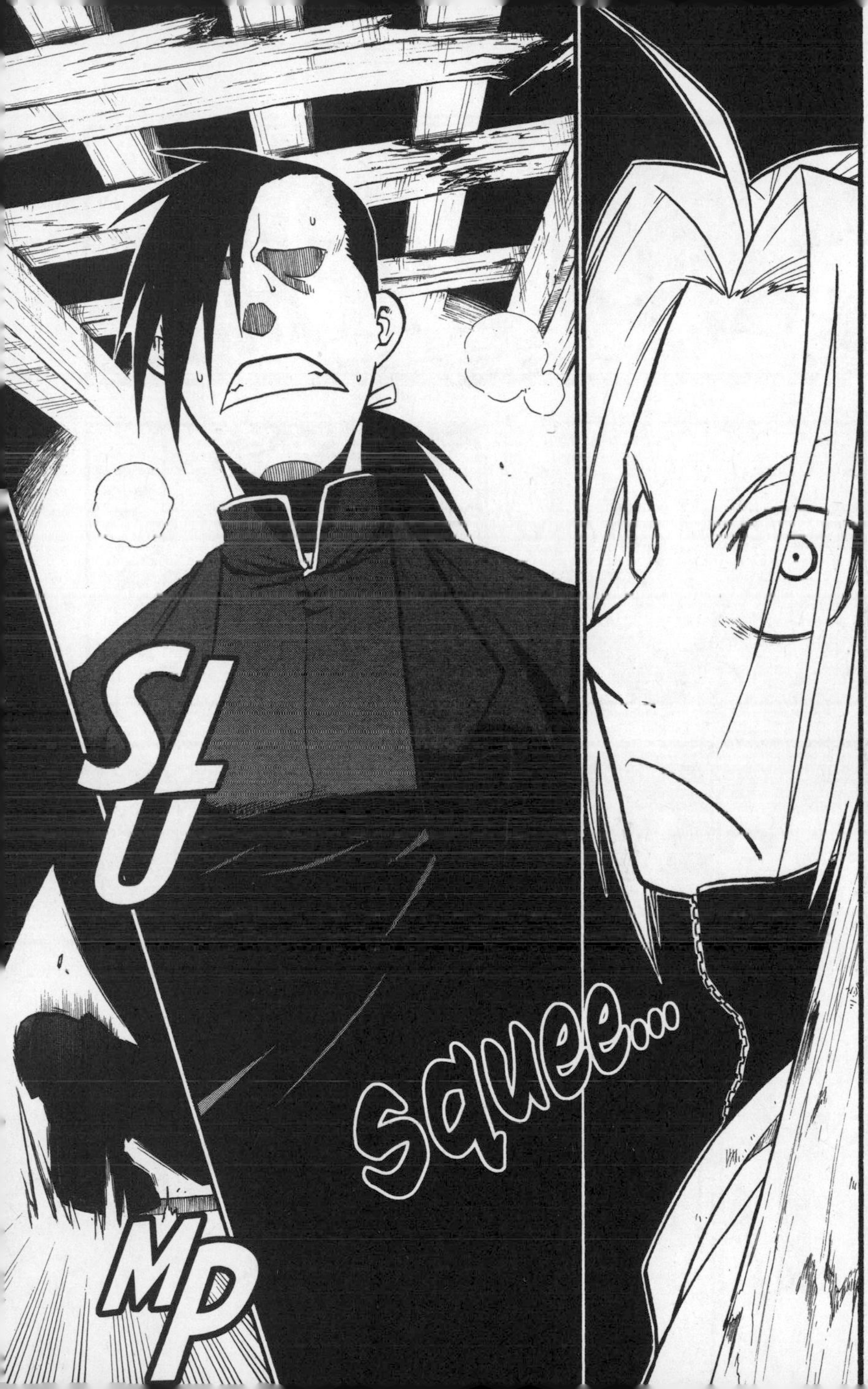
squee...
SLUMP

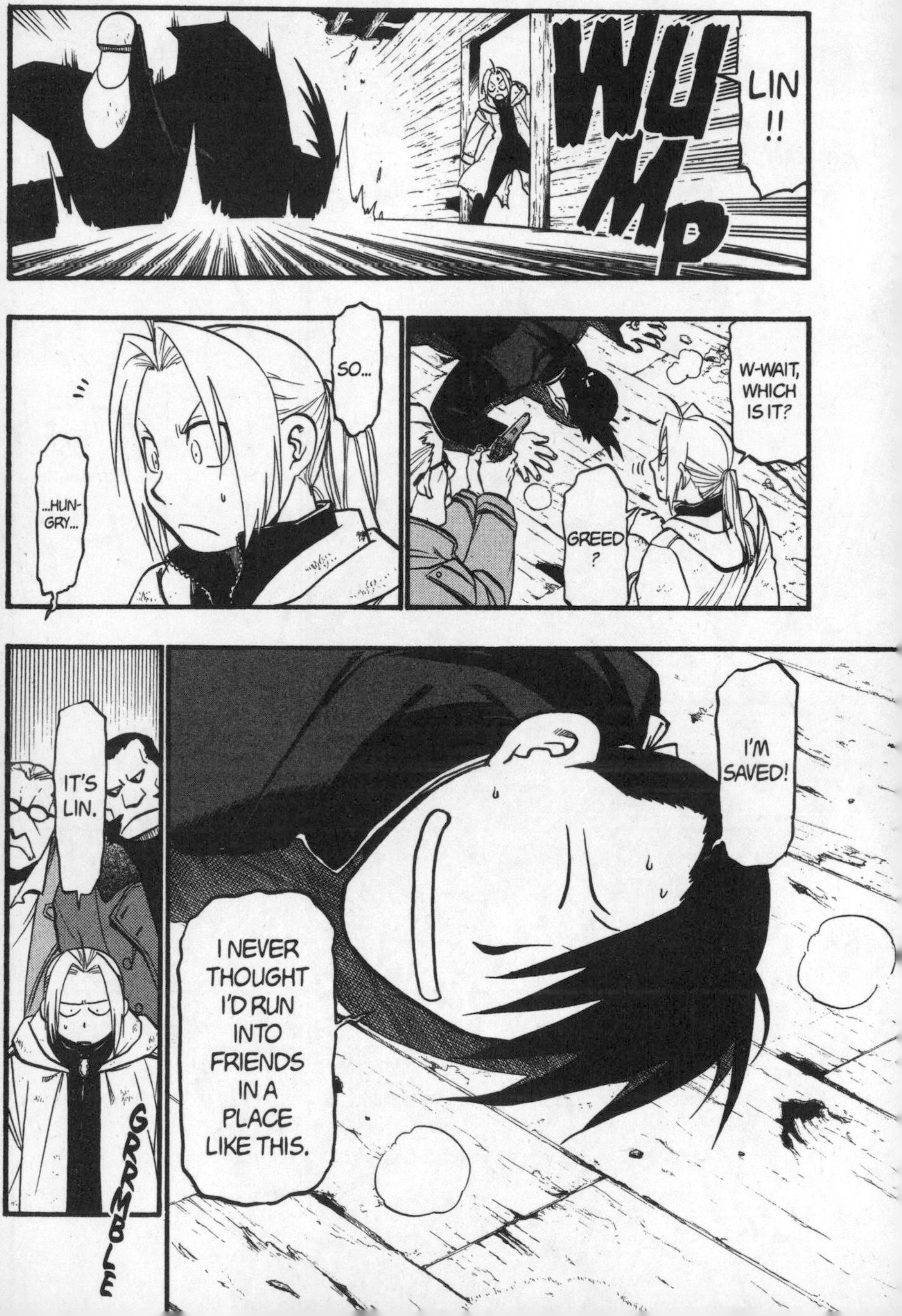
LIN !!
WUMP
W-WAIT, WHICH IS IT?
GREED ?
SO...
...HUN-GRY...
I'M SAVED!
I NEVER THOUGHT I'D RUN INTO FRIENDS IN A PLACE LIKE THIS.
IT'S LIN.
GRRMBLE

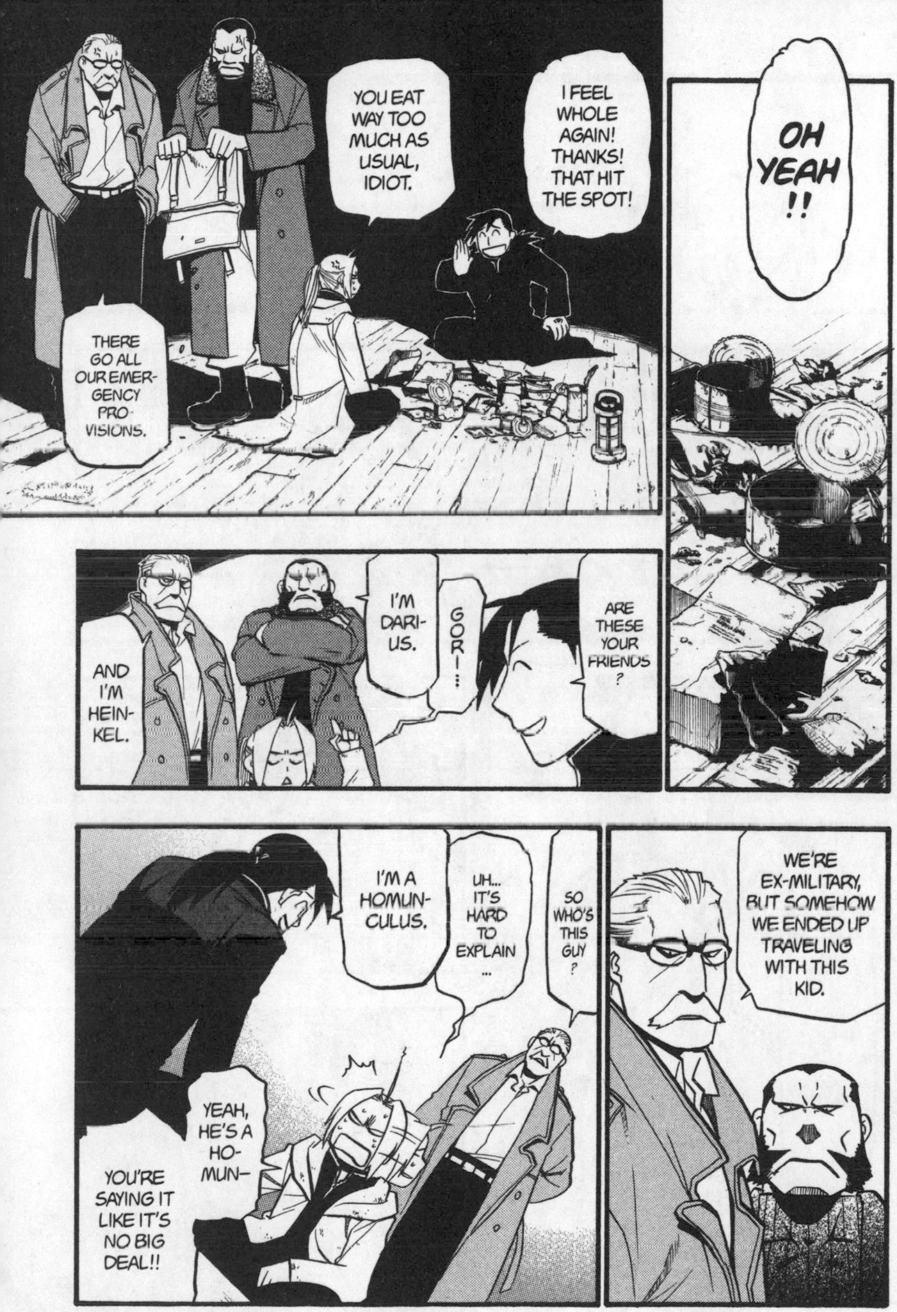
OH YEAH!!
I FEEL WHOLE AGAIN! THANKS! THAT HIT THE SPOT!
YOU EAT WAY TOO MUCH AS USUAL, IDIOT.
THERE GO ALL OUR EMERGENCY PROVISIONS.
ARE THESE YOUR FRIENDS?
GORI...
I'M DARIUS.
AND I'M HEINKEL.
WE'RE EX-MILITARY, BUT SOMEHOW WE ENDED UP TRAVELING WITH THIS KID.
SO WHO'S THIS GUY?
UH... IT'S HARD TO EXPLAIN...
I'M A HOMUNCULUS.
YEAH, HE'S A HOMUN-
YOU'RE SAYING IT LIKE IT'S NO BIG DEAL!!

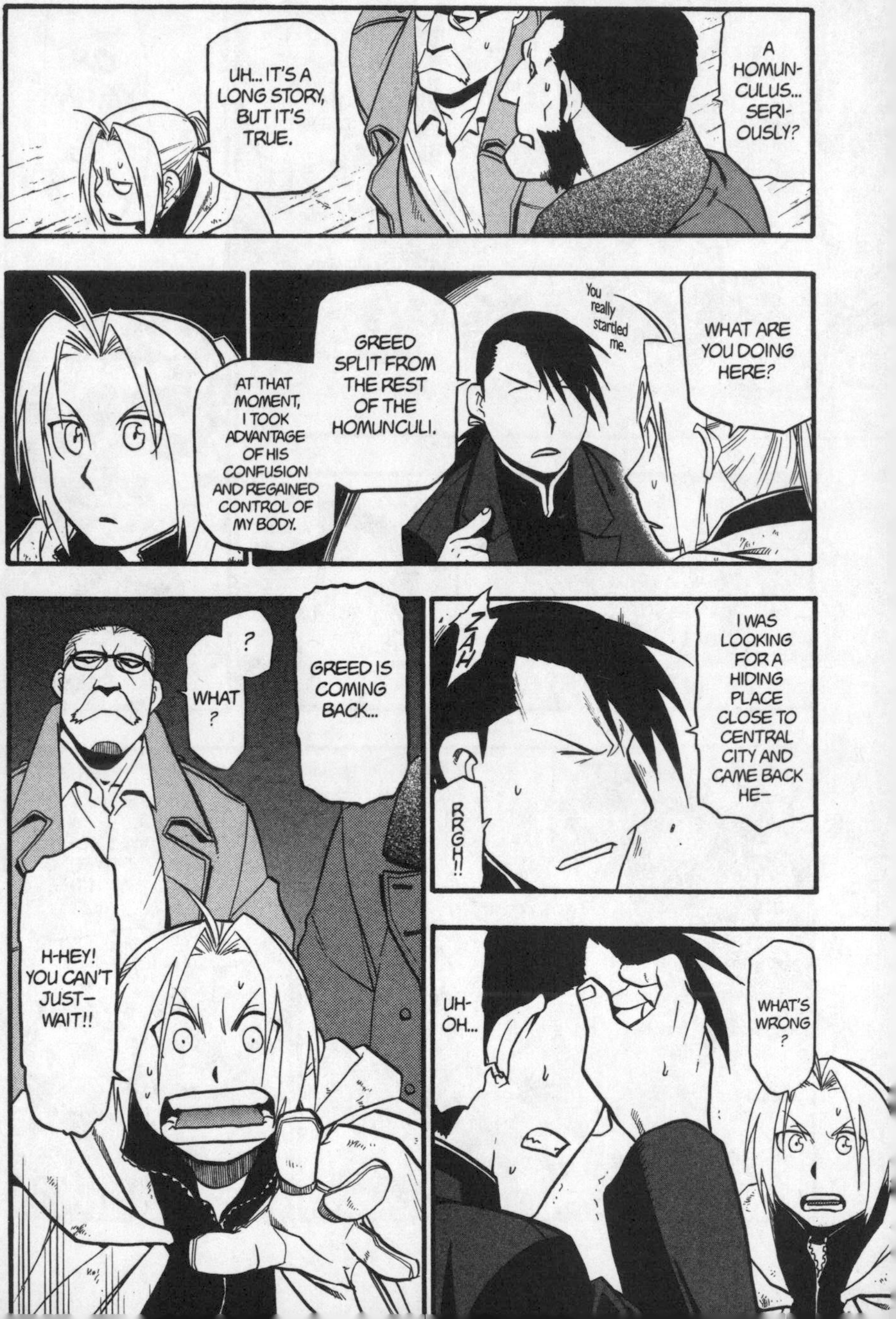
A HOMUNCULUS... SERIOUSLY?
UH... IT'S A LONG STORY, BUT IT'S TRUE.
WHAT ARE YOU DOING HERE?
You really startled me.
GREED SPLIT FROM THE REST OF THE HOMUNCULI.
AT THAT MOMENT, I TOOK ADVANTAGE OF HIS CONFUSION AND REGAINED CONTROL OF MY BODY.
I WAS LOOKING FOR A HIDING PLACE CLOSE TO CENTRAL CITY AND CAME BACK HE—
ZAH
RRGH!!
WHAT'S WRONG?
UH-OH...
GREED IS COMING BACK...
WHAT?
?
H-HEY! YOU CAN'T JUST— WAIT!!

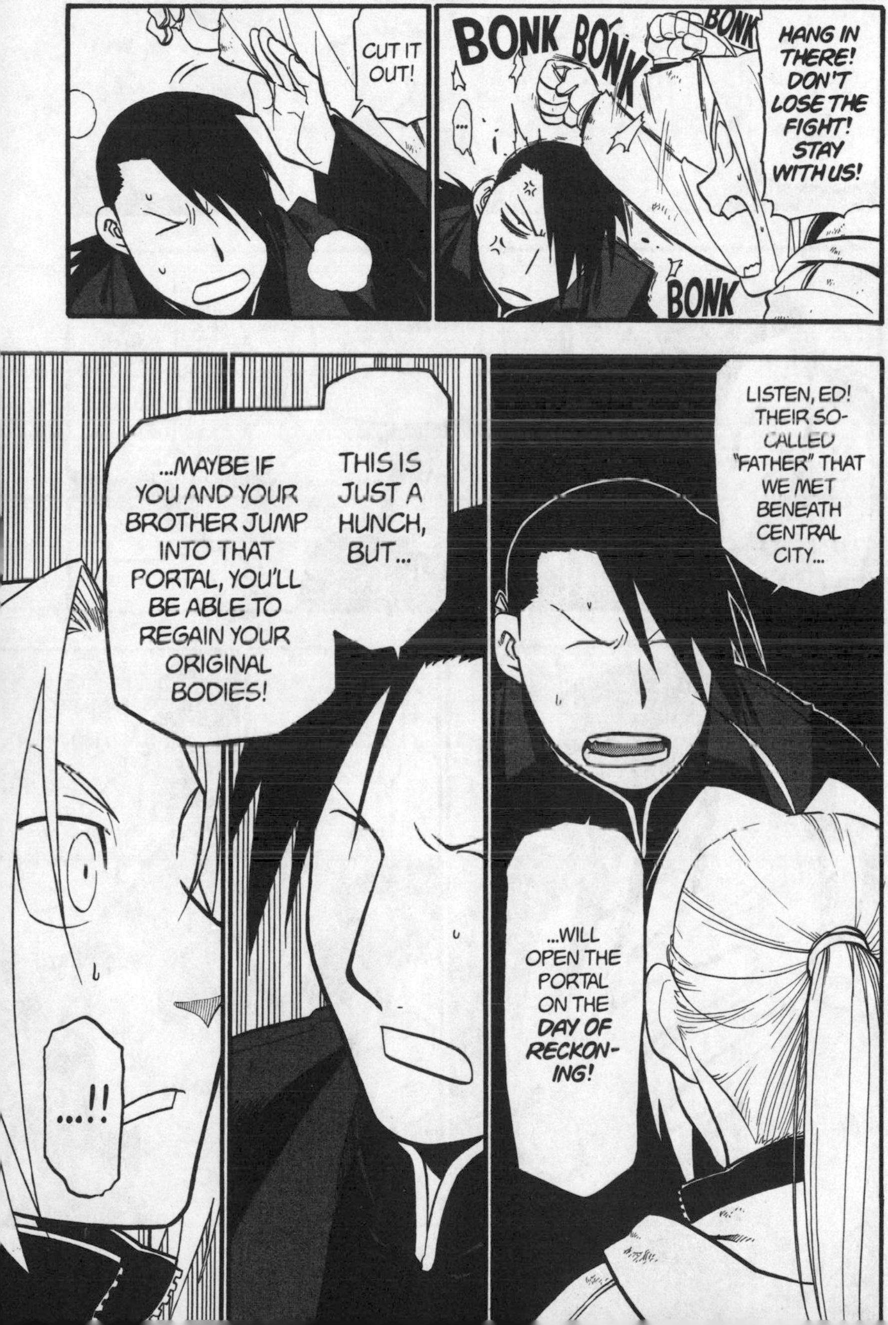
BONK
HANG IN THERE! DON'T LOSE THE FIGHT! STAY WITH US!
BONK BONK
...
BONK
CUT IT OUT!
LISTEN, ED! THEIR SO-CALLED "FATHER" THAT WE MET BENEATH CENTRAL CITY...
...WILL OPEN THE PORTAL ON THE DAY OF RECKONING!
THIS IS JUST A HUNCH, BUT...
...MAYBE IF YOU AND YOUR BROTHER JUMP INTO THAT PORTAL, YOU'LL BE ABLE TO REGAIN YOUR ORIGINAL BODIES!
....!!

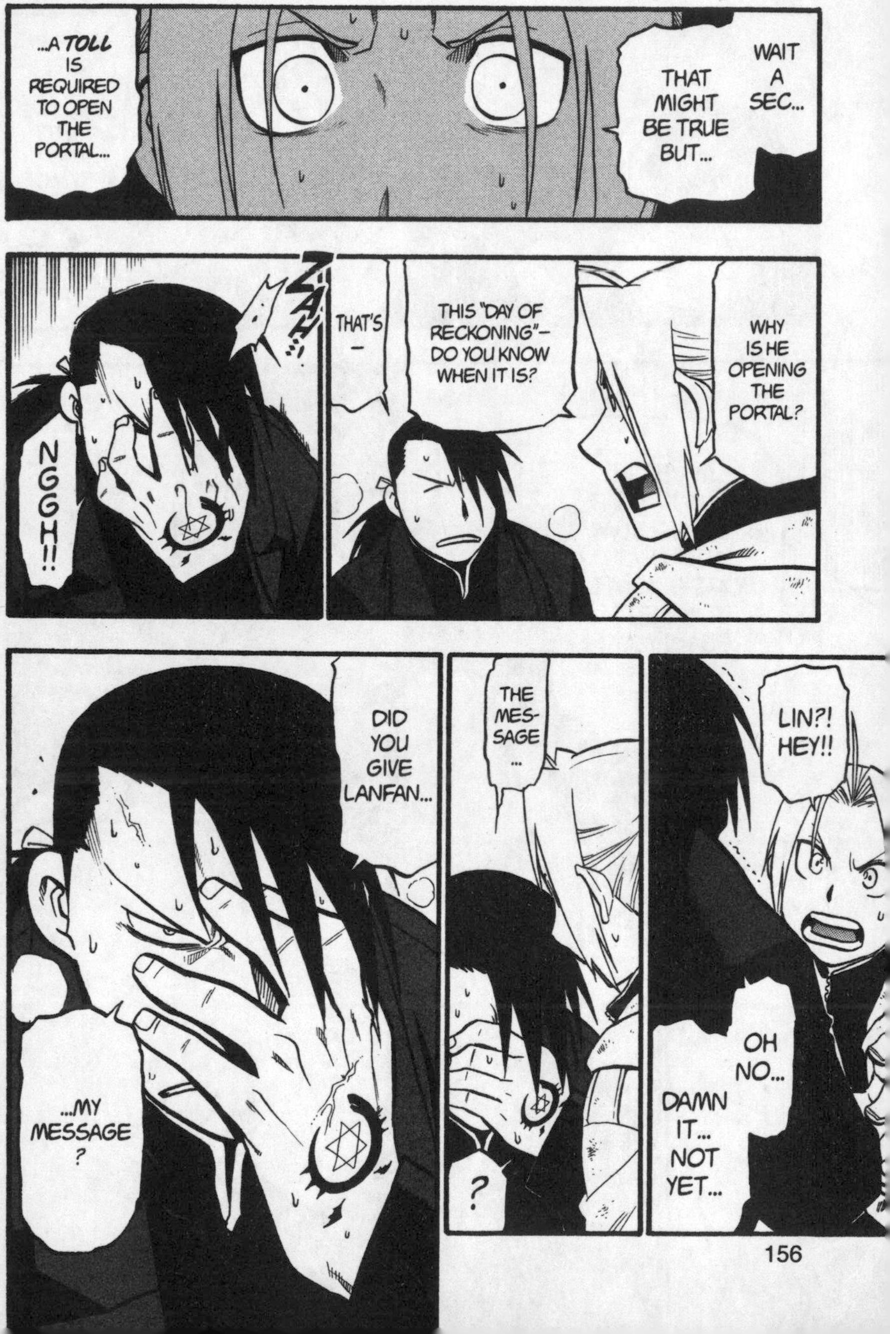
WAIT A SEC...
THAT MIGHT BE TRUE BUT...
...A TOLL IS REQUIRED TO OPEN THE PORTAL...
WHY IS HE OPENING THE PORTAL?
THIS "DAY OF RECKONING"—DO YOU KNOW WHEN IT IS?
THAT'S —
ZAH!!
NGGH!!
LIN?! HEY!!
OH NO...
DAMN IT... NOT YET...
THE MES-SAGE ...
?
DID YOU GIVE LANFAN...
...MY MESSAGE ?

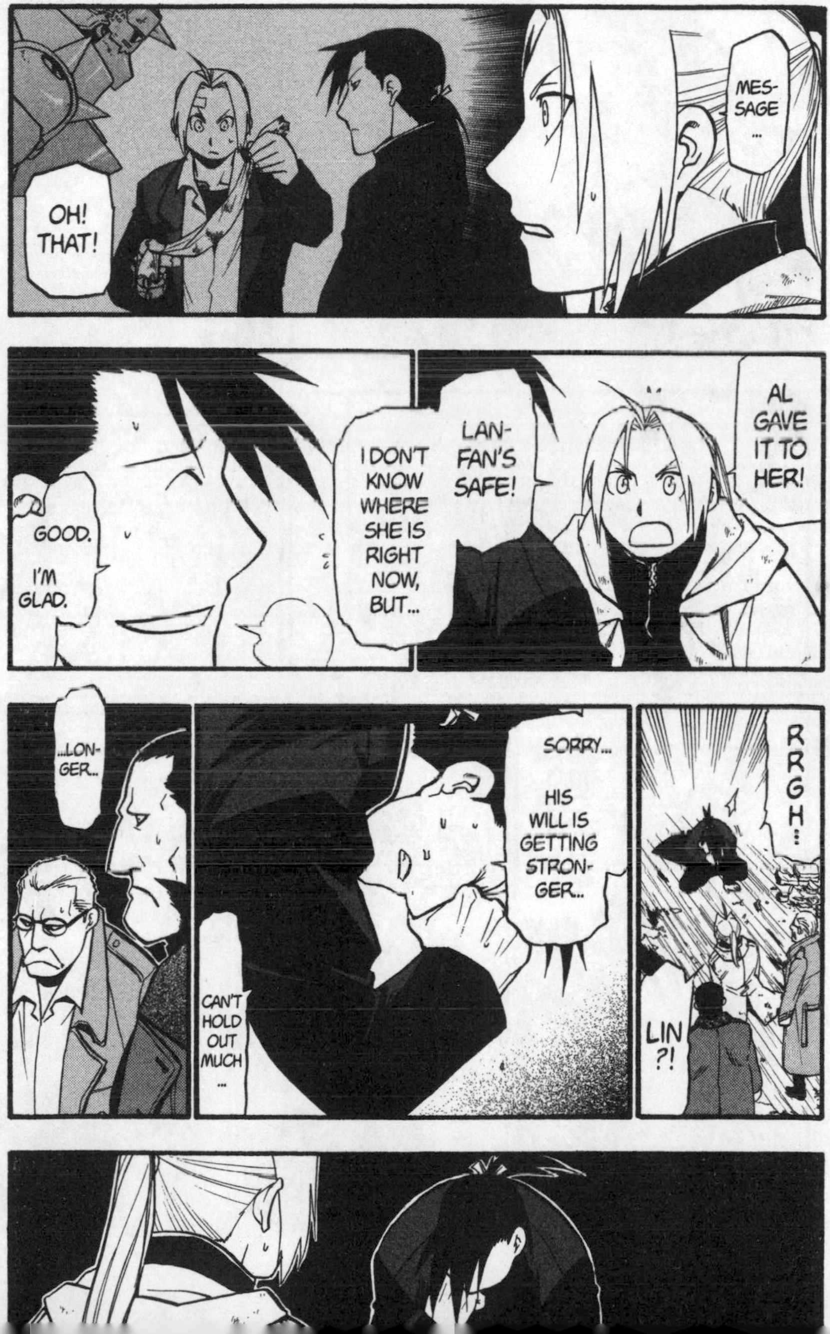
MES-SAGE ...
OH! THAT!
AL GAVE IT TO HER!
LAN-FAN'S SAFE!
I DON'T KNOW WHERE SHE IS RIGHT NOW, BUT...
GOOD.
I'M GLAD.
RRGH!!
LIN?!
SORRY...
HIS WILL IS GETTING STRON-GER...
CAN'T HOLD OUT MUCH ...
...LON-GER...

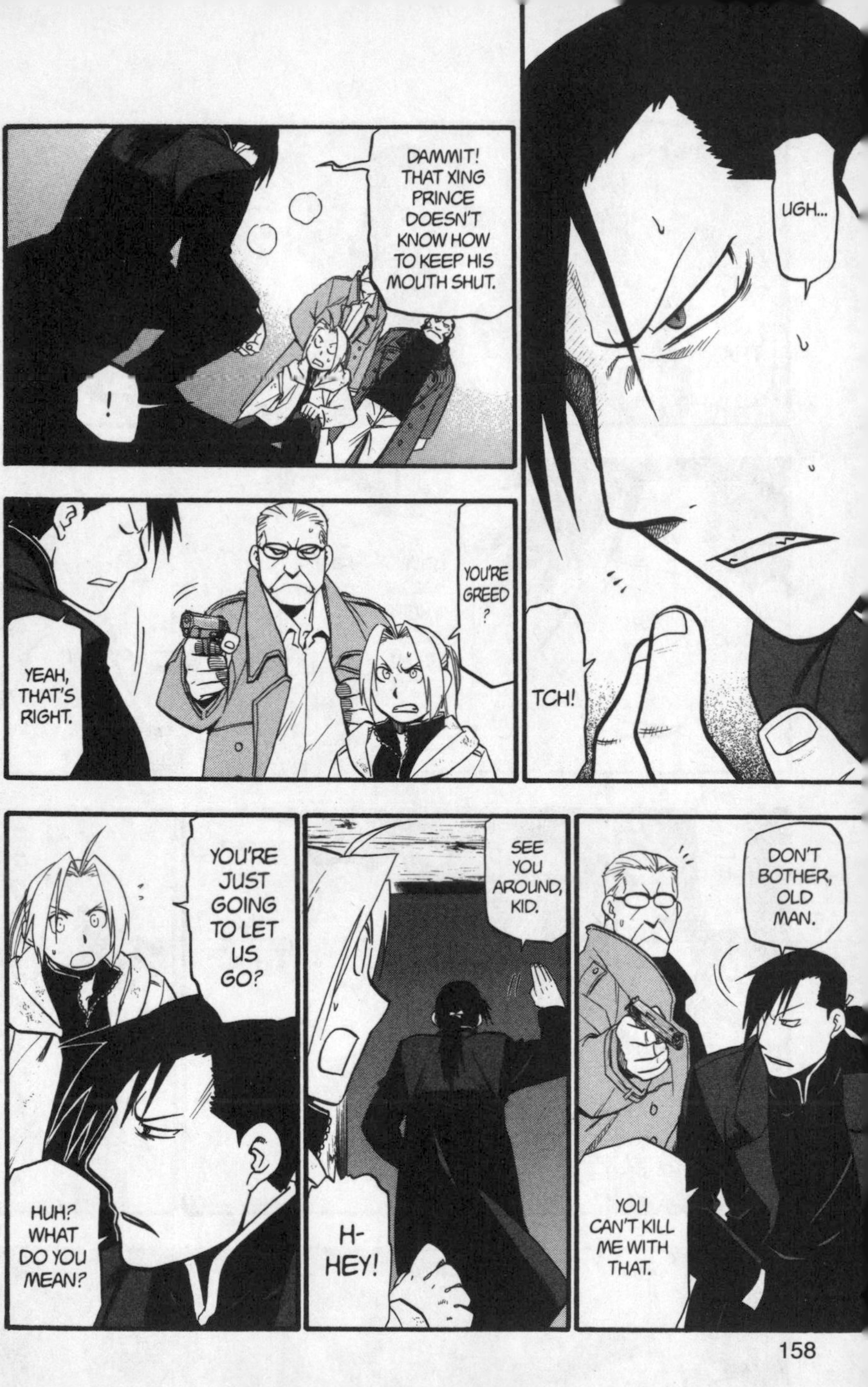
UGH...
TCH!
DAMMIT! THAT XING PRINCE DOESN'T KNOW HOW TO KEEP HIS MOUTH SHUT.
!
YOU'RE GREED?
YEAH, THAT'S RIGHT.
DON'T BOTHER, OLD MAN.
YOU CAN'T KILL ME WITH THAT.
SEE YOU AROUND, KID.
H- HEY!
YOU'RE JUST GOING TO LET US GO?
HUH? WHAT DO YOU MEAN?

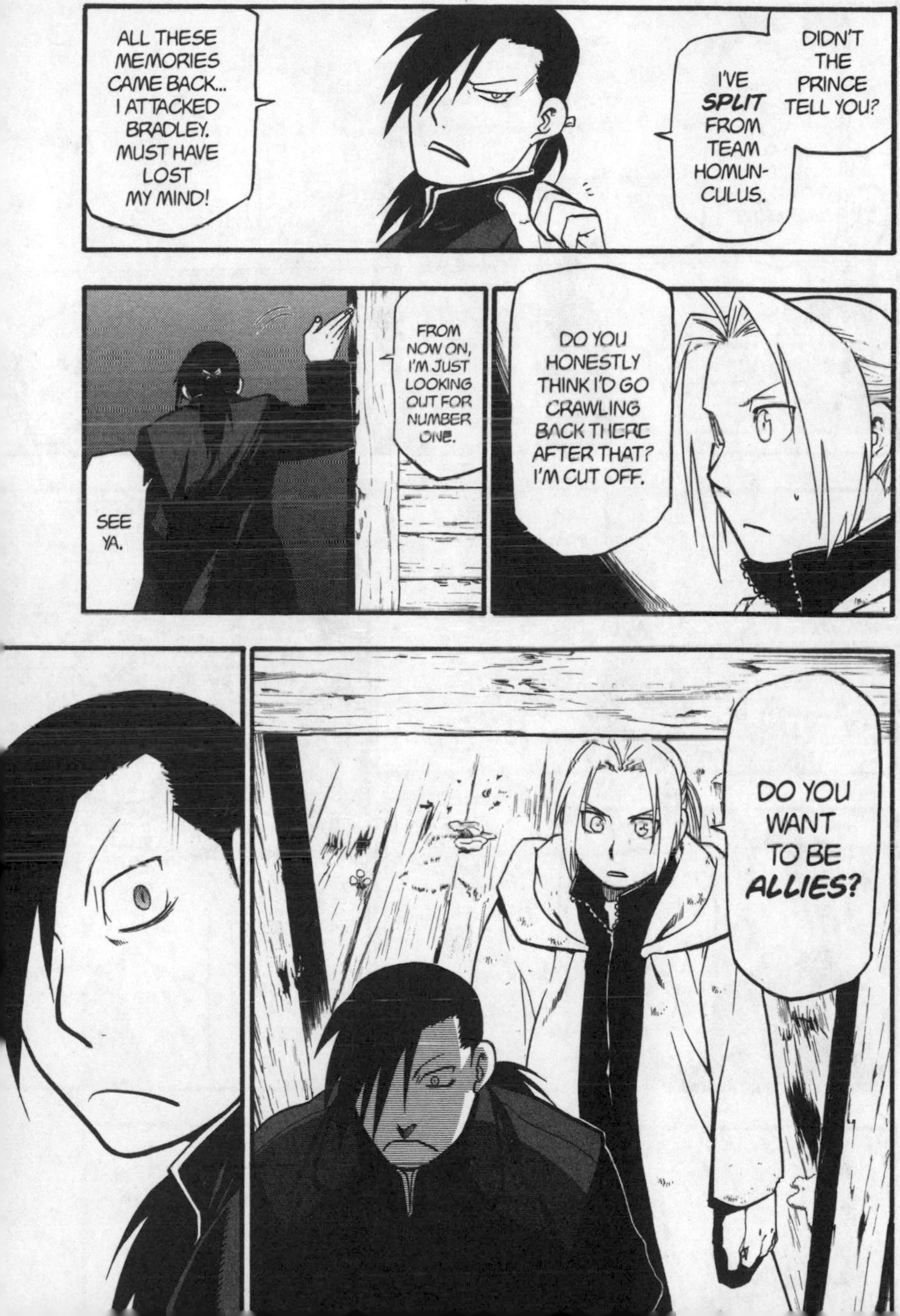
DIDN'T THE PRINCE TELL YOU?
I'VE **SPLIT** FROM TEAM HOMUN-CULUS.
ALL THESE MEMORIES CAME BACK... I ATTACKED BRADLEY. MUST HAVE LOST MY MIND!
DO YOU HONESTLY THINK I'D GO CRAWLING BACK THERE AFTER THAT? I'M CUT OFF.
FROM NOW ON, I'M JUST LOOKING OUT FOR NUMBER ONE.
SEE YA.
DO YOU WANT TO BE **ALLIES?**

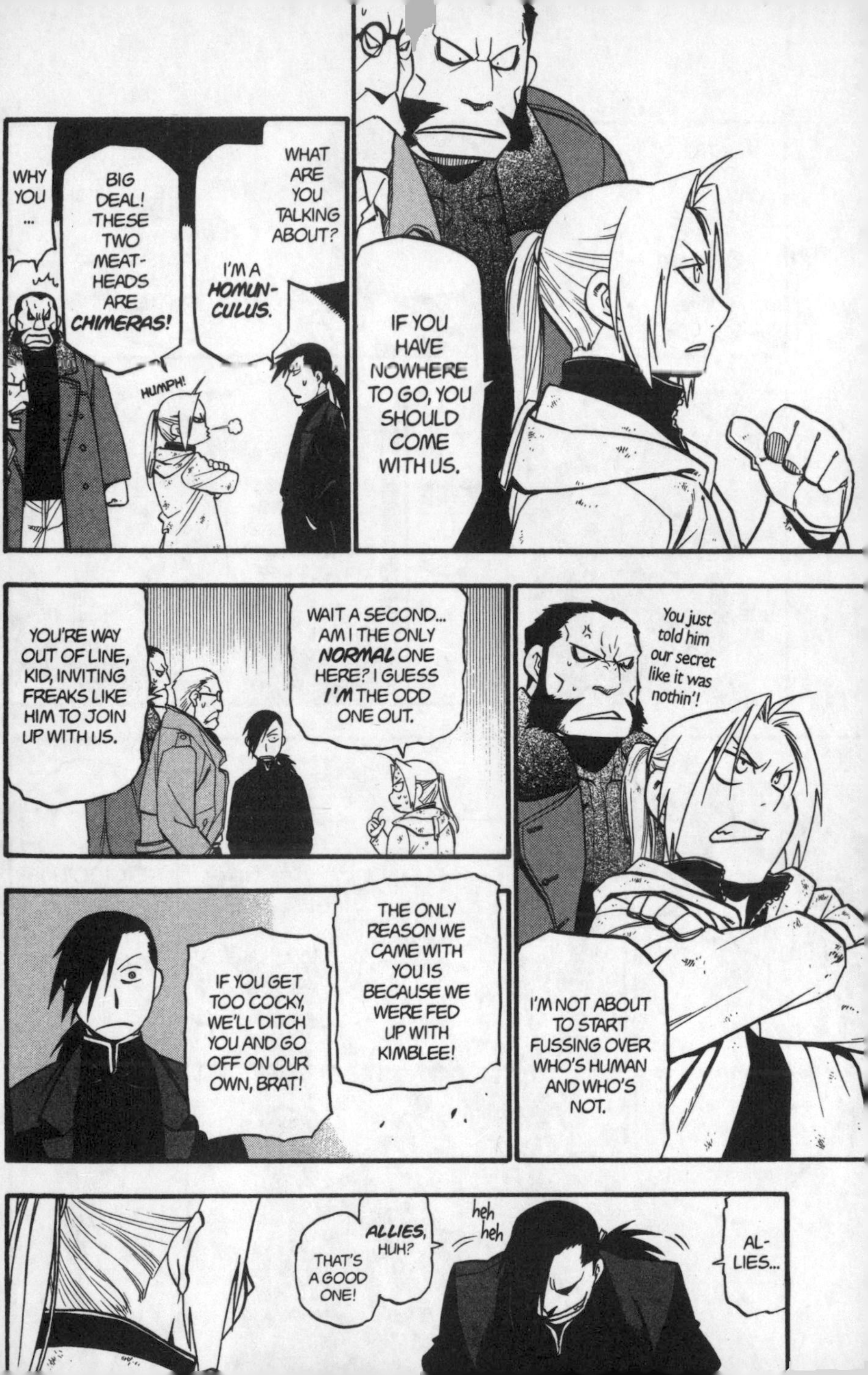
IF YOU HAVE NOWHERE TO GO, YOU SHOULD COME WITH US.
WHAT ARE YOU TALKING ABOUT?
I'M A HOMUNCULUS.
BIG DEAL! THESE TWO MEATHEADS ARE CHIMERAS!
HUMPH!
WHY YOU ...
You just told him our secret like it was nothin'!
I'M NOT ABOUT TO START FUSSING OVER WHO'S HUMAN AND WHO'S NOT.
WAIT A SECOND... AM I THE ONLY NORMAL ONE HERE? I GUESS I'M THE ODD ONE OUT.
YOU'RE WAY OUT OF LINE, KID, INVITING FREAKS LIKE HIM TO JOIN UP WITH US.
THE ONLY REASON WE CAME WITH YOU IS BECAUSE WE WERE FED UP WITH KIMBLEE!
IF YOU GET TOO COCKY, WE'LL DITCH YOU AND GO OFF ON OUR OWN, BRAT!
AL-LIES...
heh heh
ALLIES, HUH? THAT'S A GOOD ONE!

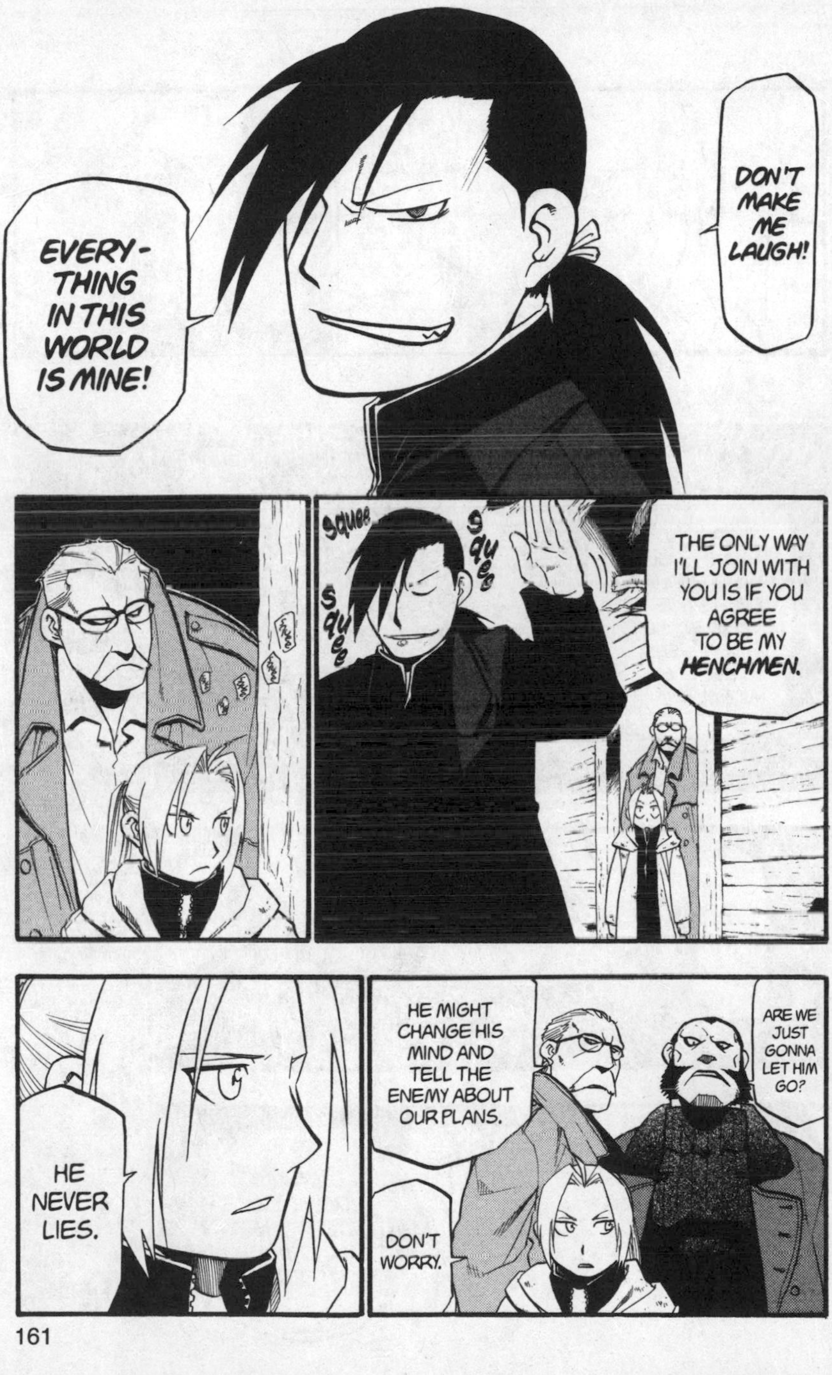
DON'T MAKE ME LAUGH!
EVERY-THING IN THIS WORLD IS MINE!
squee squee squee
THE ONLY WAY I'LL JOIN WITH YOU IS IF YOU AGREE TO BE MY **HENCHMEN.**
ARE WE JUST GONNA LET HIM GO?
HE MIGHT CHANGE HIS MIND AND TELL THE ENEMY ABOUT OUR PLANS.
DON'T WORRY.
HE NEVER LIES.

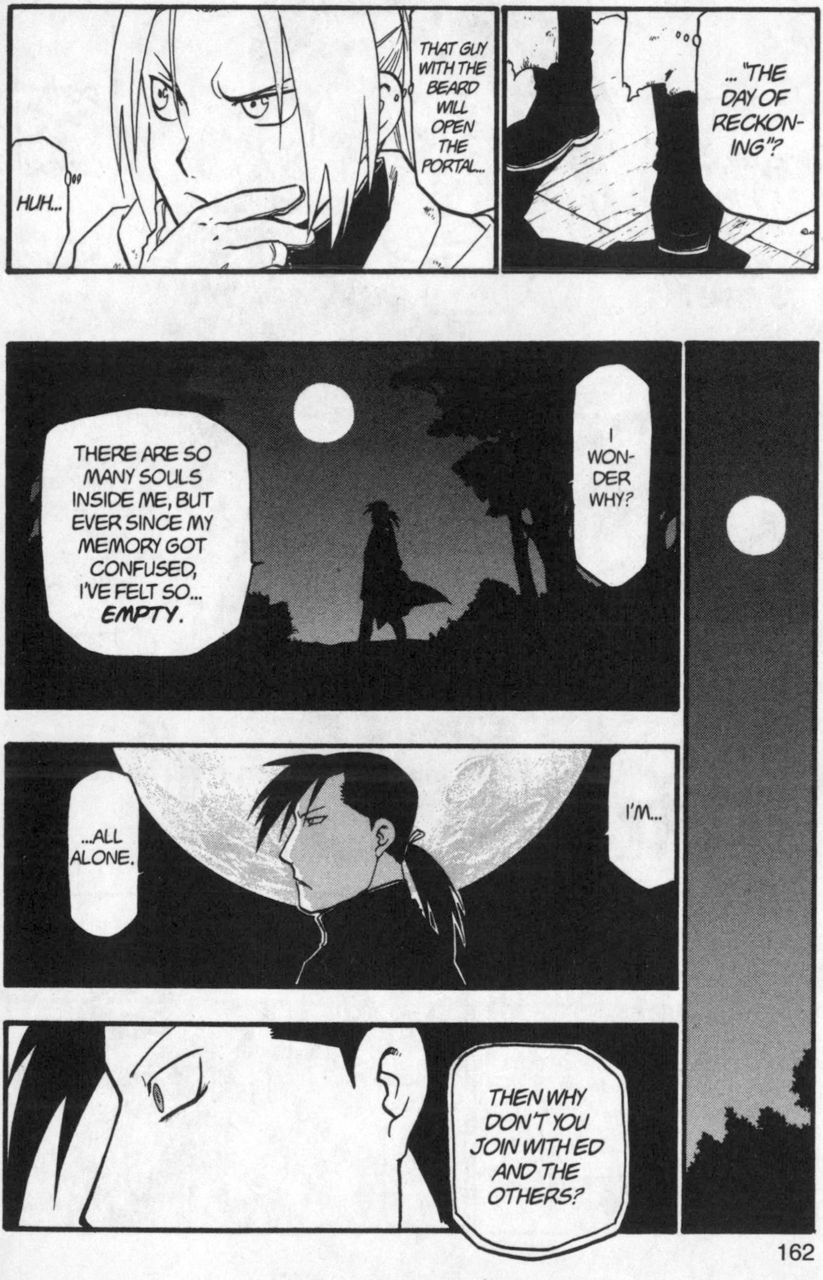
..."THE DAY OF RECKON-ING"?
THAT GUY WITH THE BEARD WILL OPEN THE PORTAL...
HUH...
I WON-DER WHY?
THERE ARE SO MANY SOULS INSIDE ME, BUT EVER SINCE MY MEMORY GOT CONFUSED, I'VE FELT SO... **EMPTY**.
I'M...
...ALL ALONE.
THEN WHY DON'T YOU JOIN WITH ED AND THE OTHERS?

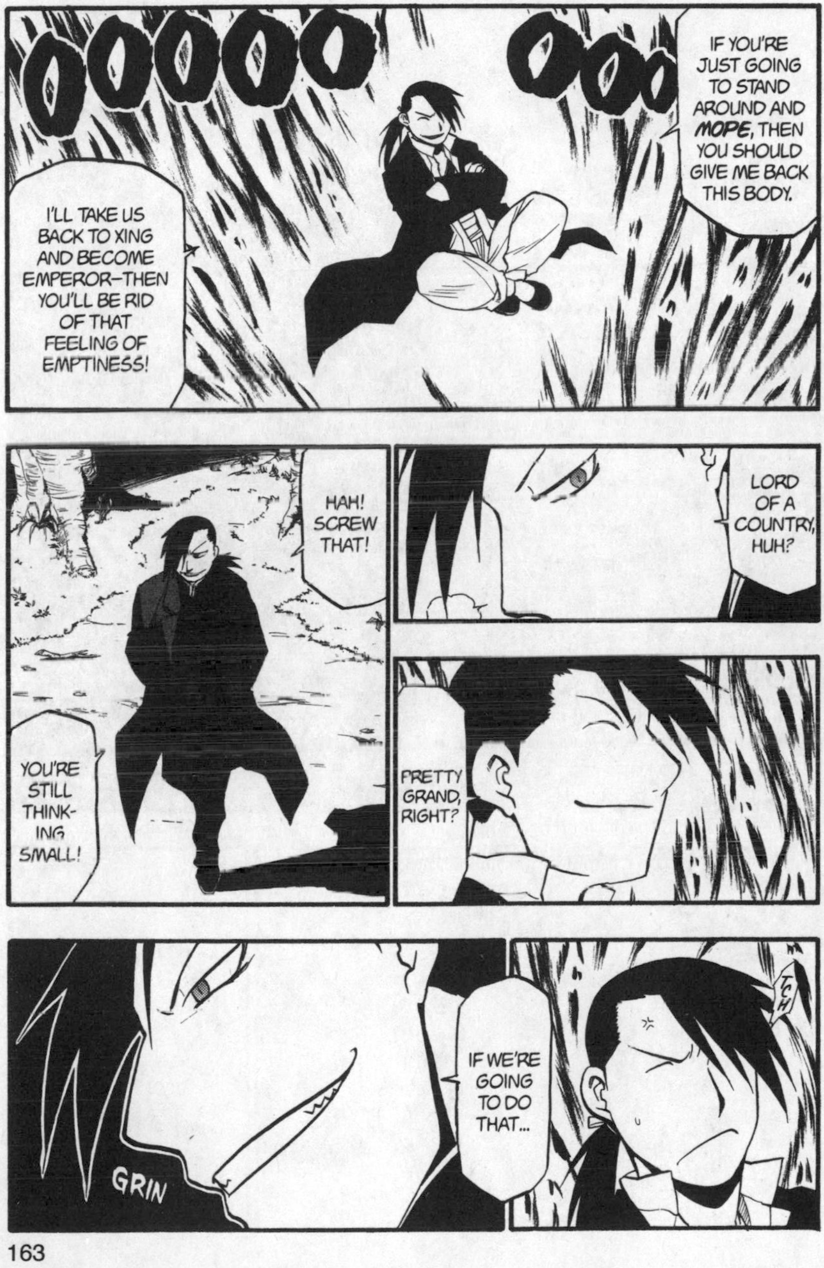
IF YOU'RE JUST GOING TO STAND AROUND AND **MOPE**, THEN YOU SHOULD GIVE ME BACK THIS BODY.
I'LL TAKE US BACK TO XING AND BECOME EMPEROR–THEN YOU'LL BE RID OF THAT FEELING OF EMPTINESS!
LORD OF A COUNTRY, HUH?
PRETTY GRAND, RIGHT?
HAH! SCREW THAT!
YOU'RE STILL THINK-ING SMALL!
TCH
IF WE'RE GOING TO DO THAT...
GRIN

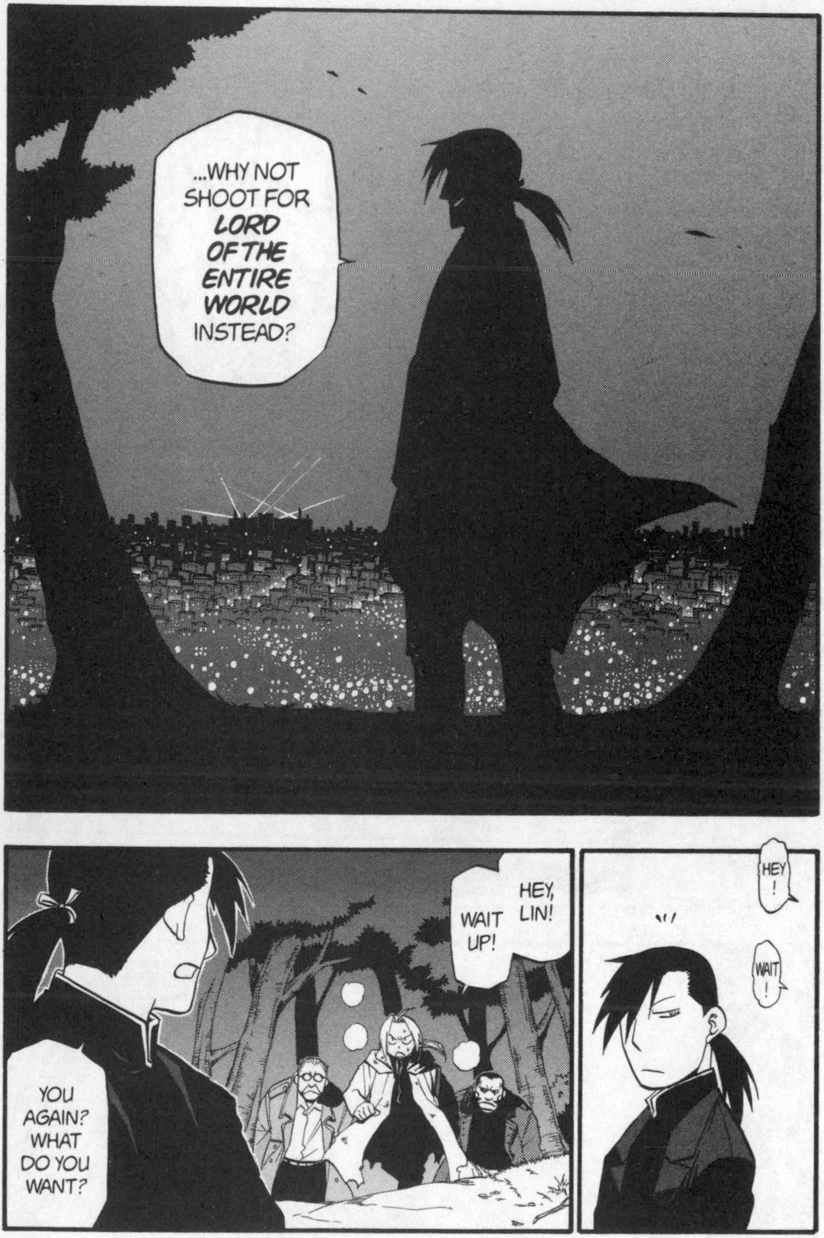
...WHY NOT SHOOT FOR **LORD OF THE ENTIRE WORLD** INSTEAD?
HEY!
WAIT!
HEY, LIN! WAIT UP!
YOU AGAIN? WHAT DO YOU WANT?

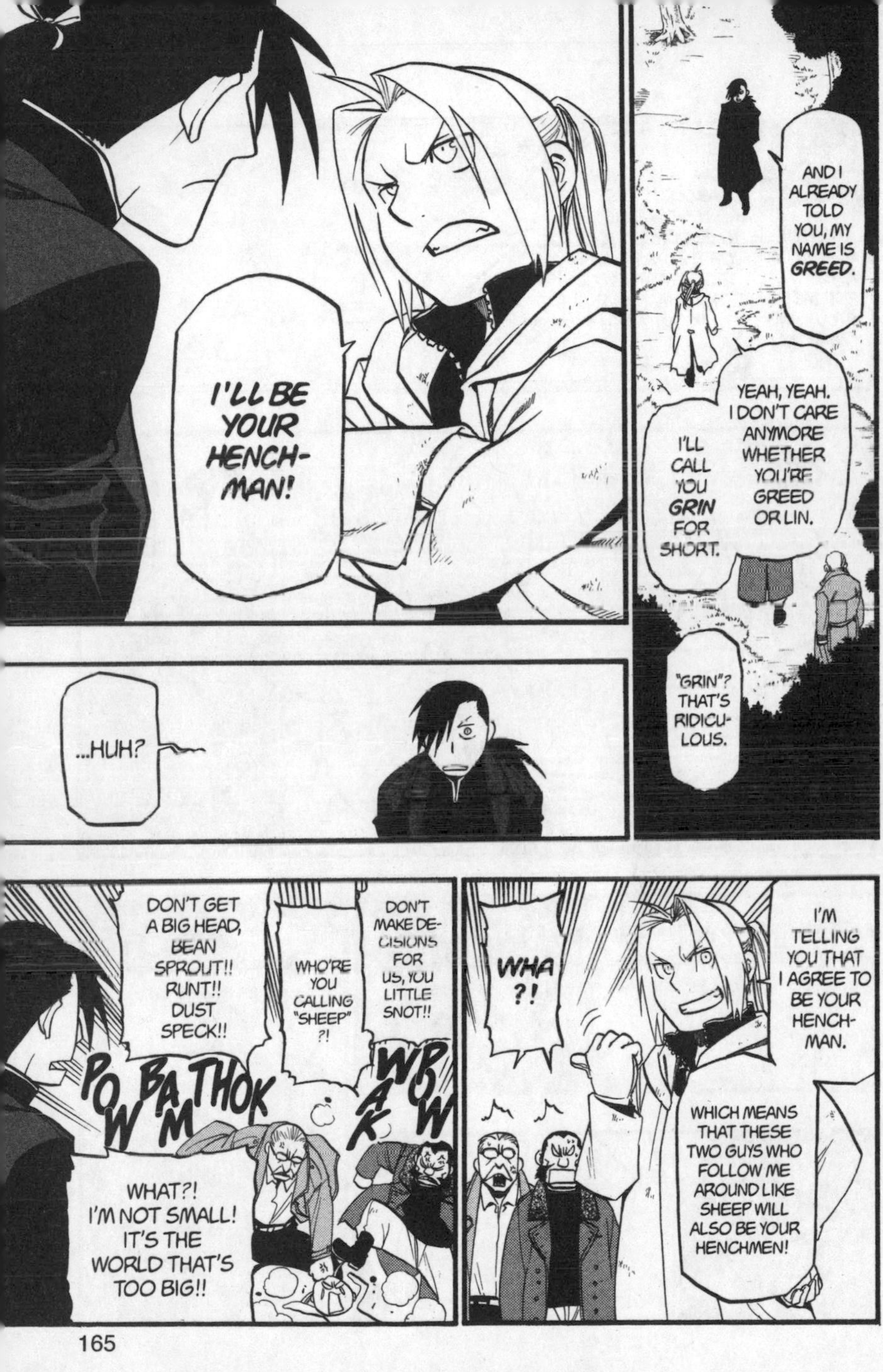
AND I ALREADY TOLD YOU, MY NAME IS **GREED.**
YEAH, YEAH. I DON'T CARE ANYMORE WHETHER YOU'RE GREED OR LIN.
I'LL CALL YOU **GRIN** FOR SHORT.
"GRIN"? THAT'S RIDICULOUS.
I'LL BE YOUR HENCH-MAN!
...HUH?
I'M TELLING YOU THAT I AGREE TO BE YOUR HENCH-MAN.
WHICH MEANS THAT THESE TWO GUYS WHO FOLLOW ME AROUND LIKE SHEEP WILL ALSO BE YOUR HENCHMEN!
WHA?!
DON'T MAKE DE-CISIONS FOR US, YOU LITTLE SNOT!!
WHO'RE YOU CALLING "SHEEP"?!
DON'T GET A BIG HEAD, BEAN SPROUT!! RUNT!! DUST SPECK!!
WPOW
WAK
THOK
BAM
POW
WHAT?! I'M NOT SMALL! IT'S THE WORLD THAT'S TOO BIG!!

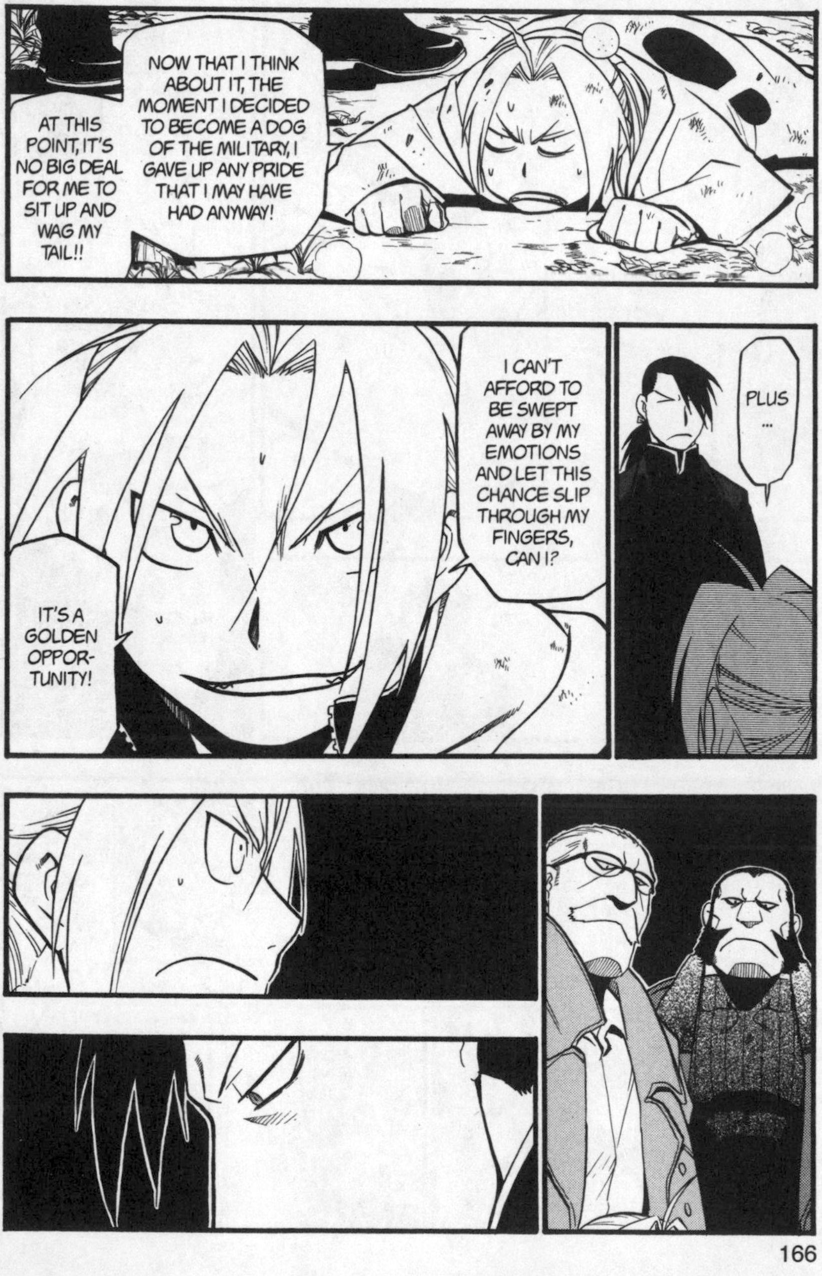
NOW THAT I THINK ABOUT IT, THE MOMENT I DECIDED TO BECOME A DOG OF THE MILITARY, I GAVE UP ANY PRIDE THAT I MAY HAVE HAD ANYWAY!
AT THIS POINT, IT'S NO BIG DEAL FOR ME TO SIT UP AND WAG MY TAIL!!
PLUS ...
I CAN'T AFFORD TO BE SWEPT AWAY BY MY EMOTIONS AND LET THIS CHANCE SLIP THROUGH MY FINGERS, CAN I!?
IT'S A GOLDEN OPPOR-TUNITY!

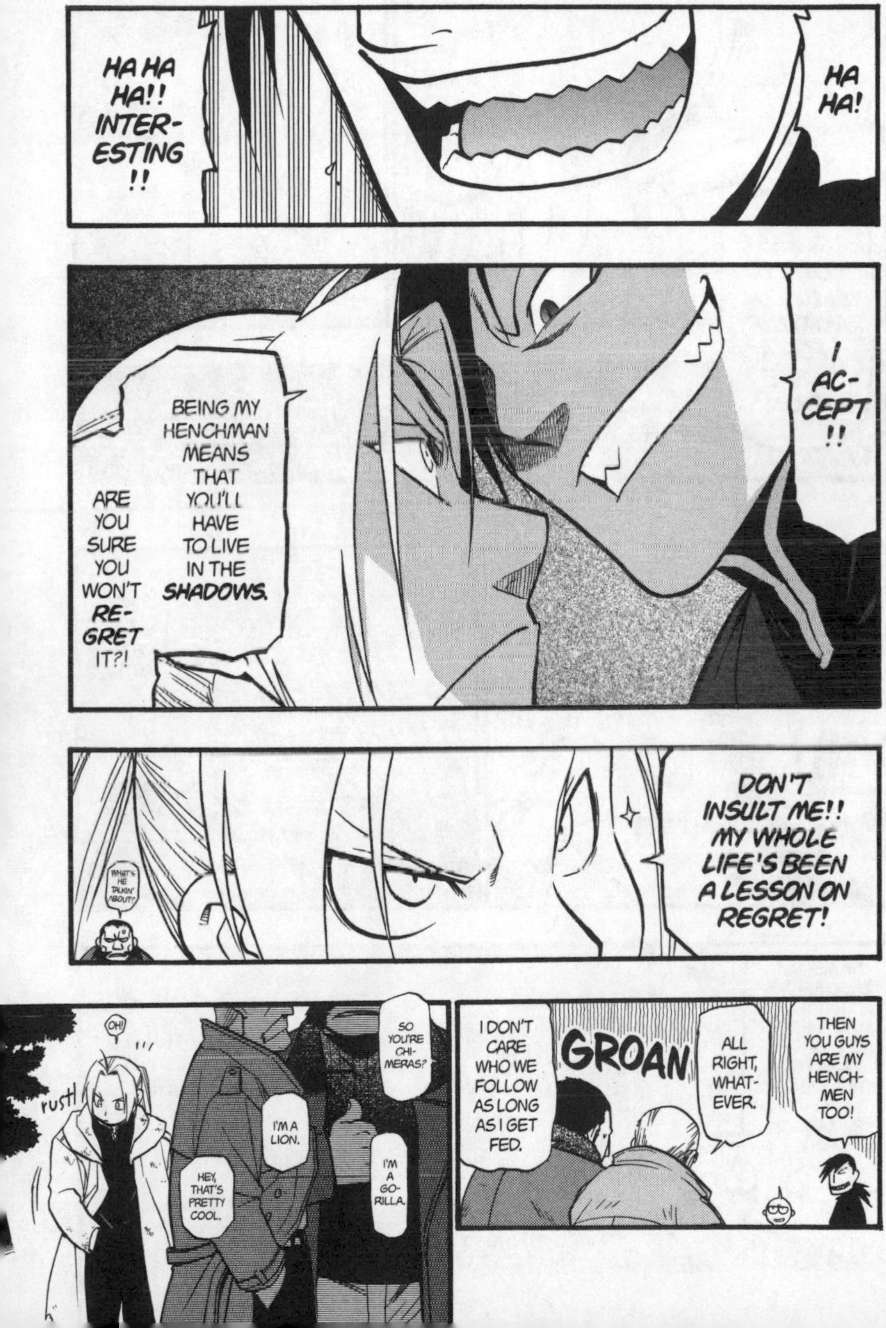
HA HA!
HA HA HA!! INTERESTING!!
I ACCEPT!!
BEING MY HENCHMAN MEANS THAT YOU'LL HAVE TO LIVE IN THE SHADOWS.
ARE YOU SURE YOU WON'T REGRET IT?!
DON'T INSULT ME!! MY WHOLE LIFE'S BEEN A LESSON ON REGRET!
WHAT'S HE TALKIN' ABOUT?
THEN YOU GUYS ARE MY HENCHMEN TOO!
ALL RIGHT, WHATEVER.
GROAN
I DON'T CARE WHO WE FOLLOW AS LONG AS I GET FED.
SO YOU'RE CHIMERAS?
I'M A LION.
I'M A GORILLA.
OH!
HEY, THAT'S PRETTY COOL.
rustl

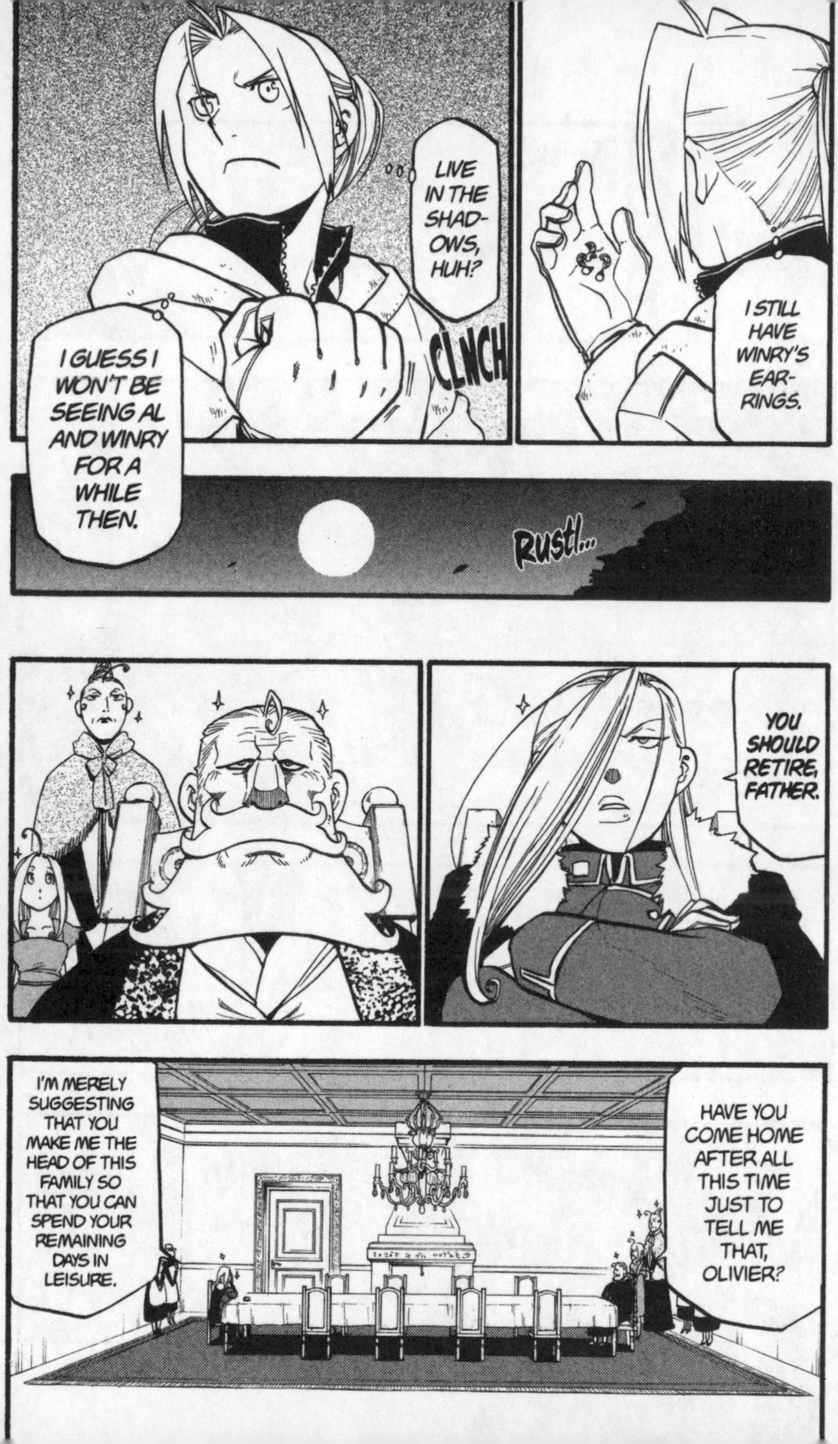
I STILL HAVE WINRY'S EAR-RINGS.
LIVE IN THE SHAD-OWS, HUH?
CLNCH
I GUESS I WON'T BE SEEING AL AND WINRY FOR A WHILE THEN.
Rustl...
YOU SHOULD RETIRE, FATHER.
HAVE YOU COME HOME AFTER ALL THIS TIME JUST TO TELL ME THAT, OLIVIER?
I'M MERELY SUGGESTING THAT YOU MAKE ME THE HEAD OF THIS FAMILY SO THAT YOU CAN SPEND YOUR REMAINING DAYS IN LEISURE.

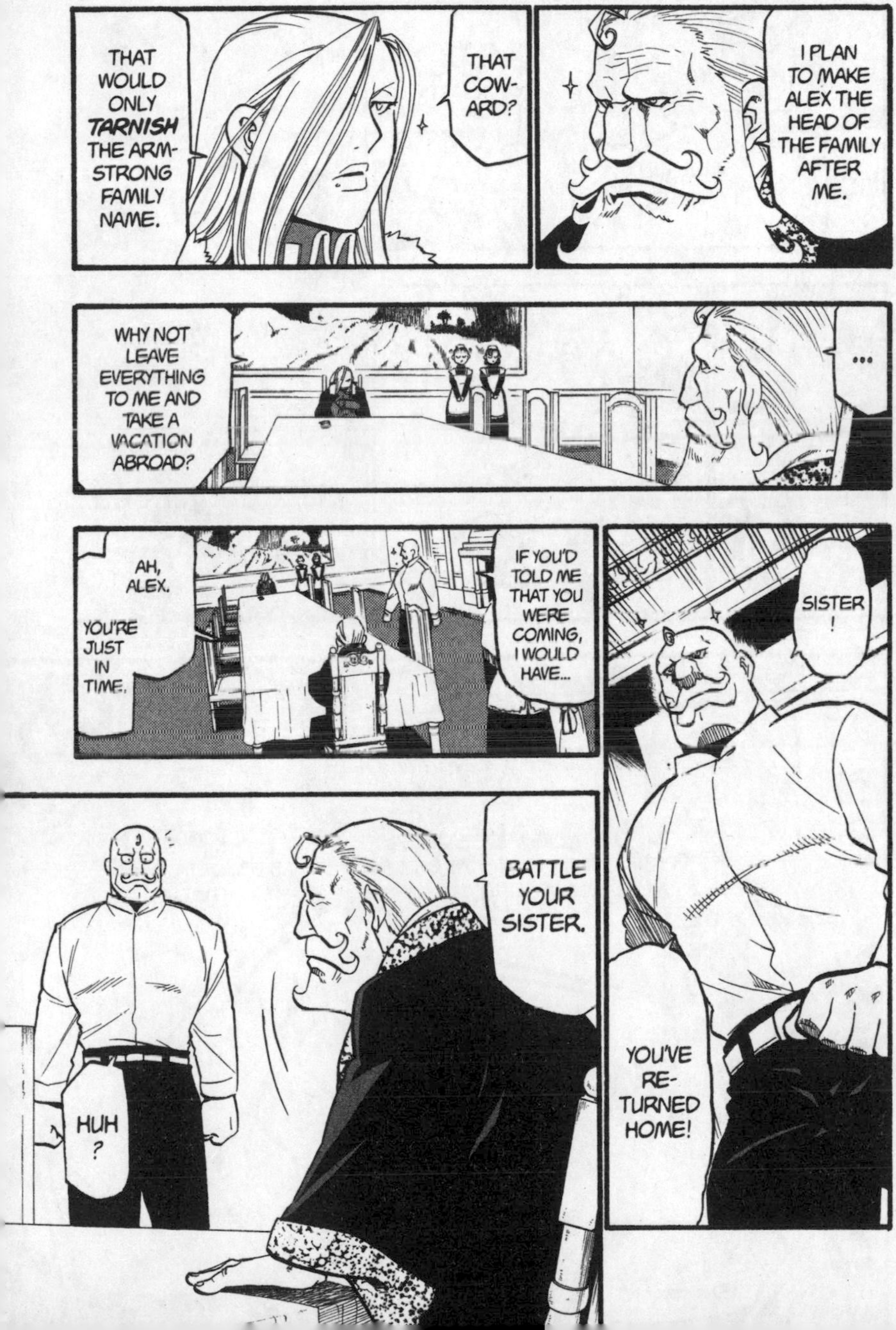
I PLAN TO MAKE ALEX THE HEAD OF THE FAMILY AFTER ME.
THAT COWARD?
THAT WOULD ONLY *TARNISH* THE ARMSTRONG FAMILY NAME.
...
WHY NOT LEAVE EVERYTHING TO ME AND TAKE A VACATION ABROAD?
SISTER!
YOU'VE RETURNED HOME!
IF YOU'D TOLD ME THAT YOU WERE COMING, I WOULD HAVE...
AH, ALEX.
YOU'RE JUST IN TIME.
BATTLE YOUR SISTER.
HUH?

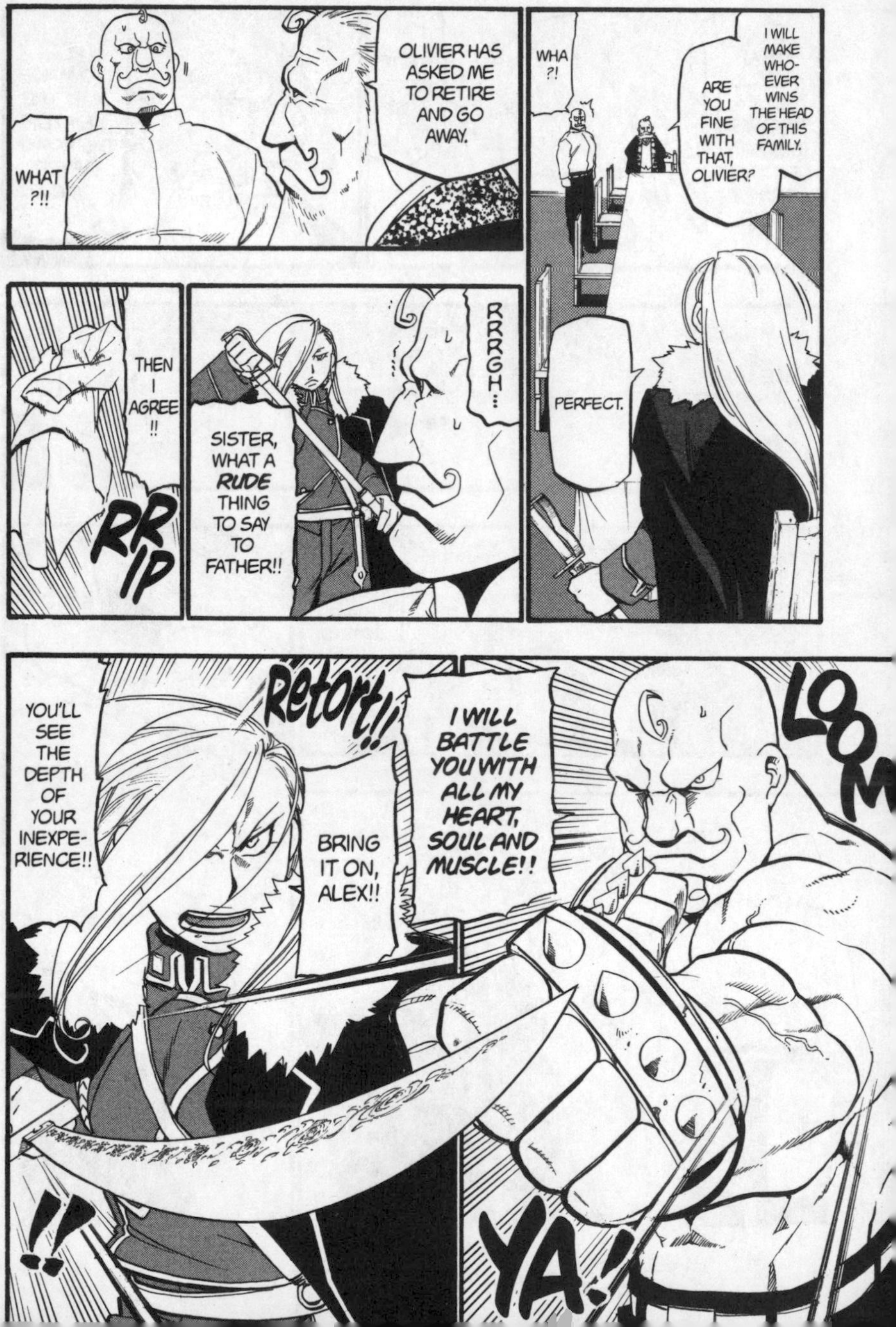
I WILL MAKE WHOEVER WINS THE HEAD OF THIS FAMILY.
ARE YOU FINE WITH THAT, OLIVIER?
WHA ?!
PERFECT.
OLIVIER HAS ASKED ME TO RETIRE AND GO AWAY.
WHAT ?!!
RRRGH...
SISTER, WHAT A RUDE THING TO SAY TO FATHER!!
THEN I AGREE !!
RRIP
LOOM
I WILL BATTLE YOU WITH ALL MY HEART, SOUL AND MUSCLE!!
YA!!
Retort!!
BRING IT ON, ALEX!!
YOU'LL SEE THE DEPTH OF YOUR INEXPERIENCE!!
!!

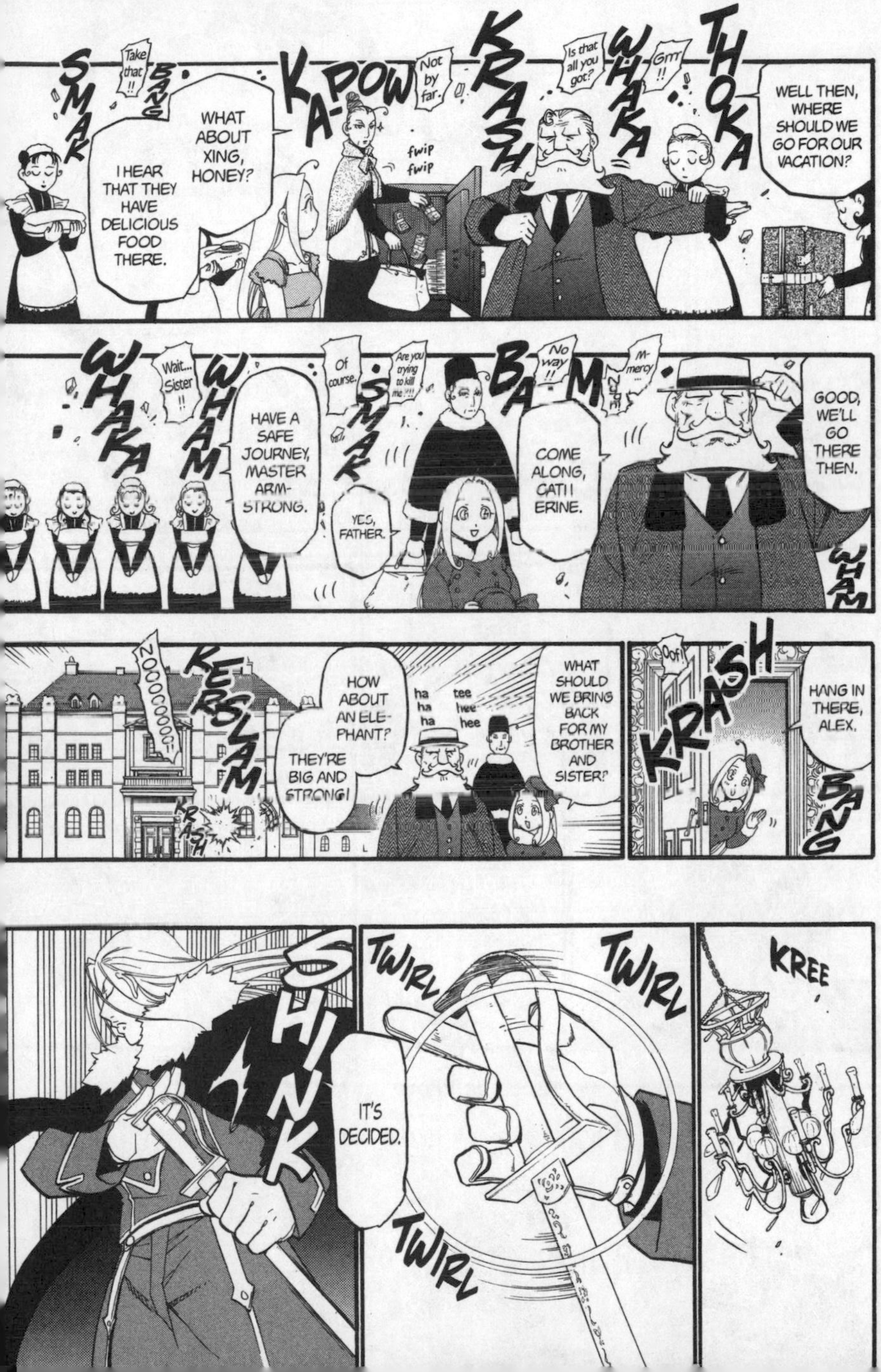
WELL THEN, WHERE SHOULD WE GO FOR OUR VACATION?
THOKA
Grr !!
WHAKA
Is that all you got?
KRASH
Not by far.
KA-POW
fwip fwip
WHAT ABOUT XING, HONEY?
I HEAR THAT THEY HAVE DELICIOUS FOOD THERE.
BANG
Take that !!
SMAK
GOOD, WE'LL GO THERE THEN.
WHAM
M-mercy...
NO!!
No way !!
BAM
COME ALONG, CATHERINE.
YES, FATHER.
Are you trying to kill me?!!
SMAK
Of course.
HAVE A SAFE JOURNEY, MASTER ARMSTRONG.
WHAM
Wait... Sister !!
WHAKA
HANG IN THERE, ALEX.
BANG
KRASH
Oof!
WHAT SHOULD WE BRING BACK FOR MY BROTHER AND SISTER?
tee hee hee
ha ha ha
HOW ABOUT AN ELEPHANT?
THEY'RE BIG AND STRONG!
KERSLAM
NOOOOOOOO!!
KRASH
KREE
TWIRL
TWIRL
TWIRL
IT'S DECIDED.
SHINK

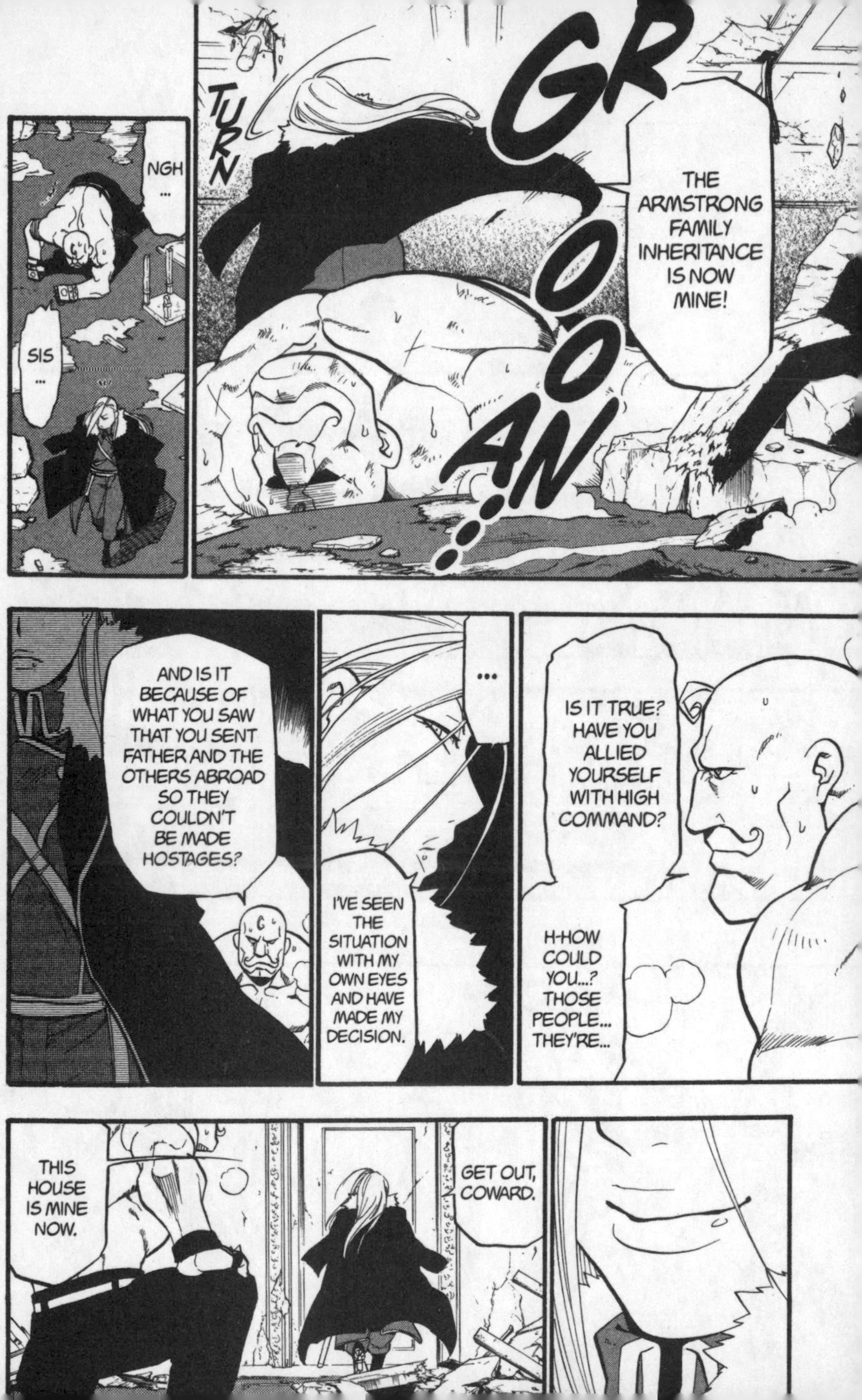
THE ARMSTRONG FAMILY INHERITANCE IS NOW MINE!
GROOOAN...
TURN
NGH...
SIS...
IS IT TRUE? HAVE YOU ALLIED YOURSELF WITH HIGH COMMAND?
H-HOW COULD YOU...? THOSE PEOPLE... THEY'RE...
...
I'VE SEEN THE SITUATION WITH MY OWN EYES AND HAVE MADE MY DECISION.
AND IS IT BECAUSE OF WHAT YOU SAW THAT YOU SENT FATHER AND THE OTHERS ABROAD SO THEY COULDN'T BE MADE HOSTAGES?
GET OUT, COWARD.
THIS HOUSE IS MINE NOW.

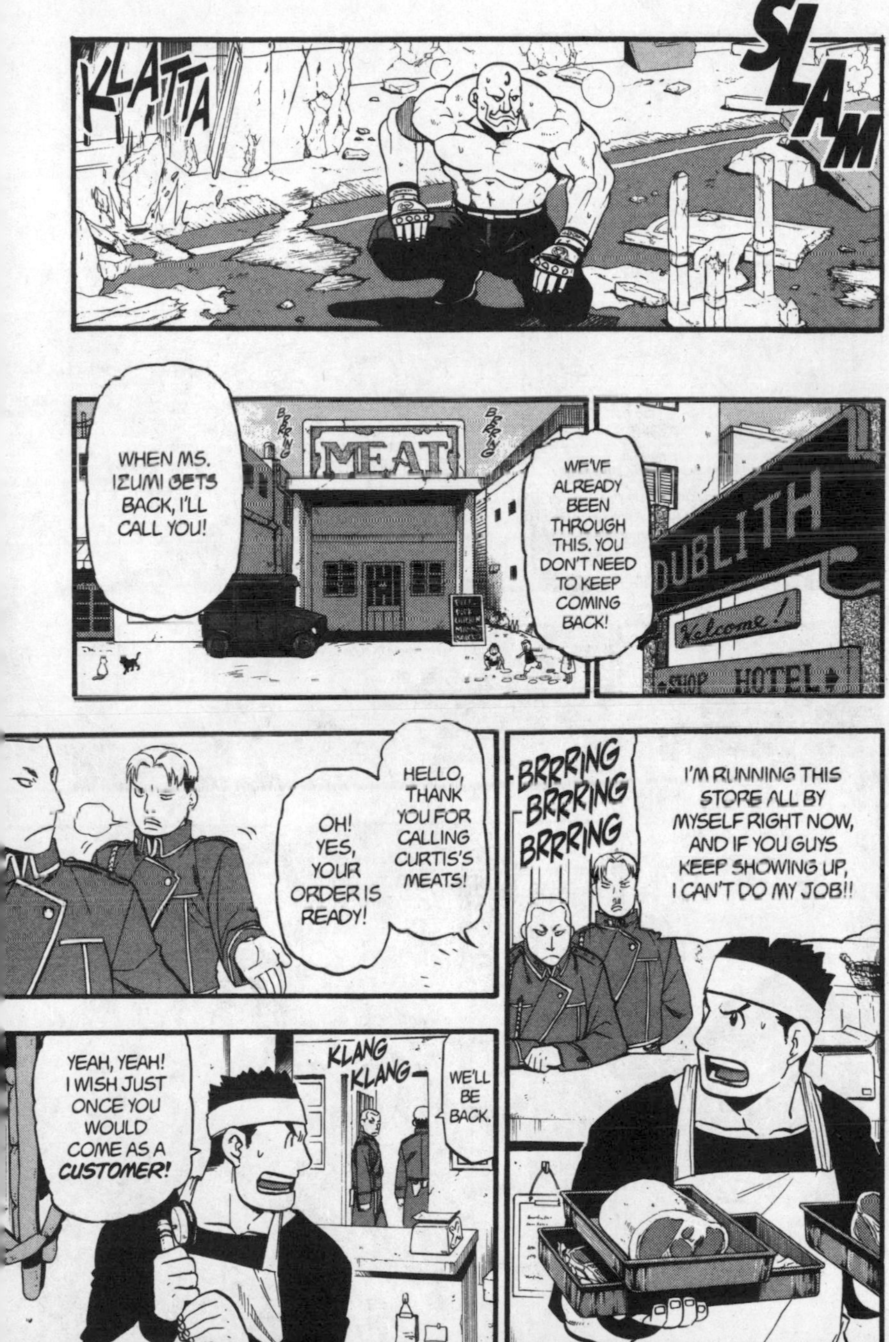
SLAM
KLATTA
DUBLITH
Welcome!
SHOP
HOTEL
WE'VE ALREADY BEEN THROUGH THIS. YOU DON'T NEED TO KEEP COMING BACK!
BRRRING
BRRRING
MEAT
WHEN MS. IZUMI GETS BACK, I'LL CALL YOU!
BRRRING
BRRRING
BRRRING
I'M RUNNING THIS STORE ALL BY MYSELF RIGHT NOW, AND IF YOU GUYS KEEP SHOWING UP, I CAN'T DO MY JOB!!
HELLO, THANK YOU FOR CALLING CURTIS'S MEATS!
OH! YES, YOUR ORDER IS READY!
KLANG
KLANG
WE'LL BE BACK.
YEAH, YEAH! I WISH JUST ONCE YOU WOULD COME AS A CUSTOMER!

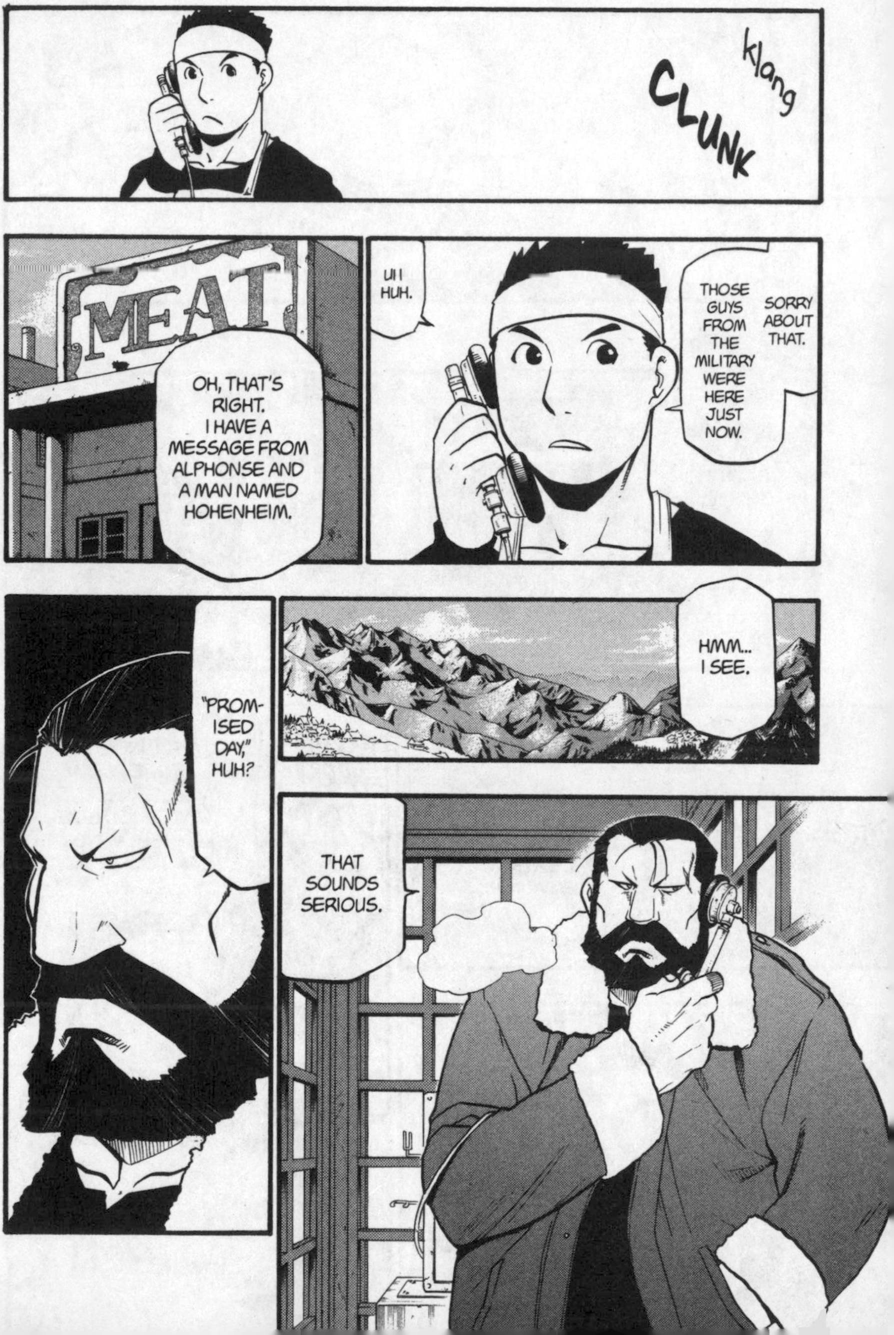
klang
CLUNK
SORRY ABOUT THAT.
THOSE GUYS FROM THE MILITARY WERE HERE JUST NOW.
UH HUH.
OH, THAT'S RIGHT. I HAVE A MESSAGE FROM ALPHONSE AND A MAN NAMED HOHENHEIM.
MEAT
HMM... I SEE.
THAT SOUNDS SERIOUS.
"PROMISED DAY," HUH?

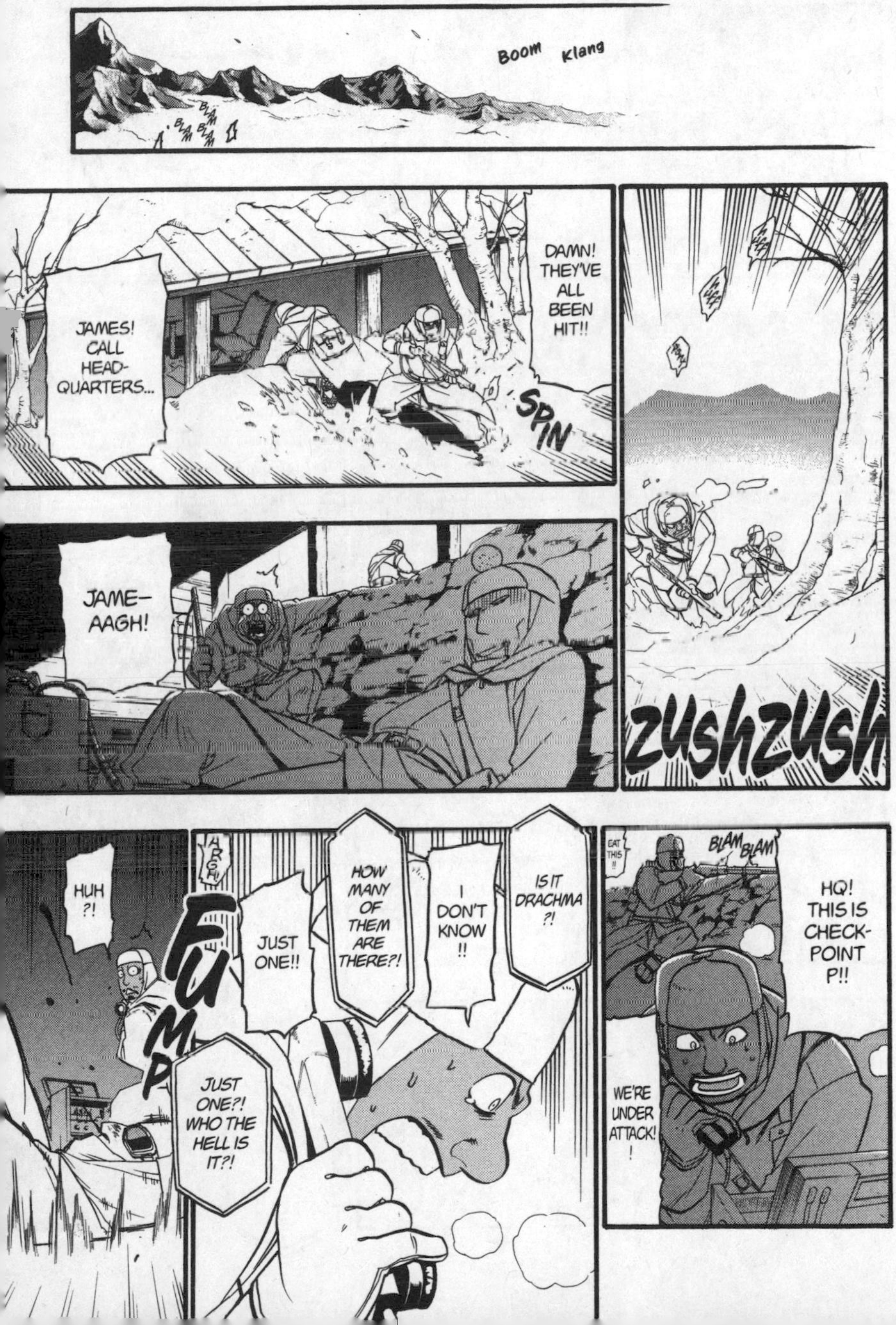
Boom
Klang
BLAM BLAM
BLAM BLAM
ZUSHZUSH
DAMN! THEY'VE ALL BEEN HIT!!
JAMES! CALL HEAD-QUARTERS...
SPIN
JAME— AAGH!
HQ! THIS IS CHECK-POINT P!!
EAT THIS!!
BLAM BLAM
WE'RE UNDER ATTACK!!
IS IT DRACHMA?!
I DON'T KNOW!!
HOW MANY OF THEM ARE THERE?!
JUST ONE!!
JUST ONE?! WHO THE HELL IS IT?!
ARGH
FUMP
HUH?!

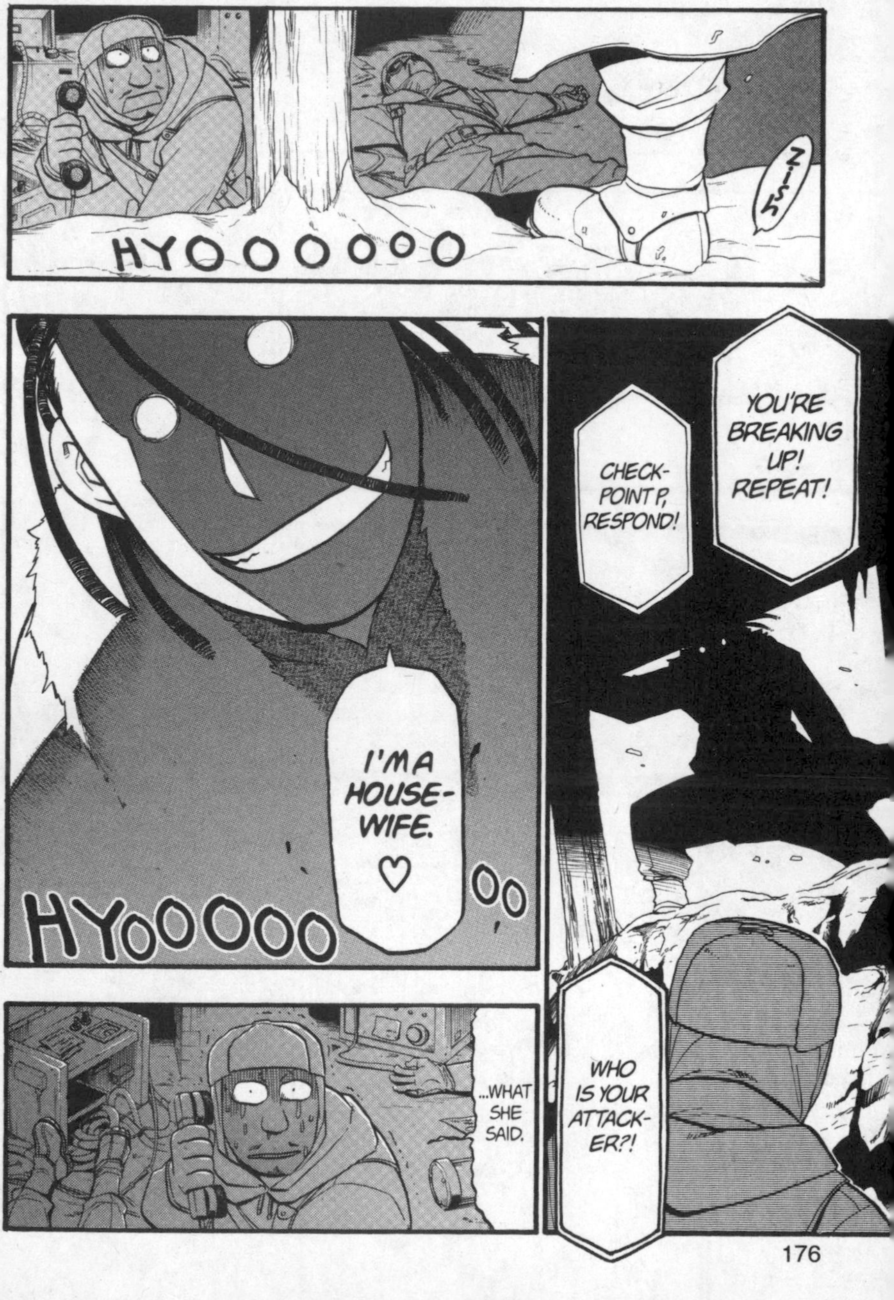
Zish
HYOOOOOO
YOU'RE BREAKING UP! REPEAT!
CHECK-POINT P, RESPOND!
WHO IS YOUR ATTACK-ER?!
I'M A HOUSE-WIFE. ♡
HYOOOOOOO
...WHAT SHE SAID.

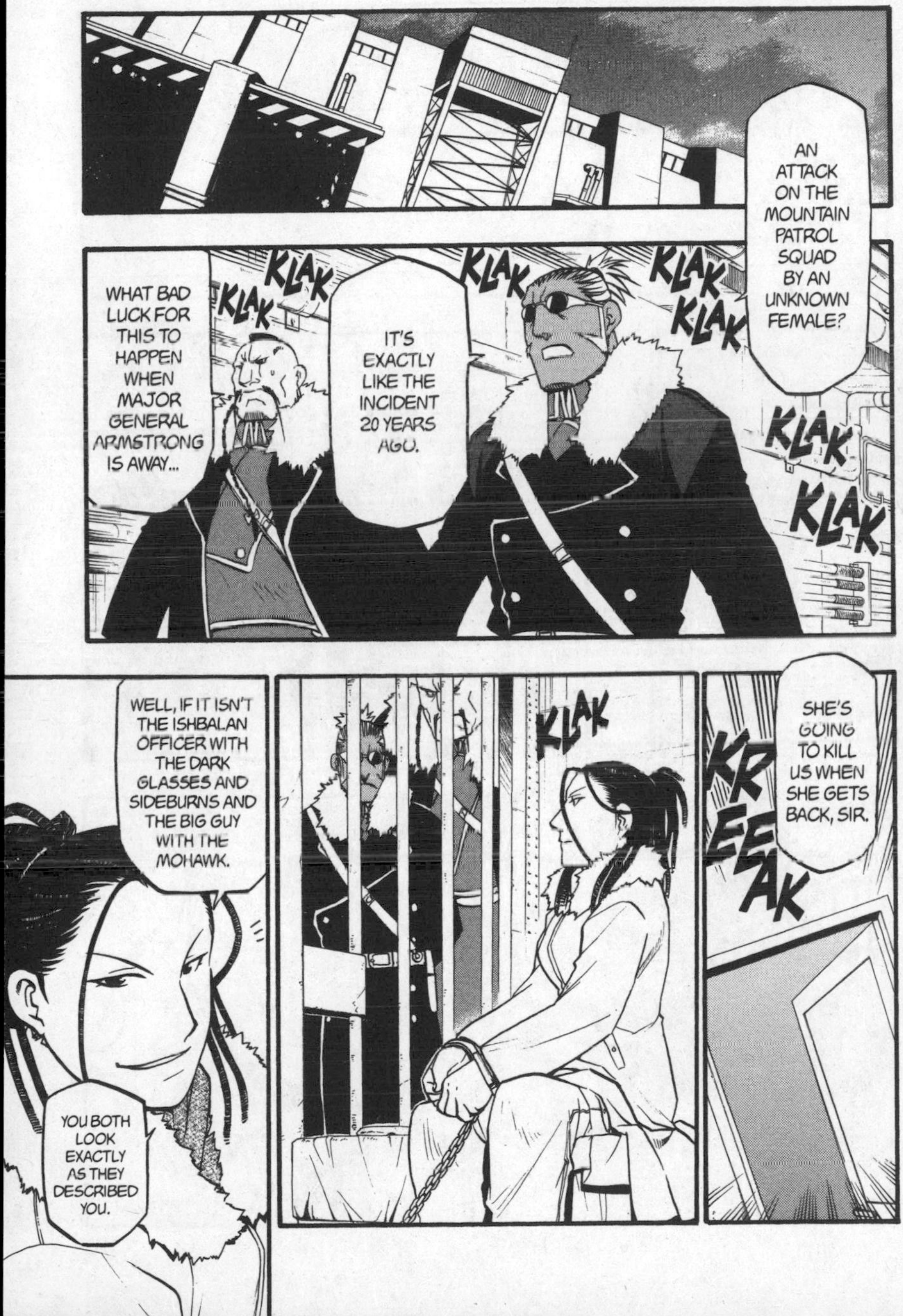
AN ATTACK ON THE MOUNTAIN PATROL SQUAD BY AN UNKNOWN FEMALE?
KLAK KLAK KLAK KLAK
KLAK KLAK
IT'S EXACTLY LIKE THE INCIDENT 20 YEARS AGO.
KLAK KLAK
WHAT BAD LUCK FOR THIS TO HAPPEN WHEN MAJOR GENERAL ARMSTRONG IS AWAY...
SHE'S GOING TO KILL US WHEN SHE GETS BACK, SIR.
KREEEAK
KLAK
WELL, IF IT ISN'T THE ISHBALAN OFFICER WITH THE DARK GLASSES AND SIDEBURNS AND THE BIG GUY WITH THE MOHAWK.
YOU BOTH LOOK EXACTLY AS THEY DESCRIBED YOU.

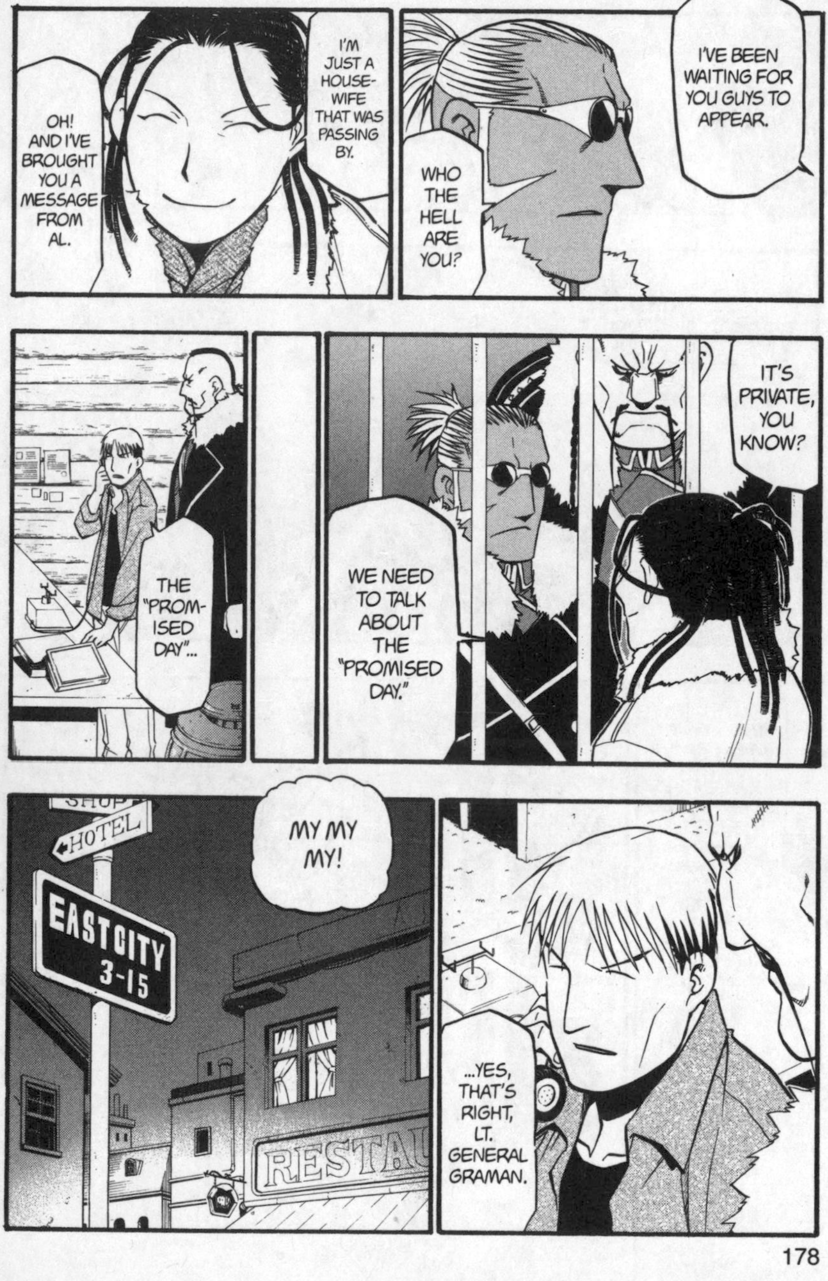
I'VE BEEN WAITING FOR YOU GUYS TO APPEAR.
WHO THE HELL ARE YOU?
I'M JUST A HOUSE-WIFE THAT WAS PASSING BY.
OH! AND I'VE BROUGHT YOU A MESSAGE FROM AL.
IT'S PRIVATE, YOU KNOW?
WE NEED TO TALK ABOUT THE "PROMISED DAY."
THE "PROM-ISED DAY"...
...YES, THAT'S RIGHT, LT. GENERAL GRAMAN.
MY MY MY!
SHOP
HOTEL
EAST CITY 3-15
RESTAU

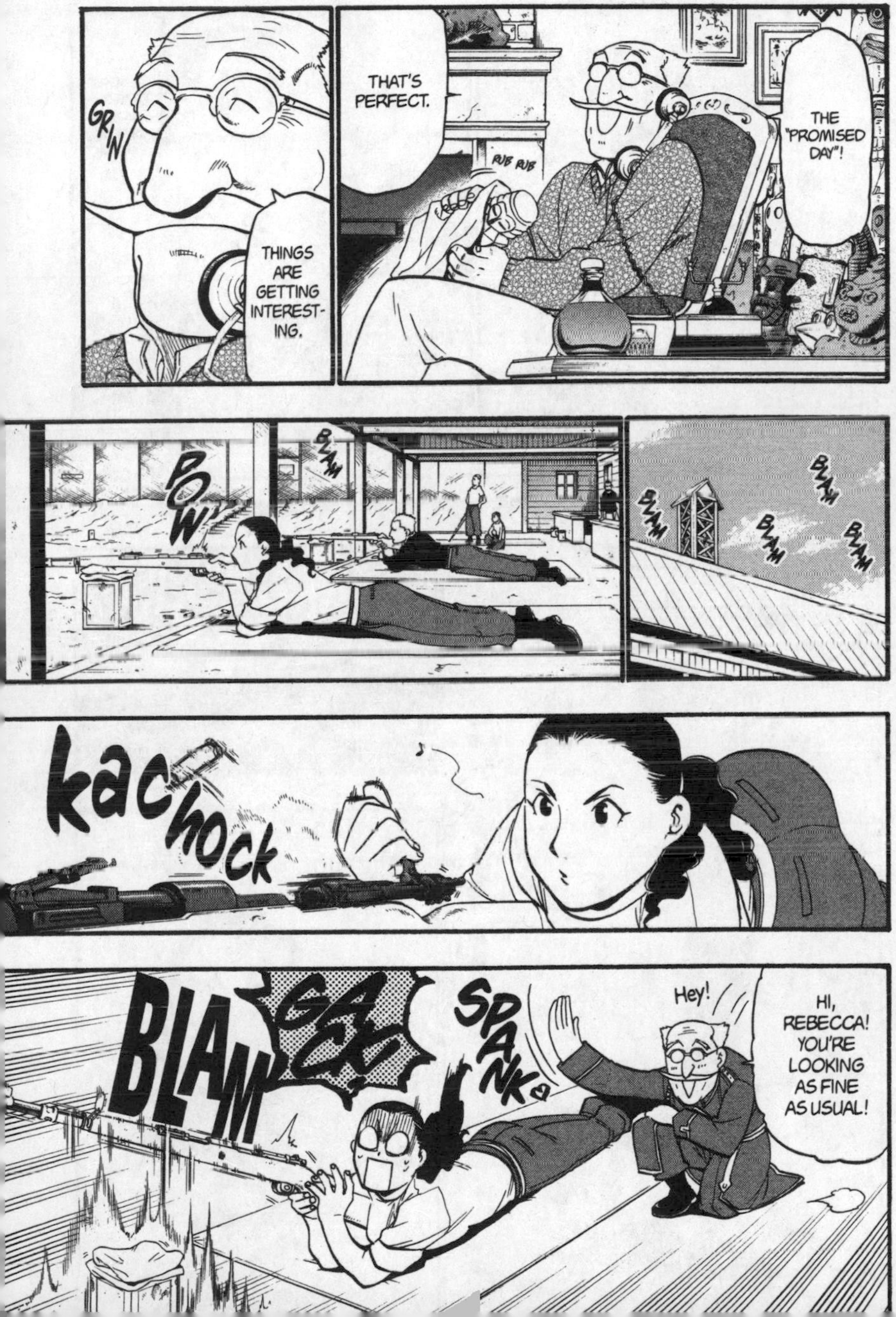
THE "PROMISED DAY"!
THAT'S PERFECT.
RUB RUB
GRIN
THINGS ARE GETTING INTEREST-ING.
BLAM
BLAM
BLAM
BLAM
BLAM
POW
kachock
HI, REBECCA! YOU'RE LOOKING AS FINE AS USUAL!
Hey!
SPANK
BLAM

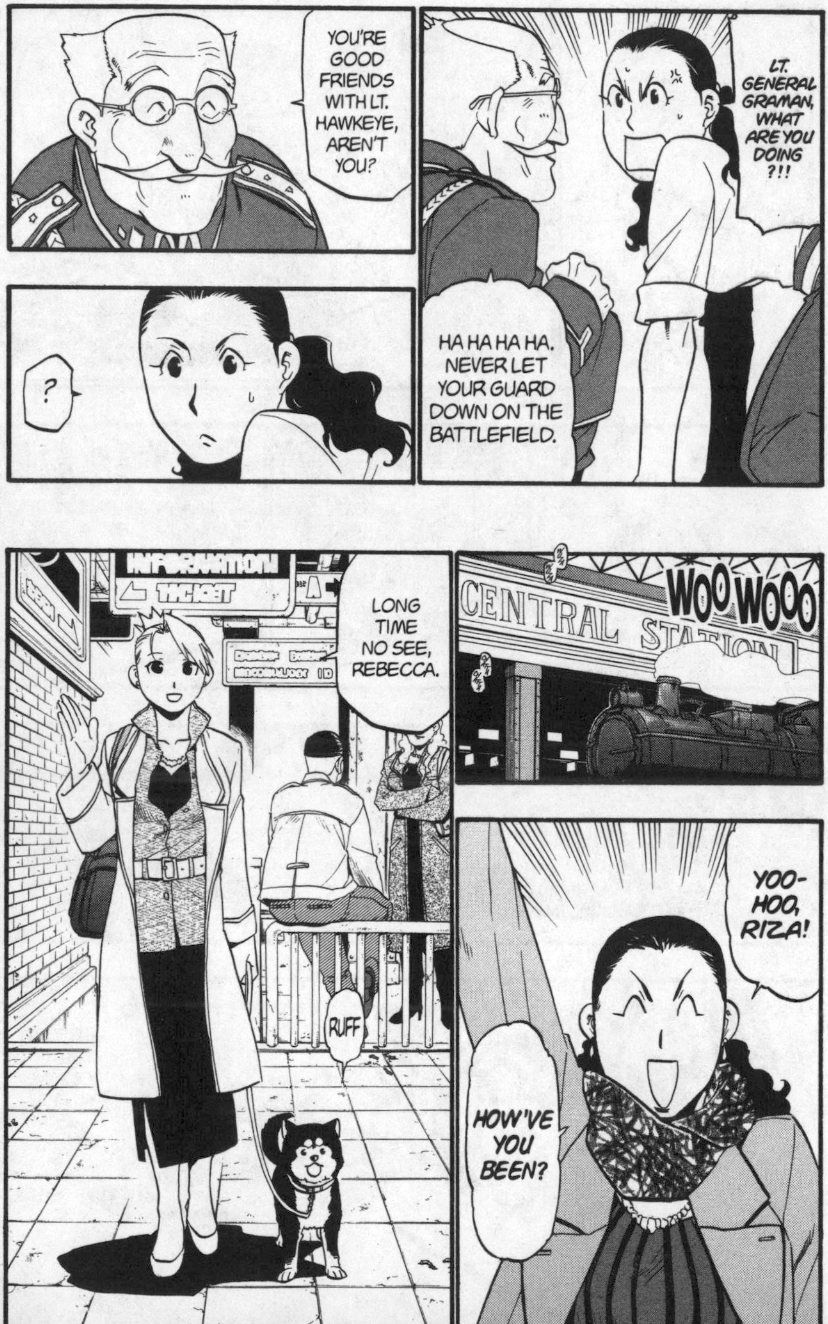
LT. GENERAL GRAMAN, WHAT ARE YOU DOING ?!!
HA HA HA HA. NEVER LET YOUR GUARD DOWN ON THE BATTLEFIELD.
YOU'RE GOOD FRIENDS WITH LT. HAWKEYE, AREN'T YOU?
?
WOO WOOO
CENTRAL STATION
YOO-HOO, RIZA!
HOW'VE YOU BEEN?
LONG TIME NO SEE, REBECCA.
RUFF

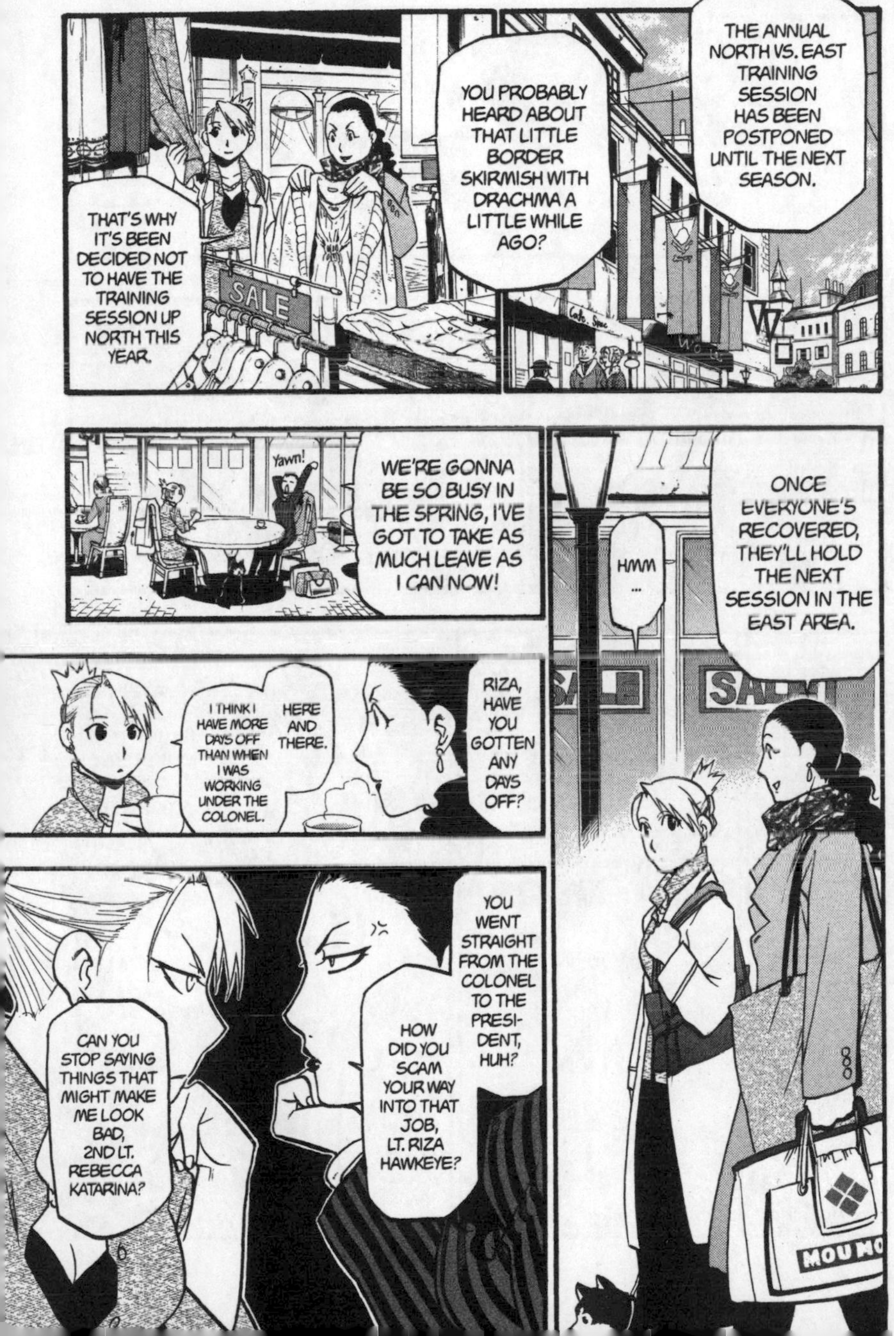
THE ANNUAL NORTH VS. EAST TRAINING SESSION HAS BEEN POSTPONED UNTIL THE NEXT SEASON.
YOU PROBABLY HEARD ABOUT THAT LITTLE BORDER SKIRMISH WITH DRACHMA A LITTLE WHILE AGO?
SALE
THAT'S WHY IT'S BEEN DECIDED NOT TO HAVE THE TRAINING SESSION UP NORTH THIS YEAR.
ONCE EVERYONE'S RECOVERED, THEY'LL HOLD THE NEXT SESSION IN THE EAST AREA.
HMM ...
WE'RE GONNA BE SO BUSY IN THE SPRING, I'VE GOT TO TAKE AS MUCH LEAVE AS I CAN NOW!
Yawn!
RIZA, HAVE YOU GOTTEN ANY DAYS OFF?
HERE AND THERE.
I THINK I HAVE MORE DAYS OFF THAN WHEN I WAS WORKING UNDER THE COLONEL.
YOU WENT STRAIGHT FROM THE COLONEL TO THE PRESIDENT, HUH?
HOW DID YOU SCAM YOUR WAY INTO THAT JOB, LT. RIZA HAWKEYE?
CAN YOU STOP SAYING THINGS THAT MIGHT MAKE ME LOOK BAD, 2ND LT. REBECCA KATARINA?

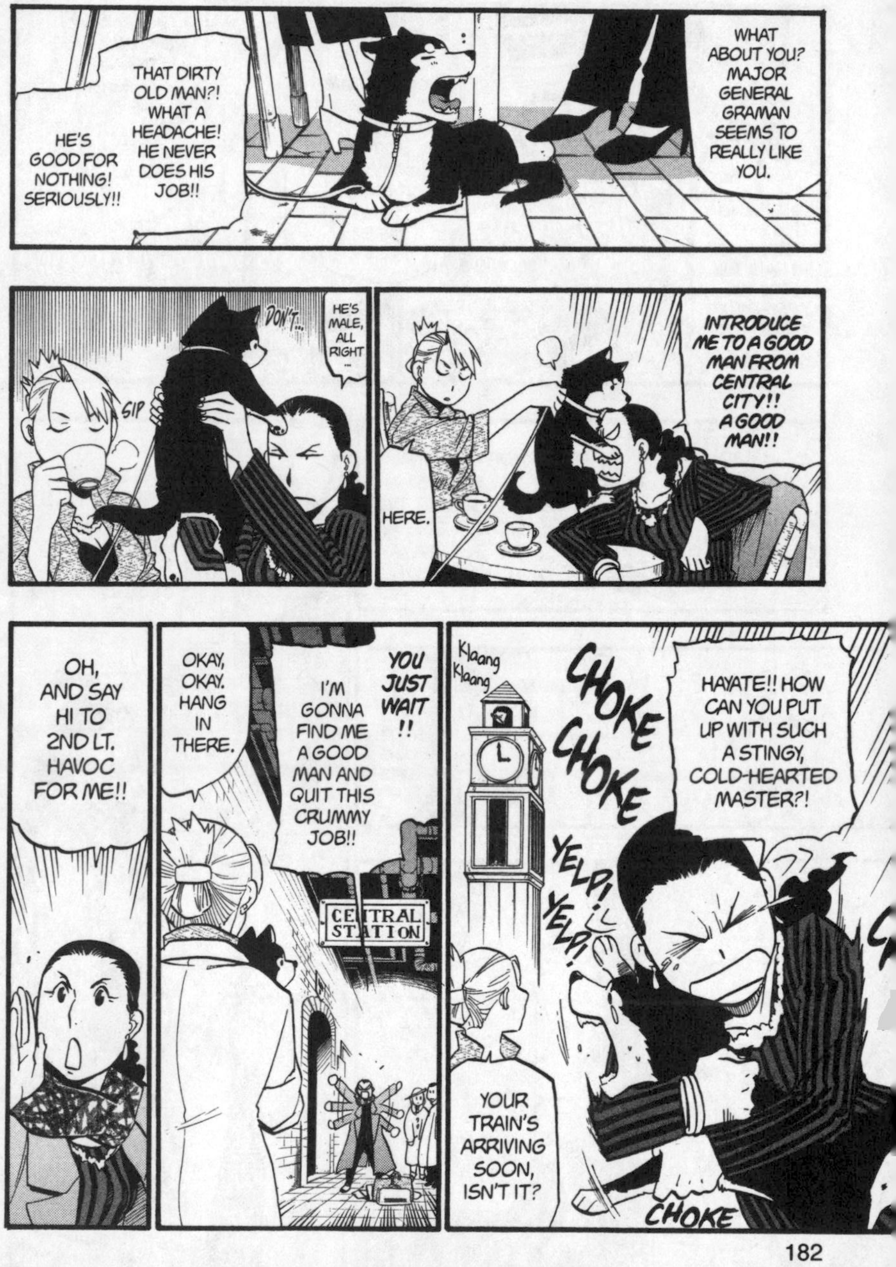
WHAT ABOUT YOU? MAJOR GENERAL GRAMAN SEEMS TO REALLY LIKE YOU.
THAT DIRTY OLD MAN?! WHAT A HEADACHE! HE NEVER DOES HIS JOB!!
HE'S GOOD FOR NOTHING! SERIOUSLY!!
INTRODUCE ME TO A GOOD MAN FROM CENTRAL CITY!! A GOOD MAN!!
HERE.
HE'S MALE, ALL RIGHT ...
DON'T...
SIP
HAYATE!! HOW CAN YOU PUT UP WITH SUCH A STINGY, COLD-HEARTED MASTER?!
CHOKE CHOKE
Klaang Klaang
YELP! YELP!
YOUR TRAIN'S ARRIVING SOON, ISN'T IT?
CHOKE
YOU JUST WAIT!!
I'M GONNA FIND ME A GOOD MAN AND QUIT THIS CRUMMY JOB!!
OKAY, OKAY. HANG IN THERE.
CENTRAL STATION
OH, AND SAY HI TO 2ND LT. HAVOC FOR ME!!

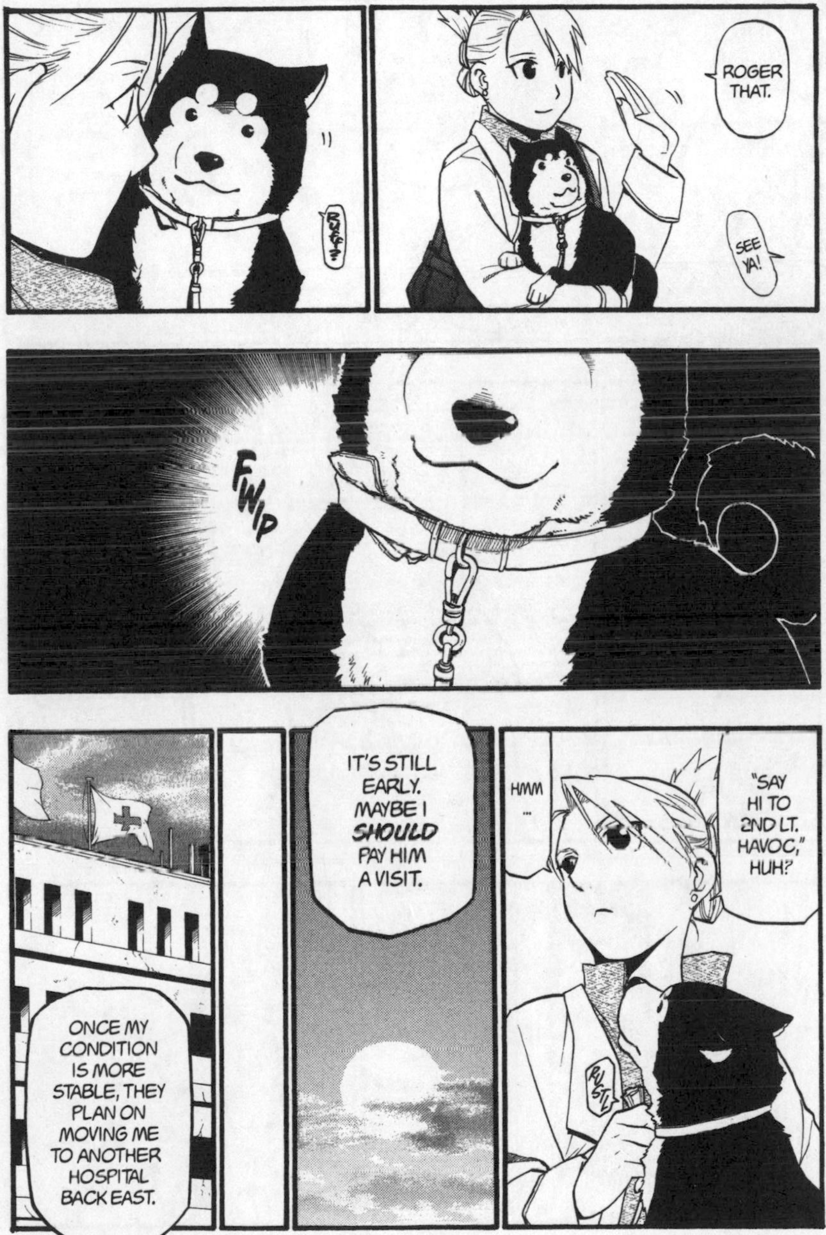
ROGER THAT.
SEE YA!
RUFF?
FWIP
"SAY HI TO 2ND LT. HAVOC," HUH?
HMM ...
RUSTL
IT'S STILL EARLY. MAYBE I **SHOULD** PAY HIM A VISIT.
ONCE MY CONDITION IS MORE STABLE, THEY PLAN ON MOVING ME TO ANOTHER HOSPITAL BACK EAST.

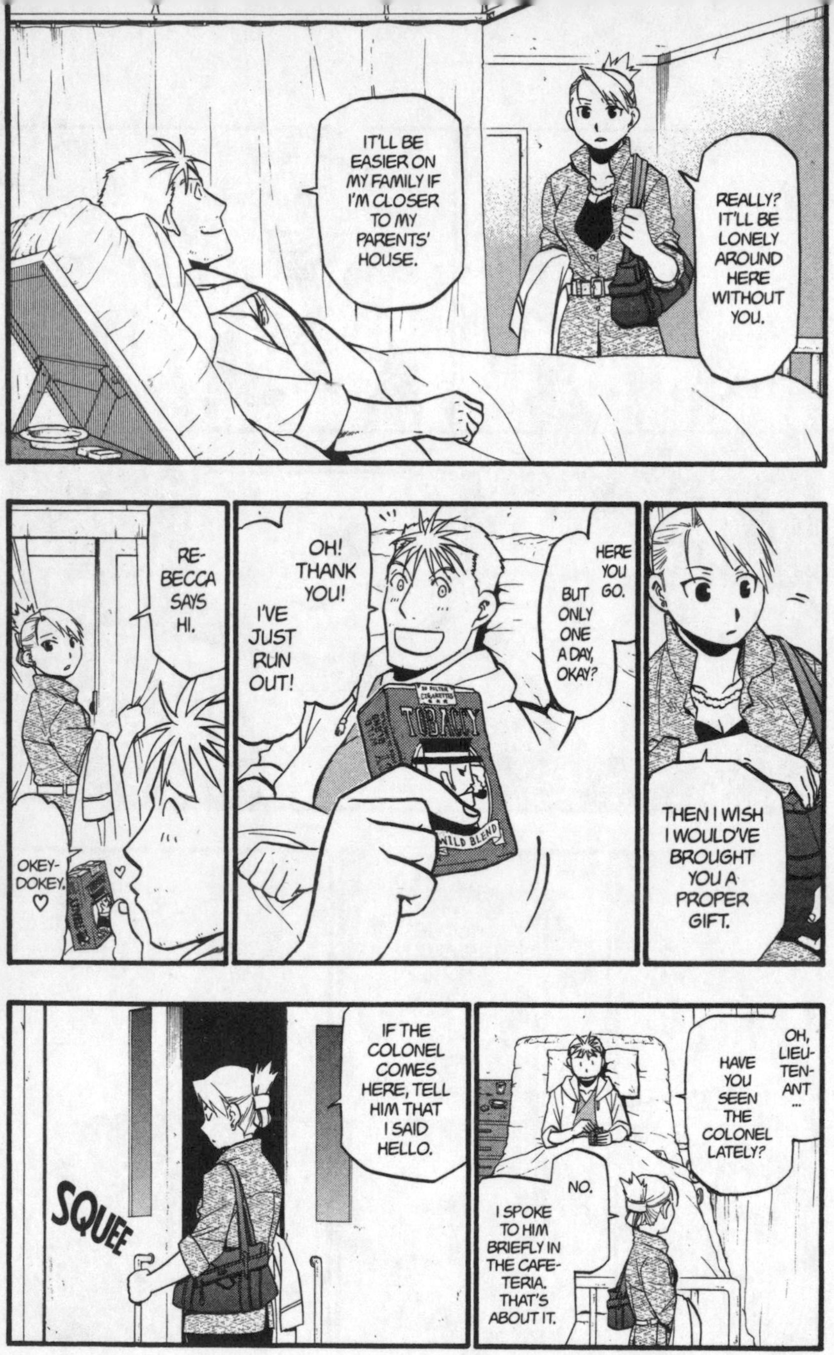
IT'LL BE EASIER ON MY FAMILY IF I'M CLOSER TO MY PARENTS' HOUSE.
REALLY? IT'LL BE LONELY AROUND HERE WITHOUT YOU.
THEN I WISH I WOULD'VE BROUGHT YOU A PROPER GIFT.
HERE YOU GO.
BUT ONLY ONE A DAY, OKAY?
OH! THANK YOU!
I'VE JUST RUN OUT!
TOBACCO
WILD BLEND
REBECCA SAYS HI.
OKEY-DOKEY. ♡
OH, LIEUTENANT...
HAVE YOU SEEN THE COLONEL LATELY?
NO.
I SPOKE TO HIM BRIEFLY IN THE CAFETERIA. THAT'S ABOUT IT.
IF THE COLONEL COMES HERE, TELL HIM THAT I SAID HELLO.
SQUEE

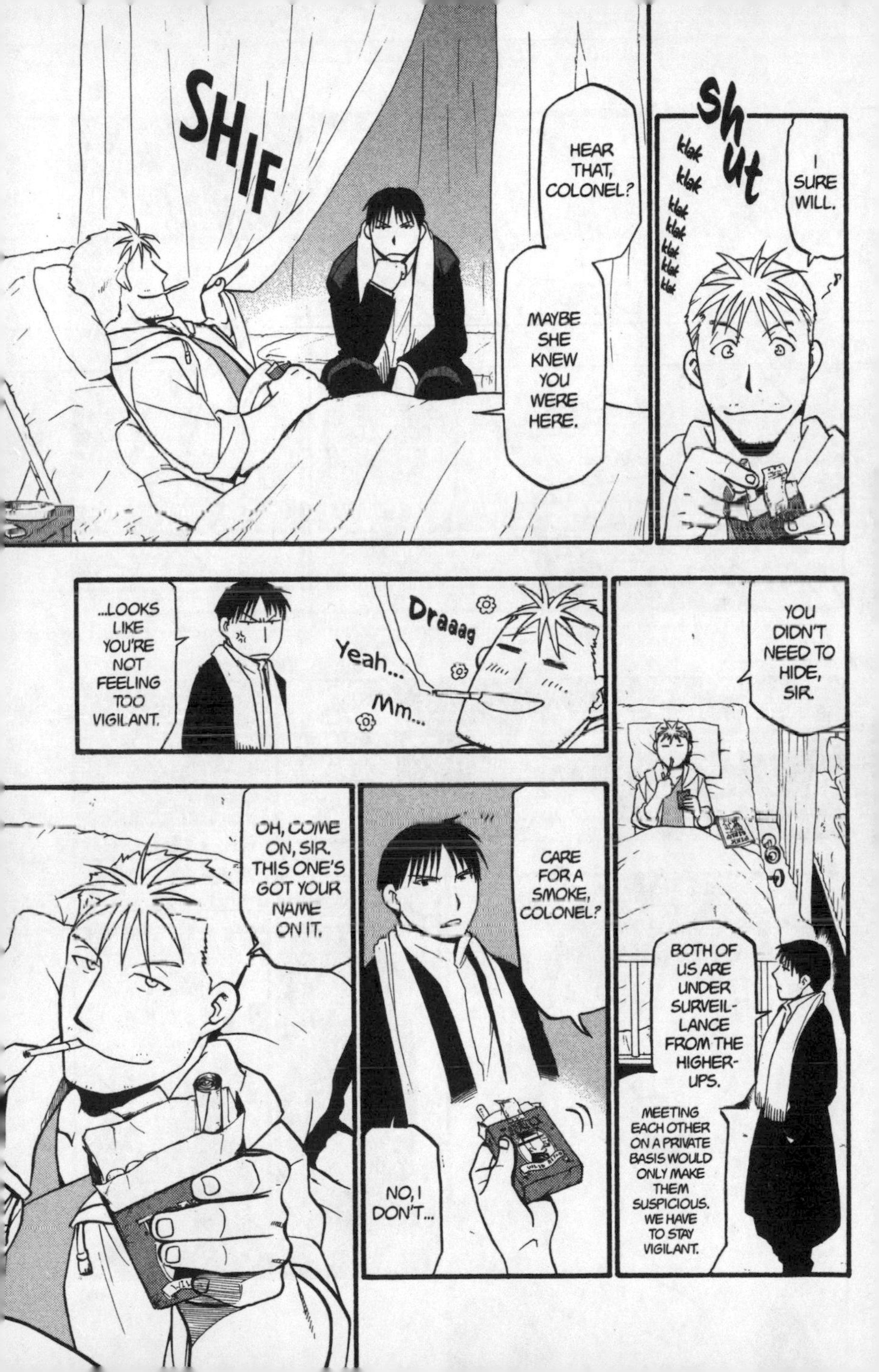
SHUT
KLAK KLAK KLAK KLAK KLAK KLAK KLAK
I SURE WILL.
HEAR THAT, COLONEL?
MAYBE SHE KNEW YOU WERE HERE.
SHIF
YOU DIDN'T NEED TO HIDE, SIR.
BOTH OF US ARE UNDER SURVEIL-LANCE FROM THE HIGHER-UPS.
MEETING EACH OTHER ON A PRIVATE BASIS WOULD ONLY MAKE THEM SUSPICIOUS. WE HAVE TO STAY VIGILANT.
Draaag
Yeah...
Mm...
...LOOKS LIKE YOU'RE NOT FEELING TOO VIGILANT.
CARE FOR A SMOKE, COLONEL?
NO, I DON'T...
OH, COME ON, SIR. THIS ONE'S GOT YOUR NAME ON IT.

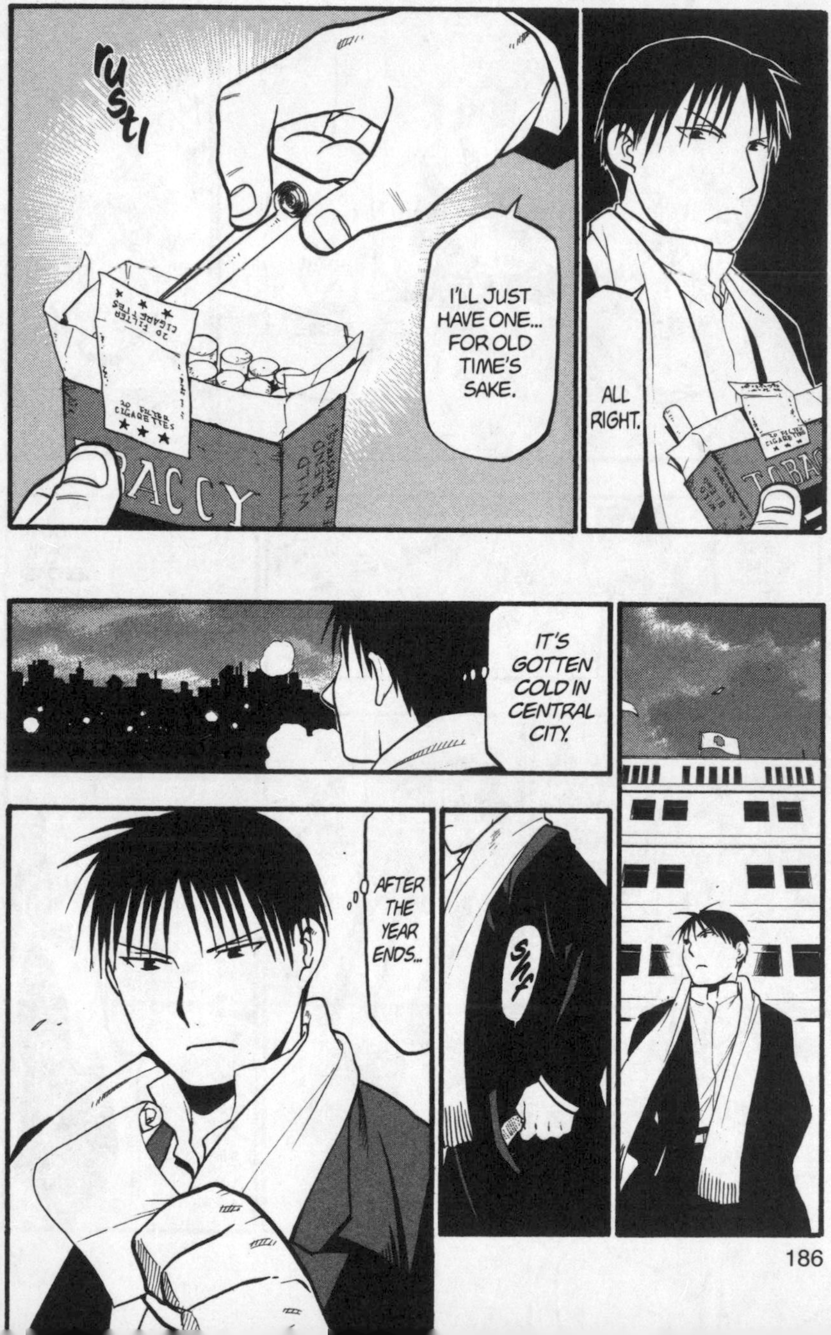
ALL RIGHT.
rustl
I'LL JUST HAVE ONE... FOR OLD TIME'S SAKE.
20 FILTER CIGARETTES
IT'S GOTTEN COLD IN CENTRAL CITY.
AFTER THE YEAR ENDS...

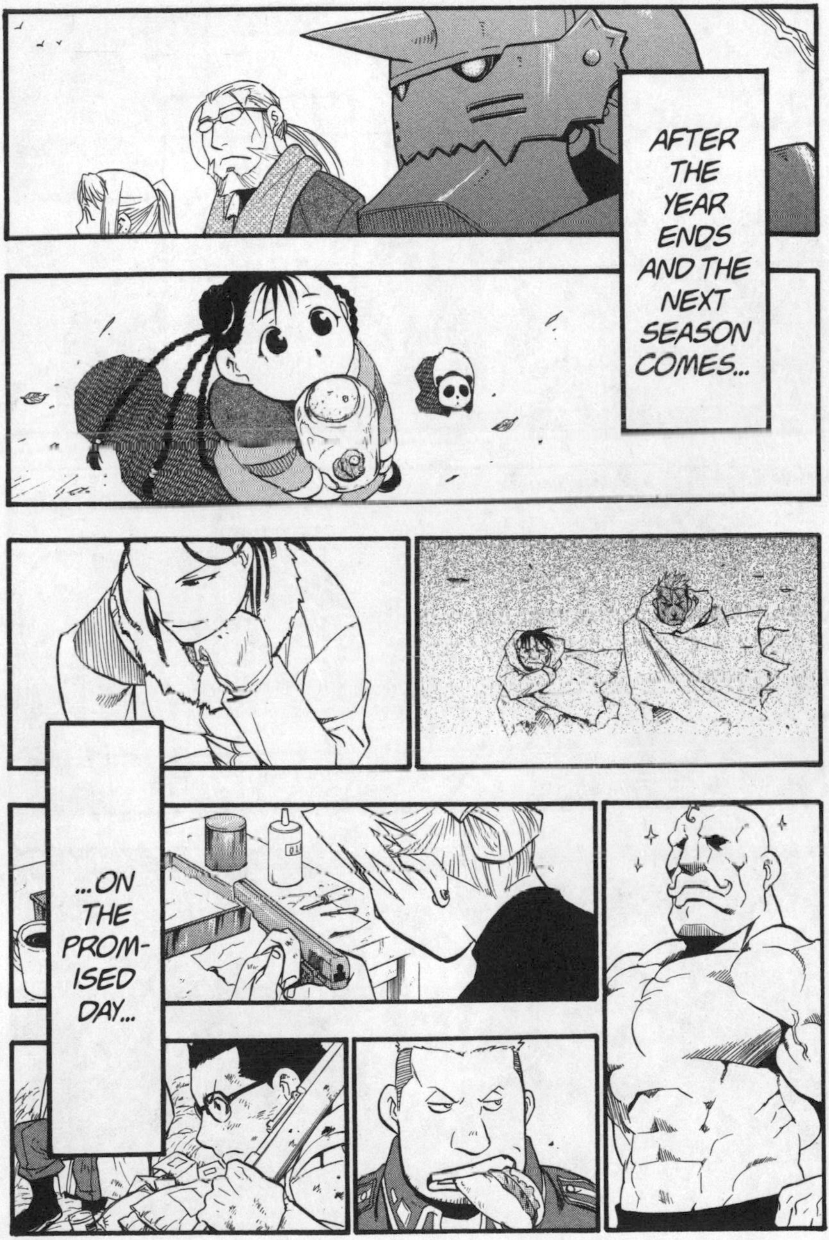
AFTER THE YEAR ENDS AND THE NEXT SEASON COMES...
...ON THE PROM-ISED DAY...

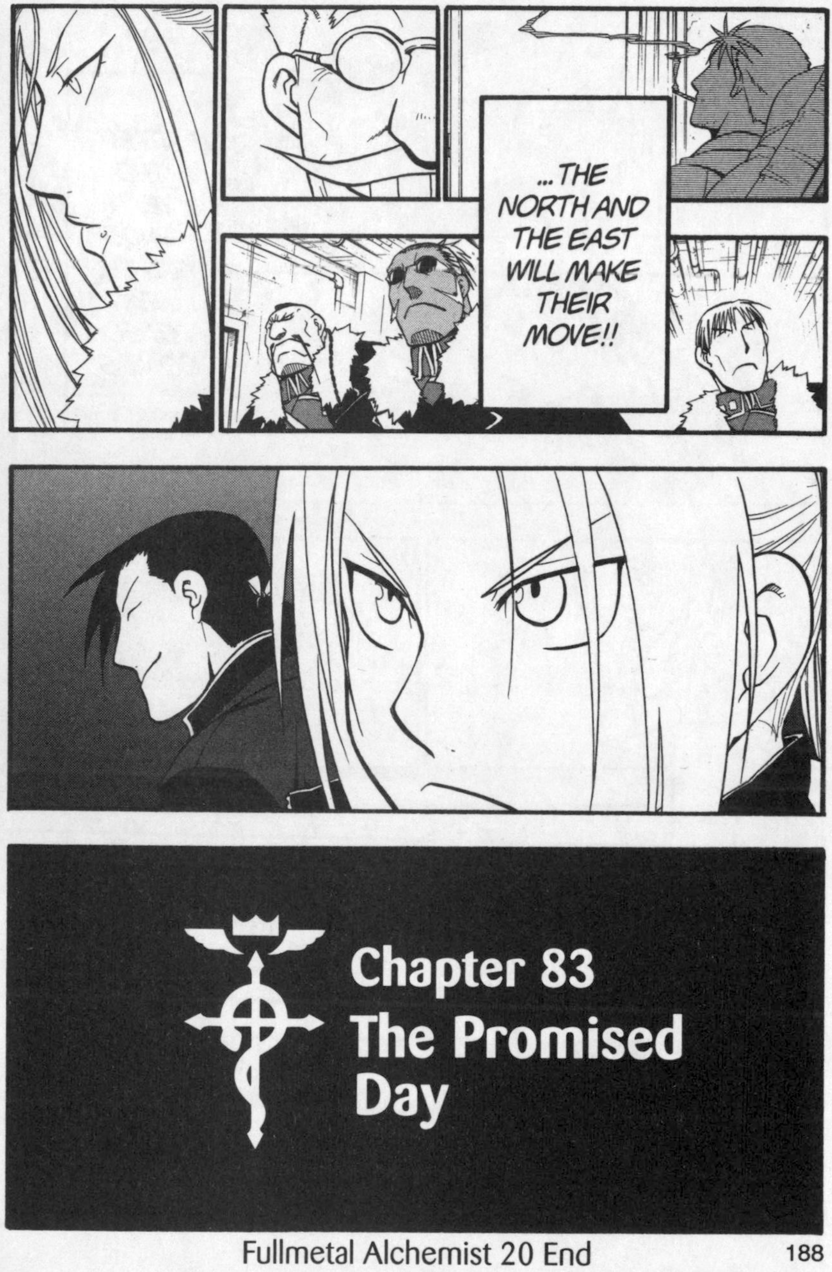
...THE NORTH AND THE EAST WILL MAKE THEIR MOVE!!

Chapter 83 The Promised Day

What if?

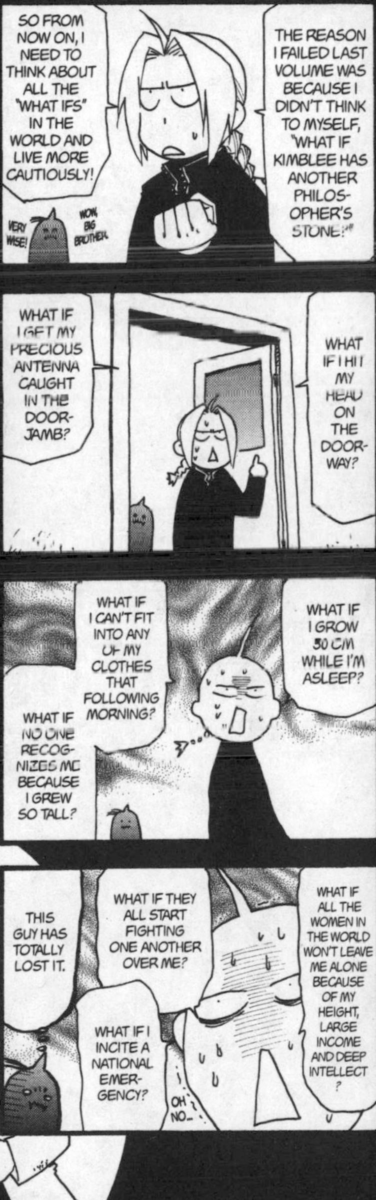
THE REASON I FAILED LAST VOLUME WAS BECAUSE I DIDN'T THINK TO MYSELF, "WHAT IF KIMBLEE HAS ANOTHER PHILOSOPHER'S STONE?"
SO FROM NOW ON, I NEED TO THINK ABOUT ALL THE "WHAT IFS" IN THE WORLD AND LIVE MORE CAUTIOUSLY!
WOW, BIG BROTHER.
VERY WISE!
WHAT IF I HIT MY HEAD ON THE DOORWAY?
WHAT IF I GET MY PRECIOUS ANTENNA CAUGHT IN THE DOORJAMB?
WHAT IF I GROW 30 CM WHILE I'M ASLEEP?
WHAT IF I CAN'T FIT INTO ANY OF MY CLOTHES THAT FOLLOWING MORNING?
WHAT IF NO ONE RECOGNIZES ME BECAUSE I GREW SO TALL?
WHAT IF ALL THE WOMEN IN THE WORLD WON'T LEAVE ME ALONE BECAUSE OF MY HEIGHT, LARGE INCOME AND DEEP INTELLECT?
WHAT IF THEY ALL START FIGHTING ONE ANOTHER OVER ME?
THIS GUY HAS TOTALLY LOST IT.
WHAT IF I INCITE A NATIONAL EMERGENCY?
OH NO...

Fullmetal Alchemist 20

Special Thanks

Jun Tohko

Nono

Masashi Mizutani

Coupon

Noriko Tsubota

Haruhi Nakamura

Kazufumi Kaneko

Mitsuri Sakano

Kei Takanamazu

Big bro Yoichi Kamitono

Aiyaball Sensei

Michiko Shishido Sensei

My Editor,
Yuichi Shimomura

AND YOU!!

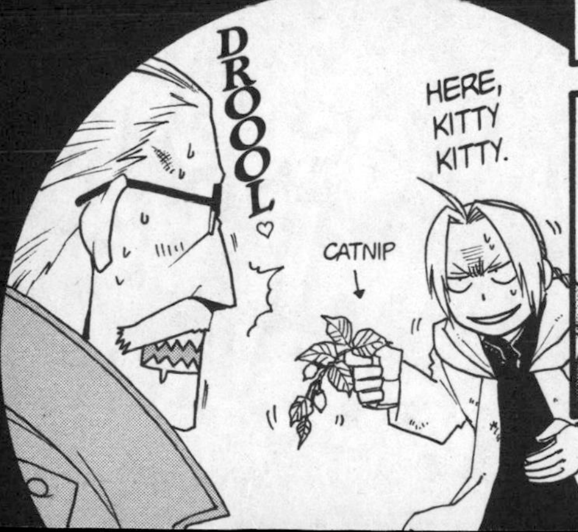
HERE, KITTY KITTY.
DROOOL ♡
CATNIP

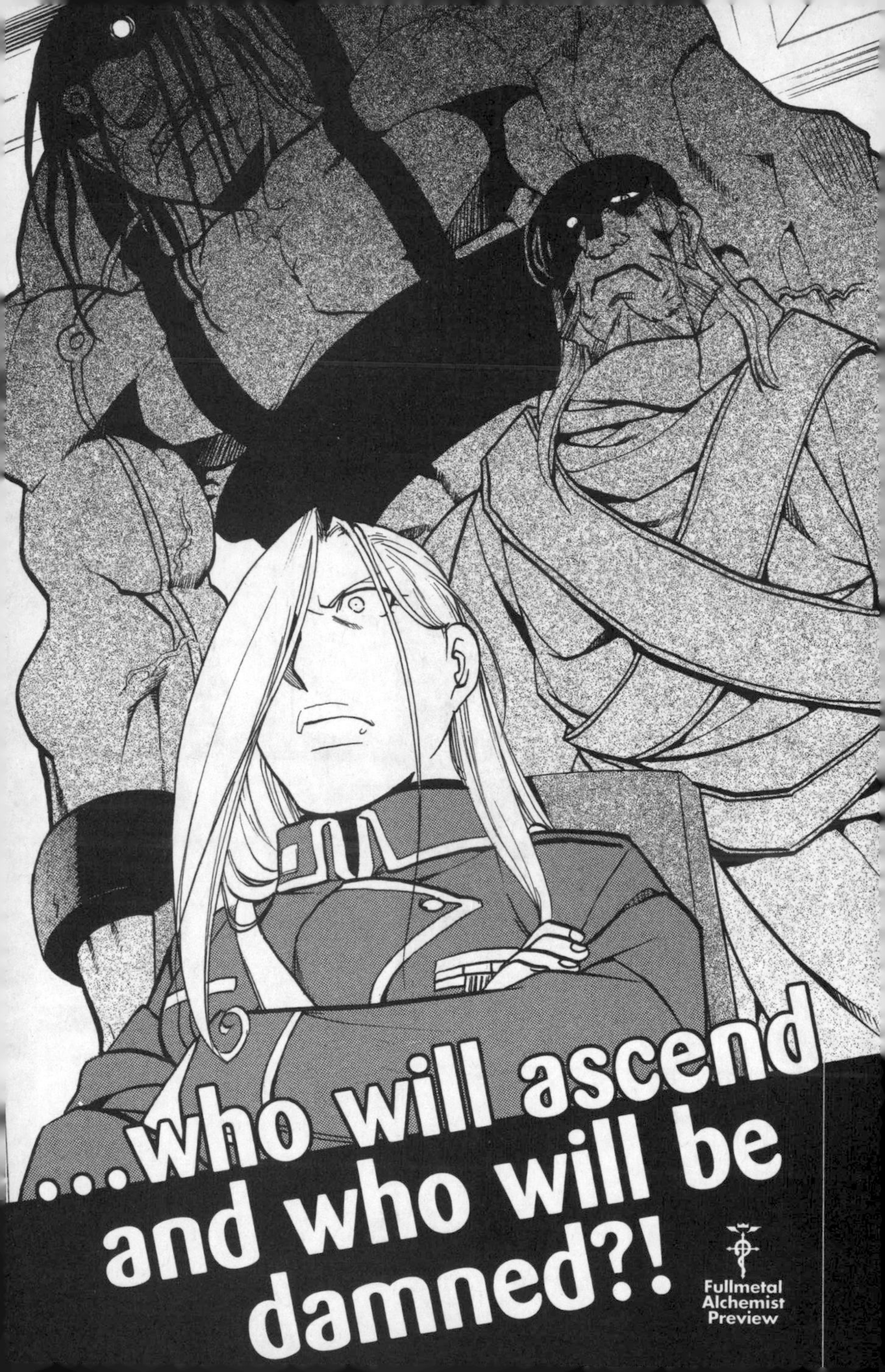
...who will ascend and who will be damned?!
Fullmetal Alchemist Preview

Fullmetal Alchemist 20

A rejected state alchemist character

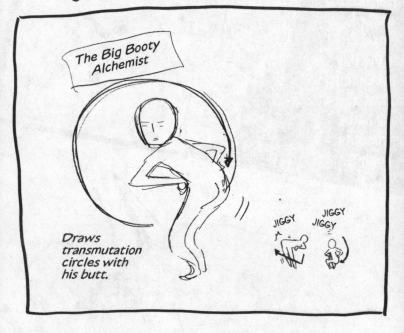

The Big Booty Alchemist

Draws transmutation circles with his butt.

JIGGY

JIGGY JIGGY

I found this while cleaning out a drawer. Now the part of me that asks, "Why did you reject this idea?!!" and the part of me that says, "Of course I rejected it!!" are engaged in an epic battle.

BOOTY ALCHEMIST?

—ARAKAWA

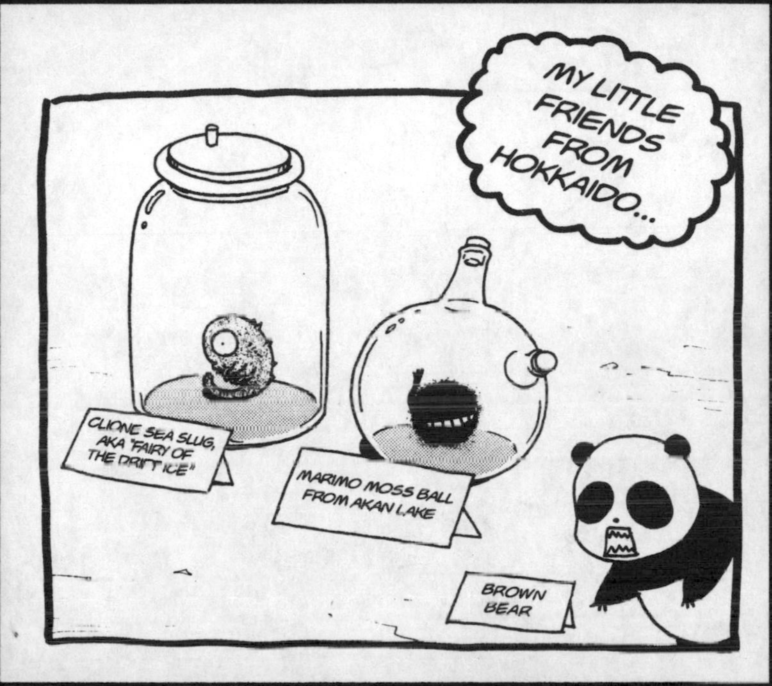
MY LITTLE FRIENDS FROM HOKKAIDO...
CLIONE SEA SLUG, AKA "FAIRY OF THE DRIFT ICE"
MARIMO MOSS BALL FROM AKAN LAKE
BROWN BEAR

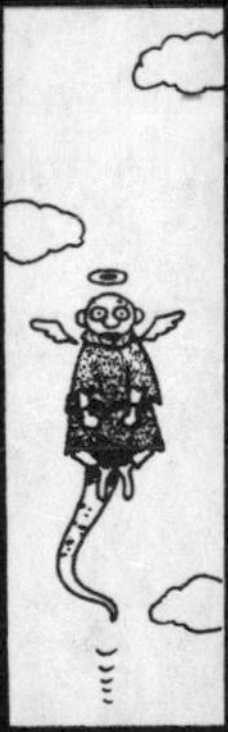

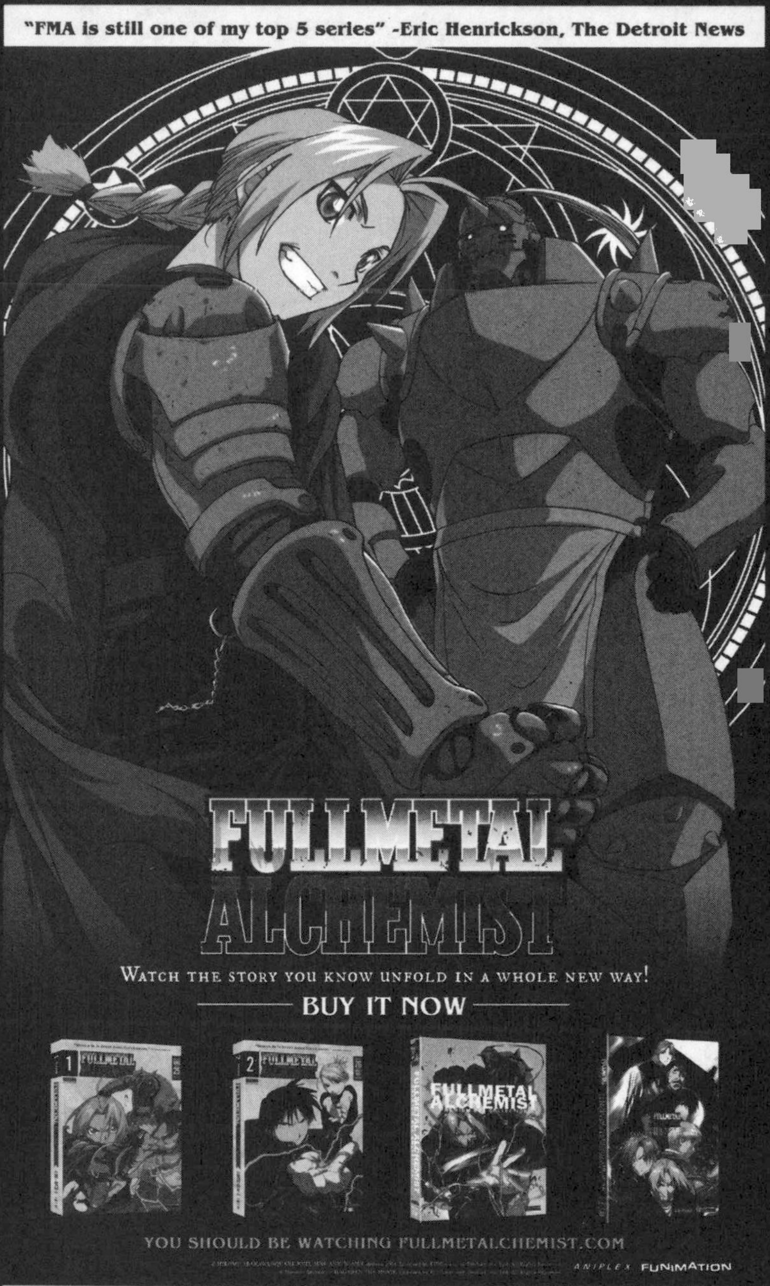
"FMA is still one of my top 5 series" -Eric Henrickson, The Detroit News
FULLMETAL ALCHEMIST
WATCH THE STORY YOU KNOW UNFOLD IN A WHOLE NEW WAY!
BUY IT NOW
YOU SHOULD BE WATCHING FULLMETALCHEMIST.COM
ANIPLEX FUNIMATION

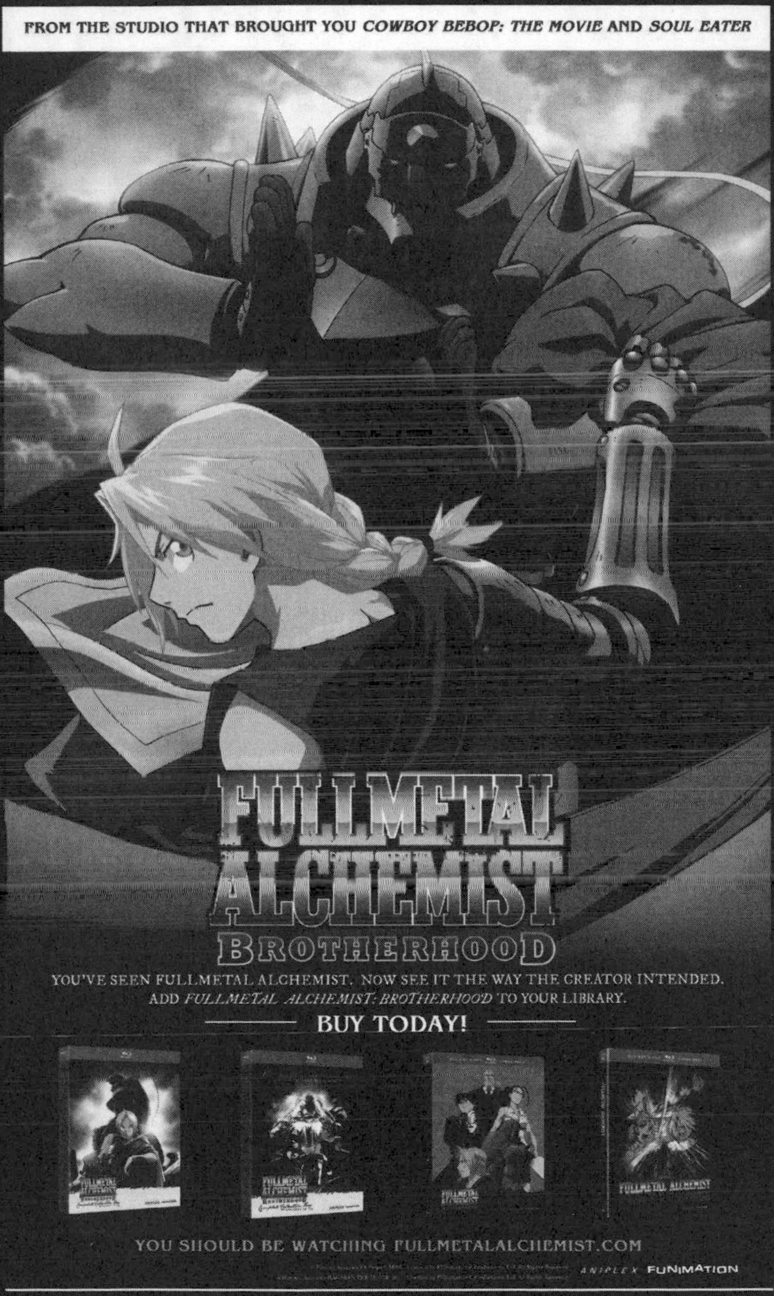
FROM THE STUDIO THAT BROUGHT YOU COWBOY BEBOP: THE MOVIE AND SOUL EATER
FULLMETAL ALCHEMIST
BROTHERHOOD
YOU'VE SEEN FULLMETAL ALCHEMIST. NOW SEE IT THE WAY THE CREATOR INTENDED.
ADD FULLMETAL ALCHEMIST: BROTHERHOOD TO YOUR LIBRARY.
BUY TODAY!
YOU SHOULD BE WATCHING FULLMETALALCHEMIST.COM
ANIPLEX FUNIMATION

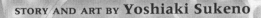

Twin ☆ Star Exorcists

ONMYOJI

STORY AND ART BY Yoshiaki Sukeno

The action-packed romantic comedy from the creator of *Good Luck Girl!*

Rokuro dreams of becoming *anything* but an exorcist!
Then mysterious Benio turns up. The pair are dubbed the
"Twin Star Exorcists" and learn they are fated to marry...

Can Rokuro escape both fates?

www.viz.com

SOUSEI NO ONMYOJI © 2013 by Yoshiaki Sukeno /SHUEISHA Inc.

Hey! You're Reading in the Wrong Direction!

This is the **end** of this graphic novel!

To properly enjoy this VIZ graphic novel, please turn it around and begin reading from **right to left.** Unlike English, Japanese is read right to left, so Japanese comics are read in reverse order from the way English comics are typically read.

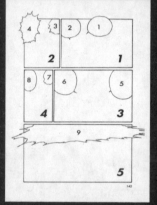

Follow the action this way

This book has been printed in the original Japanese format in order to preserve the orientation of the original artwork. Have fun with it!